NOBODY KNOWS WHERE THE BLUES COME FROM

NOBODY KNOWS WHERE THE BLUES COME FROM

Lyrics and History

EDITED BY ROBERT SPRINGER

UNIVERSITY PRESS OF MISSISSIPPI • JACKSON

www.upress.state.ms.us

The University Press of Mississippi is a member of
the Association of American University Presses.

Print-on-Demand Edition

Library of Congress Cataloging-in-Publication Data

Nobody knows where the blues come from : lyrics and history / edited by
Robert Springer.—1st ed.
    p. cm.—(American made music series)
  Includes bibliographical references and index.
    ISBN 1-57806-797-9 (cloth : alk. paper) 1. Blues (Music)—History and
criticism. I. Springer, Robert, 1946– II. Series.
  ML3521.N63   2006
    782.421643'09—dc22   2005006883

British Library Cataloging-in-Publication Data available

CONTENTS

PREFACE

Although the aesthetic appeal of African American popular music has always been its main drawing card, the lyrical content of the songs, sometimes overlooked, is at least equally to be credited for its staying power.

Two seminal works, both by Paul Oliver, can be said to have launched the study of songs and lyrics in this domain: *Blues Fell This Morning: The Meaning of the Blues* (London: Cassell, 1960; reprint: Cambridge University Press, 1990) and *Songsters and Saints: Vocal Traditions on Race Records* (Cambridge University Press, 1984), which complemented each other, covering the broad spectrum of African American popular music, secular and religious, blues and non-blues, as found on commercial recordings over a time span of four decades from the 1920s to the 1950s.

The treasure being by no means exhausted, I felt the need to organize two conferences on "The Lyrics in African American Popular Music" at the University of Metz, France, in 2000 and 2002. The former led to the publication of selected papers in *The Lyrics in African American Popular Music* (Bern: Peter Lang, 2001). The latter took place on September 27 and 28, 2002, and gathered scholars and experts, in and outside the academic world, who, almost without exception, may be seen as disciples of Paul Oliver, himself an indispensable participant in the proceedings.

Eight papers, resulting from years of thorough research, make up this volume. In all, the focus rests on the historical dimensions of the lyrics with the intention of setting the record straight or creating a record where none existed. In several, the examination of the subtext has proved enlightening, helping to establish the significance of African American popular song as a neglected form of oral history.

With "High Water Everywhere: Blues and Gospel Commentary on the 1927 Mississippi River Flood," David Evans delivers the definitive study of the repertoire of songs about the greatest natural disaster in the history of the United States. The black population having been hardest hit by the flood, this historical event "served to give focus to many of the essential personal concerns found in blues and gospel song texts in general." More particularly, Evans amply demonstrates the presence as a subtext of the application of the rigid Jim Crow system to the rescue and relief effort. This vast corpus of songs is an important supplement to the news reports and official documents of the flood and, as such, constitutes history from the point of view of the otherwise voiceless.

Similarly, in "Death by Fire: African American Popular Music on the Natchez Rhythm Club Fire," Luigi Monge makes a detailed textual analysis of songs about another, this time exclusively, African American tragedy, the Natchez Rhythm Club fire of 1940. This accident, of minor social importance at the national level, started a continuum of songs which, together, convey a historical message and are constitutive of a popular consciousness among black Americans. The author suggests that consideration of a diachronic context here, and more generally for thematic songs, may overcome the limitations of mere synchronic analysis.

In "Lookin' for the Bully: An Enquiry into a Song and Its Story," Paul Oliver, as ever stimulated by historical enigmas, retraces the origins in early black popular music and the many avatars of the "Bully song." He thus sheds more light on the generally obscure "pre-blues" period, assesses the song's durable career in the blues idiom, and suggests answers to relevant questions regarding the emotions audiences must have felt when listening to it.

In "That Dry Creek Eaton Clan: A North Mississippi Murder Ballad of the 1930s," Tom Freeland and Chris Smith choose a little-known ballad recorded in 1939 by John Lomax from a black convict at Parchman prison farm which describes and comments on a white murder and its aftermath. The question they address is how the ballad could have reached an African American singer and also remained so close to the Eatons' version of the story. The article ends with an enlightening discussion of what makes a song African American and of the target audiences of black performers.

"Coolidge's Blues: African American Blues from the Roaring Twenties" is a survey by Guido van Rijn of the blues of that decade. It delineates in effect the working-class African American point of view, leaving one with an impression in contrast with the general buoyancy of the decade as described in history books. The blues corpus of the period also reveals dreams of moving north to escape Jim Crow, often followed by disappointment after a brush with the difficulties of urban life.

My own contribution, "On the Electronic Trail of Blues Formulas," presents a number of early conclusions concerning the dissemination of blues formulas on commercial recordings, a study now made easier thanks to electronic searches. Though the database used awaits further additions, it is already possible at this stage to underline the influence of classic blues singers on their country blues counterparts but also to offer evidence of cross influences even among the reputedly most seminal blues artists.

In "West Indies Blues: An Historical Overview 1920s–1950s—Blues and Music from the English-speaking West Indies," John Cowley gives us a complete depiction of West Indian songs produced on the American mainland from the 1920s to the 1950s. With the cultural connections between the Caribbean and black America as a backdrop, the examination of aspects of cultural adjustment as well as musical and cultural interchange, informed as it is by lyric analysis, makes this a direly needed article on a treasure of black popular music which had until now received insufficient attention.

Closing the book with "Ethel Waters: 'Long, Lean, Lanky Mama,'" Randall Cherry reappraises the early career of an often maligned blues and vaudeville singer. The Ethel Waters of the 1920s indeed deserves to be rehabilitated and given pride of place in the history of the genre right next to Bessie Smith, her main rival at the time. The recorded songs studied here reveal her sensibility, her sophistication, and her multifaceted stage persona in "a perfect marriage of lyrics and performer."

Together, this collection presents African American popular music as a self-contained cultural domain and as a form of oral history which continues to be a permanent source of enlightenment as it serves to shine a light on several dark corners of official history. Another common thread is the characterization of the music as a close blending of folklore and commercial facets. Lastly, in its own way, it is a celebration of the tremendous vitality of oral tradition among African Americans, particularly in the first half of the twentieth century.

May the proceedings of our conference provide readers with an opportunity to tap into the often unsuspected wealth of African American musical texts, learn from the studies of their origins and dissemination, penetrate the historical significance of the songs, and form their own opinions about the interpretations proposed here. Though blues singer and pianist Leroy Carr once claimed that "nobody knows where the blues come from" (in "Papa's on the House Top," recorded for Vocalion in 1930), the contributors to this book, with passion and determination, have done their utmost to trace some of the roots and developments of this and other related genres.

Robert Springer
University of Metz, France
December 2004

ACKNOWLEDGMENTS

I wish to thank the Centre d'Etude des Textes et Traductions of the University of Metz and its chairperson, Annie Cointre, the Direction Générale de l'Urbanisme et du Développement Economique de la Ville de Metz, the Service d'Action Culturelle of the University and its director, Alain Billon, as well as the University itself, for funding the Second Conference on the Lyrics in African American Popular Music held on September 27 and 28, 2002. The present volume contains the proceedings of that conference.

NOBODY KNOWS WHERE THE BLUES COME FROM

HIGH WATER EVERYWHERE

Blues and Gospel Commentary on the
1927 Mississippi River Flood

DAVID EVANS

The purpose of this paper is to identify and survey the texts of blues, gospel songs and sermons recorded by African Americans about the flood of the Mississippi River and its tributaries in 1927.[1] Although to my knowledge this is the first survey of all such recordings that directly mention the flood, it benefits from earlier partial surveys of these songs and songs about other floods by Paul Oliver (to whom I would like to dedicate this paper), Chris Strachwitz and Pete Welding, Keith Briggs, and Steven J. Morrison, as well as the comments of many authors about individual songs and related matters.[2] I shall briefly compare these recordings to other songs about the 1927 flood in popular and country music, place them in the context of the unfolding events of the flood and its aftermath as well as a broader American social and historical context, and relate them to the policies, attitudes, and promotional efforts of commercial record companies as well as relevant facts about the lives and compositional and performance styles of the singers and songwriters. It will be shown that these African American recordings offer a wide variety of perspectives on the flood, including direct personal experience of it, news reporting, sentimentality, moralizing, praise and criticism of the rescue and relief efforts, and tragic, heroic, humorous, romantic, sexual, social, racial, political, economic, and spiritual themes. Thus a real historical and very public event served to give focus to many of the essential personal concerns found in the texts of blues and gospel songs in general.

If one takes into consideration the factors of geographical scope, number of people killed, injured, and left homeless, loss of property, duration of the event, and its long-term impact, the flood of 1927 would have to rank as the greatest natural disaster in the history of the United States.[3] It affected 16.5 million acres of land in seven states: Illinois, Missouri, Kentucky, Arkansas, Tennessee, Mississippi, and Louisiana. Although most of this land was owned by whites, almost all of it had a heavy, often predominantly, African American population, mostly farmers, farm workers, sharecroppers, and other rural manual laborers. It was this population that was hardest hit by the flood.

Despite the reinforcement of levees and the building of jetties in the 1870s, there were still occasional severe floods of the lower Mississippi River in 1882, 1884, 1890, 1897, 1903, 1912, 1913, and 1922. By 1927 it was widely thought that the levees had been sufficiently reinforced to be able to withstand any force of water that nature could hurl against them. No one, however, counted on the extraordinary amount of rain that would fall on the Mississippi River basin in the winter and spring of 1926–27. Severe storms occurred in the mid-South in December 1926, and, before the end of the year, there was flooding in Nashville, Chattanooga, and along the Yazoo River in the Mississippi Delta. The rains continued in January of 1927 along the Ohio River and its tributaries. Pittsburgh was flooded on January 23 and Cincinnati on January 28. Northeast Arkansas and other locations along the lower Mississippi valley experienced flooding in February, with thousands of refugees and several dozen deaths. In March there was another flood in Pittsburgh, and tornadoes accompanied by rain killed several dozen people in the lower Mississippi valley. In mid-April there were major breaks in the levee system at Hickman, Kentucky, and Dorena, Missouri, and on April 21 the worst break occurred at Mounds Landing, Mississippi, with the water rapidly inundating the city of Greenville and much of the lower Mississippi Delta over an area fifty miles wide and a hundred miles long. On the following day, President Calvin Coolidge appointed Secretary of Commerce Herbert Hoover to head the flood relief effort. Hoover had experience in similar efforts in Europe following World War One and was admired for his efficiency and organizational skills. Levees continued to break in Louisiana as the high water proceeded toward the Gulf of Mexico. The city of New Orleans was only saved from disastrous flooding by a decision to dynamite the levee at Caernarvon beginning on April 29 and lasting for several days, in order to allow the water to drain toward the Gulf. Two parishes were almost totally flooded as a result. Meanwhile, Hoover, with the aid of the Red Cross, organized the relief effort. By June, the waters had largely receded, leaving a vast mud plain. It was too late to plant, however, and many farmers in the affected area could not make a crop in 1927. Altogether, over 162,000 homes were flooded, 41,000 buildings destroyed, between 600,000 and a million people made homeless, between 250 and 1,000 people drowned, and up to a billion dollars in economic losses incurred. Over 90 percent of the flood refugees were black.

In contrast to its themes of destruction, tragedy, charity, and heroism, there were two aspects of the flood story that were especially controversial, revealing appalling portraits of selfishness, prejudice, and inhumanity. One of these centered on the decision to dynamite the levee at Caernarvon, Louisiana. While the city of New Orleans was saved from major devastation, large parts of St. Bernard and Plaquemines Parishes were inundated. Some ten thousand people were evacuated before the dynamiting, most of them to New Orleans. The decision to dynamite was purely a matter of Louisiana politics, with the political and economic power, social standing, and greater voting population of New Orleans prevailing over the forces of the two neighboring parishes. Most of the refugees lost their homes, property, and livelihoods. New Orleans political and financial leaders gave guarantees that the refugees would be compensated for their losses. Yet, when the time came for a settlement, the city proved itself to be stingy with its money. Most refugees received barely anything and were ruined economically. This episode, as important and shameful as it was, received only a single rather confused and not especially revealing mention by blues singer Sippie Wallace in the body of African American songs about the 1927 flood. The reason was undoubtedly the fact that most of the people affected in the two parishes were Spanish Isleños, descendants of earlier settlers from the Canary Islands. Blacks were a small minority, along with people of French, Portuguese, Hungarian, and Filipino descent. Although many of the residents were prosperous, they were viewed by other citizens of Louisiana as socially disreputable on account of their ethnic status and their occupations of fur trapping, fishing, bootlegging, and smuggling. Their plight simply did not capture the attention of America's black community.[4]

The second controversial and appalling aspect of the flood story was the application of the rigid southern Jim Crow system to the rescue and relief effort. This issue did affect the black community in a major way. Although it is not the exclusive or even the predominant focus of most of the blues and gospel songs about the flood, I will attempt to show that it is alluded to, often cryptically, and is a significant subtext of many of the songs. Because of the fear and horror that it evoked, most blues and gospel artists, who usually lived in the South, toured there, or had relatives and friends there, were reluctant to address this issue overtly or were perhaps prevented from doing so by white-controlled record companies. Indeed, if one were to listen to all the songs about the flood by

African American singers without knowing anything more than the fact that they were about a great natural disaster, one could easily come to the conclusion that the issue of Jim Crow is not even mentioned. It is only when one learns about the conditions that existed, the incidents of brutality and coercion, especially as reported in the African American press, that certain phrases in a number of the songs begin to reveal their deeper meaning. Some of the songs even reveal as much by what they don't say as they do by their texts.

Herbert Hoover was in a difficult position. In the midst of spreading flood waters and new breaks daily in the levee system, he had to coordinate rescue efforts over a stretch of several hundred miles of the Mississippi River and further hundreds of miles along its tributaries. He had to see that the refugees were brought to safe places and received adequate food, clothing, shelter, and health care. He had to prevent looting and other crimes, and oversee the repair of broken levees. Finally, there was the clean-up and rebuilding effort. It was a daunting organizational and logistic task, and, to his credit, Hoover handled it with an efficiency that probably prevented the death toll from climbing much higher. In his work he enlisted the aid of the U.S. Army Corps of Engineers, state and local officials, the various state units of the National Guard, and the American Red Cross. All of these institutions and agencies were entirely controlled by whites as well as made up almost entirely of whites, while the majority of victims of the flood were black. The basic policy that emerged was to herd refugees into "concentration camps" on high ground or in locations outside the flood zone so that goods and services could be delivered to them more efficiently. This term had not yet acquired the sinister meaning it would have in later years, but, by the end of the flood, it was well on its way to a new meaning as many of these camps turned into virtual prisons and slave labor markets. There were 154 camps in all, 84 percent of them in Arkansas, Mississippi, and Louisiana. They were strictly segregated by race, and the black camps were supervised and guarded by whites. Perhaps the largest and most horrible of these was the camp at Greenville, Mississippi, the city hardest hit by the flood. It ran for eight miles north of the city along the top of the levee and was only about twenty feet wide on average. It held up to 13,000 black refugees and was patrolled by armed members of the all-white Mississippi National Guard.

Herbert Hoover was nursing presidential ambitions for the election of 1928, needing only the assurance, which was eventually forthcoming, that his boss Calvin Coolidge would not run for reelection. Hoover held frequent press conferences with announcements of successes in the relief effort. He consistently under-reported the number of deaths that had occurred after he took over and lavished praise on the Red Cross, downplaying the role of the National Guard. However, reports of abuses from the black press and black leaders eventually forced him to act. Hoover was no southern racist, but he could not risk alienating southern whites and causing a breakdown in the relief system that they controlled, as this might lead to further deaths and embarrassing incidents that would harm his electoral chances. Although he knew that most of them would vote Democratic in the general election, he hoped to make inroads in this constituency through his humanitarian reputation. However, he needed the votes of southern black delegates at the Republican Convention in order to win his party's nomination, and he needed black votes in the general election in order to carry several northern states. As the chorus of complaints from the black community grew louder, Hoover finally appointed a Colored Advisory Committee at the end of May, more than a month after the major flooding in Arkansas and Mississippi. It was headed by Robert Russa Moton, President of Tuskegee Institute, and began its work on June 2. After individual members made investigations in various refugee camps, the committee assembled in Baton Rouge on June 10–11 to draft a report to Hoover. Walter White of the National Association for the Advancement of Colored People made an independent investigation and issued a separate report complaining of peonage of black flood victims, which Hoover denounced as being "without foundation." Hoover acted on the somewhat milder report of the Colored Advisory Committee, which was heavily censored before publication, and made some changes in some of the worst relief camps in late June. But by then most black refugees had been released to their plantations and were safely out of sight. Hoover managed to give the appearance of addressing wrongs against black people without upsetting the system of white domination, and he protected his reputation as a great humanitarian. He won the Republican nomination in 1928 and prevailed in the general election. Nevertheless, just as he largely ignored the needs and complaints of blacks, the black voters eventually ignored him when he ran for reelection in 1932. Certainly the black singers ignored him. His heading of the relief effort goes unmentioned in all of the songs about the 1927 flood, and he is only mentioned once during his presidential administration in a blues that describes a Depression refugee camp on the outskirts of St. Louis as "Hooverville."[5]

The abuses against blacks began with the first breaks in the levees.[6] They were simply an extension of the racist patterns that had prevailed in the South for decades. As the flood waters rose in April, blacks were ordered by armed whites to work on the levees while white families fled. Many black workers lost their lives when the levees broke, and hundreds of others lost all their possessions because they were given no opportunity to make preparations. One black convict worker was shot when he expressed disapproval on seeing an aged woman carrying large sacks of dirt.[7] At Inverness, Mississippi, a thousand black workers were prevented from fleeing the rising waters by plantation owners, fearful that they would lose their labor force.[8] Along the St. Francis River in Arkansas, two thousand blacks and four hundred whites stood on a crumbling levee, awaiting death. A rescuing steamer took on all the whites and only twenty-five blacks.[9] In the refugee camps, army cots, tents, clothing, and food were given first to the whites, while the blacks received the left-overs. A thousand dollars worth of toys donated by Chinese merchants for general distribution to children were given only to the whites.[10] Black men were forced to engage in boxing matches for the amusement of the white guards. Whites ate at sheltered tables, while blacks often stood or sat on the ground and ate without utensils. In Greenville, black refugees were forced into a camp on the levee, while white refugees were housed in local hotels and other buildings in town. Unsanitary conditions prevailed in many of the black camps. A black man was shot by a National Guard soldier when he attempted to take food and clothing into a relief camp in Vicksburg.[11] A young woman was gang raped by twenty national guardsmen at the camp in Cleveland, Mississippi, and found dead. Authorities stated that she was "drowned."[12] Blacks who died in the camps had their bodies slit, loaded with sand, and dumped in the river. Black men and women were not allowed to leave the camps, while whites could travel freely. When some women were allowed to go to Vicksburg, the men were kept behind in Greenville. Even so, the women traveled by barge, while white refugees traveled by steamboat. Black men in the camps were forced to work on the levees and the clean-up effort. Disease-breeding trash from the white neighborhoods was dumped in the black neighborhoods which were the last to be cleaned up. Black women refugees were forced to clean the houses of white people and were paid only one dollar per week. William Alexander Percy, in charge of the relief effort at Greenville, ordered that black families would receive no rations unless there was a man in the household who worked. He refused rations to any family if the man made more than one dollar per day, effectively setting a wage limit for the laborers. Visitors were not allowed into the camps, and the blacks were carefully protected from contact with labor agents. They were released only to the custody of the landlords from whose plantations they had come. On the plantations, relief supplies were given in bulk to the owner, who often charged them against his black workers, forcing them further into debt peonage. Essentially, the landowners used these provisions to run their plantations and hold their labor force. Returning refugees were often given flood-damaged rations from plantation commissaries, while the new Red Cross rations were held for sale. On top of all this misery, the tensions created by the flood led to a rise in lynchings.[13]

These horrible conditions were the inevitable result of long-established southern racial disparities as well as different understandings about the flood in the white and black communities. Most whites viewed the flood as a "tragedy" and "natural disaster," one of God's many random acts that man cannot understand. The people in the stricken area needed to rebuild and be vigilant against future floods. The black people should be grateful for the emergency relief they received and willing to work in the rebuilding effort. The furnishing they had received from white landowners before the flood and the relief supplies they received in the camps and on the flooded plantations were a debt that they needed to repay, even if they had no hope of replanting and making a crop in 1927.[14] Naturally, most black people had a different understanding. They felt that the flood was a sign of God's wrath against the sins of man, just as in the time of Noah. The flood had wiped the slate clean and cancelled all old debts. The Delta was now a new land. The soil that had been on the old plantations had been washed away and deposited elsewhere. It was now time to leave the plantations and head north for better opportunities. As the *Baltimore Afro-American* editorialized, "Thank God for the Mississippi river flood."[15] The same newspaper later reported that "one escaped refugee from Yazoo City camp, who arrived in Memphis the day of [*sic*] the earth tremors were felt, tells of being asked to 'speak to his people for the land owners,['] as he was a preacher and race leader. 'I did,' he said, 'I told my people, and others, too, the Lord sent his flood to baptize sinners, master and servant alike. They were slow in accepting salvation, so he shook the earth, giving warning to take the first train to Memphis and then to the Promised Land, north or East. I had to leave so here I am, on my way.' "[16] Blacks felt no duty to rebuild the Old South, and if they absolutely had to, at least they should be paid adequately for it.

The flood provoked a great outpouring of song and music, the majority of it from black Americans who were its primary victims. Even during the rescue effort in Arkansas, the *Pittsburgh Courier* and the *Baltimore Afro-American* reported, "In the St. Frances [*sic*] River District, situated below here, two thousand Negroes and four hundred whites stood on a crumbling levee, awaiting death. A rescuing steamer came up, took on all the whites and twenty-five Negroes, and left the others to perish. Facing almost certain death, these Negroes sang the songs of hope and triumph which their forefathers had sung during the dark days of slavery, and continued to do until a white man in a launch rescued them."[17] Another report stated that 500 people marooned for several days at Wayside, Mississippi, without food and supplies "sang plantation melodies and old time religious songs as they joyfully thronged the decks of the Wabash," a steamer that had come to rescue them.[18] Although a writer for the NAACP found a mood of "incredible melancholy" and "no music" in the refugee camps,[19] other sources describe a variety of types of song and music there. Pete Daniel reprints two photographs of musicians taken in the camps, one of a black fife and drum band taken in front of the Red Cross headquarters in Tallulah, Louisiana, and another of two Cajun fiddlers playing for dancers in front of a large tent at Lafayette, Louisiana.[20] A writer for *National Geographic* magazine, however, stated, "Now the spade is above the banjo. Pastimes are forgotten." The only songs he heard in the camps in three weeks were camp-meeting hymns like "Throw Out the Life Line" and "Shall We Gather at the River."[21] Robert Russa Moton, head of Hoover's Colored Advisory Committee, appears to have seen deeper into the hymn singing. In a memorandum to the committee he stated, "We were interested in a song that these people sang in the levee camps—that the flood had washed away the old account. . . . They felt that the flood had emancipated them from a condition of peonage."[22] Almost certainly, the song that Moton heard in the camps was a version of "The Old Account Was Settled Long Ago," which had appeared in the widely used black hymnal, *Gospel Pearls.*[23] The Norfolk Jubilee Quartette had recorded a version of it in February 1927, that was probably released a couple of months later, about the time the levees broke along the Mississippi River (Paramount 12499). It is perhaps of some significance that this record proved popular enough to be reissued on two other labels (Broadway 5051, Herwin 93020). Many listeners probably associated the song's meaning with the flood. A reporter for the Memphis *Commercial Appeal* entered the refugee camp at the Memphis Fairgrounds, which had both white and black sections, and reported that on Sunday, April 24, the whites sang "Jesus Lover of My Soul" while the blacks sang "Swing Low, Sweet Chariot." No clearer expression of the difference in attitudes toward the flood exists than this observation. The whites ask Jesus to protect them "while the tempest still is high," while the blacks are looking for a band of angels "comin' fo' to carry me home." The same reporter noted that on Sunday afternoon a band concert was given in the camp "by one of the negro musical organizations of Memphis."[24] A similar concert was given by the town band on Sunday, May 1, for refugees camped at the Agricultural, Mechanical & Normal School at Pine Bluff, Arkansas. It was reported that "even in their destitute condition the refugees gave an enthusiastic applause."[25] White Delta lawyer and businessman David Cohn was the only observer to detect a light-hearted mood in song. In the horrible refugee camp in Greenville he stated,

> Three young bucks dressed in Sunday clothes snatched from the flood sat upon a battered dresser and sang:

> *A nigger'll be a nigger, don't care what you do;*
> *Tie a bow of ribbon round the top of his shoe;*
> *Button his pants up around his th'oat,*
> *Put him on a collar, don't need no coat.*
> *He's spo'tin', we shall be free, (x2)*
> *'Cause de good Lawd done set us free.*[26]

Cohn seems to have heard what he wanted to hear at the camp and had his stereo-type of carefree blacks reinforced, even in the midst of disaster. He makes no mention of more serious spirituals or blues.[27] An equally suspect claim about music in the camp was made by Big Bill Broonzy, who was born at Scott, Mississippi, near where the levee broke above Greenville. In introducing his 1956 performance of the Bessie Smith song "Back-Water Blues," Broonzy stated, "They sent for a lot of musicians to come down and write about this big flood down there in Mississippi at that time. They didn't have to send for me, 'cause I was already there. . . . And the man said that whosoever that played, that wrote the best song, he got five hundred dollars. So Bessie got the five hundred dollars, so we always plays hers, you know."[28] Five hundred dollars was a huge sum, a year's income for a sharecropper in a good year. Broonzy's recording career had not yet begun in 1927, and he was therefore hardly in the same league as Bessie Smith. She, in any case, was nowhere near the Delta at this time and had already recorded "Back-Water Blues" on February 17, two months before the flood struck Greenville. Nevertheless, Broonzy's statement revealed an understanding that there was money to be made in composing an original song about the flood. In 1937 he would compose two songs about the Mississippi River flood of that year. Others too saw commercial possibilities in music with a flood theme. The

Pittsburgh Courier on May 21 reported a show opening at Snyder's Theater in
New York, starring Duke Ellington's Orchestra, titled "Muddy Waters." The article stated, "Muddy Waters is a corking good clean show—turning them away at
every performance. We suggest change of name for title."[29] Other theaters, however, staged benefits for the flood victims. The Lafayette Theater in New York
staged a "monster midnight performance" on May 17 that raised $2,500. Among
the stars who donated their services were Bill "Bojangles" Robinson, Butterbeans
and Susie, and Sissle and Blake.[30] A midnight benefit show at Boston's National
Theater, with a cast of lesser-known entertainers, added another $1,000, while a
program at Chicago's Apollo Theater on the afternoon of May 6 that included
blues artists May Alix and Frankie Jaxon and Louis Armstrong's Orchestra raised
a mere $200.[31] T.O.B.A. theaters in the flood zone, however, reported "almost
empty houses" and some engagements delayed because of the high water.[32]

Musical themes associated with the flood even made their way into American
literature. The great African American poet Sterling Brown, who had used the
Mississippi River and its floods as metaphors of fear and escape in "Children of
the Mississippi" and "Riverbank Blues," incorporated portions of two songs on
flood themes recorded by Bessie Smith into "Ma Rainey" and "Cabaret."[33] In the
former poem, Ma Rainey brings tears to the eyes of listeners in a town in the
Deep South by singing "Back-Water Blues." In the latter poem, set in a Chicago
"black & tan" cabaret in 1927, Brown mixes images of "rich, flashy, puffy-faced"
whites entertained by a jazz band and Creole chorus girls with images of the
flood refugee camps further south and flashbacks to slave auctions while a singer
wails the words to "Muddy Water." In Mississippi novelist William Faulkner's
The Wild Palms, which is set along the Mississippi River during the 1927 flood,
a group of black refugees emerges from a rescue boat carrying bundles of the few
possessions they could save. One young man, however, carries nothing but a guitar, which he plays as he mounts the levee. A few pages later a white man who
had been picked up from the roof of a cotton shed by another boat complains,
"Never nobody came for me. . . . I set there on that sonabitching cotton house,
expecting hit to go any minute. I saw that launch and them boats come up and
they never had no room for me. Full of bastard niggers and one of them setting
there playing a guitar but there wasn't no room for me. A guitar! Room for a bastard nigger guitar but not for me."[34] We shall encounter the mirror image of this
scene in a blues by Mississippi guitarist Charley Patton.

Besides the songs and music that were performed during the flood, in the
camps and in benefit shows in theaters, there were a number of new songs

composed about the flood itself and closely related matters, such as levee work, the refugee camps, and other natural disasters. Many of these songs were recorded during the months of the flood and for up to three years afterwards. A few became standards and were recorded many times. The greatest number of songs directly about the flood were by African American composers, who were usually the same artists who recorded these songs. Some of them had even experienced the flood directly. There was also a significant body of song commentary by white songwriters and performers, both in the popular and country music fields. Some of this material was taken up by black singers, while some of the white pieces drew from black blues and jazz sources. Although the purpose of this paper is to survey African American blues and gospel songs about the flood, we should briefly examine these white song expressions first, as they provide both a context for and a contrast to the material by black composers and performers.

Interest in the Mississippi River as a subject for popular song had already begun to develop before 1927, as the river and its way of life came to be viewed nostalgically by many Americans, now that trains, automobiles, and trucks were replacing riverboats and steamers as vehicles of transportation and commerce. The river was also frequently viewed in association with the new jazz music that was sweeping the country in the "Roaring Twenties." These associations with jazz and "the good old days" are represented by Hoagy Carmichael's 1925 composition "Riverboat Shuffle" and Ferde Grofé's classical success "Mississippi Suite" of 1926. One of the biggest popular song hits of 1926 was "Muddy Water (A Mississippi Moan)," composed by Joe Trent, Peter DeRose, and Harry Richman. It came out late in the year and was mostly recorded in the early months of 1927, before the flood struck in Arkansas, Mississippi, and Louisiana. Bessie Smith was the first African American vocalist to make a recording of it (Columbia 14197–D) on March 2. She was followed by Evelyn Preer on March 27 (Banner 19723). The song is not about a flood at all but is instead an expression of nostalgia for the Old South of "Dixie moonlight, Swanee shore." Nevertheless, in the midst of praise for the South's "grand garden spots" and its life of "ease and comfort," there is an undertone of menace as the singer describes "Muddy water 'round my feet, muddy water in the street." Various writers have speculated why such a great artist as Bessie Smith would record this song.[35] Everyone recognizes that her performance transcends the song's theme, and I must agree with Angela Y. Davis's recent conclusion that "she is summoning her audience toward a critical reading of the lyrics."[36] This conclusion gains strength from Sterling Brown's quotation of the lyrics for precisely this purpose in his poem "Cabaret." When Bessie Smith ends her performance with the line, "My heart cries out for muddy water," the listener cannot help feeling that she has penetrated the mask of the song's text. We shall see shortly that Bessie Smith was quite aware of the real meaning of "Muddy Water," when we examine the lyrics of her "Back-Water Blues" recorded two weeks earlier. Columbia Records did not immediately make a connection between "Muddy Water" and the Mississippi River flood. Even though the record was released on April 20, the day before the levee broke above Greenville,[37] it was advertised in the *Baltimore Afro-American* and *Chicago Defender* on May 14 with a caricature of a grinning barefoot black man strumming a banjo in accompaniment to a singing alligator in a pool nearby, with the caption "Bessie Smith fished up some mighty mean blues this time."[38] One week later, Columbia had changed its tune, advertising this record and Bessie Smith's "Back-Water Blues" in the *Pittsburgh Courier* with a photograph of the artist and the equally absurd description of "Muddy Water" as "a vivid soul-stirring song of the ravishing levee-breaking Mississippi, a song picture of the disastrous Mississippi flood."[39] The short-lived Black Patti record company evidently also saw a potential connection between "Muddy Water" and the flood, as it released a recording of it made by singing banjo player Herman Perry on June 29, about the time when much of the Delta flood plain would have been turning to mud. Bessie Smith's recording of the song was the only one of these to become a hit.

During the flood year of 1927 there was another veritable flood of new popular songs with themes of the Mississippi River itself, riverboats and showboats, roustabouts, levees, swamps, and cotton.[40] The popularity of these themes continued to 1931 and beyond. Interestingly enough, with one obscure exception, these songs nowhere mention the great flood of 1927 or the controversial events surrounding it, although some of them do describe the power of the river. It was as if American popular culture could not focus on the tragedy and pain of this massive current event and had to fall back on nostalgia and stereotypes. Although I have not yet been able to determine whether some of these songs were composed before or after the cataclysmic month of April 1927, that year saw the following new songs: "Slow River" (Henry Myers, Charles M. Schwab), "Blue River" (Joseph Meyer, Alfred Bryan), "Here Comes the Showboat" (Maceo Pinkard, Billy Rose), "By the Bend of the River" (Bernhard Haig, Clara Edwards), "Chloe (Song of the Swamp)" (Gus Kahn, Neil Moret), and "Mississippi Mud" (Harry Barris, James Cavanaugh). "Chloe" does contain a suggestion of fear and menace that could have been applied to the circumstances of the flood, but the song itself was set in "the distant swampland" as the singer searches for Chloe "through the smoke and flame." "Chloe" was recorded by several African American artists in 1928, among them Bessie Brown (Brunswick 3817), Jack Richmond (Paramount 12624), and Eva Taylor (OKeh 8585). The most insidious of these songs was "Mississippi Mud." Its downright insulting lyrics were recorded by Paul Whiteman's Rhythm Boys on June 20, as the receding flood waters were turning to mud. Utterly ignoring the significance of the mud and all the pain and loss it represented, Bing Crosby, Al Rinker, and Harry Barris crooned:

> *They don't need no band.*
> *They keep time by clapping their hands.*
> *Just as happy as a cow chewing on a cud,*
> *When the darkies beat their feet on the Mississippi mud.*

There were no recordings of this song by black singers, but it may have given its name to several black artists in later years, after the pain of the water and mud had diminished. Mississippi Mud Steppers was the name used for the Mississippi Sheiks string band on recordings made December 15, 1930, and released in the OKeh "Old Time" series marketed to southern whites. A black vocal quintet that recorded on January 21, 1935, for Bluebird Records in New Orleans was called the Mississippi Mud Mashers, and Mississippi Mudder was the nickname used by Jimmie Gordon, Joe McCoy, and Charlie McCoy, on various records made for Decca between 1934 and 1936. The McCoys and probably Gordon were originally from Mississippi.

On October 4, 1926, the opera *Deep River* by W. Franke Harling and Laurence Stallings opened in New York, running for 32 performances. It starred African American baritone Jules Bledsoe. The key song was "Deep River," an old Negro spiritual that had been published in an arrangement by Harry T. Burleigh in 1917. Another African American baritone, Paul Robeson, made a very popular recording of the song (Victor 20793) on May 10, 1927, during the height of the flood in Mississippi and Louisiana. Since Robeson had already made a recording of it on March 30, before the flood, that remained unissued, we cannot assume that he had the flood in mind when he chose this piece. Most likely he was simply trying to capitalize on the success of the opera of the previous year. The song, in fact, is not about a flood at all but about crossing the Jordan River, yet, because of the timing of Robeson's recording, it was widely interpreted in connection with the flood. A few years earlier, in 1924, W. C. Handy's daughter Lucille Marie Handy and Eddie Green had composed a "Deep River Blues" that was recorded that year by Katherine Handy (Edison trial recording) and Rosa Henderson (Banner 1452, etc.). Although this song also was not about a flood, its publisher W. C. Handy saw an opportunity in 1927 and began promoting it once again. The *Baltimore Afro-American* and *Chicago Defender* ran short pieces about it in June that appear to be drawn straight from a Handy press release, making connections between the song, the flood situation, and other song hits such as "Muddy Water" and even W. C. Handy's "St. Louis Blues."[41] Handy was not able to get any black vocalists to record "Deep River Blues" in 1927, but several white dance bands and vocalists did.

There was another dramatic production of 1927 with a river theme, *Show Boat*, by Jerome Kern and Oscar Hammerstein II, again starring Jules Bledsoe. It opened in New York on December 27 and ran for an extraordinary 572 performances. The production as a whole, and its key song "Ol' Man River," are by no means about the flood, yet the latter was widely interpreted in connection with the flood. The song is given a dignified treatment by a stoic black dock worker, who stands in marked contrast to the frivolous white characters who populate this musical. Paul Robeson made another highly successful recording of this song with Paul Whiteman and His Concert Orchestra on March 1, 1928, and it became his signature piece for the rest of his long career.

The year 1928 also brought forth the songs "Ready for the River" (Meil Moret, Gus Kahn) with its theme of suicide by drowning and "Pickin' Cotton" (Ray Henderson, Buddy DeSylva, Lew Brown) from the show *George White's Scandals of 1928*. Another song from that year was "Dusky Stevedore" by the black songwriting team of Andy Razaf and J. C. Johnson. Its singer is a stevedore in need of money, "workin' and singin' a song." He sings, "See my ragtime shufflin' gait; happy 'cause I'm handlin' freight." The song was recorded by blues artist Mary Dixon in 1928 (Vocalion 1199) and most famously by Louis Armstrong in 1933 (Victor 24320). The year 1929 brought a philosophical piece, "Weary River" (Grant Clarke, Louis Silvers), comparing life to a river, and 1930 brought the light-hearted "Rollin' down the River" (Fats Waller, Stanley Adams) and "High Water," the latter recorded by Paul Robeson (HMV B-3663). The year 1931 saw the philosophical "The River and Me" (Harry Warren, Al Dubin), the light-hearted "Roll On, Mississippi, Roll On" (Eugene West, James McCaffrey, Dave Ringle), and "River Stay 'Way from My Door" (Mort Dixon, Harry Woods). The latter song is about a flood threat, but it is rather trivialized in the lyrics. It was a hit for popular white singer Kate Smith (Velvet Tone 2578–D) but was also recorded by Paul Robeson (HMV B-3956) that year.

Robeson by this time was becoming a specialist in songs with river themes. In 1933 he recorded "Take Me Away from the River" (HMV B-4352), and in 1935 he starred in the British film *Sanders of the River*.

Although the 1927 flood undoubtedly inspired the composition of some of these pieces and contributed to their popularity, none of them actually mention this flood in their lyrics. The only popular song to do so was "High Water Blues" by Daryl Sinclair Conner and Clarke Tate, published in 1927 in Augusta, Arkansas, by Conner Publishing Company.[42] It is described as "a real southern blues," and the cover depicts a black man sitting on the porch of a shack in the midst of rising flood waters, with animals seeking shelter in the distance. The singer has "those triflin' high water blues" as he sits on his porch without companionship, food, or a boat, contemplating the rising waters. Clarke Tate was a popular Memphis singer and music teacher and likely contributed the music to this composition. Daryl Sinclair Conner was undoubtedly connected to the publishing company in Augusta, Arkansas, that bears his surname. He probably contributed the lyrics. Augusta itself was not flooded, but the region around it was hard hit, with three hundred people stranded at nearby Peach Orchard Bluff for several days with few provisions.[43] Although the song is written in black dialect and is a bit sentimentalized, on the whole it presents a fairly realistic picture of the ravages of the flood. Needless to say, it was not what the world of popular song was looking for in 1927, and it failed to become a hit.

In 1974, white singer-songwriter Randy Newman from Georgia recorded a retrospective "Louisiana 1927" in a lush arrangement with synthesizers on the album *Good Old Boys* (Reprise 2193). In 1977, the fiftieth anniversary of the flood, the song was reissued on a 45 rpm single record (Reprise 1387). The historically inaccurate lyrics depict the flood striking the community of Evangeline and suggest that the devastation in Louisiana was somehow a conspiracy of Yankee politicians, including President Coolidge, who pays a fictitious visit to Louisiana accompanied by "a little fat man with a note-pad in his hand." In the booklet notes to a 2002 CD reissue of *Good Old Boys* (Reprise/Rhino R2 78243), Newman changes his interpretation of the event, claiming, still inaccurately, that the "Bosses in New Orleans" probably were behind a decision to let the flood take place upriver "above Clarksdale" in order to save their city.

The field of country music contributed a few songs about the flood of 1927. First into the studio was the immensely popular Vernon Dalhart, singing "The Mississippi Flood" composed by his partner Carson Robison (Victor 20611). This was first recorded by Dalhart on April 27, 1927, only six days after the levee broke near Greenville. The text is formulaic.[44] "The springtime flowers were blooming" and the "folks along the levee were happy all the day," when suddenly the skies grow cloudy and a "mighty torrent" falls to the ground. The levees break, waters rise, and people pray. The song concludes with the thought that "we can't explain the reason these great disasters come" but that, somehow, it must be God's will. Arthur Fields (Abe Finkelstein), a northern vaudeville performer and songwriter who occasionally recorded hillbilly material, made a recording in May 1927, of "The Terrible Mississippi Flood" (Grey Gull/Radiex 2334), which he probably also composed. It gives a straightforward account of the devastation caused by the flood and concludes, "Let's hope this great stream can be harnessed." Ernest V. Stoneman recorded "The Story of the Mighty Mississippi" on May 21, 1927, when the flood waters were still high. It was composed by Kelly Harrell. The lyrics tell of people on housetops, "children clinging in the treetops," and "mothers wading in the water with their babies in their arms," and conclude with the thought, "Let us all get right with our Maker." Robison was from Kansas, Dalhart from Texas, Fields from New York, and Stoneman and Harrell from Virginia. All of their flood songs are very objective and give no hint of any involvement on their part in the events of the flood, although they express sympathy for its victims.[45] Ernest V. Stoneman recorded another flood song at the May 21 session titled "Joe Hoover's Mississippi Flood Song," but it remained unissued. Not surprisingly, its composer is credited as Joe Hoover in the Victor session files. It is reported that Stoneman learned a flood song from a black janitor at the Victor building where he recorded.[46] If this is true, it was probably this song, and it is ironic that the janitor bore the same surname as the head of the flood relief effort. Joe Hoover composed other topical songs that were recorded by artists for Victor and its Bluebird subsidiary. "L'Eau Haute" ("High Water Waltz") (Victor 22562) by Louisiana Cajun artists Bartmon Montet and Joswell Dupuis, recorded in New Orleans on November 9, 1929, is probably another song about the 1927 flood.

We come now to the main topic of this presentation, the songs by African Americans that are specifically about the great flood of 1927. Using a method established by Guido van Rijn in his monumental study of blues and gospel songs related to the administration of President Franklin D. Roosevelt,[47] we shall seek connections between song texts, information about artists and composers, recording and release dates, and historical facts. The songs will be examined in chronological order of recording dates. This sort of examination actually enables us to eliminate from consideration several recordings made from 1928 onward, which are about other unrelated floods, or depict purely imaginary flood scenarios, or are about flooding in a general sense. Even many of these later songs, however, probably owe their existence at least in a small way to the precedent that was established through the popularity and commercial success of some of the songs about the 1927 flood. Some listeners might even have associated them incorrectly with their memories of the 1927 flood. Certainly a number of researchers have wrongly associated some of them with that flood. We must, therefore, examine these other flood songs briefly.

On September 18, 1928, Reverend Sutton E. Griggs recorded a sermon titled "Saving the Day" (Victor V38516). Likening his topic to the story of the Israelites crossing the Jordan River on dry ground (Joshua 3:17), Reverend Griggs tells how a group of black levee workers repaired a break in the levee during a Mississippi River flood when they "offered their bodies as temporary sandbags. Wedging their frames into the break, they formed a human wall, and at the immanent [sic] peril of their lives held the furious waters in leash until sandbags could be rushed to the break. And thus the day was saved." The sermon concludes with members of his congregation singing "Roll, Jordan, Roll." Griggs was pastor of the Tabernacle Institutional Baptist Church of Memphis and the author of several books on Negro advancement, including *Guide to Racial Greatness or the Science of Collective Efficiency*.[48] Although he has sometimes been labeled as an "accommodationist," he actually was an advocate of the adoption of various "traits of character," most of them drawn from the Bible, by which black people could advance the race and demonstrate their virtue, thus eliminating racial hatred by whites. While his sermon criticizes the reliance on levees to control floods, which had been an issue hotly debated in the wake of the 1927 flood, the actual example he cites pertains to an earlier flood of the Mississippi River in 1912. On April 11 of that year, the *New York Times* ran a story with the headline "Human Dike Used to Hold Back Flood: Negroes Lie on Top of Weakening Levee and Save Day Near Greenville, Miss."[49] What Griggs fails to mention, but which the newspaper article reveals, is that these several hundred levee workers did not "offer their bodies" but were "ordered . . . to lie down on top of the levee and as close together as possible" by a "young engineer in charge," without doubt a white man. Although this sermon is not about the flood of 1927, the example it uses is set in the same location that drew most attention that year, and it deals with issues of compulsory dangerous levee work, race relations, and government flood control policies that were prominent during the 1927 flood.

In March 1929, severe floods struck rivers in southern and southwestern Georgia, as well as parts of Alabama, Kentucky, and Tennessee. Particularly hard hit was the town of Elba, Alabama. These floods inspired Ivy Smith's "Southern High Waters Blues" (Gennett 7101), recorded on August 27 of that year, and probably George Carter's "Rising River Blues" (Paramount 12750). Carter was almost certainly from Atlanta, and his name is likely a pseudonym for Columbia recording artist Charlie Hicks (Charlie Lincoln). The Carter recording session is usually dated ca. February 1929, but the flooding actually began on February 28 and was preceded by rising rivers, as in the song's title. The song itself provides no textual detail and soon drifts on to other themes. Whatever the song's point of reference was, it seems unlikely that it was the Mississippi River flood of 1927. Reverend J. M. Gates of Atlanta also recorded a sermon on the 1929 floods on March 21 titled "The Flood of Alabama" (OKeh 8678).[50]

On January 23, 1930, the Memphis *Commercial Appeal* ran the headline "Flood Menace Shifts to Mississippi Area: Swollen Tallahatchie Forces 400 Families Out: Ice Thwarts Rescuers."[51] One month later, on February 21 or thereabouts, a singer named Mattie Delaney recorded "Tallahatchie River Blues" (Vocalion 1480) in Memphis with the line, "Some peoples on Tallahatchie done lost everything they had." Undoubtedly, she was singing about this recent flood. It was actually part of a series of floods that struck at this time, most seriously in northeastern Arkansas, accompanied by bitter cold and ice. No one died in the flood in Mississippi, but many families lost their possessions and livestock in flood waters that were three feet deep and turning to ice over 20,000 acres north of the town of Swan Lake.[52]

On July 19, 1933, Birmingham artist Sonny Scott recorded a self-composed blues called "Rolling Water" (Vocalion 02533). There were no particularly severe floods that year, and it is hard to tell what event Scott had in mind. This was his only recording session, and it is possible that the song was drawn from some past event, possibly the 1929 floods that did severe damage in Alabama. In the song, Scott's woman loses her life in a storm that rises suddenly and causes a lake to flood. These details do not fit the Mississippi River flood of 1927.

Popular blues singer Leroy Carr recorded a song called "Muddy Water" (Vocalion 03107) on August 14, 1934, composed by someone named "Williams." This is not the song of the same title that was composed in 1926. Carr's song is vague in its details and juxtaposes the singer's love life with the menace of a rising river. The singer escapes to a mountain and looks down on the river. Since there are no mountains anywhere near the Mississippi River, it is highly unlikely that this song refers to the flood of 1927.

On January 29, 1935, Houston-based singer Joe Pullum recorded "Mississippi Flood Blues" (Bluebird B5844) in a session in San Antonio. In it the singer's woman in Mississippi sends him a telegram asking him to rescue her from a flood. He vows to save her "if through twenty feet of water I wade." He finally succeeds, and by the end of the song he sings, "I'm back in my baby's arms with those Mississippi flood blues." Blues researchers have generally assumed that this song is related to the 1927 flood, although why a singer from Texas would sing about a flood that occurred in Mississippi eight years earlier is not clear. It is actually much more likely that Pullum's song is an imaginative recasting of an event that was widely reported in newspapers through an Associated Press wire service story two days before Pullum's recording session. The *New York Times* headlined it "Heroism of Negro Saves 100 in Flood: Mississippian Rows Six Miles with Frozen Hands to Obtain Large Boat."[53] Pullum would likely have seen the story in a Texas daily newspaper, as it was not reported in the Negro weekly papers until February 2, four days after his recording session.[54] The story concerns John Little, a black man from Crenshaw, Mississippi, who, in the dead of night and in freezing temperatures, rowed for six miles in order to obtain a larger boat for rescuing a hundred flood refugees in danger of drowning. The article stated that "the Negro's hands were frozen and his clothes had to be cut from his body, the flesh of his arms cracked and his finger tips may drop off. He is receiving the best of care from the white people and he is looked upon as a hero by whites and blacks in the Crenshaw area." It seems likely that Joe Pullum wanted to be a hero too, at least in his baby's eyes, in 1935, not in 1927.

In March 1936, there was severe flooding along rivers in Pennsylvania, West Virginia, and Maryland. The city of Pittsburgh was particularly hard hit. These floods inspired Casey Bill Weldon to record "Flood Water Blues No. 1 & 2" (Vocation 03220) on March 25 and Carl Martin to record "High Water Flood Blues" (Champion 50074) on April 18. In January and February of 1937, there were very severe floods along the Ohio and Mississippi Rivers that rivaled the flood of 1927. While the waters were still raging, Bumble Bee Slim recorded "Rising River Blues" (Vocalion 03473) on January 27, and Big Bill Broonzy recorded "Southern Flood Blues" (ARC 7–04–68) on January 29 and its flip side "Terrible Flood Blues" two days later. On March 12, Kokomo Arnold recorded "Wild Water Blues" (Decca 7285). Sleepy John Estes's "Floating Bridge" (Decca 7442), recorded August 2, 1937, was also related to the flood of that year. Lonnie Johnson contributed a "Flood Water Blues" (Decca 7397) on November 8 and followed this up with "South Bound Backwater" (Decca 7461) on March 31,

1938, more than a year after the flood struck. The latter song, however, might have been about severe flooding in eastern Arkansas in late February 1938, or indeed about any flood. By this point in his career, he had already recorded six other blues on flood themes. On May 10, 1959, Roosevelt Charles recorded "Where Were You When the Archeta River Went Down?" in Baton Rouge, Louisiana, about the 1937 flood.[55]

As we focus now on recordings about the 1927 flood, we see that four record companies—Columbia, OKeh, Paramount, and Victor—engaged in a sweepstakes of sorts to see which one could come up with the biggest original "race record" song hit dealing with this theme. They had to work fast—in the months of April, May, and June 1927—as public interest in topical songs tends to wane quickly. The year 1927 was full of other interesting stories in the fields of aviation, sports, politics, crime, and further natural disasters. All of the initial entries in this sweepstakes were blues, although some gospel commentary would emerge subsequently. The initial lack of new gospel songs about the flood is probably due to the fact that themes of floods and dangerous waters already abounded in Christian imagery and especially in traditional African American spirituals and sermons. Most famously there was Noah's flood, but other popular themes were Moses' crossing of the Red Sea, the Israelites crossing the River Jordan (also used as an image for the entry into heaven), and Christ walking on the waters. Even the story of Jonah and the whale could be related to the flood theme. OKeh Records, in fact, did quite well with a sermon by Rev. J. M. Gates, "Noah and the Flood" (OKeh 8458), fortuitously recorded on February 22, 1927, and released about the time that the southern levees broke. It was well advertised in the African American press.[56] We have also already noted the Norfolk Jubilee Quartette's recording of "The Old Account Was Settled Long Ago" and Paul Robeson's recording of "Deep River." Deacon Leon Davis's recording of "Didn't It Rain" (OKeh 8426), made on November 1, 1926, probably also continued to sell during the flood months. Other spiritual and sermon recordings with themes relevant to the flood could probably be identified.

In the blues sweepstakes, the Columbia Record Company was in the lead from the start. Their most popular blues artist, and probably the most popular on any label, Bessie Smith, had already recorded "Back-Water Blues" and "Muddy Water," and Columbia had these two records on the market by the time the levees broke in the South in April. For good measure, Columbia got its most popular country blues artist, Barbecue Bob, to record a flood blues in June. All three of these records were extensively advertised in the black press, and all three were hits. Both artists also recorded follow-up blues about the flood that were less successful, Smith in September and Barbecue Bob in April 1928. Kansas Joe and Memphis Minnie did not begin their recording careers until June 18, 1929, but on their first session they recorded a flood blues for Columbia. Mary Dixon, who also began her recording career after the flood, recorded in August 1929, a cover of a flood blues waxed the previous year by James Crawford for Gennett Records, and Clara Smith, Columbia's second biggest blues star, recorded a revised version of a flood blues that Lonnie Johnson had originally made in 1927 for OKeh Records.

OKeh took a somewhat different approach. Although they had their biggest blues star, Lonnie Johnson, record a flood blues only four days after the levee broke at Greenville and put his cover of "Back-Water Blues" on the flip side, the company otherwise seems to have conducted its own in-house sweepstakes. Blue Belle and Sippie Wallace were the winners with blues they recorded in early May. Their records and Lonnie Johnson's were advertised by OKeh. The losing songs that remained unissued were Raymond Boyd's "Hard Water Blues," recorded on May 1, and Bertha "Chippie" Hill's "Mississippi Waters Blues," recorded on May 14. Lonnie Johnson evidently liked the flood theme, as he followed up with flood blues on December 12, 1927, March 13, 1928, and June 11, 1929, all of them advertised by OKeh in the black press. A blues singer from Clarksdale, Mississippi, in the Delta, known only as Keghouse, recorded a "Scott Levee Blues" for OKeh on February 17, 1928, but it remained unissued. Finally, Elders McIntorsh and Edwards, whose recording careers had not begun at the time of the flood, recorded the only original gospel song on this theme for OKeh on December 4, 1928.

Paramount Records also shot its big gun, getting its star blues singer Blind Lemon Jefferson to record a flood blues in May 1927. The record was heavily advertised in the black press. The company hedged its bets, however, by getting a newcomer, Alice Pearson, to record no less than three songs on the flood theme in July. Her records were released but were not given feature advertisements and apparently sold poorly. Reverend Moses Mason, in his first and only studio session, recorded the only sermon about the flood for Paramount in January 1928. The record was heavily advertised, but the flip side was featured. As late as October 1929, Mississippi blues artist Charley Patton recorded a two-part flood blues for Paramount. The company devoted one of its last race record newspaper advertisements to this record, which became a surprise hit as the Great Depression was setting in.

Victor Records pinned all of its hopes in the blues field on Laura Smith, a fad-
ing veteran of the vaudeville circuit. She recorded two blues about the flood on
June 7, 1927, but Victor failed to promote the record. The company was doing
well, however, with Paul Robeson's "Deep River," Paul Whiteman's Rhythm
Boys' "Mississippi Mud," and hillbilly flood songs by Vernon Dalhart and Ernest
V. Stoneman.

The efforts of other companies to record flood blues were feeble in comparison to those of Columbia, OKeh, Paramount, and Victor. The best that the new
Black Patti Record Company could do was to get Herman Perry to make a
recording of "Muddy Water" on June 29, 1927, while Cameo Records got Viola
McCoy to record a cover of "Back-Water Blues" in the same month. Pathé/Perfect
recorded another cover of the same song that month by Kitty Waters. In April
1927, possibly after the southern levees broke, Uncle Charlie Richards (Blind
Richard Yates) recorded "Levee Blues" for Pathé/Perfect. It was not on a flood
theme, however, and in fact was a cover of a song that had been recorded before
the flood by Billy Higgins (Ajax 17125, ca. March 1925) and George Williams
(Columbia 14148–D, March 31, 1926).

Vocalion, Brunswick, and Gennett Records did not even enter the flood blues
sweepstakes in 1927. Vocalion recorded a jazz instrumental tune, "Low Levee—
High Water," by Chick Webb's Harlem Stompers on August 25, 1927, but it
remained unissued. In January 1928, however, Luella Miller recorded a flood
blues for Vocalion, backed with a blues about the more recent St. Louis tornado.
The best that Gennett could do was a flood blues by James Crawford on July 11,
1928. Vera Smith's "Farewell High Water Blues," recorded for Gennett on July 2,
1928, remained unissued.

On June 18, 1927, the *Baltimore Afro-American* reported that "'Back-Water
Blues' and 'Muddy Water' (a Mississippi moan) are probably in the fore of best
sellers of the past week. Both are by Bessie Smith. Some owners of the record shops
attribute the present popularity of these records to the publicity given to the
Mississippi river floods which are laying waste to many former haunts of record
buyers."[57] "Back-Water Blues" was by far the biggest hit song of the flood of 1927.
In fact, it became a blues standard. Besides the cover records that were made in
1927, the following artists, among others, have recorded versions of it over the
years: Albert Ammons, Lavern Baker, John Henry Barbee, Big Bill Broonzy,
Dusky Dailey, Cow Cow Davenport, John Lee Hooker, Lightnin' Hopkins,
John Jackson, Skip James, Larry Johnson, Lonnie Johnson, Leadbelly, Mance
Lipscomb, Sylvia Mars, Brownie McGhee, Memphis Slim, a group of women

convicts at Mississippi's Parchman Penitentiary, Buster Pickens, Brother John Sellers, Ruby Smith, Speckled Red, Will C. Thomas, Three Brown Buddies, Josh White, and Jimmy Witherspoon. Country music versions of the song were also recorded by Byrd Moore, The Three Tobacco Tags, and Dewey and Gassie Bassett.

"Back-Water Blues" was composed by Bessie Smith herself, but it was recorded on February 17, 1927, some two months before the levees broke in the southern states. This fact has caused some scholars to feel that the song is merely "a personal narrative of the distress caused by seasonal Mississippi floods,"[58] and that its connection with the 1927 flood is a fortuitous result of its recording and release dates. Some may even have assumed that Bessie Smith was clairvoyant. In the song's lyrics, she tells a fairly typical story of a rescue by boat from rising flood waters following a five-day rain. Pianist James P. Johnson creates special effects in the accompaniment that suggest wind, rain, and rushing waters. Bessie Smith gives no clues to the place or date of this flood, and to all intents and purposes it appears to be a generic flood song. Columbia Records' initial advertisements on April 2 treated the song as a generic piece, but on May 21 they stated, "'Back Water Blues' brings to your mind the heart-rending scene of the thousands of people made homeless by the mighty flood."[59] A week later, their advertisement called it "a real blues about the great flood that you'll want to have."[60]

Bessie Smith, "Back-Water Blues" (Bessie Smith). Acc. James P. Johnson, piano. New York, Feb. 17, 1927. Columbia 14195–D.

1. When it rained five days, and the skies turned dark as night, (x2)
Then trouble taking place in the lowlands at night.

2. I woke up this morning, can't even get out of my door. (x2)
That's enough trouble to make a poor girl wonder where she want to go.

3. Then they rowed a little boat about five miles 'cross the pond. (x2)
I packed all my clothes, throwed 'em in, and they rowed me along.

4. When it thunders and lightning, and the wind begins to blow, (x2)
There's thousands of people ain't got no place to go.

5. Then I went and stood upon some high old lonesome hill. (x2)
Then I looked down on the house where I used to live.

6. Back water blues done caused me to pack my things and go, (x2)
'Cause my house fell down, and I can't live there no more.

7. Mmmn, I can't move no more. (x2)
There ain't no place for a poor old girl to go.

There is only one source of information about the circumstances that inspired
Bessie Smith to compose "Back-Water Blues," and it is both enlightening and
misleading. Her sister-in-law Maud Smith, who was a member of Bessie's traveling show in late 1926 and early 1927, stated the following to Bessie's biographer
Chris Albertson:

> After we left Cincinnati, we came to this little town, which was flooded,
> so everybody had to step off the train into little rowboats that took us to
> where we were staying. It was an undertaker parlor next door to the the-
> ater, and we were supposed to stay in some rooms they had upstairs
> there. So after we had put our bags down, Bessie looked around and said,
> "No, no, I can't stay *here* tonight." But there was a lot of other people
> there, and they were trying to get her to stay, so they started hollerin',
> "Miss Bessie, please sing the 'Back Water Blues,' please sing the 'Back
> Water Blues.'" Well, Bessie didn't know anything about any "Back Water
> Blues," but after we came back home to 1926 Christian Street where we
> were living, Bessie came in the kitchen one day, and she had a pencil and
> paper, and she started singing and writing. That's when she wrote the
> "Back Water Blues"—she got the title from those people down South.[61]

There are four clues to the location and date of the flood in this statement: "after
we left Cincinnati," "this little town, which was flooded," "an undertaker parlor
next door to the theater," and "those people down South." The first two clues are
misleading, but the last two lead to the solution of the mystery. Chris Albertson
places Bessie Smith in Cincinnati twice during this period. He states that she
opened a one-week engagement at the Roosevelt Theater there on January 17,
1927, before going on to Chicago for the following week.[62] He has the troupe
playing in Detroit on Saturday, February 5, then leaving for Columbus, Ohio,
where they presumably would have opened on Monday, February 7. They
played only one show in Columbus. Then Bessie broke her contract and fled to
avoid a fight with her husband Jack Gee. She and her niece Ruby Smith hid out

in Cincinnati for a few days before heading for New York and her recording session of February 17, when she recorded "Back-Water Blues."[63] Since Maud Smith was not with Bessie on this second visit to Cincinnati, the flood that she describes could only have been encountered following the troupe's engagement there for the week of January 17. However, the troupe was headed for Chicago, not "down South." Furthermore, it turns out that Bessie Smith was not even in Cincinnati the week of January 17. Instead, she and her troupe played at the Lincoln Theater in Louisville, Kentucky, that week, according to files of the Hatch Show Print Company, which made her tour posters.[64] We must therefore find another scenario for her flood experience.

On Thursday, December 30, 1926, the *Nashville Banner* ran an advertisement on page 20 that stated: "The World's Greatest Blues Singer/Bessie Smith/With Her All-Star Revue/Special Show for White People/Bijou Theater—Tonight 10:45/Regular Show 8:30—Colored Only/'Passed by the Board of Censorship'/Phone 6–5981 for Seats." The headline that same day on the front page of Nashville's other newspaper, the *Nashville Tennessean*, read: "River Rise Here Sets Record . . . 6,000 Homeless, 1,500 Out of Jobs; Rise to Continue."

It is not possible to tell precisely when Bessie Smith opened at Nashville's Bijou Theater. She was on the T.O.B.A. circuit, and it would have been normal to open on a Monday night and run through Saturday, with Sunday free for traveling to the next theater on the tour. This would suggest an opening on Monday, December 27. However, the listings in the *Chicago Defender*'s "On the T.O.B.A." column of December 25 stated that she was to open at the Palace Theater in Ensley, Alabama, on December 20 and at the Frolic Theater in Birmingham on December 27.[65] The latter engagement may have been for one or two nights only. Ensley was actually a suburb of Birmingham, now part of the city. Complicating this picture is the statement by Chris Albertson, apparently from information supplied by Ruby Smith that "the troupe spent Christmas of 1926 on the road somewhere in Tennessee, where Bessie threw a small party for her gang."[66] Everyone got drunk at the party, and afterward Bessie initiated one of her famed lesbian relationships with a dancer in the show.[67] According to Albertson, "Several days later, Bessie was on stage at the Frolic Theater in Bessemer, Alabama."[68] The Frolic was actually in Birmingham, but Bessemer is a suburb and could be considered as part of "greater Birmingham." In trying to piece all of this together, the best itinerary that we can come up with would have her opening at the Palace in Ensley on December 20. Christmas day, December 25, was the following Saturday, but it is likely that southern theaters observed this religious holiday and remained closed. Bessie Smith's engagement in Ensley could have been for only one or a few days, and she could indeed have gone to "somewhere in Tennessee" for Christmas. The most likely place would have been her birthplace, Chattanooga, where she had family and friends. Chattanooga is only 150 miles from Birmingham and could be easily reached by train. It does seem odd, however, that Bessie Smith would pay for train fare for her whole troupe to come to Chattanooga, or anywhere else in Tennessee, when their next engagement was in Birmingham.[69] Whatever the case, they evidently played the Frolic in Birmingham on Monday, December 27. On one of the next three days they must have traveled to Nashville, as we know she was booked at the Bijou there on December 30, if not even earlier. She continued at the Bijou for the week beginning Monday, January 3, 1927, playing on successive Mondays in St. Louis, Louisville, and Chicago.[70] Thus Bessie Smith arrived in Nashville on December 28, 29, or 30, 1926, and stayed over until January 9, 1927.

When Bessie Smith arrived in Nashville, the city was in the midst of a major flood. It struck Nashville early on Christmas morning 1926. A short report in the next day's *New York Times* sounds almost like the basis for some of Bessie Smith's song lyrics: "Flood waters from rapidly rising Tennessee rivers, caused by excessive rainfall of the past five days, tonight menaced a wide portion of middle and western Tennessee, drove refugees from their homes, flooded highways and made highway traffic generally hazardous. One thousand persons are estimated to have been made homeless in Northeast Nashville, many of them Negroes, where the Cumberland River, which winds through the center of the city, ran rampant with the holiday spirit and inundated wide areas in low-lying residential sections. . . . At least a dozen families awoke Christmas morning to find water high about their premises."[71] The number of homeless was eventually estimated at 10,000.[72] The inundated section stretched for miles, and many people had to be rescued in rowboats; disruptions in train service were reported.[73] The Bijou Theater, where Bessie Smith played, was located at 423 4th Avenue North, right on the edge of the flooded section. Next door, at 422 4th Avenue North, was the establishment of William H. McGavock, Funeral, Undertaker & Embalmer.[74] This was undoubtedly the place that Maud Smith remembered where the troupe was initially brought for lodging.

Bessie Smith's "Back-Water Blues" corresponds to many facts of the flood in Nashville: five days of rain, flood in the lowlands, people waking up to flood conditions, rescue by rowboat, water that stretches for miles, and thousands of people homeless. There is nothing in her text that overtly suggests any racial dimension to this tragic story. Nevertheless, a racial critique can be read into the events. As the *Chicago Defender* observed in reporting on this flood, "The southern economic law, which assigns members of our Race to homes in the lowlands bordering dangerous rivers and swamps, might be blamed for the suffering widespread in communities occupied by members of our Race. . . . Relief work was begun immediately in the section occupied by whites. Our people have been forgotten by the police and various reserve workers."[75] With this report in mind, the line "trouble taking place in the lowlands at night" takes on a greater meaning.

There can be little doubt that Bessie Smith composed "Back-Water Blues" about the flood that she experienced in Nashville. The Cumberland River drains into the Ohio River and eventually into the Mississippi. Its rising waters at the end of 1926 contributed to the conditions that would eventually cause the levees to break further south in April 1927. Bessie Smith's "Back-Water Blues" is thus in every way part of the complex of songs about this flood.[76]

The bursting of the levee above Greenville, Mississippi, on April 21 was the defining event of the 1927 flood, and the great rush to record flood songs began only after this catastrophe. The first artist into a recording studio was Lonnie Johnson on April 25, only four days later, in St. Louis, which is situated on the Mississippi River but outside the flood zone.

Lonnie Johnson, "South Bound Water" (Johnson). Acc. self and James Johnson, guitars. St. Louis, Apr. 25, 1927. OKeh 8466.

1. I live down in the valley; people comes from miles around. (x2)
Their little homes was washed away; they had to sleep on the ground.

2. Through the dreadful nights I stood, no place to lay my head. (x2)
Water was above my knees, and the water had taken my bed.

3. I climbed up on the mountain to find some place to stay, (x2)
'Cause the south bound water had washed my little valley home away.

4. The water was roaring down the valley just like a thunder storm. (x2)
Washed my little valley house away; there's no place I can call my home.

Johnson's performance is strong, but his text is altogether ordinary. If ever there was a generic flood song, this was it. Although Johnson was born in New Orleans, had lived for many years in St. Louis, and had toured throughout the Mississippi Delta, there were no mountains close to any of these places or anywhere else that the flood inflicted major damage. It would appear that Johnson, or someone at OKeh Records, realized that Bessie Smith's record of "Back-Water Blues" was going to get a tremendous boost in sales from the recent flood events and decided that another record on a flood theme by a star blues singer might do equally well. Six days later, Johnson was back in the OKeh studio to record the flip side. It was a cover of "Back-Water Blues," complete with storm effects on the piano by John Erby, and only the predictable change from "girl" to "man" in the first-person lyrics. OKeh's advertisement for the record appeared on June 18, featuring "Back Water Blues" and a head portrait of the singer.[77]

In addition to making his own recordings, Lonnie Johnson was acting as a studio guitarist in OKeh's St. Louis sessions of late April and early May. On May 2, he and pianist DeLoise Searcy backed up a singer known as Blue Belle on the first recordings of her career. One of the two songs she recorded was "High Water Blues." There is some uncertainty about the singer's real name. An OKeh file card calls her Bessie Martin, and the composer credit on her record is "Martin." However, she later recorded for other companies under the names Bessie Mae Smith, May Belle Miller, St. Louis Bessie, and Streamline Mae.

Blue Belle, "High Water Blues" (Martin). Acc. prob. DeLoise Searcy, piano; Lonnie Johnson, guitar. St. Louis, May 2, 1927. OKeh 8483.

1. The rivers all are rising, ships sinking on the sea.
The rivers all rising, ships sinking on the sea.
I wonder do my baby think of me.

2. The waves is dashing and roaring like a lion. (x2)
My baby's in the river drifting up and down.

3. I want to go to Cairo, but the river's all over town.
I want to go to Cairo, but the water's all over town.
I want to ride the train, but the track's all out of line.

4. I'm gonna build me a ship and buy me a rocking chair. (x2)
If this water keep on rising, gonna rock on 'way from here.

5. My daddy's got something make you talk in your sleep.
My daddy have got something make you talk in your sleep.
But these high water blues will make you hang your head and weep.

OKeh released "High Water Blues" somewhat later than Lonnie Johnson's flood record and did not advertise it until August 13. Their advertisement was spectacular, however, depicting a young woman sitting in a rowboat without oars, holding her head in her hands, while huge waves tower above her. The caption read: "The great, green waves are rising high . . . like giant, yellow-eyed monsters they have menaced BLUE BELLE with death . . . she has raised her voice in song . . . all the horror of 'HIGH WATER BLUES' is waiting for you on this record. You see the stricken maiden . . . her struggle to safety . . . she holds you like a spell with her brooding Blues."[78] The performance is effective enough, but the singer's text seems to be trying to reconcile two themes, a shipwreck at sea and the flood along the Mississippi River between St. Louis, her home as well as the recording location, and Cairo, Illinois, about 150 miles to the South. Her good loving man is "drifting up and down" in the river, with waves "dashing and roaring like a lion." Contrary to the OKeh advertisement, which depicts the singer herself in a boat, Blue Belle is safe on land, although worried about the rising water. She expresses only a desire to build a ship and escape. She also tries to go to Cairo by train but is prevented by the high water there and uprooted tracks. Cairo lies at the juncture of the Ohio and Mississippi Rivers and is in danger of floods from either direction. It was threatened by flooding as early as April 14, and, over the next several days, levee workers fought feverishly to contain the spread of the rising waters. Rail service there was reported seriously hampered on April 18.[79] It is probably these events that Blue Belle had in mind when she recorded "High Water Blues" some two weeks later. The most spectacular loss at sea shortly before this recording date was the American freighter Elkton, which disappeared in the Pacific Ocean on February 16 and was declared sunk on April 8, with a loss of 37 crewmen.[80]

In 1949, Texas blues singer Melvin "Little Son" Jackson recorded "Cairo Blues" (Gold Star 663), containing the second line of stanza three of Blue Belle's "High Water Blues." Jackson also sang "The polices on the corner don't 'low nobody 'round" and "Girl I love, she got washed away." On July 10, 1960, he recorded another version of "Cairo Blues" (Arhoolie F1004), containing the first two of these lines. The remainder of his song abandons the flood theme. Jackson was born in 1916 near the city of Tyler in East Texas, and, so far as is known, did not experience the flood of 1927. Evidently, Blue Belle's recording had reached him directly or indirectly by 1949 and the theme appealed to him. Jackson's recording of that year, in turn, appealed to James "Son" Thomas, an artist born in 1926 in Eden, Mississippi, who later settled in the nearby town of Leland. Thomas recorded versions of the song, combined with lyrics from other records by Jackson, in 1968 (Matchbox 226), 1980 (L+R 42.035), 1981 (Swingmaster unissued), 1986 (Black & Blue 33.745), and 1990 (Rooster R96100). Although Leland is located in the Delta just a few miles east of Greenville and suffered greatly in the 1927 flood, Thomas was too young to have had any memory of it, and, in any case, his song is set far to the North in Cairo, Illinois. At most, his and Jackson's song appears to reflect the influence of Blue Belle's record and a generalized community knowledge about the consequences of floods and specifically about Cairo's precarious position at the confluence of two mighty rivers, the Mississippi and the Ohio. Nevertheless, Thomas's version had sufficient resonance in the Leland community some forty years after the 1927 flood for him to receive the nickname "Cairo."[81]

Blind Lemon Jefferson recorded "Rising High Water Blues" for Paramount Records in May, most likely very early in the month, as the record was given a feature advertisement in the *Chicago Defender* on June 11.[82] The illustration depicts a man and woman with their son and daughter, dog and mule, standing on a hill or levee watching housetops float by in the water. Even the letters of the song title are afloat. Next to a sketch of Jefferson with guitar, the caption reads: "The great and terrible Mississippi River Flood was Blind Lemon Jefferson's inspiration for 'Rising High Water Blues.' This awful catastrophe is described in this sensational new Paramount record, making a selection you will always want to keep, and one you'll never grow tired of playing." This is one of the few recordings made by Jefferson on which he does not play guitar, although the record label states that a guitar is present. The only instrument that can be heard, however, is the piano, ably played by George Perkins, about whom nothing is known. Perhaps piano accompaniment was chosen in order to continue the precedent set on Bessie Smith's "Back-Water Blues." The composition is credited to Perkins, but it has all the marks of a typical Jefferson lyric. In fact, except for a probable factual inaccuracy, it is an excellent piece of blues poetry, perhaps the best among the flood songs.

Blind Lemon Jefferson, "Rising High Water Blues" (George Perkins). Acc. George Perkins, piano. Chicago, ca. May 1927. Paramount 12487.

1. Back water rising, southern people can't make no time.
I said, back water rising, southern people can't make no time.
And I can't get no hearing from that Memphis girl of mine.

2. Water all in Arkansas, people screamin' in Tennessee.
Oh, people screamin' in Tennessee.
If I don't leave Memphis, back water been all over poor me.

3. Paper states it's rainin'; it has been for nights and days.
Paper states it's rainin', has been for nights and days.
Thousand people stands on the hill lookin' down where they used to stay.

4. Children sadly pleading, "Mama, we ain't got no home."
"Oh, mama, we ain't got no home."
Papa says to children, "Back water left us all alone."

5. Back water rising, come in my windows and door.
The back water rising, come in my windows and door.
I'll leave with a prayer in my heart, back water won't rise no more.

Blind Lemon Jefferson was from Texas and had been living part of the time in Chicago, where he made his recordings for Paramount. He is known to have performed in Memphis and the Mississippi Delta and probably would have done so in his travels in 1926 following the great success of his first records released early that year. The months of the fall cotton harvest would have been a good time for him to make money in the Delta region of Mississippi and Arkansas, which he could do simply by standing in a park or on a street corner and performing for tips. In 1927, he traveled from Dallas to Atlanta by train to make records for OKeh on March 14 and 15.[83] This was just a month before the great flood, and he would have passed through regions of Louisiana and Mississippi that would be hard hit. There is no doubt that he had some familiarity with the flood zone and probably knew some people there as well. He may even have had a girl friend there, as he states in his song. He also states that he knew about the flood from newspaper reports. Although he could not see to read, his songs suggest that he had a keen interest in the world around him, and he easily could have heard news reports read by others.[84] He begins his song with an expression of sympathy for all of the "southern people" who "can't make no time." The latter expression refers to hourly or daily wage work and would have had special applicability to many black workers in the flood zone. The subject would come up once again in a flood blues by Barbecue Bob, and the issue of wages was a major theme in the complaints directed against the flood relief efforts in Greenville and elsewhere. Jefferson takes a variety of perspectives on the flood, focusing on his "Memphis girl," himself, the refugees as a whole, a typical refugee family, and himself again, ending with a prayer for something that would benefit everyone—an end to the rising waters. He mentions Memphis, the states of Tennessee and Arkansas, and a hill where people look down on the flood scene. Memphis, Tennessee, is located on bluffs high above the flood level of the Mississippi River. It experienced only relatively minor street flooding and back-water from its creeks. Its Tri-States Fairgrounds, however, were one of the largest refugee camps in the flood zone, and it served as the Red Cross headquarters for the entire relief effort. The camp began taking in refugees around April 23 and eventually held thousands, most of them from the St. Francis River area in Arkansas.[85] Thus, Jefferson's line in stanza two, "Water all in Arkansas, people screamin' in Tennessee," is quite accurate historically, although his fears about back water in Memphis had little foundation. The hill that Jefferson mentions in stanza four could well be Crowley's Ridge, which runs parallel to the St. Francis River for much of its length. Just west of the river, it would have been a natural place of immediate refuge before people could be evacuated to the Fairgrounds in Memphis.

The remaining singer in the initial rush to record topical flood blues was Sippie Wallace. Originally from Houston, Texas, she had settled in Chicago and Detroit in the 1920s. She was probably familiar with the flood zone through her travels on the vaudeville theater circuit. "The Flood Blues" was recorded by her in Chicago on May 6. It has the fullest accompaniment of any of the flood songs, a four-piece all star jazz combo featuring Louis Armstrong on cornet. In 1982, Wallace told Eric Townley and Ron Harwood, "'The Flood Blues' was about the 1927 Mississippi floods. Now Bessie Smith had done 'Backwater Blues' and Mr. Peer came to my brother in Chicago and said they wanted me to do a flood blues so George and I wrote it."[86] George W. Thomas, her brother, was a successful Chicago blues songwriter and publisher and often supplied his sister with song material. Yet, the record credits composition of the song to "Wallace-Granger." The second name would likely be the pianist on the recording session, probably Cleo Granger. Mr. Peer was Ralph Peer, who had supervised Wallace's early recording sessions for OKeh, beginning in 1923. By 1927, however, he was working for Victor Records and would not have been involved in Wallace's recording of "The Flood Blues." Nevertheless, it is quite possible that some other representative of OKeh suggested the topic to Wallace's brother.

Sippie Wallace, "The Flood Blues" (Wallace-Granger). Acc. Louis Armstrong, cornet; Artie Starks, clarinet; unknown, piano (Cleo Granger ?); Bud Scott, guitar. Chicago, May 6, 1927. OKeh 8470.

1. I'm standing in this water, wishing I had a boat. (x2)
The only way I see is take my clothes and float.

2. The water is rising, people fleeing for the hills.
Lord, the water will obey if you just say "Be still."

3. They sent out alarms for everybody to leave town. (x2)
But when I got the news, I was high water bound.

4. They dynamite the levee, thought it might give us ease. (x2)
But the water still rising, doing as it please.

5. I called on the Good Lord and my man too. (x2)
What else is there for a poor girl to do?

The text is quite focused on the singer's immediate peril in the rising flood waters. It is notable for its religious imagery in stanzas two and five and its attention to factual detail in stanzas three and five. Alarms were sounded in advance of the flood waters in many towns, including Greenville. There was also dynamiting at many points along the levee system, both planned by authorities and in illegal acts by individuals, all hoping to divert flood waters and save selected sites from inundation. The most famous dynamiting, which, as we saw, began at Caernarvon, below New Orleans, on April 29, was widely publicized in newspapers and newsreels, and was very likely the scenario for Sippie Wallace's song. The evacuation preceding the dynamiting was orderly and no one was stranded in the manner described in the lyrics. The affair was controversial, but Wallace gives no hint of this in her lyrics, although she does suggest that the plans of men are futile against the power of nature and that only God (and perhaps her man) can help.

Victor Records entered the flood blues sweepstakes last, bringing Laura Smith into a Chicago studio to record two flood songs on June 7, a month after

Sippie Wallace's session. She was a vaudeville veteran, now near the end of her career and suffering from bouts of ill health, but back in 1910 and 1911 she had toured in theaters all over the Mississippi and Arkansas Deltas in the Tri-State Circuit headquartered in Memphis.[87] "Lonesome Refugee" and "The Mississippi Blues" were composed by Sidney Easton and Joe Simms respectively, according to Victor session files. Both were veteran vaudeville singers and comedians and had made a few recordings of their own. Laura Smith probably knew them from her many years on the circuit. Simms and Easton were co-producers of a musical comedy, *Sons of Rest in Shiloh*, making the rounds of northeastern black vaudeville theaters in May. On May 14, 1927, about three weeks before Laura Smith's recording session, the *Baltimore Afro-American* reported that Simms, in Philadelphia at the Gibson Theater with the show, was planning a benefit program there for the flood sufferers. It added that Simms was originally from Vicksburg, Mississippi, and that his father, Rev. David Simms, had been pastor of King David Baptist Church there for twenty-five years. Rev. Simms at this time was "directing his church workers in the care and relief of flood victims."[88]

Laura Smith, "Lonesome Refugee" (Sidney Easton). Acc. Clarence M. Jones, piano. Chicago, June 7, 1927. Victor 20775.

Tracks all washed away, wires down,
Levee is busted; good-bye, town.
All I had went floating down the stream.

You'll never know 'less you've been there.
Oh, what a cross I had to bear.
Always I'll remember what the levee watchman said.

Tide is rising, water's everywhere.
Trouble in its wake and much despair.
Once a rosy lawn, but now a muddy pond
Floods the fields of cotton and the sugar cane,
And wrecks the shanties down in Pleasant Lane.
I'm so weary, heavy laden, and blue,
With no one to tell my trouble to.
I'm just a wandering homeless lonesome refugee.

I'm so weary, heavy laden, and blue,
With no one to tell my trouble to.
I'm just a wandering homeless lonesome refugee.

Laura Smith, "The Mississippi Blues" (Joe Simms). Acc. Clarence M. Jones,
piano. Chicago, June 7, 1927. Victor 20775.

I'm blue; you'd be too,
If your home was washed away.
Mine's gone, so long,
I'm weeping every day.
So sad, too bad,
Lost everything I had.
That's why I sigh and sometimes cry,
I get so raving mad.

Water, water, more than I've ever seen.
The water is still rising from Memphis down to New Orleans.
I feel so bad, I don't know what I'll ever do,
And as long as I live, I'll have the Mississippi River blues.

Mmmm, mmmm. (x3)

Now it's water, water, more than I've ever seen.
Yes, the water is still rising from Memphis down to New Orleans.
I feel so bad, I don't know what I'll ever do,
And as long as I live, I'll have the Mississippi River blues.

The lyrics of both songs have an oddly dated, at times even flippant, quality ("Levee is busted; good-bye, town"; "Once a rosy lawn, but now a muddy pond"; "So sad, too bad, lost everything I had"). This compositional style was more typical of popular songs than of blues in 1927. The lyrics depict more or less generic flood scenes, even in the one specific location that is given: Pleasant Lane. There is, however, a specific historical detail embedded in the second song, when Smith sings, "The water is still rising from Memphis down to New Orleans." Although the initial devastation of late April and early May had long passed by the date of recording, a second rising of the Mississippi River was feared, and ferocious levee reinforcement was carried out near Greenville in the first week of June. It ended on June 7, the date of Laura Smith's recording session, and the town was saved from further destruction.[89] The work was done entirely by compulsory Negro labor, and many of the workers must have muttered something like Laura Smith's lines, "I get so raving mad" and "As long as I live, I'll have the Mississippi River blues."

By mid-June, the flood stories were centered on the topics of mud, the clean-up effort, and taking toll of the losses. Atlanta artist Robert Hicks (Barbecue Bob) was in a New York studio to sing about them for Columbia Records in his "Mississippi Heavy Water Blues."

Barbecue Bob, "Mississippi Heavy Water Blues" (—). Acc. own guitar. New York, June 15, 1927. Columbia 14222–D.

1. I was walking down the levee with my head hanging low,
Looking for my sweet mama, ah, but she ain't here no more.
That's why I'm crying "Mississippi Heavy Water Blues."

2. Lord, Lord, Lord, I'm so blue; my house got washed away,
And I'm crying "How long 'fore another pay day?"
That's why I'm crying "Mississippi Heavy Water Blues."

3. I'm sitting here looking at all of this mud,
And my gal got washed away in that Mississippi flood.
That's why I'm crying "Mississippi Heavy Water Blues."

4. I hope she comes back some day kind and true.
Can't no one satisfy her like her sweet papa do.
That's why I'm crying "Mississippi Heavy Water Blues."

5. I think I heard her moan on that Arkansas side,
Crying "How long before sweet mama ride?"
That's why I'm crying "Mississippi Heavy Water Blues."

6. I'm in Mississippi with mud all in my shoes.
My gal in Louisiana with those high water blues.
That's why I'm crying "Mississippi Heavy Water Blues."

Spoken: *Lord, send me a sweet mama.*

7. Got plenty mud and water, don't need no wood or coal.
All I need's some sweet mama to slip me jelly roll.
That's why I'm crying " 'Sippi Heavy Water Blues."

8. Nothin' but mud and water far as I could see.
I need some sweet mama come and shake that thing with me.
That's why I'm crying "Mississippi Heavy Water Blues."

9. Listen here, you mens. One more thing I'd like to say.
Ain't no womens out here, for they all got washed away.
That's why I'm crying "Mississippi Heavy Water Blues."

10. Lord, Lord, Lord, Mississippi's shaking, Louisiana's sinking.
The whole town's a rinking [sic]; Robert Hicks is singing.
That's why I'm crying "Mississippi Heavy Water Blues."

Columbia advertised the record on August 13 with a photograph of the artist in a chef's outfit serving a plate of barbecue, with the caption: "When Barbecue Bob mixes the notes for a vocal dish, you are sure that nothing better ever came off the fire."[90] Despite the inappropriate promotion, the record was a hit, and the song was covered years later in 1959 by Robert Pete Williams (Folk Lyric LP 111), then incarcerated at the Louisiana State Penitentiary in Angola, located on the Mississippi River. Since convicts were frequently drafted for levee work when floods threatened in the southern states, Williams probably knew what he was singing about. It is not known, however, whether Barbecue Bob had ever been in the flood zone, but surely he had heard details about the flood and its aftermath.[91] He mentions the three states hardest hit, Arkansas, Mississippi, and Louisiana, distributing the action among them equally. The first six stanzas depict a tragic scene of a man searching the levee for his "sweet mama," eventually to conclude that she was washed downstream in the Mississippi River flood. If he has any specific location in mind, it would have to be Greenville, as it is across the river from Arkansas, just a few miles above that state's border with Louisiana. There must have been many there who walked through the eight-mile refugee camp on the levee looking for loved ones. The line in stanza two expressing uncertainty about "another pay day" could also be related to the conditions at Greenville and the controversy over payment for the flood relief work done by African Americans. Following a pause in which Barbecue Bob says, "Lord, send me a sweet mama," the remaining verses are focused on sex, or rather the lack of it. Several of the flood blues had mentioned spouses, boy friends, or girl friends, and Blue Belle had even stated, "My daddy's got something make you talk in your sleep." Barbecue Bob, however, leaves absolutely no doubt that he is really horny and sex is uppermost on his mind. Although this preoccupation may seem crass in light of scenes of death and destruction he has described earlier in the song, the disruption of many refugees' sex lives under crowded camp conditions with little privacy and exhausting forced labor must have been a real factor in the flood zone. It is a topic that goes unmentioned in the press accounts and histories of the flood, and we are dependent on Barbecue Bob to reveal it. "Robert Hicks is singing" indeed!

Sometime in July, Alice Pearson and her piano accompanist Freddie Coates appeared in Paramount Records' Chicago studio to record six blues. This would be Ms. Pearson's only recording session, and three of her songs would be concerned with recent natural disasters, "Memphis Earthquake," "Greenville Levee Blues," and "Water Bound Blues." From their titles and lyrics, it would appear that Pearson experienced the flood at Greenville on April 21, spent some time in the refugee camp on the levee, and eventually made her way north to Memphis in time to experience an earthquake there on the morning of May 7. The only published information about her comes from an interview of Johnny Watson, better known as Daddy Stovepipe, made by Paul Oliver in Chicago in 1960. Recalling his days in Greenville, Mississippi, Watson stated, "There was another lady used to sing—Alice—Alice Pears think her name was and she had a pianner player call him Freddy. They used to be there."[92] These would seem to be Alice Pearson and Freddie Coates, but we cannot be certain whether Watson's memory extended back to 1927. He and his wife Sarah recorded a "Greenville Strut" (Vocation 1662) in 1931, and Watson told Oliver he stayed in Greenville until 1937 when Sarah died. But in July 1927, he was in Birmingham, not too far from his birthplace of Mobile, recording with a male partner, Whistlin' Pete, and before that, in 1924, he recorded alone in Richmond, Indiana, both times for Gennett Records. Whatever the period was that Watson remembered, there can be little doubt that Alice Pearson had some familiarity with Greenville. Her pianist, Freddie Coates, however, was a well-known musician in Memphis and had accompanied blues singer Sadie James there in a February 1927 session for

Victor Records. Fred Coates (wife Ruth) is listed in the 1927 Memphis City Directory as a musician living at 223 Hernando St. He is not listed in 1928, but he reappears in 1929 as a musician living at 479 E. Iowa Avenue with a wife named Thelma. Whether Alice Pearson met him for the first time before her Chicago session or worked with him for some time is not known, but her first blues on a natural disaster certainly indicates that she had been in Memphis not long before the recording session.

Alice Pearson, "Memphis Earthquake" (−). Acc. Freddie Coates, piano. Chicago, ca. July 1927. Paramount 12507.

1. Earth quaked last night just about two o'clock. (x2)
You might have seen my bed began to reel and rock.

2. I wheeled and turned in my bed from side to side. (x2)
I'll overcome next summer some day bye and bye.

Hoo hoo hoo hoo hoo hoo hoo.
Hoo hoo hoo hoo hoo hoo.
Hoo hoo hoo hoo hoo hoo.

3. When the sun looked funny and the doves began to moan, (x2)
Lord, I knowed right then that something was going on wrong.

4. 'Fore the sun went down, I felt so sad and blue.
When the sun went down, I felt so sad and blue.
I knowed some[thing] was going to happen, and I didn't know what to do.

On Sunday, May 8, 1927, Mothers' Day, the Memphis *Commercial Appeal* replaced the latest flood news on its front page headline with the following report: "New Madrid Fault Caused Earthquake: Shocks Here Early Yesterday Felt Over 250–Mile Radius: Memphis' 37th Quake: Shifting of Rocks Cause Temblors That Shook Houses, Caused Chimneys to Topple—No Connection Between Flood and Quake." The article went on to state that the quake occurred between 2:30 and 2:35 on the morning of May 7 and lasted for six to seven seconds. The shocks were felt in five states but did only minor damage. Nevertheless, the newspaper noted, "The quakes yesterday morning just about put on the finishing touch to a series of weather freaks that have accompanied the worst flood in the history of the valley." These "weather freaks" included tornadoes, lightning storms, and incessant rains. The paper reassured readers, "There is no connection between the flood and the earthquake, Meteorologist F. W. Brist said yesterday. He pointed out that the two are caused by different elements of nature, and declared that earthquakes are more frequent when there is no flood than when there is a flood."

Memphis lies in the New Madrid fault zone. Tremendous earthquakes occurred in this zone in 1811 and 1812 that caused the bed of the Mississippi River to shift in several places and created Reelfoot Lake in northwestern Tennessee. If the area had been heavily settled, as it was only a few decades later, the loss of lives would have been huge. There have been many lesser earthquakes reported along the New Madrid fault in the years since then. Dr. Arch Johnston, Director of the Center for Earthquake Research and Information at the University of Memphis, states that the epicenter of the 1927 quake was somewhere between Marked Tree and Jonesboro, Arkansas, about fifty miles from Memphis, and that it was actually felt over seven states and had an estimated magnitude of 4.8, perhaps as high as 5, on the Richter Scale.[93] Johnston adds, "The question whether the earthquake was in some way related to the 1927 flood is intriguing, but the bottom line is that it is impossible to say with certainty. The location is right along the SW extension of the New Madrid fault zone so in one sense it was routine, just part of the ongoing or background earthquake activity of the New Madrid zone. But earthquakes can be induced or triggered by external changes of surface conditions. One of the best examples is earthquakes induced by artificial reservoirs, and they correlate best with sudden changes in the reservoir water level rather than the absolute level itself. The great 1927 flood would qualify as 'sudden.'"

The *New York Times* reported, "Some brick chimneys were tumbled down in North Jonesboro, Ark., and numbers of residents of other towns were shaken up, but there apparently was no effect on river levees, which at first it was feared might have been weakened by the earth movements. Residents of many towns, however, were badly frightened for they seemed to connect the shocks in some way with the flood."[94] It would certainly appear that Alice Pearson thought there was a connection. If she had just recently experienced the flood at Greenville, as she states in her songs, surely her nerves as well as her bed were shaken by the earthquake. In fact, in stanza two, she declares that it will take her a year to recover. She admits in her final stanza that she had been worried on the evening before the earthquake, and in the preceding stanza she recalls warning signs from nature. Folk beliefs that nature gives signs of impending calamities are universal. Dr. Johnston states that there are many reports of peculiar behavior by animals prior to earthquakes.

"Memphis Earthquake" was the first song Alice Pearson recorded at her Paramount session. Two songs later, she recorded "Greenville Levee Blues," followed immediately by "Water Bound Blues."

Alice Pearson, "Greenville Levee Blues" (—). Acc. Freddie Coates, piano. Chicago, ca. July 1927. Paramount 12547.

1. I woke up this morning, couldn't even get out of my door. (x2)
The levee broke, and this town is overflowed.

2. And you could hear people screaming all over town. (x2)
And some was hollering, "Please don't let me drown."

3. When the water was rising, creeping up in my door, (x2)
I had a mind to leave, and I didn't know where to go.

4. They was rowing little boats five and ten miles away.
They was rowing little boats, Lord, five and ten miles away.
They were picking up people didn't have no place to stay.

5. Living on the levee, sleeping on the ground. (x2)
I will tell everybody that Greenville's a good old town.

6. Delta water caused me to lose my clothes and shoes. (x2)
You can tell by that it's left me with the Delta water blues.

Alice Pearson, "Water Bound Blues" (—). Acc. Freddie Coates, piano. Chicago, ca. July 1927. Paramount 12507.

1. High fever and sufferin' really got me barred. (x2)
I can't even get away. High water's all in my yard.

2. I went to bed last night, water was easing over my white floor. (x2)
I got up this morning, water creeping all in my door.

Hey, hey, hey, hey, hey, hey.
Hey, hey, hey, hey, hey, hey, hey.
Hey, hey, hey, hey, hey, hey, hey, hey.

3. I went and climbed a tall old lonesome tree.
I went and climbed up a tall old lonesome tree.
I couldn't stand to see my house float away from me.

4. All down the road the water's all 'cross the tracks. (x2)
And I've left my home; you see I can't go back.

"Greenville Levee Blues" clearly owes some lyric as well as melodic debts to
Bessie Smith's "Back-Water Blues," yet Alice Pearson's song has a greater immediacy and sense of terror. It is the difference between a song composed by someone
who experienced the rapidly rising waters and one by someone who arrived in a
flooded city a few days after a flood had hit. The "levee" that she has in mind in
the song's title is not the broken levee that let the flood waters into the Delta, but
the levee that served as a "concentration camp," with thousands of black people
"sleeping on the ground." Where did Alice Pearson stand on the controversies that
surrounded the refugee camp at Greenville? We may never know for certain, and
that is probably how she wanted it to remain. The last line of stanza five, "I will tell
everybody that Greenville's a good old town," would seem to indicate approval of
"living on the levee, sleeping on the ground." Or does it? No doubt all of the
refugees felt gratitude for their rescue and whatever provisions they received, since
many had lost everything they possessed. No doubt they realized also that they
were living under emergency conditions and that hardships were to be expected.
The resentment arose only when it became clear that white refugees were systematically receiving better treatment and had greater freedom of movement. If "good
old town" is meant in the same way as the common southern phrase "good old
boy," it would mean "typical," with an added connotation of "wild, hell raising."
Alice Pearson used this ambiguous phrase to "tell everybody" about the conditions
in the camp without challenging anyone's sensibilities or inviting retaliation.

In "Water Bound Blues," Pearson's opening line, "High fever and sufferin' really
got me barred," seems to describe a present state, while the remainder of the song
recounts her experience in the flood, essentially stating how she came to be in this
condition. Many of the refugees were not in the best of health even before the flood.
Rickets, pellagra, and hookworm were common diseases in the rural South, but the

unsanitary conditions in the camps led to outbreaks of typhoid fever, venereal disease, smallpox, and anthrax among cattle, with fears of epidemics. The Red Cross initiated a policy of compulsory inoculation. A correspondent from Natchez for the *Chicago Defender* described conditions in the camps in several locations in Mississippi, conditions that undoubtedly prevailed in Greenville. "To check epidemics of typhoid fever and smallpox in refugee camps here and throughout the state, the medical division of the Mississippi flood relief forces have ordered antitoxins for more than 90,000 persons, the majority of whom are members of our Race. The dread diseases are beginning to destroy hundreds of men, women and children who have been driven from their homes along the banks of the Mississippi. Members of our Race have been especially affected by the epidemic because of the poor sanitary conditions in refugee camps. Many of them are dying from the poor food they are receiving at the hands of white relief workers."[95] This article was written on May 13. The conditions were much worse in the camps two and three weeks earlier when Alice Pearson was presumably still in Greenville. She states that these conditions "really got me barred," but it is hard to imagine she did not also have in mind the National Guard troops that patrolled the camp and prevented refugees from leaving. Somehow, she got out of Greenville. Perhaps she was among the refugees transferred to the camp at Memphis to relieve overcrowding. She concluded her song with the line, "And I've left my home; you see I can't go back." In 1928, Alice Pearson was listed in the Memphis City Directory as rooming at 249 S. Third St., in the Beale Street entertainment district. She had said in "Memphis Earthquake" that it would take her until the next summer to "overcome."

By the end of July, the waters had largely receded, and blues singers could now even inject a bit of humor into flood themes. No doubt even the verses about Barbecue Bob's sexual cravings in his "Mississippi Heavy Water Blues," recorded on June 15, had raised a few chuckles. On July 30, Columbia blues artist Clara Smith recorded "Black Cat Moan" (Columbia 14240–D), a song evidently composed by her pianist Stanley Miller. It is not a flood song but a song about bad luck and the loss of the singer's man, all brought about by a black cat that moans and crosses her path. In the third stanza, however, she sings:

> *You heard about the flood way down South.*
> *I'll tell you how it come about.*
> *Two black cats had a fight.*
> *I didn't hear which one was right.*
> *The black cats squabbled, and it rained every night.*

Although it would be dangerous to read too much into these lyrics, the choice of flood imagery to express fear was an appropriate one. In the song's next and final stanza Clara Smith sings:

Mmmm, I'm scared to death.
Mmmm, I can't get my breath.
Mmmm, somebody hold my hand.
I'm getting weak in my knees, and I can't stand.
I heard a black cat moaning like a natural man.

Bessie Smith and Columbia Records must have been pleased with the success of her "Back-Water Blues," and between them it was decided to record a follow-up, "Homeless Blues," on September 28. This time, the lyrics were composed by Bessie Smith's pianist, Porter Grainger. The record was released shortly before Christmas, and Columbia advertised it extensively in the black press. The illustration was inappropriate, however, depicting a male hobo sitting dejectedly on a porch step and holding a cigar.[96] The caption makes no mention of the flood, but the lyrics certainly do.

Bessie Smith, "Homeless Blues" (P. Grainger). Acc. Ernest Elliott, alto saxophone; Porter Grainger, piano. New York, Sept. 28, 1927. Columbia 14260–D.

1. Mississippi River, what a fix you left me in.
Lord, Mississippi River, what a fix you left me in.
Mudholes of water clear up to my chin.

2. House without a steeple, didn't even have a door. (x2)
Plain old two-room shanty, but it was my home sweet home.

3. Ma and Pa got drownded; Mississippi, you to blame.
My Ma and Pa got drownded; Mississippi, you to blame.
Mississippi River, I can't stand to hear your name.

4. Homeless, yes, I'm homeless, might as well be dead.
Ah, you know I'm homeless, homeless, yes, might as well be dead.
Hungry and disgusted, no place to lay my head.

5. Wished I was an eagle, but I'm a plain old black crow. (x2)
I'm gonna flop my wings and leave here and never come back no more.

In this song, the flood is definitely along the Mississippi River, not in Nashville. There are two strong expressions of racial pride here, even in the face of disaster, poverty, hunger, and homelessness. Just before lamenting the deaths of her mother and father, she describes their lost dwelling as "plain old two-room shanty, but it was my home sweet home." One thinks here of the thousands of black people restricted in the camps and prevented from checking on their two-room shanties and their belongings, then forced to help clean up the grand homes of the white people. In her final stanza, she cannot be the king of birds, just "a plain old black crow." But for all that, she is flying just the same and getting out of the flooded region never to return. This is precisely what thousands of flood refugees did as soon as they could. It was what the white authorities and plantation owners feared and tried to prevent with their "concentration camps," but they could do so only temporarily.

Reverend J. M. Gates of Atlanta would record many sermons on current events in a career that stretched from 1926 to 1941. He had recorded "Jonah and the Whale" (OKeh 8478) and "Noah and the Flood" (OKeh 8458) on February 22, 1927, and these records sold well during the months of the flood. He was not in a recording studio again, however, until early October, and by then other natural disasters had been in the news. On October 6 in Atlanta, he recorded "God's Wrath in the St. Louis Cyclone" (OKeh 8515), assisted by Deacon Leon Davis and Sisters Norman and Jordan. The sermon is mainly about the tornado that struck St. Louis on September 29, 1927, and left ninety-one dead and 5,000 homes destroyed. But Rev. Gates extends his theme of God's wrath to Sodom and Gomorrah, Memphis (which suffered Yellow Fever epidemics in 1879 and 1880), Miami, Florida (which had suffered a hurricane on September 18, 1926, that left over 1,000 dead), Atlanta (which was burned by the Union army in 1864), and Chicago (which was devastated by fire in 1871). In the midst of relating these acts of God's wrath, Rev. Gates states that "God not only rode through St. Louis, ah, in the cyclone, but He passed through Louisiana, and down Tennessee, Mississippi and Tennessee in a flood of water." This theme of God's anger at sin would recur in the lone religious song composed about the 1927 flood.

On December 12 Lonnie Johnson recorded "Low Land Moan" (OKeh 8677). It was not released, however, until a year and a half later. The song is not about a flood, but it describes work on the levees and in "the freight house yards." The work pays a dollar an hour, good pay for manual labor in 1927, but it is "too long and hard." He suggests that "six months in the lowlands has made some change in me," making him mean and hard-hearted, and he threatens to kill his woman "just to see her fall." The song may have a peripheral relationship to the 1927 flood, in the sense that there was plenty of levee restoration work to be had in the months following the flood, if one was willing to work "too long and hard." On September 9, 1930, Clara Smith recorded a version of this song (Columbia 14580–D) recomposed from a woman's point of view.

The only sermon completely devoted to the 1927 flood was recorded in Chicago by Moses Mason in January 1928. It was titled "Red Cross the Disciple of Christ Today" (Paramount 12601). Paramount advertised him in the *Chicago Defender* as "Uncle Mose Mason, the singing elder from the Delta land."[97] The company even advertised the record in May, July, and August 1928, in *The Crisis*, the journal of the NAACP, which had been highly critical of the flood relief effort and even the Red Cross. The advertisements, however, featured the record's flip side, another sermon titled "Judgment Day in the Morning." Moses Mason may have been a man of that name, listed in the 1930 U.S. Census for Washington County, Mississippi, Enumeration District 76–3, sheet 10–A, recorded April 26, 1930. He is described as fifty-one years old, married at age twenty-one, literate, born in Mississippi of parents born in Virginia, a farmer, and living with his wife Katie, age fifty. Greenville is the county seat of Washington County. Apparently the same Moses Mason was recorded in nearby Bolivar County in the World War One Civilian Draft Registration, said to be born June 1, 1878. The *Chicago Defender* advertisement contains a photograph of a man who appears to be about fifty years of age. A Moses Mason, who worked on the levee when the flood struck and who is still living in Greenville, is not the man who recorded this sermon. His wife told me over the telephone recently that her husband "wasn't nothin' but a boy" when he worked on the levee.[98]

Moses Mason, "Red Cross the Disciple of Christ Today" (–).
Unaccompanied. Chicago, ca. Jan. 1928. Paramount 12601.

My subject will be the Mississippi flood of Nineteen and Twenty-Seven. My text will be "The Red Cross a Disciple of Christ." Bretherens, I saw, when Jesus Christ came down here on this earth, I saw all humanity, Master, come running after Him. I saw all His people from Judea and from Galilee come running unto Christ. And when they were hungry,

Jesus Christ took five, five little loaves and three fishes and fed five thousand. I want to call your attention today, ah, the Red, the Red Cross, a disciple of Christ, ah, obtained right there down in Greenville, Mississippi, and food to feed the suffering humanity, just what Christ was to the world. I saw, ah, when the water begin to rise, and as she rise, I'm told that boils got in the levee, and I heard the men that were watching the levee begin to notify, "Aaah, it's danger. Aaah, it's dangerous." I want to call your attention, er, at that time, ah, when men was doomed, ah, to deaths in hell, ah, I saw heaven's chariot begin swaying, ah, and, ah, He had no gun on His side, ah. It was then that Jesus Christ came, ah, and redeemed man, ah, upon his trust of the Lord. I saw the Red Cross when she heard the cry of men and women that was runned out from their home by the water that was coming down, ah, through the breaks it caused. I heard, I heard, ah, men crying, "Where is my son? Where is my son?" Women crying, "Where is my daughter?" Oh, look at the water as it washing down buildings. Look at the water, aah, as it washes through the land, ah, washing down corn cribs, ah, washing away cotton houses, ah, aaah, destroying railroads. Aaah, think on rebuilding. If you only hold up your arms, the Red Cross, she will take care of you. Amen.

Moses Mason was clearly impressed with the Red Cross relief effort, comparing it to Christ feeding the multitude. It is possible that he was one of the "Uncle Tom" and "jackleg" preachers of Greenville, ready to support the white authorities in return for their patronage. Such preachers were bitterly denounced by the *Chicago Defender*.[99] However, he is not among the preachers of this sort specifically named by the newspaper. Actually, there were many refugees that appreciated the work of the Red Cross and viewed it in contrast with the cruelties of the National Guard and other authorities, even though some of the most militant black spokespersons saw the Red Cross as complicit in the pattern of discrimination against black refugees. Mason seems to have taken the milder view. In fact, he appears to contrast Christ in his chariot with the armed Guardsmen. Christ, he says, "had no gun on His side." Mason does speak of "rebuilding," but he fails to mention Herbert Hoover or any of the authority figures. His praise is entirely restricted to the Red Cross.

Vocalion Records had not entered the flood blues sweepstakes in 1927. However, on January 24, 1928, the company recorded Luella Miller in Chicago singing "Muddy Stream Blues." Miller was from St. Louis, and the flip side of her

record was "Tornado Groan" about the tornado that had struck her home city on
September 29, 1927. She had tried to record both songs earlier, on October 11,
1927, but those recordings remained unissued.

*Luella Miller, "Muddy Stream Blues" (−). Acc. unknown piano. Chicago,
Jan. 24, 1928. Vocalion 1147.*

1. Mississippi muddy water rose from bank to bank. (x2)
Prayed to the good Lord that the man I love won't sink.

2. Sun rise in the east, and it sets in the west. (x2)
The way rain have did the people, left all their homes in a mess.

3. I'm going back South, going back there to stay.
Going back South, going back there to stay.
And I'll see you, daddy, most any old rainy day.

4. I got the muddy stream blues; I ain't got no time to lose.
I got the muddy stream blues; got no time to lose.
All this rain down South give all the farmers the blues.

The singer alternates verses about her personal problems with ones expressing
concern for the people in the South. Her obvious presence in the North and her
mention of east, west, and south seem to give her lyrics a universal significance. Her
final line, "All this rain down South give all the farmers the blues," refers to the fact
that the flood waters had ruined the planting season and left many farmers unable
to raise a crop. White plantation owners, knowing this situation, still kept many
sharecroppers in peonage on their plantations to rebuild, charging their provisions
to their accounts. Sometimes they even charged the relief supplies that were given
free but delivered in bulk to the plantation owners for distribution to the workers.

The flood blues with the most overt theme of protest was "Broken Levee
Blues," recorded by Lonnie Johnson for OKeh on March 13, 1928. If he had
recorded it ten months earlier instead of the rather sentimental "South Bound
Water," it would have created a sensation.

*Lonnie Johnson, "Broken Levee Blues" (−). Acc. own guitar. San Antonio,
March 13, 1928. OKeh 8618.*

1. I wants to go back to Helena; the high water's got me barred. (x2)
I woke up early this morning, high water all in my back yard.

2. They want me to work on the levee; I have to leave my home.
They want to work on the levee; then I had to leave my home.
I was so scared the levee might break, Lord, and I may drown.

3. The water was 'round my windows and backing all up in my door.
The water was all up 'round my windows and backing all up in my door.
I'd rather to leave my home 'cause I can't live there no more.

4. The police run me from Cairo all through Arkansas,
The police run me all from Cairo all through Arkansas,
And put me in jail behind those cold iron bars.

5. The police say "Work, fight, or go to jail." I say, "I ain't totin' no sack."
Police say, "Work, fight, or go to jail." I say, "I ain't totin' no sack."
"And I ain't buildin' no levee; the planks is on the ground, and I ain't drivin'
no nails."

If this song is based on a specific incident, the details are a bit difficult to figure out. The general picture is clear enough, however. The area south of Helena,
Arkansas, was hard hit by the flood, beginning April 15, 1927. Although Helena
itself was safe behind five miles of high levees, railroad service to the town was
almost completely suspended. A "concentration camp" was established there for
refugees from the surrounding region of Arkansas. Men worked feverishly to
reinforce the top of the levee that had been weakened by steady rains and tried
to spot sand boils created by the river waters rushing by. Electric lights were
strung along the levee so that the work could continue at night. The scene was
no different in many other towns along both banks of the Mississippi River.
In many places, black men who tried to leave the area, even those who were simply passing through, were arrested by white police and National Guard troops
and forced to work on the levees. Some were even removed from trains.
Questions were seldom asked. Blacks, who had no stake in the physical or social
order of these towns, who were valued merely for their labor, were forced to
work in extremely dangerous conditions to save and rebuild the world that the
white folks had made and ruled. The defiance that Lonnie Johnson expresses in
his final stanza very likely would have earned him a severe beating. If southern

white people heard his record, they might have made life uncomfortable for him there. OKeh advertised the record in the black press, but the other side, "Stay Out of Walnut Street Alley," was featured.[100] One wonders what kind of illustration and caption OKeh might have run, had they featured "Broken Levee Blues."

Like Bessie Smith, Barbecue Bob evidently felt that there was more material to be extracted from the flood theme. On April 21, 1928, the anniversary of the levee break at Greenville, he recorded "Mississippi Low-Levee Blues" in his home city of Atlanta. Columbia advertised the record in the *Chicago Defender*.[101] A sketch depicts a hen and two ducks floating on debris in the river, as well as a floating house containing three black people. A woman in an upper window looks distressed, but two men lounge lazily on the rooftop, one holding an umbrella in apparent sunshine. The caption reads: "Stop cultivating the corn and cotton. Barbecue Bob's singing the 'Mississippi Low-Levee Blues.' Mama and Daddy, it sure will make you step out with the best of them. Joining in, the guitar has a mean, wicked strumming."

> *Barbecue Bob, "Mississippi Low-Levee Blues" (−). Acc. own guitar. Atlanta, April 21, 1928. Columbia 14316–D.*

Spoken: *Oh, it won't be long now. Bob is back in Mississippi. Remember last summer I sung you "Mississippi Heavy Water Blues"? Now I'm gonna sing you "Mississippi Low-Levee."*

1. I'm back in Mississippi, worried over this mud,
Thinking 'bout that gal that went down in the flood.
Now I'm gonna sing "Mississippi Low-Levee Blues."
Mmmm, mmmm.
Lord, Lord, Lord, Lord, Lord, Lord.
Now I'm gonna sing "Mississippi Low-Levee Blues."

2. I've been around here ever since last spring.
Nothing to do but shake that thing.
Now I'm gonna sing "Mississippi Low-Levee Blues."

3. We can't plant no cotton, can't raise no corn.
Our house got washed away, and we ain't got no home.
Now I'm gonna sing "Mississippi Low-Levee Blues."

4. Oh, it thunders and it lightnin', rain and storm.
We had a hard time since this flood been on.
Now I'm gonna sing "Mississippi Low-Levee Blues."

5. Ain't nothin' but muddy water for miles or more.
Them low levee womens ain't puttin' out no more.
Now I'm gonna sing "Mississippi Low-Levee Blues."

Mmmm, mmmm.
Lord, Lord, Lord, Lord, Lord, Lord.
Now I'm gonna sing "Mississippi Low-Levee Blues."

6. I'm in Mississippi, mud all in my shoes.
Gal in Louisiana got the low levee blues.
Now I'm singing "Miss-Low Low-Levee Blues." [sic]

7. I walked down on the levee, where the water's heavy,
Trying to find where my gal went down.

8. Lord, Lord, low levee's shaking, river's all ringing,
Barbecue Bob is singing.
Now I'm gonna sing "Mississippi Low-Levee Blues."

9. We ain't burnin' no oil, ain't usin' no coal.
The low levee women won't sell no good jelly roll.
Now I'm gonna sing "Mississippi Low-Levee Blues."

Musically and lyrically the song is quite obviously a continuation of the singer's earlier "Mississippi Heavy Water Blues," as he announces in his opening statement. He continues his preoccupations with mud, the death of his woman in the flood, poverty and loss of income, and sex, but here they are all mixed together. The singer has lost his woman and his home, he "can't plant no cotton, can't raise no corn," and has "nothing to do but shake that thing," but the women seem uninterested in him and "ain't puttin' out no more." Perhaps they were preoccupied with other problems and immune to Bob's "mean, wicked strumming." Sometime around July 11, 1928, an otherwise unknown singer named James Crawford recorded "Flood and Thunder Blues" for Gennett Records, another company that had stayed out of the flood blues sweepstakes of 1927. This song is possibly about severe flooding that struck parts of Arkansas and Missouri and routed thousands of people between June 16 and 26, 1928. The yodeling and mention of a mountain in stanza four even suggest a hillbilly setting. But it is more likely that this was simply a song composed about the 1927 flood that the artist was unable to record earlier. His 1928 session was the only one of his career.

James Crawford, "Flood and Thunder Blues." Acc. unknown trumpet, clarinet, piano. New York, ca. July 11, 1928. Gennett 6536.

1. Moanin' and cryin', people all dyin',
Lightnin' and rain in store.
Houses all swimmin', children and women,
Stormin' like it never did before.

2. Black cats whinin', white dogs want to bite. (x2)
Clouds are wide open, days are lookin' black as night.

3. Heaven's angry, someone's done some wrong.
Oh, heaven's angry, someone's done some wrong.
Trouble is spreadin', been rainin' too doggone long.

4. Fire burnin' on the mountain high, oh lee oh lay-ee-hoo.
Fire burnin' on the mountain high, oh lee oh lay-ee.
Wind's a-blowin', thunder rumblin' in the sky.

5. Muddy water, nothin' but sad news.
Oh, just muddy water, nothin' but sad news.
Sad and I'm weary, got the flood and thunder blues.

Crawford mostly concentrates on the storm and the flood water, but his line in stanza two, "Black cats whinin', white dogs want to bite," could easily have relevance to the complaints of black flood refugees and the harsh policies of the white authorities. There is no other logical reason why the colors of cats and dogs should be of any importance. The singer's line in stanza three, "Heaven's angry, someone's done some wrong," echoes the sentiments about the flood expressed in religious songs and sermons.

On December 4, 1928, a group of singers from the Church of God in Christ in Memphis recorded "The 1927 Flood" for OKeh Records in Chicago. The group was under the direction of Elders McIntorsh and Edwards, but the strongest singers were Sisters Bessie Johnson and Melinda Taylor. This is the only known original gospel song about the flood, and it packs a powerful message. The singers were not yet recording artists in 1927.

Elders McIntorsh and Edwards, "The 1927 Flood" (−). Vocal duet, assisted by Sisters Johnson and Taylor. Tambourine, clapping, two guitars. Chicago, Dec. 4, 1928. OKeh 8647.

1. It was in Nineteen Twenty-Seven. It was an awful time to know.
Through many towns and countries God let the water flow.
The people worked in vain, but God wouldn't stop the rain.
Lord, He poured out His flood upon the land.

2. He sent a flood to the land, and He killed both beast and man,
'Cause the people got so wicked, they wouldn't hear God's command.
All praying the water would yield, but for God they had no zeal.
Well, He poured out His flood upon the land.

3. Many sacks of dirt was gathered; men worked with all their power,
But the levees still was breaking, water rising more each hour.
They did all they could do, but God's judgment must go through.
Lord, He poured out His flood upon the land.

4. He sent a flood to the land, and He killed both beast and man,
'Cause the people got so wicked, they wouldn't hear God's command.
They prayed the water would yield, but for God they had no zeal.
And He poured out His flood upon the land.

5. The evil hearts of men have brought this land to shame,
But God looked down from heaven to invade the Delta plain.
It's we should be content with the flood that He had to send.
And He poured out His flood upon the land.

6. He sent a flood through the land, and He killed both beast and man,
'Cause the people got so wicked, wouldn't hear God's command.
They was praying the water'd yield, but for God they had no zeal.
And He poured out His flood upon the land.

7. God sent a flood through the land, killed both beast and man.
Them people got so wicked, they wouldn't hear God's command.
They prayed the water would yield, but for God they had no zeal.
And He poured out His flood upon the land.

8. Many sacks of dirt was gathered; men worked with all their power,
But the levees still was breaking, water rising more each hour.
They did all they could do; God's judgment must go through.
Lord, He poured out His flood upon the land.

The heterophonic singing style and apparent inattention of the singers to the recording microphone make the text difficult to decipher. Nevertheless, it is clear that this group of singers believed, like Reverend Gates, that God had sent this flood to punish the sins of man. The song does not specify what these sins were or who were the sinners. The sin seems to pertain to all the Delta residents, black and white. The Delta had a reputation for being a place where huge fortunes were won and lost each year, where there was rampant exploitation of the land and human labor, where liquor and gambling ran unchecked, and where the blues, the devil's music, was born.[102] There was enough sin there to go around for everyone. The performance by the Sanctified singers is most effective, with the rough voices and urgent rhythm nicely matching the frantic levee work described in the lyrics.

On June 11, 1929, Lonnie Johnson recorded "The New Fallin' Rain Blues" for OKeh Records. It was based on his earlier "Falling Rain Blues" (OKeh 8253), recorded November 4, 1925. It had been Johnson's first recorded hit, his first release in fact, but it was not about a flood. The new record was, however. On both records he played violin instead of his more usual guitar.

Lonnie Johnson, "The New Fallin' Rain Blues" (Johnson). Acc. own violin; unknown piano. New York, June 11, 1929. OKeh 8709.

1. Storm is rising, rain begin to fall. (x2)
Think some poor people ain't got no home at all.

2. The dark clouds risin', trouble in the low land, I know.
Dark clouds risin', trouble in the low land, I know.
Lord, I wants to leave this old shack, but I'm afraid to go.

3. It's been raining in this town forty days and nights.
Been raining in this town forty days and nights.
When the world turned dark, know it was trouble in the low land that night.

4. Storm started at midnight and never stopped until day. (x2)
Seen nothing but empty houses floating down the river all day.

5. Started to raining on Monday, rained forty days and nights. (x2)
When the world turned dark, I know it's trouble in the low land that night.

6. When the wind start to howlin', poor people begin to scream and cry. (x2)
The water roared like a lion and taken poor people as it passed by.

Lonnie Johnson might have had in mind the floods that struck Georgia, Alabama, Tennessee, and Kentucky in March 1929, when he composed this blues. However, it is more likely that the song is simply an extension of his series of blues inspired by the 1927 flood. Whatever the case, the text has a generic quality, as if Johnson were more concerned with capitalizing on his earlier hit than with the flood theme itself. He borrows phrases and imagery from the biblical flood and Bessie Smith's "Back-Water Blues," and he repeats one of his stanzas. The text adds little to our understanding of the flood theme.

Kansas Joe and Memphis Minnie were two more blues artists whose recording careers had not yet begun in 1927. They were both based in Memphis, but on June 18, 1929, they were in New York for their first session to record "When the Levee Breaks" for Columbia Records. The singer is Kansas Joe, whose real name was Wilber McCoy. He had grown up in Vicksburg, Mississippi, spent some time in Jackson, but, by the time of this session, had settled in Memphis and hooked up with the guitar-playing Lizzie Douglas, who became Memphis Minnie as he became Kansas Joe. The song may well be autobiographical if he was still in Vicksburg at the time of the flood, as his home city lies on the Mississippi River.

Kansas Joe and Memphis Minnie, "When the Levee Breaks" (—). Kansas Joe, vocal and guitar; Memphis Minnie, guitar. New York, June 18, 1929. Columbia 14439–D.

If it keeps on raining, levee's going to break. (x2)
And the water gon' come, and have no place to stay.

Well, all last night I sot on the levee and moaned, (x2)
Thinking 'bout my baby and my happy home.

If it keeps on raining, levee's going to break, (x2)
And all these people have no place to stay.

Now look here, mama, what am I to do?
Now look here, mama, now what I should do?
I ain't got nobody to tell my troubles to.

I worked on the levee, mama, both night and day. (x2)
I ain't got nobody to keep the water away.

Oh, crying won't help you, praying won't do no good.
Now crying won't help you, praying won't do no good.
When the levee breaks, mama, you got to move.

I works on the levee, mama, both night and day.
I worked on the levee, mama, both night and day.
Done worked so hard to keep the water away.

I had a woman; she wouldn't do for me. (x2)
I'm going back to my used to be.

Oh, mean old levee, caused me to weep and moan.
It's a mean old levee, caused me to weep and moan.
Gonna leave my baby and my happy home.

The singer sounds nervous and rushed in this, his first recording session. He garbles his lyrics in stanzas one and five and has to repeat them. It is also not clear how the levee has caused him to be separated from his woman in the final stanza. Perhaps he has been kept away from her by compulsory labor for so long that she has found another man. Whatever the case, the stanzas that deal with levee work, two, three, six, and seven, present a chilling portrait of the desperation of the workers. The work did indeed go on "both night and day," and if the levee broke, there was no doubt that "you got to move," either scrambling to safety or being carried away by the rushing waters. Many black workers, under the guns of white police and National Guardsmen, were lost when sudden crevasses opened in the levees during the 1927 flood.

On August 15, 1929, Sister Cally Fancy recorded "Everybody Get Your Business Right" (Brunswick 7110) in Chicago. Here the 1927 flood is merely alluded to vaguely in a catalog of natural disasters of the sort that struck the Mississippi Valley in that year:

> *God's warning you in tornadoes,*
> *Earthquakes and windstorms too.*
> *He's sending high water overflowing your land.*
> *Friends, what are you going to do?*

Another flood song was recorded on August 24, 1929, "Fire and Thunder Blues" (Columbia 14459–D) by vaudeville singer Mary Dixon. The song is a cover of James Crawford's "Flood and Thunder Blues" recorded a year earlier, but the composition of Ms. Dixon's piece is credited to "Cole." Her text omits Crawford's introductory stanza, but she adds two others:

> *Lost my daddy, he got washed away. (x2)*
> *Oh, destruction; have some mercy, please, I pray.*
>
> *If I must die, I'd rather die on land, (x2)*
> *Than to be buried under all this mud and sand.*

In his first recording session on June 14, 1929, the great Mississippi Delta blues singer and guitarist Charley Patton sang the following lines in his "Pea Vine Blues" (Paramount 12877), a song that memorialized a train that wound between Boyle, Mississippi, and Patton's home plantation, Dockery's, a few miles to the East.

> *And the levee's sinking, and I, babe, and I . . .*
> (Spoken: *Baby, you know I can't stay.)*
> *The levee's sinking; Lord, you know I ain't gonna stay.*
> *I'm going up the country, mama, in a few more days.*

These lines were merely a precursor for a much fuller treatment of the flood theme that Patton would deliver in his next recording session in October of that year, a two-part blues that he called "High Water Everywhere." Why he waited until his second session to record it is unknown.[103] Paramount did not release the record until the spring of the following year, but the company saw fit to devote one of its last feature advertisements to it, and they were rewarded with a hit during the depth of the Depression.[104] The illustration depicts a family sitting dejectedly on the porch of a shack, looking at the rising waters. The caption reads: "Everyone who has heard this record says that 'HIGH WATER EVERY-WHERE' is Charley Patton's best and you know that means it has to be mighty good because he has made some knockouts." Paramount was not exaggerating. Although this is the last original blues to be recorded about the 1927 flood, some two and a half years after the event, it conveys the greatest sense of immediacy and involvement. The listener is taken right back to April 1927, and deposited into the midst of the rising waters. Patton moans, growls, beats his guitar, snaps the strings, stomps on the floor, and carries on conversations with imaginary fellow flood victims. As in many of his other songs, the intensity of Patton's performance, his speech accent and phrasing, his allusive compositional style, all combined with the surface noise on the records themselves, make transcription of his lyrics highly problematical. I offer the transcriptions here as my latest thinking on the matter, the product of many years of listening, revising, and considering the transcriptions of others.[105]

While the two sides of Patton's record are called Parts I and II, they are really two separate songs about the 1927 flood. They differ in the events they describe, in mood, tempo, melody, and to some extent in their guitar parts. Thus it will be most instructive to examine them separately.

Charley Patton, "High Water Everywhere, Part 1" (Patton). Acc. own guitar. Grafton, Wisconsin, ca. October 1929. Paramount 12909.

1. *The back water done rose all around Sumner, Lord, drove me down the line.*
Back water done rose at Sumner, drove poor Charley down the line.
And I'll tell the world the water done struck Drew'ses town.

2. *Lord, the whole round country, Lord, creek water is overflowed.*
Lord, the whole round country, man, it's overflowed.
(Spoken: You know, I can't stay here. I'm . . . I'll go where it's high, boy.)
I would go to the hill country, but they got me barred.

3. Now looky here now at Leland, Lordy, river was rising high.
Looky here, boys around Leland tell me river is ragin' high.
(Spoken: *Boy, it's rising over there. Yeah.*)
I'm gonna move over to Greenville. Bought our tickets. Good-bye.

4. Looky here, the water dug out, Lordy (Spoken: *Levee broke*), *rose most*
everywhere.
The water at Greenville and Leland, Lord, it done rose everywhere.
(Spoken: *Boy, you can't never stay here.*)
I would go down to Rosedale, but they tell me it's water there.

5. Lord, the water now, mama, done struck Shaw'ses town.
Well, they tell me the water done struck Shaw'ses town.
(Spoken: *Boy, I'm going to Vicksburg.*)
Well, I'm going to Vicksburg on a high[er] mound.

6. I am going out on high water where land don't never flow. [sic]
Well, I'm going on a hill where water, oh, it don't never flow.
(Spoken: *Boy, Sharkey County and Issaquena's drowned and inched over.*)
Bolivar Country was inchin' over in Tallahatchie's shore.
(Spoken: *Boy, I went in Tallahatchie. They got it over there.*)

7. Lord, the water done rushed all over that old Jackson Road.
Lord, the water done raised up over the Jackson Road.
(Spoken: *Boy, it got my clothes.*)
I'm going back to the hill country. Won't be worried no more.

Part I is clearly set in Patton's home state of Mississippi. In fact, all of the
places he mentions are in the Delta region, the part of the state that was most
affected by the flood. It would be impossible to read his text either as an account
of the progress of the flood waters or as his personal odyssey through the Delta
flood zone. Patton's nephew Tom Cannon placed him in the town of Gunnison,
close to the Mississippi River, when the flood struck, while Patton's niece Bessie
Turner had him ten miles to the east at Shelby.[106] Patton's musical partner Son
House claimed that Patton stated he was at Rolling Fork, some eighty miles to
the South, when the flood struck.[107] None of these towns is mentioned in "High
Water Everywhere," although Rosedale in stanza four is less than ten miles from
Gunnison. Patton was probably in several locations during the weeks of the

flood, moving about in the manner described in his lyrics. The specific details and locations in the lyrics, however, are probably based on a combination of personal experience, experiences of friends, news reports, and perhaps even Patton's imagination. Whatever the basis of the lyrics in fact, Patton places himself in the Tallahatchie County town of Sumner in his opening stanza, some twenty-five miles northeast of his home on Dockery's plantation and on the outer edge of the flood zone. Over the course of the song, he takes us into areas of the Delta that were much harder hit. This is against all logic for someone fleeing the flood waters, and it must be viewed as a dramatic device of Patton the blues composer. His lyrics perfectly convey the sense of confusion that must have affected thousands of Delta residents as they observed and heard reports of "high water everywhere." In some cases, they were driven "down the line," as in stanza one. In other cases, they were able to get on the trains that were still operating, as in stanza three. But the waters kept rising. In stanza six, Patton presents a frightening image of two entire counties, Sharkey and Issaquena, totally inundated, and another county, Bolivar, deposited two counties over to the east on the shores of the Tallahatchie River. In this stanza, he has more or less described the range of the flood in the state of Mississippi. Except for those located close to the Mississippi River, the logical place to flee to was the "hill country" to the east or south of the Delta. Like many black Delta residents, Patton and his family had migrated from the hills some years earlier, in his case from a place near Bolton, located between Vicksburg and Jackson. He still had relatives there and in Vicksburg in 1927 and visited these places frequently in his travels. Vicksburg, safe on hills overlooking the Mississippi River, was the location of a large refugee camp. But it was mainly Delta whites who were sent there, especially from the area around Greenville and Leland. Patton, like many black people in the Delta, may have wanted to go there or elsewhere in the hills, but, as he sings in stanza two, "they got me barred." This almost certainly refers to the conditions at the "concentration camp" on the Greenville levee or a similar camp elsewhere in the Delta. Patton, who continued to live in the Delta, manages to state his case and that of thousands of other black flood victims, while deflecting attention and potential retaliation through the use of the seemingly innocuous word "they." Robert Springer has pointed out that this word often serves as an indirect and coded expression for oppressive white people in blues rhetoric.[108]

Charley Patton, "High Water Everywhere, Part 2" (Patton). Acc. own guitar. Grafton, Wisconsin, ca. October 1929. Paramount 12909.

1. Back water at Blytheville, backed up all around.
Back water at Blytheville, done struck Joiner town.
It was fifty families and children. "Tough luck; they can drown."

2. The water was rising up in my friend's door. (x2)
The man said to his womenfolk, "Lord, we'd better go."

3. The water was rising, got up in my bed.
Lord, the water was rolling, got up to my bed.
I thought I would take a trip, Lord, out on the big ice sled.

4. Oh, I hear the horn blow, blowin' up on my shore.
(Spoken: You know, I couldn't hear it.)
I heard the ice boat, Lord, was sinking down.
I couldn't get no boat, so I let 'em sink on down.

5. Oh-ah, the water rising, islands sinking down.
Sayin', the water was rising, airplanes was all around.
(Spoken: Boy, they was all around.)
It was fifty men and children. "Tough luck; they can drown."

6. Oh, Lordy, women is groanin' down.
Oh, women and children sinkin' down.
(Spoken: Lord, have mercy.)
I couldn't see nobody home, and wasn't no one to be found.

Part II is set in Arkansas, or at least its first stanza is. Blytheville and Joiner are both located in northeast Arkansas, close to the Mississippi River. The country around Blytheville was very hard hit by back water in mid-April 1927, especially from an overflow of nearby Big Lake. I have not seen any specific flood reports for Joiner, which is a few miles to the south, but no doubt it experienced flooding as well. One would assume that the first two lines set the scene for the remainder of the lyrics, but with Charley Patton's lyrics anything is possible. The song seems to describe the abandonment and apparent drowning of fifty families (or men) and children, with a concentration on one particular family in stanza two. However, in all of my reading about the 1927 flood, I have not been able to find an incident that matches this description. Most of the hundreds of people who lost their lives in the flood did so individually or in small groups, as part of a single household. One rescue boat perished when a crevasse opened near Helena, Arkansas, but this is far to the south of Blytheville and Joiner. An untold number of workers were lost when the levee broke above Greenville, and there were similar incidents on a smaller scale. None of these events fits the picture drawn by Patton. However, it is clear that the Red Cross, and particularly Herbert Hoover, under-reported the number of deaths in the flood. Many families must have perished with no witnesses, their bodies washed far away or buried in mud. Their loss would be felt in the black community but would never become part of the official statistics. Patton mentions ice boats and reconnaissance airplanes that were used in the rescue effort, but the scene he describes here seems to be a failed rescue attempt, with a serious implication that the rescuers either did not care or did not make as strong an effort as they might have. There are many difficulties in interpreting this song, beginning with trying to establish the text itself. Patton compounds this problem through his compositional technique of taking multiple perspectives on the situation. He is a reporter, an eye-witness, a flood victim himself, and one of the rescuers. In truth, it was not unusual for someone in the flood zone to be all of these. The failed rescue is described in stanzas one and four through six, and it culminates in the cruel phrase, "Tough luck; they can drown," uttered by one of the rescuers. This must have been the reality in all too many cases. We cannot automatically assume that there was a racial dimension to the particular incident Patton sings about, but there is no doubt that black housing was more often located in low lying areas, both in the towns and the rural districts. The housing pattern of the South, controlled by whites, assured that blacks would be the chief victims of floods. One other blues by a Mississippi singer-guitarist has a flood theme. It is Tommy Johnson's "Slidin' Delta," recorded in December 1929. Johnson also had not begun his recording career in 1927, but this record was made at his third and last session. The song's title is not, as it would appear, about the movement of water or mud, but is simply the name given to a railroad branch line running to Greenwood, Mississippi, from the Mississippi River. Different blues with this title were recorded by Mississippi artists John Hurt and J. D. Short.[109]

Tommy Johnson, "Slidin' Delta" (Johnson). Acc. own guitar. Grafton, Wisc., ca. Dec. 1929. Paramount 12975.

Delta Slide done been here and gone.
Well, the Delta Slide, baby, done been here and gone.

Take me out o' the Delta, baby, 'fore the water rise.
Take me out o' the Delta 'fore the water rise.
If I don't get drownded, baby, gonna sure, Lord, lose my mind.

Crying, Lord, Lord, Lord, Lord, Lord.
Lord, I wonder what is I'm gon' do.
Lord, I can't do nothing but hang my head and cry.

Babe, when I leave, I ain't comin' here no more.
When I leave here, coming here no more.
Lord, I'm going away to wear you off my mind.

Crying, Lord, Lord, Lord, Lord, Lord.
Lord, I wonder, wonder to myself.
Crying, you know that I wonder, that I wonder to myself.

Tommy Johnson lived most of his life in Crystal Springs and Jackson, Mississippi, but he frequently went to the Delta to play blues and pick cotton in the fall.[110] The second stanza of his song clearly deals with a flood there, the most recent of which would have been the flood of 1927, and he expresses a strong desire to get away. It is impossible to tell, however, whether his final three stanzas are related to his flood experience or are simply general statements about having the blues.

Clara Smith recorded a woman's answer to Lonnie Johnson's "Low Land Moan" (Columbia 14580–D) on September 9, 1930, but this song is more about levee camp life than about a flood. The last original blues statement about the 1927 flood was made once again by Charley Patton in "Love My Stuff," recorded on January 31, 1934, almost seven years after the event.

Oh, I'm gonna leave Mississippi now, babe, 'fore it be too late.
I'm gonna leave Mississippi 'fore it be too late.
(Spoken: Boy, you know I got to leave Mississippi.)
It may be like Twenty-Seven high water; swear it just won't wait.

Oh, I once had a notion, Lord, I believe I will.
(Spoken: Oh, sure.)
I once had a notion. Lord, I believe I will.
I'm gonna boat 'cross the river and stop at Dago Hill.

By now the flood has become a symbol of some pressing circumstance that compels one to leave Mississippi. Patton had survived the 1927 flood, the 1930 dry spell, numerous fights, an attempted throat slashing, and recently had been driven from Dockery's plantation by a white overseer angry at Patton's popularity among the sharecroppers.[111] He knew he suffered from heart disease, and, in fact, he would die only three months after recording this song. Dago Hill, a mixed black and Italian immigrant community in St. Louis, must have seemed like the closest thing to heaven on earth at this point near the end of his life.

The last original mention of the 1927 flood in a gospel song occurred in Charles Haffer's "The Song of the Great Disaster (Storm of '42)," a field recording made by Alan Lomax in Clarksdale, Mississippi, on July 23, 1942, for a joint recording expedition of the Library of Congress and Fisk University (AFS 6624–A-1). Fifteen years after the event, the singer merely mentions the flood in a list of disasters that had struck Mississippi. A recent storm is declared to be the most serious of them all. Although some listeners would no doubt have disagreed about the flood's relative importance, it is clear that it had now become part of history. In 1942, America was at war, and several other natural and man-made disasters had occurred in the intervening years.

Our survey of blues and gospel songs about the 1927 flood has taken us through themes of fear, tragedy, love, sex, comedy, the wrath of God, heroism, sacrifice, race relations, and social protest. These are many of the major themes of blues and gospel songs in general, given focus here in this group of more than two dozen songs about the flood. The singers were both male and female, from the North and the South, from within and outside of the flood zone, performing in styles representative of the country frolic, the street corner, the urban house party, the vaudeville stage, and the holiness church. These songs serve as an important supplement to the news reports and official documents of the flood. They come from the flood's victims, their friends, and members of their communities. Often they were people farthest down the social ladder, but they managed, in the words of Charley Patton, to "tell the world" their experiences, thoughts, and opinions about the flood and its aftermath.

NOTES

1. An earlier and less complete paper on this subject, "Blues and Gospel Songs about the 1927 Mississippi River Flood," was read at the meeting of the Mississippi Folklore Society at Delta State

University, Cleveland, Mississippi, April 21, 1990, and at the Delta Blues Museum, Clarksdale, Mississippi, on December 20, 1997. I gratefully acknowledge the support of the Mississippi Humanities Council for these presentations. I would like to thank the following people for their help in the research for the present study in supplying recordings and information: Lynn Abbott, Mary Katherine Aldin, Barry Jean Ancelet, John M. Barry, William Clements, John Cowley, Pete Daniel, Bob Eagle, Michael Fu, Bob Groom, Scott Hines, Elliott Hurwitt, Sylvia Jackson, Arch Johnston, Sue Loper and the staff of the Nashville Public Library, Robert Macleod, Roger Misiewicz, Luigi Monge, Tony Russell, Doug Seroff, Randi Sherman, Chris Smith, Richard Spottswood, Richard Sudhalter, Alex van der Tuuk, Guido van Rijn, and Charles Wolfe.

2. Paul Oliver, *Blues Fell This Morning: Meaning in the Blues*, Second ed. (Cambridge: Cambridge University Press, 1990), pp. 215–25; Paul Oliver, *Songsters and Saints: Vocal Traditions on Race Records* (Cambridge: Cambridge University Press, 1984), pp. 193–96; Chris Strachwitz and Pete Welding, eds., *The American Folk Music Occasional* (New York: Oak, 1970), pp. 53–57 ("The Words"); Keith Briggs, "High Water Everywhere: Blues and the Mississippi Flood of 1927," *Living Blues* 87 (August, 1989): 26–29; Steven J. Morrison, "Downhome Tragedy: The Blues and the Mississippi River Flood of 1927," *Southern Folklore* 51 (1994): 265–84. Also useful was an article about songs on the related topic of levee camps and levee work by John Cowley, "Shack Bullies and Levee Contractors: Black Protest Songs and Oral History," *Juke Blues* 3 (Dec., 1985): 6–12; 4 (Spring, 1986): 9–15; reprinted as "Shack Bullies and Levee Contractors: Bluesmen As Ethnographers," *Journal of Folklore Research*, 28, nos. 2–3 (May–Dec., 1991): 135–62; and in *Songs about Work; Essays in Occupational Culture*, ed. Archie Green, Special Publications of the Folklore Institute, No. 3 (Bloomington: Indiana University, 1993), pp. 134–62.

3. Two books are especially important sources of information about the flood. Pete Daniel, *Deep'n As It Come: The 1927 Mississippi River Flood* (Fayetteville: University of Arkansas Press, 1996), containing many extraordinary photographs, is especially good in describing the flood itself and the conditions it created. John M. Barry, *Rising Tide: The Great Mississippi Flood of 1927 and How It Changed America* (New York: Simon and Schuster, 1997) complements Daniel's work with a description and analysis of government policies with regard to flood control and disaster relief and the personalities who set and directed these policies. The notes and bibliographies in these books contain references to much previous literature. My description of the flood is drawn from these sources.

4. On the dynamiting of the levee and its aftermath see Barry, pp. 211–58, 337–60; Daniel, *Deep'n As It Come*, pp. 68–73; and "Moving into the City They Hate," *Pittsburgh Courier*, May 14, 1927, sec. 2, p. 7.

5. Guido van Rijn, *Roosevelt's Blues: African American Blues and Gospel Songs on FDR* (Jackson: University Press of Mississippi, 1997), pp. 24–25. For an interesting sidelight on Hoover's "good intentions" but failure in implementing them see Bruce A. Lohof, "Herbert Hoover's Mississippi Valley Land Reform Memorandum: A Document," *Arkansas Historical Quarterly* 29 (1970): 112–18.

6. For representative descriptions of these abuses see Pete Daniel, *The Shadow of Slavery: Peonage in the South, 1901–1969* (Urbana: University of Illinois Press, 1990), pp. 149–69; Walter White, "The Negro and the Flood," *The Nation* 124, no. 3233 (June 22, 1927): 688–89; "The Flood, the Red Cross and the National Guard," *The Crisis* 35, no. 1 (Jan., 1928): 5–7, 26, 28; 35, no. 2 (Feb., 1928): 41–43, 64; 35, no. 3 (Mar., 1928): 80–81, 100, 102; J. Winston Harrington, "Rush Food, Clothes, to Flood Area," *Chicago Defender*, Apr. 30, 1927, p. 1; "Thousands Homeless in Delta," *Pittsburgh Courier*, Apr. 30, 1927, pp. 1, 8; "Death Stalks in Mississippi Floodpath," *Baltimore Afro-American*, Apr. 30, 1927, pp. 1, 7; J. Winston Harrington, "Use Troops in Flood Area to Imprison Farm Hands; Herd Refugees Like Cattle," *Chicago Defender*, May 7, 1927, pp. 1, 13; "First Flood Refugee Tells Tragic Story," *Chicago Defender*, May 7, 1927, pt. 1, p. 4; "Death and Famine Grip Delta Section As Surging Rivers Take Frightful Toll," *Pittsburgh Courier*, May 7, 1927, pp. 1, 8; "Dixie Farm Owners Want Labor Guarded," *Baltimore Afro-American*, May 7, 1927, p. 1; "Conscript Labor Gangs Keep Flood Refugees in Legal Bondage, Claimed," *Pittsburgh Courier*, May 14, 1927, pp. 1, 8; J. Winston Harrington, "Troops Drive Refugees to Forced Labor," *Chicago Defender*, May 21, 1927, pp. 1, 2; James N. Smith, "Eye-Witness Tells Amazing Story of Barbarism in Flood District," *Pittsburgh Courier*, May 28, 1927, pp. 1, 8; J. Winston Harrington, "Deny Food to Flood Sufferers," *Chicago Defender*, June 4, 1927, pp. 1, 2; "Tragedy, Comedy, Walk Hand in Hand As Flood Victims, Called 'Heroes of '27' Prepare to Return to Mississippi's 'No Man's Land'," *Pittsburgh Courier*, June 4, 1927, pp. 1, 8; "Walter White Finds Peonage Rife in Refugee Camps, Bayonets Bar Flood Victims," *Baltimore Afro-American*, June 4, 1927, pp. 1, 4; "Miss. Has Third Flood Lynching," *Baltimore Afro-American*, June 4, 1927, p. 1; J. Winston Harrington, "Work or Go Hungry Edict Perils Race," *Chicago Defender*, June 11, 1927, pp. 1, 4; "Seek Probe in Flood Area," *Chicago Defender*, June 18, 1927, p. 1; "Conditions in Flood Area Being Probed," *Pittsburgh Courier*, June 18, 1927, pp. 1, 8; "Hoover to Correct Abuses," *Pittsburgh Courier*, June 18, 1927, p. 11; Ida B. Wells-Barnett, "Flood Report Found Untrue to Conditions," *Chicago Defender*, July 9, 1927, pp. 1–4; "Flood Likely to Wipe Away Picturesque 'Old Plantation'," *Pittsburgh Courier*, July 30, 1927, p. 3; "Moton Wants Red Cross Head Fired," *Baltimore Afro-American*, Dec. 17, 1927, p. 1; "Hoover Ousts Woman Worker in Mississippi," *Baltimore Afro-American*, Dec. 24, 1927, p. 1.

7. J. Winston Harrington, "Many Die of Exposure as Tornado Rages," *Chicago Defender*, April 23, 1927, pt. 1, p. 4.

8. "1,000 Held on Plantation," *Baltimore Afro-American*, May 7, 1927, p. 1.

9. "Death and Famine Grip Delta Section As Surging Rivers Take Frightful Toll," *Pittsburgh Courier*, May 7, 1927, pp. 1, 8.

10. "Girl in Flood Area Victim of Soldiers," *Chicago Defender*, May 14, 1927, pt. 1, p. 12.

11. J. Winston Harrington, "Use Troops in Flood Area to Imprison Farm Hands; Herd Refugees Like Cattle," *Chicago Defender*, May 7, 1927, pp. 1, 13.

12. "Girl in Flood Area Victim of Soldiers," *Chicago Defender*, May 14, 1927, pt. 1, p. 12.

13. "Miss. Has Third Flood Lynching," *Baltimore Afro-American*, June 4, 1927, p. 1.

14. For white apologist accounts of the flood relief activity at Greenville see William Alexander Percy, *Lanterns on the Levee* (New York; Alfred A. Knopf, 1941), pp. 242–69; and David Cohn, *Where I Was Born and Raised* (Notre Dame: University of Notre Dame Press, 1967), pp. 43–56.

15. "Flood," *Baltimore Afro-American*, May 7, 1927, p. 16.

16. Julian Moyse, "Dixie Farmers Fear They Will Lose Laborers," *Baltimore Afro-American*, May 21, 1927, p. 5.

17. "Death and Famine Grip Delta Section As Surging Rivers Take Frightful Toll," *Pittsburgh Courier*, May 7, 1927, pp. 1, 8; "2,000 Awaited Death," *Baltimore Afro-American*, May 7, 1927, p. 1.

18. "Thousands Homeless in Delta," *Pittsburgh Courier*, Apr. 30, 1927, pp. 1, 8; "Way Down upon the . . . ," *Pittsburgh Courier*, May 7, 1927, p. 1.

19. "The Flood, the Red Cross and the National Guard," *The Crisis* 35, no. 1 (May, 1927): 5.

20. Daniel, *Deep'n As It Come*, pp. 159, 169.

21. Frederick Simpich, "The Great Mississippi Flood of 1927," *National Geographic* 52, no. 3 (Sept. 1927): 265. For further reports of the singing of spirituals by refugees see Lyle Saxon, *Father Mississippi* (New York: Century, 1927), pp. 310, 349.

22. Daniel, *The Shadow of Slavery*, p. 161.

23. *Gospel Pearls* (Nashville: Sunday School Publishing Board, 1921), pp. 97–98 (as "The Old Account Settled Long Ago," comp. F. M. Graham).

24. Turner Catledge, "Refugees Sing Praise to God for Deliverance from Flood," *The Commercial Appeal* (Memphis), April 25, 1927, p. 8.

25. "Arkansas Victims in Flight," *Pittsburgh Courier*, May 7, 1927, pp. 1, 8; "As Floods Engulfed Arkansas," *Baltimore Afro-American*, May 7, 1927, p. 7.

26. Cohn, p. 50.

27. Another stereotyped account of black singing during the flood comes from William Alexander Percy. When he went to a black church in Greenville to explain to a hostile audience the policies he had instituted in the relief camps, he was greeted by a hymn. He wrote, "It was a hymn I had never heard, a droning, monotonous thing that swelled, as they repeated verse after verse, from an almost inaudible mutter to a pounding barbaric chant of menace." Percy, pp. 266–67.

28. Big Bill Broonzy, spoken introduction to "Backwater [sic] Blues," Evanston, IL, autumn, 1956, Verve VFW LP 9008. Broonzy made an even more outlandish claim that talent scout Mayo Williams chartered a boat for the purpose of blues singers witnessing the devastation of the flood. Among the alleged passengers, besides Broonzy, were Lonnie Johnson, Kansas Joe McCoy, Springback James, Sippie Wallace, and Bessie Smith. See Paul Oliver, *Bessie Smith* (London; Cassell, 1959), p. 47.

29. Chappy Gardner, "Along the Rialto," *Pittsburgh Courier*, May 21, 1927, sec. 2, p. 2.

30. Ibid.

31. "Boston Adds $1,000 to Flood Fund," *Baltimore Afro-American*, May 28, 1927, p. 3; "Sylvester Russell's Review," *Pittsburgh Courier*, May 7, 1927, sec. 2, p. 2; "Sylvester Russell's Review," *Pittsburgh Courier*, May 14, 1927, sec. 2, p. 2.

32. "T.O.B.A. Houses in Flood Districts," *Baltimore Afro-American*, May 7, 1927, p. 9.

33. Michael S. Harper, ed., *The Collected Poems of Sterling A. Brown* (New York: Harper & Row, 1980), pp. 62–63, 66–67, 90, 101–03.

34. William Faulkner, *The Wild Palms* (New York: Random House, 1939), pp. 74, 78–79.

35. Edward Brooks, *The Bessie Smith Companion* (Wheathampstead, UK: Cavendish, 1982), pp. 119–20; Chris Albertson, *Bessie* (New York: Stein and Day, 1972), pp. 128–29.

36. Angela Y. Davis, *Blues Legacies and Black Feminism* (New York: Vintage, 1998), p. 89.

37. Dan Mahony, *The Columbia 13/14000–D Series*, Second ed. (Highland Park, NJ: Walter C. Allen, 1966), p. 36.

38. *Baltimore Afro-American*, May 14, 1927, p. 8; *Chicago Defender*, May 14, 1927, p. 9.

39. *Pittsburgh Courier*, May 21, 1927, sec. 2, p. 2.

40. For a selection of recordings of these songs see the CD *Riverboat Shuffle*, Memphis Archives MA 7004 (1994).

41. "Deep River Blues," *Baltimore Afro-American*, June 4, 1927, p. 7; Dave Peyton, "The Musical Bunch," *Chicago Defender*, June 11, 1927, pt. 1, p. 8.

42. Reprinted in Richard L. Riley, comp., *Early Blues*, vol. 2 (Roseville, CA: Piano Mania, 1996), pp. 79–81.

43. "300 Marooned by Flood at Peach Orchard Bluff with Scanty Provisions," *The Commercial Appeal* (Memphis), April 19, 1927, p. 10.

44. For Robison's formulaic approach to the composition of "event" songs see Hugh Leamy, "Now Come All You Good People," *Collier's* 84, no. 18 (Nov. 2, 1929): 20, 58–59; reprinted in *A History and Encyclopedia of Country, Western, and Gospel Music*, Second ed., ed. Linnell Gentry (Nashville: Claremont, 1969), pp. 6–13. Dalhart recorded this song for ten different record companies between April 27 and August 3. An unissued version was recorded by Lawrence Woods for Gennett on July 7. See Guthrie T. Meade, Jr., Dick Spottswood, and Douglas S. Meade, *Country Music Sources: A Biblio-Discography of Commercially Recorded Traditional Music* (Chapel Hill, NC: Southern Folklife Collection, 2002), pp. 86–87.

45. Their texts are printed in Strachwitz and Welding, eds., *The American Folk Music Occasional* (New York: Oak, 1970), pp. 53–57.

46. Ivan M. Tribe, *The Stonemans: An Appalachian Family and the Music That Shaped Their Lives* (Urbana: University of Illinois Press, 1993), p. 56. "Joe Hoover's Mississippi Flood Song" was reportedly recorded in May, 1927, by Larry Holton (an apparent pseudonym) for Plaza and released on Oriole 912. I do not know anyone who has heard this record.

47. van Rijn, *Roosevelt's Blues*.

48. For more information on Griggs see David M. Tucker, *Black Pastors and Leaders: Memphis, 1819–1972* (Memphis: Memphis State University Press, 1975), pp. 71–86.

49. "Human Dike Used to Hold Back Flood," *New York Times*, April 11, 1912, p. 12.

50. Three different songs were recorded by white "country" singers on this flood. See Meade, Spottswood, and Meade, *Country Music Sources*, pp. 87–88. "Levee Breaking Blues, Parts 1 & 2" (Vocalion 5332), recorded by hillbilly yodeler Happy Bud Harrison on May 29, 1929, was probably about this flood also. Harrison's record was advertised in the *Chicago Defender*, Aug. 3, 1929, pt. 1, p. 6.

51. "Flood Menace Shifts to Mississippi Area," *The Commercial Appeal* (Memphis), Jan. 23, 1930, pp. 1, 3.

52. The facts of the 1930 flood throw considerable doubt on the claim by Stephen Calt and Gayle Wardlow that Mattie Delaney was a pseudonym for a Mattie Doyle, who moved to Memphis shortly after the 1927 flood from her home between the towns of Howard and Tchula. These towns are some seventy miles south of the area where the 1930 flood struck. See Stephen Calt and Gayle Wardlow, *King of the Delta Blues: The Life and Music of Charlie Patton* (Newton, NJ: Rock Chapel Press, 1988), pp. 197–98. The 1950 U. S. Census for Tallahatchie County, Mississippi, Enumeration District 68–13, sheet 3–A, taken on April 5, 1930, lists a Mattie Delaney, age 25, living in Glendora with her grandfather Jeff Melton, age 70, a blacksmith in a farm shop. Delaney is described as married since the age of 22, literate, born in Mississippi and having no occupation. Glendora is about three miles south of Swan Lake. Almost certainly this is the Mattie Delaney who recorded "Tallahatchie River Blues" some six weeks earlier about a flood a few miles north of her home.

53. "Heroism of Negro Saves 100 in Flood," *New York Times*, Jan. 27, 1935, p. 24.

54. "Half Frozen Boatman Saves Scores in Mississippi Flood," *Baltimore Afro-American*, Feb. 2, 1935, p. 6; "Mississippian Hailed As Hero for Saving 100 Lives," *Chicago Defender*, Feb. 2, 1935, p. 1.

55. Harry Oster, *Living Country Blues* (Detroit: Folklore Associates, 1969), pp. 283–84. The Dellinger Family, a hillbilly group, also recorded "The Ohio River Flood" (Bluebird B-6852) on Feb. 20, 1937, in Charlotte, North Carolina.

56. *Pittsburgh Courier*, May 14, 1927, sec. 2, p. 2; *Baltimore Afro-American*, May 14, 1927, p. 9; *Chicago Defender*, May 14, 1927, p. 9.

57. "Preaching Records Vie with Blues As Best Sellers," *Baltimore Afro-American*, June 18, 1927, p. 7.

58. Brooks, p. 116.

59. *Pittsburgh Courier*, May 21, 1927, sec. 2, p. 2.

60. *Chicago Defender*, May 28, 1927, pt. 1, p. 9.

61. Albertson, *Bessie*, pp. 126–27. Albertson repeats this quotation and the other statements cited here without any changes in his revised and expanded edition of *Bessie* (New Haven: Yale University Press, 2003), pp. 134–47.

62. Ibid., p. 121.

63. Ibid., pp. 122–26.

64. Doug Seroff, "Blues Itineraries," *Whiskey, Women, and . . .* 11 (June, 1983), unpaginated.

65. "On the T. O. B. A.," *Chicago Defender*, Dec. 25, 1926, pt. 1, p. 8,, and "Bessie Smith Unit," *Chicago Defender*, Jan. 8, 1927, pt. 1, p. 6. Hatch Show Print received an order for Bessie Smith posters on December 16 for an upcoming show at the "Palace Theater, Birmingham." There is evidently a mistake here. It is impossible to determine whether this meant the Palace in Ensley or the Frolic in Birmingham, as the date of the appearance is not given in the Hatch files. See Seroff, "Blues Itineraries."

66. Albertson, p. 118.

67. Ibid., pp. 118–19.

68. Ibid., p. 119.

69. In his highly romanticized biography of Bessie Smith, *Somebody's Angel Child: The Story of Bessie Smith* (New York: Thomas Y. Crowell, 1969), p. 87, Carman Moore reported, evidently based on the testimony of Bessie's husband Jack Gee, that she "wrote it [i.e., 'Back-Water Blues'] on the train as she and Jack rode northward from Alabama to Chattanooga." Moore, however, states that the song was inspired by flooding she had witnessed along the Mississippi River. This is clearly impossible because there was no flooding along the Mississippi at any time when Bessie Smith was there during her 1926–27 tour. There actually was flooding in Chattanooga beginning on December 25, 1926, but it was relatively minor and did not conform to the description in the lyrics of "Back-Water Blues." It had, in any case, not reached its greatest level when Bessie Smith would have had to return to Birmingham on December 27. See "Crest Nears Chattanooga," *The Commercial Appeal* (Memphis), Dec. 28, 1926, p. 2.

70. Seroff, "Blues Itineraries"; "A Note or Two," *Chicago Defender*, Jan. 8, 1927, pt. 1, p. 6; "On the T. O. B. A.," *Chicago Defender*, Jan. 8, 1927, pt. 1, p. 8.

71. "1,000 Made Homeless by Nashville Flood," *New York Times*, Dec. 27, 1926, p. 23.

72. "Skiffs Capsized in Flood; Pair Believed Lost," *Nashville Tennessean*, Jan 3, 1927, pp. 1, 5.

73. "2,000 Are Homeless in Nashville Flood," *New York Times*, Dec. 27, 1926, p. 17; "2,000 Persons Flee from Homes, Driven by Swollen Floods," *The Commercial Appeal* (Memphis), Dec. 27, 1926, pp. 1, 2; "New Flood Record; Water Still Rising," *The Commercial Appeal* (Memphis), Dec. 30, 1926, pp. 1, 2.

74. Information in Nashville City Directory, courtesy of the Nashville Public Library.

75. "Rain Storms Sweep South; Many Killed," *Chicago Defender*, Jan. 1, 1927, pt. 1, p. 3. Cf. Davis, p. 109. The report in the *Defender* was accurate in respect to the "southern economic law" that resulted in poor housing conditions for black citizens in lowland areas, but it was incorrect about the quality of the flood relief effort in Nashville. Two weeks later, reporting on the annual meeting of the Tennessee State Interracial Committee, the newspaper noted that blacks and whites had "worked together with the utmost harmony for relief of the flood sufferers" and that relief

efforts were carried out "with scrupulous fairness." See "Unite for Rescue Work after Flood," *Chicago Defender*, Jan. 15, 1927, p. 2.

76. This song and its background are discussed in greater detail in David Evans, "Bessie Smith's 'Back-Water Blues': The Story behind the Song," *Popular Music*, in press. A different song about 1926–27 flood in Nashville, also titled "Back Water Blues" (Vocalion 5164), was recorded by that city's Grand Ole Opry stars Uncle Dave Macon and Sam McGee on May 11, 1927.

77. *Pittsburgh Courier*, June 18, 1927, sec. 2, p. 4; *Chicago Defender*, June 18, 1927, pt. 1, p. 9.

78. *Pittsburgh Courier*, Aug. 13, 1927, sec. 2, p. 2; *Chicago Defender*, Aug. 13, 1927, pt. 1, p. 8; *Baltimore Afro-American*, Aug. 13, 1927, p. 4.

79. "Hopes Are Revived in Cairo Territory," *The Commercial Appeal* (Memphis), Apr. 18, 1927, p. 2.

80. "American Freighter Elkton Believed Sunk with Crew of 37 in the Pacific Ocean," *New York Times*, Apr. 8, 1927, p. 2.

81. William Ferris, *Blues from the Delta* (Garden City, NY: Anchor, 1978), p. 23.

82. *Chicago Defender*, June 11, 1927, pt. 1, p. 9. The same advertisement appeared in the *Defender* on July 2, 1927, pt. 1, p. 9.

83. Roger Brown, "Recording Pioneer Polk Brockman," *Living Blues* 23 (Sept.–Oct., 1975), p. 31.

84. On Jefferson's blindness and his textual references to sight, reading, etc., see Luigi Monge, "The Language of Blind Lemon Jefferson: The Covert Theme of Blindness," *Black Music Research Journal* 20 (2000): 35–81.

85. "Over Million Acres Will Receive Water of New Madrid Area: St. Francis Basin to Catch Brunt of Dorena Gap Flood: Water Flowing over St. John's Levee Takes Winding Course: Highlands Will Escape: Most of Section Now Flooded from St. Francis, Little Rivers: Relief Appeals Are Made: Memphis to Care for Part of Arkansas Refugees: Lower Levees Holding," *The Commercial Appeal* (Memphis), Apr. 20, 1927, pp. 1, 2.

86. Eric Townley and Ron Harwood, "The Texas Nightingale: An Interview with Sippie Wallace," *Storyville* 108 (Aug./Sept., 1983), p. 229. OKeh advertised the record on July 2 in the *Pittsburgh Courier*, sec. 2, p. 2; the *Baltimore Afro-American*, p. 7; and the *Chicago Defender*, pt. 1, p. 9.

87. Lynn Abbott and Doug Seroff, " 'They Cert'ly Sound Good to Me': Sheet Music, Southern Vaudeville, and the Commercial Ascendancy of the Blues," *American Music* 14 (1996): 430–34. For more information on Laura Smith see Laurie Wright, "Pieces of the Jigsaw," in *Storyville 1996/7*, ed. Laurie Wright (Chigwell, UK: L. Wright, 1997), pp. 227–29.

88. "Comedian Began Career in a Chicago 'Beer Garden'," *Baltimore Afro-American*, May 14, 1927, p. 9.

89. Barry, pp. 324–27.

90. *Pittsburgh Courier*, sec. 2, p. 3; *Baltimore Afro-American*, p. 9; *Chicago Defender*, pt. 1, p. 9.

91. Bruce Bastin reported that Barbecue Bob composed "Mississippi Heavy Water Blues" on the train to New York for his recording session. Bastin adds that the song was mentioned by the preacher at Barbecue Bob's funeral in 1931. See Bruce Bastin, *Red River Blues: The Blues Tradition in the Southeast* (Urbana: University of Illinois Press, 1986), p. 108. The white singer and guitarist Roscoe Holcomb recorded a version of Barbecue Bob's song in Daisy, Kentucky, as late as 1972 (Folkways FA 2374).

92. Paul Oliver, *Conversation with the Blues* (New York: Horizon, 1965), p. 64.

93. Arch Johnston, personal communication to the author, Aug. 20, 2002.

94. "Towns in 6 States Rocked by Quakes," *New York Times*, May 8, 1927, p. 25.

95. J. Winston Harrington, "Wage War on Disease in Flood Area," *Chicago Defender*, May 14, 1927, p. 1.

96. *Chicago Defender*, Dec. 17, 1927, pt. 1, p. 11; *Pittsburgh Courier*, Dec. 17, 1927, sec. 2, p. 3; *Baltimore Afro-American*, Dec. 17, 1927, p. 8.

97. *Chicago Defender*, Mar. 17, 1928, pt. 1, p. 11.

98. This Moses Mason was interviewed in 1993 about the flood. See Barry, pp. 199, 201.

99. J. Winston Harrington, "Deny Food to Flood Sufferers," *Chicago Defender*, June 4, 1927, pp. 1, 2; Ida B. Wells-Barnett, "Flood Report Found Untrue to Conditions," *Chicago Defender*, July 9, 1927, pp. 1, 4.

100. *Chicago Defender*, Oct. 27, 1928, pt. 1, p. 8; *Pittsburgh Courier*, Oct. 27, 1928, p. 2.

101. *Chicago Defender*, June 9, 1928, pt. 1, p. 10.

102. On the Delta's reputation, history, and relationship to the blues see James C. Cobb, *The Most Southern Place on Earth: The Mississippi Delta and the Roots of Regional Identity* (New York: Oxford University Press, 1992); and Alan Lomax, *The Land Where the Blues Began* (New York: Pantheon, 1993).

103. Stephen Calt and Gayle Wardlow speculate that Patton "was resurrecting a discarded song subject in the studio" and even that it "was an elaboration of a previous song about another flood." See Calt and Wardlow, p. 199. The latter speculation is certainly a possibility, as Patton had lived through earlier floods in the Delta. Very likely, he composed a blues about the 1927 flood shortly after the event and performed it for a while but had laid it aside by June 14, 1929, when he made his first recordings, other than the brief allusion to the theme in "Pea Vine Blues." Perhaps the recordings of Lonnie Johnson and Kansas Joe, made within days of Patton's first session, caused him to resurrect the flood theme for his second session.

104. *Chicago Defender*, April 12, 1930, p. 11.

105. I have previously published slightly different transcriptions in David Evans, "Charley Patton: The Conscience of the Delta," in *The Voice of the Delta: Charley Patton and the Mississippi Blues Traditions—Influences and Comparisons* (Liège: Presses universitaires de Liège, 1987), pp. 193–94. I also contributed to the transcriptions in the notes to *Screamin' and Hollerin' the Blues: The Worlds*

of Charley Patton, ed. Dick Spottswood, Revenant RVN-CD-212 (7–CD album, 2001), and in *Yazoo 1–20*, comp. R. R. Macleod, rev. ed. (Edinburgh: PAT Publications, 2002), pp. 201–03, but my own transcriptions differ from the final versions established by these editors.

106. Evans, "Charley Patton: The Conscience of the Delta," p. 192.

107. Calt and Wardlow, p. 200.

108. Robert Springer, "Text, Context and Subtext in the Blues," in *The Lyrics in African American Popular Music*, ed. Robert Springer (Bern: Peter Lang, 2001), pp. 12–16.

109. I have previously published a slightly different transcription in David Evans, *Tommy Johnson* (London: Studio Vista, 1971), pp. 63–64.

110. Ibid., pp. 22–29.

111. Evans, "Charley Patton: The Conscience of the Delta," pp. 109–217 passim.

DEATH BY FIRE

*African American Popular Music
on the Natchez Rhythm Club Fire*

LUIGI MONGE

*Fire and heat provide modes of explanation in the most varied domains,
because they have been for us the occasion of unforgettable memories.*
—Gaston Bachelard, *La Psychanalyse du Feu*, 1938

Behold how great a matter a little fire kindleth.
—St. James 3:5

INTRODUCTION[1]

Like other tragic historical events such as the sinking of the *Titanic* in 1912 and the Mississippi River flood in 1927, the death of over 200 people in the Natchez Rhythm Club fire on Tuesday, 23 April 1940, inspired a relatively large number of songs. Unlike the aforementioned disasters that occurred on both sides of the color line, this event seems to have remained almost exclusively an African American tragedy. The vitality of black people's oral tradition, augmented by the help of phonograph records, has caused this essentially regional news item to be the theme of no less than ten original compositions and a few covers, which span a period of almost sixty years up to the present day. These recordings also cover a broad spectrum of black music genres, from vocal group harmony to blues, from gospel to juke joint music, thus offering different perspectives on the dichotomy of sacred versus secular in and about the Mississippi Delta.

Apart from commemorating so many young people's untimely death, the main purpose of this contribution is to remind both black and white younger generations of the rich cultural heritage inherent in African American music. Its continuity is here shown through a textual and historical analysis of the lyrics specifically dealing with the burning of the dance hall. The result of my research shows the important role to be attributed to memory as a powerful means of expression and creativity for African Americans in the development of their popular consciousness.

THE NATCHEZ FIRE: AN AFRICAN AMERICAN TRAGEDY

Although a few facts remain obscure, the newspaper reports agree that on Tuesday evening, 23 April 1940, Walter Barnes and his band were booked to play at the Rhythm Club located in St. Catherine Street, Natchez, Mississippi. The 190–by–80–foot venue—reportedly a former church turned into a blacksmith's shop and then into a garage[2]—was packed with a few hundred people coming from Mississippi and nearby Louisiana, including Baton Rouge and even as far as New Orleans.[3] Albert McCarthy, who first did historical research based on newspaper reports, summarized that "the interior was attractively redecorated; the outside, however, was not altered, and the metal sheathing on the exterior was allowed to remain in place. It was a long frame building and, to prevent anyone's entering without payment, the rear door was kept heavily bolted and the windows solidly barred."[4] About fifteen minutes after eleven, probably due to a lighted cigarette carelessly thrown away, a hissing roar was heard and the fire broke out near the front door of the building, which could only be opened inward.[5] Again in McCarthy's words, the propagation of the flames was favored by an "extractor fan turning at top speed and masses of dried Spanish moss festooning walls and rafters on the interior of the galvanized-iron framework." As soon as the fire was discovered, Walter Barnes instructed his band to continue playing in order to quiet the dancers and let them get out of that raging inferno, but the building was already wholly enveloped in flames. A few people tried to break and climb out of the boarded up windows but only a handful managed to do so, the others forming increasingly higher stacks of dead and fainted bodies on the floor, especially near the bandstand. Fire and smoke spread very quickly, and in a few minutes the tragedy was consummated. According to official sources, most people died of asphyxia or were trampled before being burnt by the flames. Nine of the twelve members of Walter Barnes's band plus the leader lost their lives in the fire, the drummer and bassist being the only musicians who managed to escape, together with the chauffeur and valet. Dwight "Gatemouth" Moore, one of the vocalists in Walter Barnes's band at the time of the fire, stated he was saved because he was talking to a girl between sets on the band's bus.[6] Former Memphis Jug Band members Willie Shade and Charlie Burse, who were supposed to be playing the Rhythm Club later that night but were late due to a flat tire, are also said to have escaped death. In any case, it is very likely they saw the aftermath of the catastrophe. Willie Borum, who claimed to be part of the Shade group, provided a less reliable account of the tragedy. His description of the building does not correspond to the characteristics of the Rhythm Club and he even included the late Charley Patton among the musicians who played the venue that night. Perhaps he was referring to another place.[7]

From the journalistic coverage, it is clear that the burning of the Natchez Rhythm Club was mainly a black and local tragedy. Being a daily, the white-owned town newspaper, the *Natchez Democrat*, was the first to cover the event the day after the fire. Most of the other papers that sent special correspondents, such as the *Chicago Defender*, the *New York Amsterdam News*, and the *Washington Afro-American* were African American, but, being weeklies, they reported the facts only on Saturday, 27 April. The *Pittsburgh Courier* published a long report on 4 May, while on the same day the national edition of the *Baltimore Afro-American* only gave the news of the tragedy.

Despite its favorable position and opportunity to relate the events fully, the *Natchez Democrat* did not deal with the news item in great detail and devoted comparatively more space to voluntary donations after the event, the passing of a bill for a fire relief fund to be administered by the American Red Cross, the organization of burials, up-to-date lists of victims and contributors, etc. Relatively few or no mentions were made of the cause of the fire, of an unproven suspicion of arson, of Walter Barnes as a bandleader, and so forth. Although in general the town of Natchez was considered (and in fact turned out to be not only on this occasion) a relatively moderate environment with respect to racial discrimination in the South, here is one of the few significant sentences quoted in the local newspaper, which illustrates the submerged atmosphere of hostility towards blacks in Mississippi at the time:

> Deputy Fire Marshal J. D. McDonald from Jackson refused to answer yesterday when asked if he had any clue indicating the fire might have been of incendiary origin. Asked his opinion of the windows of the Rhythm Club, where the fire occurred, being boarded up, he said: "You will find Negroes are like that. They like to be secretive and close everything up."[8]

The influential *Chicago Defender* proved much less evasive and detached in the treatment of the holocaust, so much so that McCarthy reports (without mentioning the source) that it won an award for its thorough reportage. In the 27 April edition, a lot of space was obviously given to details, but also to the history of the club, to the suspects arrested, and especially to Walter Barnes's heroic deed of playing amidst the flames that were sweeping the dance hall. The 4 May issue published a complete three-page coverage of the event, ranking it fourth in the last seventy-five years among fire disasters in the world for number of victims and defining it as "the greatest loss of life that a strictly racial group has suffered in the history of the nation."[9] In a short notice, the doubts concerning the exact amount of the admission charge to the dance that evening were settled by pointing out that tickets sold for 50¢ in advance and 65¢ at the door, and not for $2.50 as stated in the *Natchez Democrat* and in the *Chicago Defender* itself the previous week (and reported elsewhere) to demonstrate the relatively affluent circumstances of the Natchez black population in the 1940s. This is in contrast with the following statement by "Gatemouth" Moore: "wasn't no paid dance, it was an invitational for society people."[10] Perhaps most curious—albeit likewise revealing— were the articles "Thirteen Is Unlucky and Here's Proof" and "Dance Hall Fire Trap Was Once a Church," which dealt with the topic superstitiously or suggested all the possible interpretations of the fire from different perspectives, including the religious.[11]

The black-owned *New York Amsterdam News* was no less informative than the *Chicago Defender*. J. Robert Smith, who was the first *Amsterdam News* staff correspondent to arrive on the scene of the accident, was the only one to report that the incumbent Natchez Mayor W. J. Byrne received words of condolence from a number of black organizations but not from the President of the United States, Franklin Delano Roosevelt, who was busy following the developments of Hitler's expansionist policy two weeks before his invasion of Belgium and Holland. Smith also dealt with the unconfirmed suspicion that the fire might not have been accidental but rather the result of a vengeful act by a young man who had not been allowed to get into the dance hall. In a succinct unsigned article, an explanation was provided as to why most victims were between fourteen and eighteen years of age, i.e., students accompanied by their teachers. In a first-hand account of the tragedy, one of the survivors confirmed that the admission price was 50¢. Both the *Amsterdam News* correspondent and the Mayor of Natchez interviewed by him stated that the tragedy would not be forgotten by the community for many years to come.[12]

The Pittsburgh Courier's pictorial coverage of the catastrophe was perhaps the most gruesome of all.[13] Four photographers and as many correspondents described the event in detail, not limiting themselves to reconstructing the facts, but providing some interesting extra information including (like the *Defender*) a list of previous great fire disasters, further vivid recollections from survivors, and a brief but exhaustive article shedding more light on the cause of the fire and ensuing investigations. On the whole, the *Courier* seems to have focused its attention on underlining Natchez white people's attempts to sympathize with their colored fellow-citizens. A fortnight after the burning, the articles "Suggests Memorial for Natchez Victims" and "Race Businesses Efficient in the Inferno Services" were written with the aim of loosening the presumably high tension between the two races.[14] No less meaningful in this connection was the following editorial note at the end of an article reporting a touching interview with the widow of Walter Barnes, who had been an entertainment correspondent for the *Courier*, reporting on the Chicago scene: "There are plenty of white people who would appreciate our side of the story . . . if they knew it! Pass your Courier along to such a friend."[15] Eighteen days after the blaze, staff correspondent O. C. W. Taylor glossed that "Today the debris is being cleaned away. Natchez has ceased its weeping, though it can never forget its dead. Today Natchez prepares for the living."[16] His words would not prove as rhetorical as they may sound at first.

The national edition of *The Baltimore Afro-American* and the *Washington Afro-American* printed the same photos. They were not as instructive as the other black-owned newspapers; nevertheless they published a short editorial and made mention of the fact that a few people were being held for questioning.[17]

Two among the unfortunately many macabre occurrences in connection with this tragedy are worth mentioning. The first is the special delivery letter that Walter Barnes sent to his wife on the day he died, where he informed her that he would arrive in Chicago the following Friday. Ironically he did, after his lifeless body was shipped from Natchez.[18] The second is the grotesque death of Ed Frazier, the Rhythm Club's owner, who according to some witnesses was on the sidewalk when the fire started, but went back into the hall to collect ticket money and never came out.[19] There were also two lucky events within the tragedy. The first was the case of school teacher Jessie Elizabeth Craig, who survived the fire by sticking her head in the ice box.[20] The second was the case of "young" R. A. Dunna, who arrived at the club five minutes after the fire broke out because he had stopped at a jeweler's shop to have his crucifix repaired.[21]

To conclude, two factors emerge from the journalistic coverage at the time of the holocaust:

1. Though sometimes inferable only by contrast, the Natchez Fire was mainly a tragedy that struck black people, as individuals as well as a racial group. At a national level its resonance was scarce. The whites were hit only indirectly. Generally speaking, the black and white inhabitants of Natchez and surrounding areas seem to have had a very positive attitude and constructive reaction to the catastrophe from a social viewpoint.

2. In consequence of the above, the way the Natchez newspaper covered the event differs greatly from that of the black-owned newspapers, especially in the stronger emotive participation and impact the latter conveyed. However understandable *it* may be, in the *Natchez Democrat* there is no reference whatsoever to memory. From the very first journalistic comments, it was clear that black people would not forget this tragedy. That music would play an important role for this purpose is made clear by the textual analysis of the lyrics below.

THE SONGS

Lewis Bronzeville Five, "Mississippi Fire Blues," Chicago, 9 May 1940, Bluebird B8445

(Moaned verse*) It was in Natchez, Mississippi, just about a quarter to twelve, (x2)
When I thought I heard my poor girl crying for help.*

*Then I put on my duds and I was driven close by,
When I got there, the folks was gathered around.*

*Her eyes was sad and her face was full of pain,
Just to think of this, I just can't keep from crying.*

*Then I followed the crowd to the burying ground,
And I watched the pallbearers put my sweet gal down.*

Then I fell on my knees, lifted my head to God,
Oh, Lord, have mercy on this town.

That was the last time I saw my poor girl's face,
And I loved that gal; no one else can take her place.

The Lewis Bronzeville Five were the first to record two topical songs on the burning of the Rhythm Club. These recordings were cut in Chicago only sixteen days after the holocaust.[22]

"Mississippi Fire Blues" is a guitar-accompanied vocal blues sung by a group of five vocalists. This song has only the first of its six stanzas in the AAB verse structure. Line A in the following stanzas is not repeated, which may indicate the improvisational character of this composition or it may have been deliberately compressed in order to fit all the verses in three minutes. Some of the stanzas do not rhyme, while others seem to be derived from earlier textual sources.[23]

After the introductory moaned verse, the song opens with a reference to the moment when the tragedy starts, a typical feature of many African American narrative prewar lyrics. Yet, unlike songs where the wrong time in which the tragedy occurred is intentionally reported for commentary purposes,[24] the time when the fire broke out is in this case accurate enough. Throughout the text, we can find only one non-personal reference ("Oh, Lord, have mercy on this town"). All the rest is a recollection of events and feelings seen from the singer's perspective.

Lewis Bronzeville Five, "Natchez Mississippi Blues," Chicago, 9 May 1940, Bluebird B8445

Night time is falling, day is almost done, (ooh, yeah, yeah) (x2)
My baby left last night; she left to have some fun. (ooh, yeah, yeah)

At two o'clock in the morning by the clock on the wall (x2)
Yes, I thought I heard my poor baby call.

Ooh, the nights are long; I can't sleep at all, (x2)
Since my sweet mama burned in that Rhythm Hall.

Yes, the day is breaking, sun refuse to shine, (ooh, yeah, yeah) (x2)
I'm leaving Natchez, Mississippi, moving on down the line.

This song was recorded by the Lewis Bronzeville Five on the same date and place, as well as with the identical personnel, as "Mississippi Fire Blues," of which it is clearly a complement and sequel. Although unimaginatively reusing the line presented in the first stanza of the previous composition ("I thought I heard") and stating the wrong time ("At two o'clock in the morning"), "Natchez Mississippi Blues" seems to be more carefully and originally constructed in the use of exact rhymes and more vivid imagery. Analyzing the song's structure, we notice that the text is divided into two parts. In the former, the first stanza summarizes the antecedent fact, while the second describes the singer's presentiments of the catastrophe. At the beginning of the second half of the song, line A creates a strong suspense. The tragedy has already taken place, and one is left to wonder what happened that night until line B in the third stanza introduces a "moving and horrifying"[25] flashback that explains the cause of the singer's distress. As for the fourth stanza, both lines present specifically black distinctive features. The former introduces the spiritual setting of Judgment Day ("the sun refuse to shine") clearly deriving from gospel music and including antiphonal choral response, the latter the worldly image of the wandering bluesman ("moving on down the line"). It is known that the black population in Natchez in 1940 was about 50 percent of the total. It is difficult to determine if it diminished right after the fire, but as this already was a time of out-migration of blacks lured by northern industrial jobs and the build-up to the war, the last verse may be assumed to depict the truth.

All in all, the historical value of the two Lewis Bronzeville Five sides is not to be questioned, if only because they were the first topical recordings on the subject, but their artistic quality and textual inventiveness leave much to be desired. The justifiable somber tone of the former song and the sentimental delivery of the latter obviously try to mirror the presumably still lingering emotion and compassion stirred by the tragedy in the hearts of the victims' loved ones. The choice of a fashionable vocal style must have sounded out of place, ergo the naïveté in the third edition of *Blues and Gospel Records* in defining this group as "of no blues interest."[26] Contrary to what was stated in the *Chicago Defender*, the Bronzeville Five's songs did not eulogize Walter Barnes (who is *never* mentioned in either and was *not* a Natchez citizen) and there is only one passing reference to "the many who lost their lives in the fire."[27] The songs focus on an intimate first-person description of the story and on the psychological reactions to it. As we will see, this represents the main difference between the Lewis Bronzeville Five recordings on the Natchez Fire and all of the following ones, where blues

songs reveal a higher sense of social responsibility and community life, while
gospel songs are pervaded with a strong sense of catharsis.

Gene Gilmore, "The Natchez Fire," Chicago, 4 June 1940, Decca 7763

Lord, I know, I know how you Natchez people feel today, (x2)
Some of them are thinking of the fire that took their children's life away.

Lord, it was late one Tuesday night, people had come from miles around, (x2)
They was enjoying their lives when that Rhythm Club went down.

Lord, wasn't it sad and misery when the hearses began to roll? (x2)
It was over two hundred dead and gone, Lord, and they can't come here no more.

I'm gon' tell all you people to listen to what I have to say, (x2)
Don't be uneasy about your children, because they all is at rest today.

Goodbye, goodbye, fare you well, goodbye, (x2)
I just come to let all you people know what happened in that Natchez fire.

Again in Chicago, on Tuesday, 4 June 1940, that is exactly six weeks after the
fire, two different vocalists, Gene Gilmore and Baby Doo (Leonard Caston),
recorded one more song each on the tragedy, and the coupling was issued on
Decca 7763.[28] The singer credited on side A is Gene Gilmore, accompanied by
Caston on piano and Robert Lee McCoy on harmonica.

"The Natchez Fire" is a circular blues showing the alternation of narrative
and commentative stanzas. The circularity is inherent in the reprise of the words
"know," "Natchez," "people," and "fire," which are all present both in the first
and last stanzas and interact by means of contrasts and associations in a manner
typical of country blues lyrics.[29] Although at first sight the use of these terms
may sound predictable and almost inevitable due to the theme of the song, their
collocation is original and perfectly conveys the final meaning. The place name
"Natchez," which is used as the adjective of "people" in the first line of stanza
one merely to address the whole town plunged in mourning, is placed side by
side with "fire" at the end of the song. The weak usage of the verb "know" in
stanza one acquires a much stronger connotation in the phrase "let all you people
know" in the last verse. Commentative stanzas (one, four and five) prevail over

narrative ones (two and three) because the tragedy is here given as a known fact. Rather than telling a story, the composer seems to be concerned with how the inhabitants of Natchez will react to the demise of their loved ones ("Don't be uneasy about your children") and with the importance of spreading the news of the accident amongst black people ("I just come to let all you people know"). This focus on *collective* rather than *personal* memory will from now on more or less explicitly constitute the most relevant element shared by all the following black recordings on the Natchez Fire, apart from their common theme.

Trying to show the "contradiction to perceptions of the blues as irreligious," Jon Michael Spencer confutes Paul Oliver's definition of the Gilmore song as "epitaph" and defines it as a "eulogy."[30] Though conscious of the existence of a number of personal eulogistic blues, Spencer brings together the Lewis Bronzeville Five's double-sided disc and Gene Gilmore's "The Natchez Fire," affirming that they were "sung for all who lost friends and loved ones among the two hundred victims." This is definitely true of Gilmore's recording but only psychologically (as opposed to logically or textually) inferable from the Lewis Bronzeville Five's two texts, whose emotive impact on the African American community—however strong immediately after the burning—seems to have been entirely lost in time because of their individualistic rather than communal treatment of the subject. From a diachronic perspective, the Bronzeville Five songs seem to be losing much of their original appeal. On the other hand, one may argue that a reference to memory was unnecessary at the time of the Lewis Bronzeville Five recordings in that the tragedy had only recently occurred. Yet this holds true also one month and a half after the event, that is, when the two sides by Gene Gilmore and Baby Doo Caston were cut.

Baby Doo [Leonard Caston], "The Death of Walter Barnes," Chicago, 4 June 1940, Decca 7763

Lord, I want everyone now to listen, listen to my lonesome song, (x2)
Lord, I want to state what happened to poor old Walter Barnes.

Lord, it was just about midnight, just about twelve o'clock, (x2)
Poor Walter played his theme song, the dance hall began to rock.

Lord, and the peoples all was dancing, enjoying their life so high, (x2)
Just in a short while, the dance hall was full of fire.

This song is attributed to Baby Doo, Leonard Caston's nickname.[31] Textual and stylistic similarities with Gene Gilmore's "The Natchez Fire" may lead one to maintain that the two songs issued on Decca were composed by the same person, the most apparent and supposedly pre-arranged dissimilarity being that Caston pays homage to Walter Barnes, Gilmore to the young victims. Despite his more narrative approach, at the very beginning Baby Doo Caston draws the people's attention to the cruel fate of Walter Barnes, who is therefore rightfully inserted in the list of African American heroes. Interestingly, both Gilmore and Caston present the same image of the youngsters who were "enjoying their life" during the dance. This is not a casual remark, as it reflects early twentieth century people's two-decade-old controversy over a moralistic or materialistic outlook on life with respect to sacred and secular music and musicians. The ultimate result of this dispute was that it was difficult to find secular music players in Natchez immediately after the fire, as brought out by the following quotation: "Any songs besides spirituals are hard to get here; for that terrible dance hall fire of several months ago has sent the Negro population to the mourners' bench, and they will not sing 'reels' or 'wor'ly' songs."[32]

Charles Haffer Jr., "The Natchez [Theater] Fire Disaster," Clarksdale, 23 July 1942, Library of Congress 6623–B-2

Spoken: *The title of this song is "The Natchez Fire Disaster."*

One Tuesday night in April,
'Tween eleven and twelve o'clock,
A tragedy happened in Natchez,
Will never be forgot.

A crowd of youngsters gathered
Filled with joy and glee,
When fire of a unknown origin
Destroyed two hundred and three.

(Refrain) It was a sad time in Natchez,
So many people died.
Dead bodies were piled up
Almost shoulder high.

The night were calm and beautiful,
The skies were bright and fair,
The crowd were being jubilant
And knew not death were there.

They were eating and drinking and smoking,
Dancing and having a time,
And in less than a half an hour, brethren,
Hundreds of people were dying.

(Refrain twice)

The place was once a church house
Used for the service of God,
Later turned into a blacksmith shop
And finally to a dancing hall.

That's where the people had gathered,
So we are informed,
And were dancing to the music
Of the famous Walter Barnes.

(Refrain)

The building were crudely constructed,
Covered over with galvanized tin,
Twenty feet wide, two hundred feet long,
With one door to enter in.

Satan had them bewildered
And lured them into his den,
And then sent a sudden destruction
Which destroyed both women and men.

(Refrain twice)

Fire broke out in front,
The people run to the rear.
Moans, groans, and screams
Were pitiful to hear.

They trampled on each other
In an effort to break through,
But seeing they was, seeing they was destroyed,
They said, "Lord, what shall we do?"

(Refrain twice)

There was a number of people there
Whose name were on church rolls.
But what's the hope of a hypocrite
When God take away his soul?

(Refrain)

Some was refined and cultured, I said some was refined and cultured,
Highly honored on earth,
Claimed to have been converted
And had a spiritual birth.

Some teachers in the Sunday school,
Some singing in the choir.
Alas, like Saul, they played the fool
And perished in the fire.

(Refrain)

After the ball was over,
The news broadcast around,
Doctors, medicines, and nurses,
Rushed there from nearby towns.

All hospitals were crowded,
[That's all he can remember. The song ends here.]

Specifically taking the Rhythm Club burning as a possible source of inspiration, immediately after the tragedy John Wesley Work III made a serious proposal to conduct field work on folk music in the community of Natchez, but he failed to obtain funds.[34] Later in 1940, John A. and Ruby T. Lomax did do field work in Natchez but recorded no songs about the fire. It was only less than two

years later, on 23 July 1942, that Alan Lomax recorded for the Library of
Congress a blind ballad writer, Charles Haffer Jr., who had been making a living
by composing, singing, and selling broadsheets in the streets and in front of
churches for over thirty years. Alan Lomax's interview and recollections, as well
as an unpublished manuscript in the Alan Lomax Archive—which from internal
evidence it is reasonable to suppose was written by Lewis W. Jones—constitute
most of the information that is available on this prolific composer of religious
songs.[35] Because of his little known role in the black music panorama, I here provide some sketchy biographical information taken from the unpublished manuscript mentioned above to help put Haffer's figure in context.

Born in Desha County, Arkansas, in 1885, Charles Haffer, Jr., became blind very
early in life. When he was about five, his family moved to the Mississippi Delta.
His father being a minister, he joined the church in 1904 and started teaching in
Sunday school. He got married in 1919 and improved his already remarkable linguistic skills and critical attitude towards life by listening to his wife read him
books and newspapers. Beside writing and singing, he also organized a school for
the blind and, in 1927, a lodge named "The Ancient Order of Watchmen." After
living in Clarksdale, Mississippi, for many years, he moved to nearby Greenville,
but on weekends he would come back to his adopted town to sell "ballets."

The following portion of the interview between Alan Lomax and Haffer
about "The Natchez [Theater] Fire Disaster" illustrates the ultimate purpose of
this and other similar compositions of his:

Alan Lomax (A. L.): Now. How many copies of this song did you sell?
Charles Haffer Jr. (C. H.): The Natchez song?
A. L.: Yeah. Was that a very popular one?
C. H.: Oh, popular, popular. Sold about two thousand copies. I don't
have any direct record. I'm just guessing, but I sold around two thousand
copies of it all right.
A. L.: After you make a song from singing around the country, do peo-
ple, do you hear other people singing them then?
C. H.: Sure. Lots of people sing 'em; they buy 'em and sing 'em.
A. L.: Do they sometimes change them?
C. H.: Sometime they change it, sometime they revise it, call themselves,
and sometimes they take it and reprint it, put their name on t, claimed
they composed it. I come across lots of that.
A. L.: Well, what's your purpose in making a song like this Natchez Fire?

C. H.: It's a warning. The title, it's called a warning song. When we write about disasters, our object is to warn.

A. L.: To warn who?

C. H.: Warn the people, the unconverted or the careless and unconcerned Christians.

A. L.: Do you find that the ministers approve of what you do?

C. H.: Yes, sir. Yes, sir. Three-fourths and a part of the other fourth.

A. L.: Do you think it's really true that if a man dies in sin, he goes right straight to the bad place?

C. H.: Oh, well, now that, that brings a whole lot of . . . . I don't know about that. I think he goes to the grave.

A. L.: You're not sure of that, 'cause that's what your song tells the people.

C. H.: That song, well, it. . . . The thing in that song, that song tell the people that they were destroyed by Satan. That song don't consign 'em to no eternal torture, but it does consign that the wicked is to be destroyed.[36]

Haffer's text is basically a moralistic interpretation of the Rhythm Club tragedy, based on news reports read to him by his wife. Most of the song's 14 whole stanzas present a ballad-like ABCB rhyme structure, as does the refrain, which is inserted every two stanzas (except for one case) and sung once or twice. In the first two narrative stanzas, the emphasis is put on memory and on the time and place where the tragedy occurred. The information provided is accurate from the historical point of view, but the general perspective and linguistic approach to the treatment of the topic are very different from those in the blues songs analyzed above and below. Before reserving the right to deliver his sermon, Haffer introduces, and at the same time summarizes, the facts by making use of a high-level lexicon ("Filled with joy and glee," "fire of a unknown origin"). In light of the sermonic development of the song, even the seemingly neutral recall to memory ("A tragedy happened in Natchez/Will never be forgot") acquires an accusatory meaning. After the estranging effect caused by the refrain, and again by means of a very refined language, the third and fourth stanzas seem to go on recounting the story, but in fact bring in one concealed moralistic observation each, which are both disguised as narrative ("The crowd were being jubilant" and "They were eating and drinking and smoking/Dancing and having a time"). After the second refrain (repeated twice), we are informed not only of the fact that the dance hall had once been a church (see note two), but also of its more and more irreligious employment, a key observation in Haffer's text. The ethical condemnation is implicit in the next

two stanzas, the former of which provides the detailed—almost journalistic—
description of the causes pre-existing the fire, whereas the latter turns the tables and
identifies the ultimate Prime Mover of the tragedy, Satan.[37] The ninth and tenth
stanzas are narrative, but the end of the latter shows the hypocrisy of the victims,
who call for God's help only when they realize they have no more hope of physical
salvation. Not surprisingly, and in a very effective crescendo, the next stanza is the
most commentative of all, making the implicit accusation of hypocrisy in the previous quatrain explicit ("But what's the hope of a hypocrite/When God take away
his soul?"). From the general song structure and knowledge of the events, this may
be assumed to be the central stanza of the whole composition. Apart from being the
only isolated quatrain in between two refrains, which is in itself a sign of peculiar-
ity, it is clear that the last stanza and the truncated final line suggest the continuation of a meticulous chronicle (and, in all likelihood, of a parallel harsh paraphrase)
of the events that occurred after the burning. If my hypothesis holds true, almost
seven stanzas would be missing, a remarkably high but plausible number in view of
Haffer's other long compositions. After the refrain, the evidence of the sinful revel-
ers' immoral behavior is provided in the twelfth and thirteenth quatrains, where
social ("Some was refined and cultured/Highly honored on earth"), spiritual
("Claimed to have been converted/And had a spiritual birth"), biographical and
journalistic ("Some teachers in the Sunday School/Some singing in the choir"), as
well as biblical ("Alas, like Saul, they played the fool") references concur to
strengthen the accusation. The fourteenth stanza and the first verse of the fifteenth
restart the narration beginning from the end of the tragedy. Unfortunately the
recording breaks off here, leaving us wanting for more.

After sixty years, the impact of Haffer's musicianship is difficult to ascertain, but
the blind musician's quotation above concerning the high number of copies of this
and other ballets he managed to sell demonstrates that his influence on black popular music should not be overlooked, especially in Northern Mississippi and surrounding areas. Shortly, we will see how Haffer may have greatly contributed to the
endurance of this substantially local topic even after the ravages of World War II.

*Howlin' Wolf [Chester Burnett], "The Natchez Burnin'," Chicago, 19 July
1956, Chess 1744*

*Did you ever hear about the burning that happened way down in
Natchez, Mississippi, town? (x2)
The whole building got to burning. There my baby laying on the ground.*

Sarah Joan was there.
Louisa was there.
Rosie Mae was there.
Louise was there.

Did you ever hear about the burning that happened way down in Natchez,
Mississippi, town?
I stood back, was looking, and the whole building done tumbled down.

Ooooh, oooh.
Oooh, oooh, ooooh

The first postwar song dealing with the Rhythm Club fire was Howlin' Wolf's "The Natchez Burnin'," which was cut in Chicago for Chess on 19 July 1956.[38]

The meaning and ultimate purpose of this blues is again to preserve the memory of the tragedy that occurred, of all the people who perished in the blaze and of the individuals involved in it. This is apparent not only in the repeated opening lines, which feature the eulogy as such, but also, by means of contrastive and associative juxtapositions, in the expedient of dramatizing the narration by referring to the singer's "baby laying on the ground." In this connection, in his extremely useful and well-researched guide to Mississippi Blues,[39] Steve Cheseborough maintains that "the song personalizes the tragedy." Though this is basically true, the composition as a whole and that particular hemistich are indeed far from being merely a personal annotation. The *coup de théâtre* of mentioning the singer's girlfriend as one of the fatalities does symbolize personal bereavement, but it is just a spark, as is clear from the closely related following stanza, which has all the dramatic qualities of a Greek chorus. The novelty of commemorating some of the victims name by name in a sort of recitative aside is in fact meaningfully introduced into the brief but intense text to suggest (whether it was true or not) that Wolf knew victims personally, and consequently to associate the cruel fate shared by *all* the people who perished in the accident and by their relatives alike. By adding four more casualties (not by chance all women and excluding Walter Barnes) to the list, Howlin' Wolf makes clear that grief is no less collective than individual. In the third stanza, the slightly modified restatement of the opening lines clinches the idea, while the rhyming line adds nothing but the image of Howlin' Wolf's petrified impotence in front of the scene. The final moaned verse describes the singer and the other people mourning over the loss of their beloved.

What is really striking in this thematic composition are its textual cohesiveness, consistency and minimalism, which are achieved by means of a handful of essential verbal and non-verbal utterances. As we will see, these qualities would make this the most influential and covered of all the recordings on the theme of the Natchez Fire.

Robert Gilmore, "Wasn't That a Awful Day in Natchez," prob. Plaquemines Point, Louisiana, 1956–1957, **A Sampler of Louisiana Folksongs,** *Louisiana* **Folklore Society LFS-1**[40]

(Chorus) Wasn't that a awful day in Natchez,
Hear them sinners groan, (x2)
In the year of 1940.

On April, the twenty-fourth,
Death stepped in that dance hall,
'Round that mighty host.

(Chorus)

Tell me that destruction was really sad,
Done used all the graves that the section had.
Messenger brought the news, looking sad,
"Dry your eyes at some other grave."

(Chorus)

During his 1956–1957 field work in Louisiana, Harry Oster met Robert Gilmore, a previously unrecorded singer and guitarist, about whom nothing is known except for the scanty notes reported in the booklet accompanying the LP where the song was issued. Apart from the name and title of the song, the only information provided is the singer's place of origin, Plaquemines Point, Louisiana, hence the presumable place of recording.

From the textual and structural point of view, Robert Gilmore's religious composition has some features in common with Haffer's recording, especially in the unambiguous condemnation of the "sinners," but it is an altogether different song. It is unlikely that Robert Gilmore was acquainted with Haffer's composition, and it is also doubtful that Robert was in some way related to Gene Gilmore, so this mysterious singer probably drew inspiration from another source, also in light of the wrong date reported in the song.

John Lee Hooker, "Natchez Fire [Burnin']," Detroit, 20 April 1959, Riverside LP 008

Did you read about the fire, Nineteen and Thirty-Seven?
Did you read about the fire, Nineteen a Hundred and Thirty-Seven?
Walter Barnes and his big band, they was swinging that night.
The building had one door. It was on the side.
The fire broke out late that night.
People was screaming, they couldn't get out.
Everybody running, running to the door.
The door got jammed, nobody got out.
All you could hear crying, "Lord, have mercy.
Hmm, hmm, save me, save me, save me."
It must have been a plan, a plan from above.
Hmm, a plan from above.
'Cause who, no, no one was saved,
Not as I know, hmm, hmm.
The band was swinging late that night, hmm,
When the fire broke out,
Natchez, Natchez, Mississippi, hmm.
A great big barn, a great big barn,
A many lives was gone down that night.
Hmm, you'll never forget, you'll never forget,
Hmm, hmm, hmm, Natchez, Mississippi, Natchez, Mississippi,
Hmm, hmm.

In 1959, that is nineteen years after the catastrophe and in April as if to conjure up the past, John Lee Hooker recorded for Orrin Keepnews and Bill Grauer's Riverside label his first version of the song, "Natchez Fire," which was included in an album that was issued five years later in the U.K. only.[41]

As we will see, the wrong date at the beginning of this typical Hooker talking blues was likely due to the mistaking of events with its twin song "Tupelo Blues."[42] Compared to the latter composition and to other accounts of the

Natchez tragedy, Hooker's "Natchez Fire" sounds lifeless. The poor imagery and incisiveness—perhaps the result of his tendency to improvise lyrics in the recording studio—make this the least inspired of his three recordings on the topic. Yet it is possible to find some interesting (albeit not plainly visible) textual connections, especially with Haffer, whose influence on the general atmosphere of the song was still clearly felt seventeen years after his recording. The reference to a superior entity as the cause of the tragedy ("It must have been a plan, a plan from above") and the final thematic concordance with most of the texts analyzed so far ("you'll never forget") urging African Americans not to let the accident fall into oblivion constitute the outstanding messages of this blues.

John Lee Hooker, "Fire at Natchez" ("The Great Disaster of 1936"), Culver City, Los Angeles, California, 9 March 1961, Galaxy LP (8)201[43]

Now, people, listen real good. A story I'm got to tell you 'bout the great fire of Natchez, Mississippi. It happened in Nineteen and Thirty-Six. Walter Barnes and his band was playing there at night when the fire broke out. Everybody broke to the door, screaming and hollering, "Have mercy!" What have happened now? A story I can't 'tempt to tell it all. It's a story that will go from the end of time and from on and on, never be forgotten, and the Great Disaster in Natchez, Mississippi. It's all you could hear, people moaning and screaming, crying, "Lord, have mercy!" Mmmm, wasn't that a mighty time? Little town called Natchez, Mississippi, got 'stroyed. Oooh. The whole dance hall was wiped away that night. People, thousands of people was in there that night. Mmmm. Little town, Natchez, Mississippi. What made it so bad, nobody got saved that night, Natchez, Mississippi. The great dance hall and the great band and the great people went down that night. That was a mighty time. Oh, yeah. Nobody was saved that night. Mmmm.

The once again mistaken (though different) year in the title and at the beginning of the song clearly shows that this loosely structured talking blues is a tangible proof of how lyrics in African American popular music periodically regenerate themselves without necessarily taking the exactness of historical facts into account.

Still, in this case, it is possible to speculate on the reasons why this mistake was made. Unlike what was reported by Alan Lomax, the first Sunday evening of April 1936 was the day when a devastating storm hit "the little country town" of Tupelo, Mississippi.[44] So it would not be a groundless assumption that Hooker, who wanted or was asked to make songs about calamities (natural or not) that were dimly recalled, might have muddled the years in which the disasters in Tupelo and Natchez took place. The fact that they occurred in the same month four years apart and in the same state when Hooker was working outside music in the Cincinnati, Ohio, area, and that he recorded them for the same label in the same year certainly had something to do with his possible confusion. When Hooker's biographer, Charles Shaar Murray, states that " 'Tupelo' is a one-chord, free-form talking blues which . . . evokes the terrible flood which devastated the Delta in 1927," he further contributes to the mix-up, adding one more unnecessary ingredient to the hodgepodge.[45] The 1927 Mississippi River flood did not affect Tupelo, which is in the hills and not in the Delta.[46] It is therefore worth pointing out once and for all that Tupelo was struck by a tornado (not a flood as sung by Hooker in his various versions of the songs) on 5 April 1936 on a *Sunday* evening (not Saturday as wrongly quoted by Lomax nor Friday as sung by Hooker),[47] as reported in the stories that appeared in newspapers the following day.[48]

If one hastily listens to "Fire at Natchez," there seems to be no musical or textual connection whatsoever with any of the above-examined topical prewar recordings preceding it. Conversely, at a closer look one can find at least one biographical and some textual clues proving the contrary. If one does engage in some historical, bibliographical, and discographical research, one may discover so many coincidences and points in common shared by Haffer and Hooker to lead one to surmise that the former must have exerted a deeper influence on the latter than one might expect. It is known that Hooker was born near Clarksdale in 1917, and spent his youth in nearby Vance, Mississippi. After that, in his early teens, he first moved to Memphis for a few months where he worked outside music, then went back to Mississippi and finally left the South in 1933, settling in Cincinnati for about three years and then in Detroit in 1943. So, it is very likely for young Hooker to have seen and listened to Charles Haffer perform in front of the church in Clarksdale where the would-be bluesman used to sing spirituals in the late 1920s. As for the influence deriving from Haffer's religious ballad on the Natchez fire, obviously Hooker cannot have heard "The Natchez [Theater] Fire Disaster" before 1940, i.e., the year Haffer presumably composed it. Yet Hooker may have come back to Clarksdale after April 1940, and it is in any case plausible that he bought, borrowed or read a copy of Haffer's ballad, or simply that he remembered him and his "disaster songs" from childhood. From the linguistic point of view, my contention is substantiated by Hooker's song's textual similarities with the Haffer composition. The first (and least revealing) is the inevitable reference to how the tragedy started ("when the fire broke out"). The second is more interesting because it further corroborates the main assumption of this article, that is, the key role played by popular music as glue keeping together the pieces of African American spiritual consciousness ("It's a story that will go from the end of time and from on and on, never be forgotten"). The third is that Hooker drew from Haffer the same specific words ("moaning and screaming"; "'stroyed") that the latter had used to vividly describe the tragedy in progress. One more textual concordance with the blind composer of religious ballads is traceable in the sentence "Mmmm, wasn't that a mighty time" and in its antiphonal response "That was a mighty time." Though its origin certainly derives from the spiritual tradition,[49] the rhetorical question also appears in the refrain of Haffer's version of the "Titanic," which he claimed to have written in 1912 immediately after the sinking and to have been his first song about a disaster.

John Lee Hooker, "The Mighty Fire" ["Great Fire of Natchez"], Newport, Rhode Island, 28 July 1963, Vee Jay 107[50]

Spoken: *Right now I'm gonna do a little tune they call about the great fire of Natchez, Mississippi, the mighty fire, happened in Nineteen and Thirty-Six. The great fire of Natchez.*

Nineteen and Thirty-Six, the mighty fire of Natchez, Mississippi,
Nineteen and Thirty-Six, people, the mighty fire of Natchez, Mississippi,
They had a big dance that night and when the fire broke out.

Walter Barnes was there,
Louise was there,
Ida Mae was there, she was my heart.

Saturday morning I read the paper,
I saw Ida Mae's name, I couldn't read no more.
The mighty fire, the mighty fire in Natchez, Mississippi,
Nineteen and Thirty-Six, people.
The place was full and jammed with people when the fire broke out.
Mmmm, talking about Natchez, Mississippi.

I'm talking about Natchez, Mississippi, Nineteen and Thirty-Six.
Louise was there (spoken: my girlfriend buddy) [sic]
Ida Mae was there.

That Saturday morning I bought myself a paper,
I read about the news,
I saw Ida Mae's name.
She went down in the mighty fire.
I felt so bad, ooohoooh, hmmhmm, the mighty fire, the mighty fire.

Despite the many textual similarities with the previous two versions and the artistically speaking irrelevant insistence on the wrong year, a few substantial differences are noticeable. The most evident is the novelty of using Howlin' Wolf's device of listing the names of the victims, which gives the song a more constrained structure. Unlike Wolf and as in his two preceding studio recordings on the topic, however, Hooker mentions Walter Barnes among the dead. Though still perceivable in the spoken introduction, in the word "people," and in the calling of the deceased people's names, the sense of sharing in the grief of the community is partially lost in the two parenthetic references to his girlfriend and her "buddy" and in the two overtly personal recollections the day after the event.

According to Leadbitter and Slaven,[51] in November 1968 in Chicago Howlin' Wolf also recorded "Natchez Is Burning" for Cadet, a subsidiary of Chess Records. This song, presumably a cover of Howlin' Wolf's earlier version, was originally planned to be included in Wolf's psychedelic album, which he hated so much that he called it "dog shit," so his second tribute to the Natchez victims has never been released.[52]

After at least a couple of versions by white musicians,[53] the Howlin' Wolf 1956 original recording prompted a few black covers, of which I have traced two so far. The first is "The Natchez Burning," which was recorded on 7 April 1976 by Macon, Georgia, native Willie Wright at Sweet Home, Arkansas.[54] A Little Rock, Arkansas, resident since World War II, Wright worked as a sideman on King Biscuit Time in the early 1950s and often played with harmonica player Sunny Blair in his adoptive town. Wright's version of "The Natchez Burning" is strongly influenced by the Delta blues tradition and presents evidence of his indirect knowledge of the tragedy. In fact, Wright sings the verse "Did you ever heard of the burning, way down in the *messy* Mississippi town," thus showing that he did not know nor understand from Howlin' Wolf's recording where the disaster had happened, and substituted the word "Natchez" with "messy" to approximate the sound of what he had learned from Wolf's topical song.

"Natchez Fire," another cover of Howlin' Wolf's 1956 song, was cut in 1997 for Fat Possum Records by Natchez natives Elmo Williams and Hezekiah Early in Waterproof, Louisiana, situated a few miles from Natchez on the boundary line with the state of Mississippi along the Mississippi River.[55] A typical energetic juke joint piece, from the textual viewpoint it adds nothing to what was stated in relation to the Howlin' Wolf text. The fact that the two performers come from or near Natchez perhaps shows that the breadth of the theme is being restricted to regional boundaries, but it also confirms African American lyrics' power to help preserve the memory of a decades-old historical event and musical tradition.

CONCLUSION

From the detailed textual analysis above, it is clear that memory is the thread that runs through most of the lyrics dealing with the Natchez Fire. Not accidentally, the only exceptions seem to be the two Lewis Bronzeville Five songs which, having been recorded just a few days after the burning, obviously need not mention memory and have a more individualistic, subjective and narrative tone. Starting from the Decca sides by Gene Gilmore and Caston, recorded six weeks after the event, the attitude toward the circumstance becomes more communal, objective and commentative. An increasing awareness of the importance of solidarity and of the thaumaturgical consoling power of time is perceptible throughout the lyrics. This African American strong sense of popular consciousness, which is usually associated with literary, social and political movements such as the Harlem Renaissance in the 1920s and the Civil Rights Movement in the 1960s, in fact also permeates a large part of twentieth century black popular music, both sacred and secular, including topical prewar blues and gospel lyrics.[56] Perhaps one would have expected that such a tragic event that would normally elicit a gospel- rather than a blues-oriented commentary would be faced in a different way. Spencer is right when he upholds the historical and sometimes even thematic common origin of blues and gospel music, and Gene Gilmore's song represents a good example in this connection. There is no denying the hybrid origin and common source and milieu of religious and secular African American music, but when Spencer defines preaching, prayer, and eulogy as "kinds of blues expressions," he denies that meaning and intentions are what differentiate sacred from secular lyrics. Black people in general, and musicians in particular, were well aware of these songs' moral and spiritual implications. In this respect, though treating the same topic as the blues eulogies, Charles Haffer Jr.'s composition and Robert Gilmore's fragment are emblematic of this divergence, also in light of the different meaning to be ascribed to the concept of "memory," which in both Haffer's and Gilmore's songs is meant as a reminder not to indulge in sin.

The standard of imagery in the compositions is not as high as in songs dealing with similar natural or accidental disasters such as the 1927 Mississippi River Flood, the sinking of the *Titanic*, the 1930 drought, etc.[57] The minor historical importance of the Natchez Fire at a national level, especially for the white community, is probably only one of the many possible reasons why this topic has never drawn the attention it deserved. Over the course of years, the songs on the Natchez Fire have been greatly overlooked: as noted earlier, the two Lewis Bronzeville Five sides were once labeled as "of no blues interest" (see note twenty-six), the Decca coupling by Gene Gilmore and Leonard Caston went unobserved, Alan Lomax's recording of Haffer for the Library of Congress and the Robert Gilmore field recording collected by Harry Oster were non-commercial, and even Hooker's "The Mighty Fire" was not as successful as its twin song "Tupelo."[58] However, these types of neglect are in my opinion also due to the tendency to study thematic compositions only synchronically, thus viewing them as separate from one another and not as a continuum to be put in its diachronic context. Especially after such a long time from the tragedy, their importance lies in the historical message they convey as a whole, which makes them—as Son House suggests in his thematic "Dry Spell Blues"—"worthwhile to be heard," but not only at the time of the disaster. Despite the marginality of the topic, history, memory and the issue of African American identity account for the resilience of the Rhythm Club burning theme that, if one excludes the covers by white artists, was the subject of an average of two songs per decade up to the 1980s, though no versions were recorded in that decade.

In spite of the unavoidable loss of interest in the subject matter over time, even a secondary topic such as this contributed to the creation of other songs on different accidents. Apropos of the Natchez Fire, in 1994 Big Jack Johnson composed "Ice Storm Blues, Part One and Part Two," a song on the February 1994 ice storm in Clarksdale, Mississippi, whose words are sung to the tune of Howlin' Wolf's "The Natchez Burnin':"[59]

Have you heard about the ice storm that hit Clarksdale, Mississippi, town? (x2)
Well you could lay in your bedroom, and you could hear the leaves and
branches falling down.

In Tuscaloosa, Alabama, in February 1995, Ralph, Alabama, native Little Whitt and Emelle, Alabama, native Big Bo McGee recorded "The Burning," a downhome blues clearly inspired by Howlin' Wolf's "The Natchez Burnin'," from which it almost integrally takes the opening stanza, adapting it to a separate incident, the arson of a Natchez schoolhouse with a racist motive during Lyndon Johnson's presidency:[60]

Little Whitt & Big Bo McGee, "The Burning," Tuscaloosa, AL, February 1995, Vent Records VR 30009

Have you ever heard about the burning that happened way down in a Mississippi town? (x2)
Well, those evil people there burned the schoolhouse down to the ground.

When least expected, African American popular lyrics are reborn like the phoenix from the ashes of memory. Their unpredictable nature of reviving themselves acquires new significance and is particularly revelatory in the case of a typically black theme and historical event such as this, barely influenced by white culture.

NOTES

1. This article is a revised version of the paper I read on 11 April 2002 in Jonesboro, Arkansas, at the Delta Blues Symposium VIII titled "The Sacred and the Secular," and on 20 and 21 April 2002 in Natchez, Mississippi, respectively at the NAPAC (Natchez Association for the Preservation of Afro-American Culture) and at the Copiah-Lincoln Community College. I would like to thank Prof. William Clements of Arkansas State University and Bettye J. Mullen, Director of Student Support Services at Copiah-Lincoln Community College in Natchez for supporting my research project. Special thanks to Joan M. McLemore, Librarian at the Copiah-Lincoln Community College, and to David Evans, Rev. "Gatemouth" Moore, Alan Balfour, Chris Smith, John Cowley, James Segrest, Edward Komara, Stefano Danielli, Gianfranco Scala, Guido Van Rijn, and Flavio Mancini for their help.

2. This piece of information was reported in various sources such as "Dance Hall Fire Trap Was Once A Church," *The Chicago Defender*, 4 May 1940, p. 8, O. C. W. Taylor, "Disaster Suspects Released," *The Pittsburgh Courier*, 4 May 1940, p. 2, and "240 at Dance Die in Fire," *The Washington Afro-American*, 27 April 1940, p. 1, but is rejected by two survivors of the fire, Ethel Lee Porter and Frank R. Robinson, whom I spoke to separately at the end of the Natchez lectures mentioned in footnote 1. Without prompting, they insisted that the Rhythm Club had never been a church.

3. Althea Dumas, "Eyewitness Account of Tragedy," *New York Amsterdam News*, 27 April 1940, p. 1.

4. Albert McCarthy, *Big Band Jazz* (London: Barrie & Jenkins, 1974), 29–32, 38; see also Albert McCarthy, "Life & Death of Walter Barnes," *Jazz Monthly* 179 (January 1970), 7–10. Thanks to Alan Balfour for providing a copy of the latter article.

5. David Kellum, "Identity of Scores of Victims Still Lacking," *The Chicago Defender*, 27 April 1940, p. 1.

6. Johnny Otis, "The Otis Tapes 4: Dwight 'Gatemouth' Moore," *Blues Unlimited* 109 (August-September 1974), p. 13; see also Dave Penny and Tony Burke, "Stand Up and Shout the Blues: Dwight 'Gatemouth' Moore," *Blues and Rhythm* 15 (December 1985), p. 4. This fact was confirmed by Rev. "Gatemouth" Moore in an interview with the author made at the Comfort Inn in Yazoo City, Mississippi, on 18 April 2002.

7. Samuel Charters, *The Country Blues* (New York: Rinehart, 1959), pp. 126–27. Bengt Olsson, *Memphis Blues and Jug Bands* (London: Studio Vista, 1970), p. 70.

8. "Sidelights on Disaster," *The Natchez Democrat*, 27 April 1940, pp. 1, 4. On race relationships in Natchez see Jack E. Davis, *Race Against Time: Culture and Separation in Natchez Since 1930* (Baton Rouge: Louisiana State University Press, 2001).

9. "Natchez Fire Ranks Fourth in Disasters," *The Chicago Defender*, 4 May 1940, p. 8.

10. Peter Lee and David Nelson, "Bishop Arnold Dwight 'Gatemouth' Moore: From Shoutin' the Blues to Preachin' the Word," *Living Blues* 86 (May–June 1989), pp. 11–12. Rev. "Gatemouth" Moore, interview with the author, 18 April 2002.

11. See respectively *The Chicago Defender*, 4 May 1940, p. 8, and *The Chicago Defender*, 27 April 1940, p. 1.

12. J. Robert Smith, "Natchez Mayor Says Fire Paralyzed Town," *New York Amsterdam News*, 4 May 1940, p. 3; J. Robert Smith, "Natchez Buries Its 203 Victims," *New York Amsterdam News*, 4 May 1940, p. 7.

13. "Disaster! in Natchez," *The Pittsburgh Courier*, 4 May 1940, p. 3.

14. Both articles were published in *The Pittsburgh Courier*, 11 May 1940, p. 13.

15. Editorial note at the end of the article by Luther Hill, "Last Birthday with Walter 'Best Memory'," *The Pittsburgh Courier*, 4 May 1940, p. 20.

16. O. C. W. Taylor, "Natchez Forgets Color Line in Recovery Drive: Only Casket Trucks Halt Four Days of Funeral Parades," *The Pittsburgh Courier*, 11 May 1940, p. 2.

17. "215 Die in Natchez, Miss., Dance Hall Fire," *The Baltimore Afro-American*, 4 May 1940, p. 12, and *The Washington Afro-American*, 4 May 1940, p. 24; "Opinion: The Rhythm Club Fire Panic," *The Washington Afro-American*, 4 May 1940, p. 16.

18. See "'Be Home Friday'—Barnes," *The Chicago Defender*, 27 April 1940, p. 1, and "'I'll Be Home This Friday'—Barnes," *Down Beat*, 15 May 1940, p. 7.

19. John R. Williams, "Natchez Quivers in Stunned Grief As Dead Are Buried," *The Pittsburgh Courier*, 4 May 1940, p. 2, and J. Robert Smith, "Fatal Dance Had Showed Big Profit Before Blaze," *New York Amsterdam News*, 4 May 1940, p. 6.

20. "Put Her Head in Dance Hall Ice-Box; Lived," *The Pittsburgh Courier* 11 May 1940, p. 2; "School Teacher Came Thru Flames Unhurt," *New York Amsterdam News*, 4 May 1940, p. 6.

21. "Natchez Man Says Cross Saved Life," *The Chicago Defender*, 4 May 1940, p. 8.

22. These songs were reissued on *Black Secular Vocal Groups, Volume 3 (1923–1940)*, Document Records DOCD-5604, 1998.

23. In the Bronzeville Five's song it is interesting to note a textual borrowing from Ida Cox's "Death Letter Blues," a composition this vaudeville blues singer had recorded for Paramount Records about sixteen years prior to "Mississippi Fire Blues." Precisely, the Lewis Bronzeville Five's fourth stanza is a slight variant of Cox's third stanza ("I followed my daddy to the burying ground/I watched the pallbearers slowly let him down"), while their final stanza faithfully follows the last stanza of Ida Cox's song: "That was the last time I saw my baby's face/'Mama loves you, sweet papa, but I just can't take your place'." See Ida Cox, "Death Letter Blues," Chicago, ca. August 1924, Paramount 12220, reissued on Ida Cox, *Complete Recorded Works 1923–1938 in Chronological Order, Volume 2 (1924–25)*, Document Records DOCD-5323, 1995. For more textual connections with the Lewis Bronzeville Five's songs see Ishman Bracey, "Trouble Hearted Blues — take 1" (Victor 21691) and "Trouble Hearted Blues—take 2" (Victor unissued), Memphis, 31 August 1928, reissued on Ishman Bracey and Charley Taylor, *Complete Recorded Works in Chronological Order*, Document Records DOCD-5049, 1991; Blind Willie McTell, "Cooling Board Blues," Chicago, 25 April 1935, Decca unissued, reissued on Blind Willie McTell, *Complete Recorded Works in Chronological Order, Volume 3 (1933–1935)*, Document Records DOCD-5008, 1990; and Buddy Moss's "Undertaker Blues," Chicago, 21 July 1935 (Vocalion 04380), reissued on *Complete Recorded Works in Chronological Order, Volume 3 (1935–1941)*, Document Records DOCD-5125, 1992. For an interpretation of this and other songs by Blind Willie McTell and other unsighted prewar blues and gospel recording artists, see Luigi Monge, "Blindness Blues: Visual References in the Lyrics of Blind Pre-War Blues and Gospel Musicians," in *The Lyrics in African American Popular Music*, edited by Robert Springer (Bern, Switzerland: Peter Lang, 2001), pp. 91–119.

24. For an example and analysis see "Hi" Henry Brown's "Titanic Blues," New York City, 14 March 1932 (Vocalion 1728), reissued on Charlie Jordan, *Complete Recorded Works in Chronological Order, Volume 2 (1931–1934)*, Document Records DOCD-5098, 1992, and Luigi Monge, "Titanic Blues," in *La Lingua Inglese dei Negri d'America e i Blues: Analisi Critica di Alcuni Testi* (Black English and the Blues: A Critical Analysis of Some Lyrics), degree thesis, University of Genoa, Italy, 1985, pp. 237–68.

25. Steve Tracy, liner notes to *Black Secular Vocal Groups, Volume 3 (1923–1940)*, Document Records DOCD-5604, 1998.

26. John Godrich and Robert M. W. Dixon, *Blues & Gospel Records 1902–1942*, 3rd edition (London: Storyville Publications, 1969), p. 445. Many thanks to Stefano Danielli for this and other discographical pieces of information. The annotation is not present in the latest edition. See also "Natchez Burning!," *Blues Unlimited* 70 (February–March 1970), p. 8.

27. "Natchez Fire Brings Songs by Lewis Set," *The Chicago Defender*, 29 June 1940, p. 21. Reference and quotation from Jon Michael Spencer, *Blues and Evil* (Knoxville: The University of Tennessee Press, 1993), p. 6.

28. The two sides were reissued on *Chicago Blues Volume 2 (1939–1944)*, Document Records DOCD-5444, 1996.

29. For an explanation of the contrastive/associative phenomenon in folk blues lyrics, see David Evans, *Big Road Blues: Tradition and Creativity in the Folk Blues* (Berkeley: University of California Press, 1982). Reprint, New York: Da Capo Press, 1987, pp. 58, 146, 219, 318.

30. Jon Michael Spencer, *op. cit.*, p. 48; Paul Oliver, *Blues Fell This Morning: Meaning in the Blues* (Cambridge, UK: Cambridge University Press, 1990), p. 231. "Epitaph" is also the term used in "Natchez Burning!," *Blues Unlimited* 59 (January 1969), p. 14.

31. In the following quotation Caston claims to be the composer and the pianist of the song: "So they had a song out called 'Natchez Fire Blues' by Eugene Gilmore. I played the piano for him to sing the 'Natchez Fire' and on the flip side was my 'Death of Walter Barnes'. I played piano. Robert Nighthawk blowed harp on that. Robert Lee McCoy. I don't remember whether there was a guitar on that or not". Quoted in Jeff Titon, *From Blues to Pop: The Autobiography of Leonard "Baby Doo" Caston*, John Edwards Memorial Foundation Special Series, no. 4 (Los Angeles: University of California at Los Angeles, 1974), pp. 1–30, especially 14. Aural and discographical evidence confirms the unmistakable presence of Robert Lee McCoy on harmonica and enables us to answer Caston's doubt in the negative. Moreover, it may be speculated that the pianist in "The Death of Walter Barnes" sounds like Walter Davis rather than like Caston himself. Regardless of Caston's quotation above, however, it is more likely that the pianist is in fact Caston playing in a style similar to Walter Davis's, who was very popular at the time as a soloist in the St. Louis area. The day after the recording, Robert Lee McCoy cut a solo session and also accompanied Sleepy John Estes, as is evident in "Jailhouse Blues" (Decca 7814), where the harmonica sounds exactly as in the two Natchez Fire songs. There was no piano player in this session, which strengthens Caston's assumption that he was the pianist on both Decca sides. The sessions were reissued on Robert Lee McCoy (Robert Nighthawk), *Complete Recorded Works in Chronological Order (1937–1940)*, Wolf Records WBCD-002, 1990, and on Sleepy John Estes, *Complete Recorded Works in Chronological Order, Volume 2 (1937–1941)*, Document Records DOCD-5016, 1990.

32. Excerpt from "Ruby T. Lomax letter to family, 19 October 1940," John A. Lomax and Ruby T. Lomax 1940 Natchez, Mississippi, field notes, Library of Congress Archive of Folk Culture files, Washington, D.C., U.S.A. Many thanks to John Cowley for drawing my attention to and providing a copy of this interesting document. Perhaps the only exception to the dearth of secular music

in Natchez in this period was the John A. and Ruby T. Lomax session made on 19 October 1940, when they recorded George Boldwin, Lucious Curtis, and Willie Ford. See Howard Rye, liner notes to *Mississippi Blues and Gospel: 1934–1942 Field Recordings*, Document Records DOCD-5320, 1995. See also Bob Groom, "Natchez, Mississippi Blues," *Blues World* 38 (Spring 1971), pp. 3–7, and John H. Cowley, liner notes to *Mississippi River Blues*, Flyright-Matchbox Records SDM 230, 1973.

33. Still unavailable in any format, this incomplete non-commercial recording is obtainable only from the Library of Congress. In spite of what is reported in the Library of Congress files and consequently in the standard prewar discography by Robert M. W. Dixon, John Godrich, and Howard W. Rye, *Blues and Gospel Records, 1890–1943*, 4th ed. (New York: Oxford University Press, 1997), p. 335, when Haffer announces the title of the song, he does not mention the word "Theatre," which is thus written in brackets here. I wish to thank the Library of Congress in the person of Judith A. Gray, Reference Specialist at the American Folklife Center, and Christel Schmidt, Public Services Assistant, M/B/RS Division, for their invaluable help and patience.

34. Bruce Nemerov, "John Wesley Work III: Field Recordings of Southern Black Folk Music, 1935–1942," in *Tennessee Folklore Society Bulletin*, volume LIII, No. 3 (Fall 1987), pp. 82–103, especially 89 and 91. See also Robert Gordon, *Can't Be Satisfied: The Life and Times of Muddy Waters* (Boston: Little, Brown and Company, 2002), pp. 35–36.

35. See respectively Alan Lomax, *The Land Where the Blues Began* (New York: Pantheon Books, 1993), pp. 48–58, 495–96, and prob. Lewis W. Jones, typescript report of Coahoma County Project. Nashville: Fisk University, ca. 1943 (courtesy of Alan Lomax Archive).

36. Charles Haffer, Jr. interviewed by Alan Lomax, Clarksdale, 23 July 1942, Library of Congress 6623-B-2.

37. It is very likely that Haffer's wife read this and other pieces of information to her husband, as they are reported in "Dance Hall Fire Trap Was Once a Church," *The Chicago Defender*, 4 May 1940, p. 1, and "This Mother Keeps Her Daughters Home at Night," *The Chicago Defender*, 4 May 1940, p. 8.

38. Howlin' Wolf's song was reissued on *The Real Folk Blues/More Real Folk Blues*, MCA Records 088112 820, 2002. For a thorough biography of Chester Burnett aka Howlin' Wolf, see James Segrest and Mark Hoffman, *Moanin' at Midnight: The Life of Howlin' Wolf*, (New York: Pantheon Books, 2004).

39. Steve Cheseborough, *Blues Traveling: The Holy Sites of Delta Blues* (Jackson: University Press of Mississippi, 2001), pp. 178–79.

40. I am very grateful to Chris Smith for alerting me to and providing a copy of this rare field recording collected by Dr. Harry Oster.

41. John Lee Hooker's song was reissued on *Burning Hell*, Original Blues Classics OBCCD-555, 1992.

42. John Lee Hooker, "Tupelo Blues," Detroit, April 1959, Riverside LP 838, reissued on *The Country Blues*, Original Blues Classics OBCCD-542, n.d.

43. Only ten years ago did the song title and exact recording date and place appear in the booklet listing Hooker's complete recordings, compiled by Les Fancourt, *Boogie Chillen: A Guide to John Lee Hooker on Disc*, edited by Tony Burke (Cheadle, Cheshire, England: A Blues and Rhythm Publication, 1992), p. 35. The title was not reported in the standard postwar blues discography by Mike Leabitter & Neil Slaven, *Blues Records 1943 to 1970. A Selective Discography. Volume 1. A to K* (London: Record Information Services, 1987). Inexplicably, also the notes to the compact disc where "Fire at Natchez" was later issued with the title "The Great Disaster of 1936" assumed a very unlikely 1948–1952 recording date. See discographical notes to John Lee Hooker, *Alternative Boogie: Early Studio Recordings, 1948–1952,* Capitol Blues Collection 8 33912 2, 1996, p. 33.

44. In his book (page 52), Alan Lomax reports in inverted commas that Haffer stated that the storm in Tupelo occurred on a Saturday, whereas in the Library of Congress recording Haffer explicitly refers to "the first *Sunday* night in April 1936." For "Tupelo" as a "warning" song and the history behind it, see Alan Lomax, *op. cit.*, pp. 35–36, 52; see also Paul Oliver, "Tupelo Blues," in *Blues Off the Record: Thirty Years of Blues Commentary* (New York: Da Capo Press, 1988), p. 118.

45. Charles Shaar Murray, *Boogie Man: The Adventures of John Lee Hooker in the American Twentieth Century* (New York: St. Martin's Press, 2000), p. 214. For further biographical information on John Lee Hooker, see also Sheldon Harris, *Blues Who's Who: A Bibliographical Dictionary of Blues Singers* (New York: Da Capo Press, 1989), pp. 238–41, and Jim O'Neal and Amy Van Singel (eds.), *The Voice of the Blues: Classic Interviews from Living Blues Magazine* (New York: Routledge, 2002), pp. 202–25, originally published as *"Living Blues* Interview," *Living Blues* n. 44 (Autumn 1979), pp. 14–22.

46. John M. Barry, *Rising Tide: The Great Mississippi Flood of 1927 and How It Changed America* (New York: Simon & Schuster, 1997), pp. 170–71.

47. John Lee Hooker, "Tupelo," Palo Alto, California, September 1977, *The Cream,* Tomato CDX 22, 1988, reissued with the same title on Fuel 2000 Records 302 061 139 2, 2001.

48. "Tupelo, Miss., Wrecked," in *The New York Times,* 6 April 1936, p. 1, col. 4. I am indebted to David Evans for providing the exact historical and bibliographical information on the Tupelo tornado.

49. For similarly titled prewar recordings see Robert M. W. Dixon, John Godrich, and Howard W. Rye, *op. cit.*, p. 1298.

50. Hooker's third tribute to the Natchez Fire victims was reissued on John Lee Hooker, *Live at Newport,* Vanguard Records VCD 79703-2, 2002.

51. Mike Leadbitter and Neil Slaven, *op. cit.*, p. 631.

52. James Segrest, personal communication with the author, 12 October 2002.

53. So far I have traced: The Groundhogs, "Natchez Burning," London, June 1969, Liberty 83253, reissued on *Blues Obituary,* BGO Records BGOCD6, 1997; and Captain Beefheart, "Natchez Burning," Boston, MA, 1972, interview first issued on *Captain Beefheart & His Magic Band: Grow Fins—Rarities (1965–1982),* Revenant 210, 1999.

54. This blues was first issued on the compilation *Keep It to Yourself: Arkansas Blues Volume 1: Solo Performances*, Rooster Blues Records R7605, 1983, reissued with the same title on P-Vine Records PCD 5290, 1997.

55. For the song and information on the two musicians, see liner notes to Elmo Williams and Hezekiah Early, *Takes One to Know One*, Fat Possum Records 0313-2, 1997, David Evans, liner notes to *Hezekiah and the House Rockers*, High Water Recording Company LP 1011, 1990, and David Evans, "Since Ol' Gabriel's Time: Hezekiah and the Houserockers," *Louisiana Folklife* 7, no. 2 (October 1982), pp. 1–34.

56. See Lawrence W. Levine, *Black Culture and Black Consciousness: Afro-American Folk Thought from Slavery to Freedom* (Oxford: Oxford University Press, 1977).

57. For literature on these subjects see respectively: David Evans, "High Water Everywhere: Blues and Gospel Commentary on the 1927 Mississippi River Flood" in this book; Chris Smith, "The Titanic: A Case Study of Religious and Secular Attitudes in African American Song," in *Saints and Sinners: Religion, Blues and (D)evil in African-American Music and Literature*, edited by Robert Sacré (Liège: Société Liégeoise de Musicologie, 1996), pp. 213–27; Luigi Monge, "Preachin' the Blues: A Textual Linguistic Analysis of Son House's 'Dry Spell Blues'," in *New Perspectives on the Blues*, edited by David Evans, forthcoming.

58. In his review of *Newport Folk Festival: Best of the Blues 1959–68* (Vanguard Records 193/95-2, 2001) in *Blues and Rhythm* 162 (September 2001), p. 38, Neil Slaven defined Hooker's "The Mighty Fire" as "vague as it ever was."

59. See Big Jack Johnson's "Ice Storm Blues, Parts One & Two," Rooster Blues Records R-60-C, 1994. I am indebted to Edward Komara for providing information on this song and the transcription of the lyrics sung by Johnson.

60. Little Whitt & Big Bo [McGee], *Moody Swamp Blues*, Vent Records VR 30009, 1995.

LOOKIN' FOR THE BULLY

An Enquiry into a Song and Its Story

PAUL OLIVER

For those among us who research the early development of the blues, Henry Thomas—Ragtime Texas—is of particular importance, for the breadth of his repertoire, his use of the quills while playing guitar, and the quality of his playing, singing and even half-spoken narrative. In *Songsters and Saints* I discussed a number of his songs, including "Bob McKinney," which commences with a fragmentary version of the ballad before a brief medley of verses of other songs. Henry Thomas moves rapidly on to a verse from another early blues, "Make Me a Pallet on the Floor," recorded in classic versions, if much later, by Estelle Mama Yancey, and concludes his record with a snatch of "The Bully of the Town":

> . . . *One of these mornings, won't be long,*
> *You gonna call me, I'll be gone.*
> *She turned around, two or three times,*
> *Begged my baby, "Take me back,*
> *Take me back, take me back,"*
> *Begged my babe, "Take me back."*
>
> *"Oh make me a pallet on yo' floor,*
> *Hey, make me one pallet on yo' floor,*
> *Oh, make me a pallet on your floor,*
> *Won't you make it so your man will never know?"*
>
> *"Yes I'm lookin' for that bully, laid me down,*
> *Eeh, I'm lookin' for that bully laid me down,*
> *I'm lookin' for that bully, the bully that can't be found*
> *I'm lookin' for that bully laid me down."*[1]

It is possible to find the thread of meaning running through Henry Thomas's song medley, with the threatening Bob McKinney being the "bully" and the woman who appeals, perhaps to Ben Ferris, to take her back, being Mar'get. But there are aspects of the record that are significant irrespective of the tracing of a narrative, notably its combination of an early African American ballad with the late nineteenth-century composition "Take Me Back, Babe," written by Barrett McMahon. Further, it combines one of the earliest blues, "Pallet on the Floor," with a ragtime "coon" or "bully" song which in this version is sung to the tune of the blues. Henry Thomas's medley is a remarkable synthesis of the genres that were in circulation some thirty years before.

Of the songs that Henry Thomas drew upon, perhaps the most unlikely was one that was frequently termed the "bully song," which reinforced the stereotypes of the razor-totin', watermelon-suckin', chicken-stealin' "nigger" of that period. Before going further—what *was* the "Bully of the Town?" I discussed the history of the song briefly in *Songsters and Saints*[2] but there were several issues that should be raised. Where it has been cited in books on turn of the century song, such as in the works by Gilbert or Spaeth cited below, the discussion has mainly centered on the "bully" who had "just come to town":

He's round among de niggers a-layin' their bodies down
I'm a-lookin' for dat bully and he must be found.
I'm a Tennessee nigger and I don't allow,
No red-eyed river roustabout with me to raise a row,
I'm lookin' for dat bully and he must be found.

I'll take my long razor, I's going to carve him deep,
And when I see dat bully, I'll lay him down to sleep,
I'm lookin' for dat bully and he must be found.

As noted above, there are several published versions of the song, but most agree on these words, sung by a threatening figure who appears to be a competitor. Of interest is the location of the event at which the bully was encountered and met his desserts. In one version of the text the singers states that "I went to a wingin' down at Parson Jones'. . . ." A wingin' was a local dance or ball, the word being derived from the name of the traditional kicking and arm-flapping dance, the "buck and wing." Another version declares "now I went to a wingin' down to Brother Jones," while still another is more explicit, stating:

> *I went to a party down to Deacon Jones',*
> *I took my razzer wid me to carve dat Bully's bones,*
> *Just lookin' for dat Bully to hear his groans,*
> *When I got dar the darkies, dey was prancin' high,*
> *An' for dat Savannah nigger I peeled my weather eye,*
> *Jus' lookin' for dat Bully but he wasn't nigh.*

The singer turned to a young woman, Susie or Pansy Blossom, and suggested a dance which she was "flustrated"[*sic*] to do, or "feeling nice," even "high" when doing it: "Den you ought to see me shake ma niggah heels," she declares in one version.

> *I sanded down a Mobile buck just to cut a shine,*
> *When some niggah cross' my smeller swiped de watermelon rind,*
> *I drew my steel dat genmen fer to find.*

The singer "riz up" on his or her "hind legs," or "like a black cloud," and having found the bully, engaged him in a fight.

> *De razors went a-workin', de nigs begin to squawk,*
> *I fell upon dat bully just like a sparrow hawk,*
> *O' dat genmen was just dyin' to take a walk.*

By the time the singer had "got through" with him, the doctor and the nurse couldn't do much for him, "so dey put him in a hearse," neither "a cyclone nor a buzz-saw could have cut him or chawed him worse," according to the various texts, which agree on the story and make only minor changes in the words. No more would you hear of a "bully that treats folks so free," or "dat wicked folks so feared."

> *Go down upon de levee and his face you'll never see,*
> *Dere's only one boss bully now, dat one's me.*[3]

From where did the "bully song" come? The African American composer and "Father of the Blues," W. C. Handy wrote of wishing to compose "a down-home ditty fit to go with twanging banjos and yellow shoes. Songs of this sort could be tremendous hits sometimes. On the levee at St. Louis I had heard *Looking for the Bully* sung by the roustabouts, which later was adopted and nationally popularized by May Irwin. I had watched the joy-spreaders rarin' to go when it was played by the band on the *Gray Eagle*, or the *Spread Eagle*." At the time in the fall of 1893, he was nineteen years old and had "slept on the cobblestones of the levee of the Mississippi," trying to avoid arrest for vagrancy. "Two popular songs grew out of brutality of the police in those days, *Brady, He's Dead and Gone* and *Looking for the Bully*." Though he wanted to forget his sufferings in St. Louis, he didn't want to forget Targee Street and "the high-roller Stetson hats of the men or the diamonds the girls wore in their ears. Then there were those who sat for company in little plush parlors under gaslights."[4]

Not far from there was South Sixth Street where, at No. 210, Babe Connors ran "the Castle" which "to the initiated meant a rendezvous that was virtually the hub of St. Louis' red light wheel." The pianist at the Castle Club was the pioneer ragtime pianist Tom Turpin, who later operated his own saloons on Targee and Chestnut Streets.[5] Inside the Castle "one was blinded by the brilliance," as Douglas Gilbert noted of Babe who, "in full panoply, resembled a Tiffany window" with diamonds in her teeth and ears and all over her person. A "handsome, bronze-complexioned Negress" who weighed 165 pounds, she was proprietress of a celebrated show place and brothel, with light-hued octoroon girls from Louisiana who wore "long skirts without underclothing. Thus costumed they would dance on a huge mirror." A main attraction, nevertheless, was her singer Mama Lou who was "short, black, often belligerent and always herself. . . . She wore a calico dress, gingham apron, and head bandanna and nine tenths of her songs were obscene." They included "Ta-Ra-Ra-Boom-Der-E," "Hot Time in the Old Town Tonight," "Who Stole the Lock"—and the "bully song."[6]

It seems likely that Mama Lou had picked up a song which was popular on the levee district at the time. Though precise details of collecting the song at that date are missing, it was definitely collected as a "social song" by Howard Odum a few years later.[7] While it may have been in general circulation, there is the likelihood that the song filtered down through the black community from the stage shows. But if it did, there were very few others except "Who Stole the Lock" that did, and this too might have been acquired from the river roustabouts. Whatever the origin, a song entitled "The New Bully," with words and music by Lee Johnson, was published in 1895 by The Zeno Mauvais Music Co. The tune was clearly enough of a hit for the Zeno Company to publish it as a two-step march,

under the name of J. Donigan, in the same year. The Pacific Music Company
also published a version of "The New Bully," with music by Jos. Hirschbach and
words attributed to J. P. Wilson, also in 1895.[8]

The following year yet another version, written by Will C. Carlton with
music by J. M. Cavanagh was published, but it was the song variously entitled as
"Dat New Bully," "The Bully" or "The New Bully," composed by Charles E.
Trevathan, which became the hit of the season when it was performed by May
Irwin. Charles Trevathan was a judge of horse races and a popular writer on sports
when he was encountered by the celebrated singer while on a train en route to
Chicago from San Francisco following the races there. Amusing fellow passengers by playing his guitar and singing while they traveled, Trevathan came up
with a tune which he acknowledged he had collected from black singers in
Tennessee. May Irwin, who had been singing with a traveling show, *The Country
Sport*, was excited by the tune and encouraged Trevathan to produce some lyrics
for it.[9] She included it in her highly successful show *The Widow Jones*, which
played in Brockton, Massachusetts, before becoming a hit at Tony Pastor's celebrated New York show-house, and eventually the Bijou Theater. May Irwin herself was noted as a comedienne and doubtless wielded the razor herself while
acting her part and singing the "bully song." She recorded the song in May
1907 for Victor, the single-sided twelve-inch disc being recorded with an orches-
tral accompaniment. It was issued just a couple of months after, and was still in
the Victor catalogue a decade later.[10]

Its strong and memorable tune was undoubtedly one reason for its popularity, which permeated rural as well as urban America. It was recorded by at least
a score of white hillbilly soloists and bands such as Fiddlin' John Carson, Sid
Harkreader, Gid Tanner and the Skillet Lickers, Ernest Stoneman's Dixie
Mountaineers, the Cherokee Ramblers and many more.[11] Most of these reduced
the lyrics to a verse or two, or even just to the refrain, possibly because the words
would have been known to most purchasers. But the hillbilly singers were not
the only ones to record it; there were a few versions by other black singers besides
Henry Thomas. They included the Memphis Jug Band at their second session,
in June 1927, though their words hardly reflected the character of the original.

> *Oh, I'm lookin' for the bully, oh, the bully can't be found,*
> *I'm lookin' for the bully, the bully of the town,*
> *Oh he's a bad man, he was the baddest man in town,*
> *I'm lookin' for the bully of the town.*

Oh, and it's honey babe, oh honey, take your time,
Honey babe, oh, honey, I love you,
Oh honey babe, oh, honey take your time,
I'm lookin' for the bully of the town.[12]

The Louisiana street and juke singers Kid West and Joe Harris recorded a version for the Library of Congress in Shreveport in October, 1940.[13] It seems that they were aware that the song was a long one, even if they remembered only a verse and the chorus, both of which they repeated:

Well then it's when you walk that levee round, round, round, round
When you walk that levee round, round, round, round,
When you walk that levee round,
Yes, I'm lookin' for that bully of the town.

Oh, I'm lookin' for that bully, that bully can't be found,
I'm lookin' for that bully, that bully can't be found,
'Cause I'm lookin' for the bully of the town.[14]

At this date it was still in wide circulation. Just a few months later, in March 1941, John Work recorded a veteran banjo player Sidney Stripling, at the Fort Valley State College in Fort Valley, Georgia. In strained accents he hollered his version of "Looking for the Bully of the Town" to his own old-style "boom-ching" banjo accompaniment. His words were similar to those of other singers of the period, including those of West and Harris, with a verse that declares that he is looking for the bully that couldn't be found, and a reference to walking the levee round. But he added a verse which set the song back in its turn-of-the-century context:

I went to Chicago, tell me there was a Fair,
Well, I was lookin' for bully and the bully was not—
Well, I'm lookin' for the bully of this town.

Soon as I walk this levee round,
Soon as I walk this levee round,
Soon as I walk this levee round,
Well, I'm lookin' for the bully of this town.[15]

Even later, it was recorded in a similarly limited version by Leadbelly at his "last sessions" in 1948. In his version of the ballad "Ella Speed" Leadbelly had incorporated several verses or phrases from "The Bully."[16] Clearly, the song lived on as a tune for half a century among veteran songsters, even if the words appear to have been assimilated or to have had little appeal. May Irwin was widely reputed to have initiated the craze for "coon" songs with the "bully song," though the word does not even occur in most versions. If "bully songs" were regarded as part of the "coon" fad, "Dere's a Bully Gone to Rest" and "De Bully's Wedding Night" were just a couple of the published songs of the late nineties on the bully theme, but both the theme and May Irwin figure in virtually all the analyses and histories of ragtime, while one or two authors have noted its hint of the emergent blues of the period. Jon W. Finson sums it up: "In any event, ragtime provided the means by which the song became popular: the verse features a goodly amount of syncopation to the beat of an extroverted march. The chorus had a particularly attractive melody with just a hint of a 'blue' note (a chromatic ornament found in the blues), all supported by an alternating bass." Finson concluded that " 'The Bully Song' is a prime example of 'realistic' art, where ethnic music (or at least elements of it) has been used to support a stereotype."[17]

As we have seen, the "bully song" may well have had its origins in the black music community of St. Louis and levees in the second half of the nineteenth century, and through the period of commercial exploitation, it may still have retained its appeal as music, if not as song. Are we to assume that the bully had been found, that he was no longer looked for, and the circumstances of the "wingin'" in which he exercised his power no longer applied? Was there a parting of the music, which in some degree lived on, and of the lyric and story line, which was now an unacceptable stereotype? There would seem to be an argument in favor of this, as expressed in the recordings of both black and white musicians and singers. Yet there remains the problem that the song was apparently of southern Black origin, stereotypical though it may have been. We have some idea of what happened to the music—but what happened to the bully, to the razor-wielding heroine and the "winging" dance where their encounter took place? Are they still to be found in the songs of the subsequent generation?

Not, it would seem, in published song after the middle of the first decade of the twentieth century when May Irwin, at her only recording session, recorded the full text of "The Bully." Recordings, however, gradually began to reveal a range of music which was not necessarily published, and even when it was, largely remained in the milieu of black vaudeville or other popular entertainment in which songs about the "ball," or locally promoted dance, were prominent. As is well known, Mamie Smith was the first black artist to record in the popular vein for a major company. Her sixth record, issued in early 1921 was a good-natured song about "The Jazzbo Ball."[18] Though the description was innocuous enough, it included a reference to one "Razor Jim," clearly a bully who had laid down the rules of behavior at the ball, with threats of dire penalties if he was not obeyed.

It was only a fragment, but it may indicate that a song on the theme was already current, though a year was to pass before a full version appeared on record, sung by Edith Wilson as "Rules and Regulations Signed Razor Jim":

Down in old Bones, Kentucky, near Cemetery Hill,
Lives old, bad Razor Jim, and he's known to kill.
Just across the street, lives old Pistol Pete,
Well, the meanest man in town which I did meet.
Every Friday night Razor Jim give a ball;
Before you dance in that hall,
You have to read them
Rules and Regulations on the wall, that's all.

The first rule was "Now you can dance and glide,
You must do it neat and have a girl by your side.
Scratchin' the Gravel and Ballin' the Jack
If you do them rough dances you mustn't come back.
If you shimmy in here you'll wobble outside
If you break these rules, Jim'll cut your hide.
Don't none of you brothers get out on that limb:
Rules and Regulations, Signed Razor Jim."[19]

Pistol Pete "would not obey the law" and got into a fight. Sluefoot Joe came to the rescue, telling him to put his mind on the Rules, for "Jim can use a razor with so much vim." The victim of such a fight is the subject of the recently found recording of Eddie Hunter, accompanied by the ragtime pianist Luckyeth Roberts, narrating and singing "At the Bootlegger's Ball." Ed Hunter returns to his woman, Mahalie, who, on seeing him at the door, cries, "Aw look at your head! So where did you come from, honey? Where did you get all them bandages around your head?" "Ain't none of your business—I got 'em at the hospital; where did you think I got 'em?" Hunter replies, "Let me lay down here somewhere, my head feels like it weighs a hundred pounds." "Oh, look at this extra knot on the back here; looks like a little house," Mahalie exclaims. Getting Eddie to rest on the sofa, Mahalie asks him to tell her what happened. "Well you see, mama, it was just like this," he explains:

Ninety-nine and nine new members' names were listed on the call,
And so Bill Budd plumb decided that they'd better hire a hall,
To initiate and celebrate with a high-class free-for-all,
Where each person brings his own liquor,
And each of them carries it to Bootleg Ball
(I see.)
When they opened the hall on the night of the ball,
Here's what happened before the dance started at all:
(Describe it to me, honey.)
Bill Budd bounced a billiard ball,
Off Bob the Barber's big bald bean,
Sneaky Steve and Slapstick Sam,
Shut off Slapstick Samuel's scene;
Kit Cutler carved Cal Cummins keenly,
Causin' Calvin cops to call;
Then the bold big billies broke Bad Big Bullies',
That's Bad Big Bully's at the Bootlegger's Ball,
At bad Bill Budd's big bootleg ball.
(Go on, honey, that's interestin'.)
You could hear the brass knucks moanin' and a-groanin' through the air,
You could hear the night-sticks ringin', and singin' everywhere.
(Sounds like a concert.)
Bullets fizzin' and a-whizzin' same as in a big war zone.
(Regular movin' picture!)
Blackjacks swayin' and they's playing same as any xylophone,
Every human there got either hit, cut or shot,
Everybody enjoyed themselves quite a lot.
(What tune did they play on your head, honey?)
Bill Budd bounced a billiard ball.[20]

Eddie repeats the verse, until they hear a bell: "What's that, the police wagon?" he asks, and Mahalie explains to his alarm, that it is an ambulance. "Mahalie, lock that door. I said lock the door! And it they ask for me, tell 'em I said that I ain't here. Oh honey, my head! Get me some ice. That bootleg ball! Um, um! Um, um!"

Though it seems that the weapons had moved from razors to guns, it was still the big bad Bully, Bad Bill Budd, who reigned over the function—perhaps the last recording, apart from the "Bully of the Town" in which the "bully" is specifically mentioned. By no means every song about a ball concluded with a razor fight; Gladys Bryant could have been excused a little aggressiveness as she struggled against Porter Grainger's hard-hitting, clattering piano on "The Dark Town Flappers Ball," but it was a cheerful paean to the "black brigade" who could strut their stuff at the event.[21] Josie Miles, who was not one to avoid violence in her songs, might have been expected to have given a less optimistic view of the social dance, yet her recording of "At the Cake Walk Stepper's Ball" made three years later, in 1925, was in similar vein.[22] Nevertheless, a less roseate image of the ball of the day was still being depicted, together with a more precise identification of the characters at the function. Reflecting the role that May Irwin must have played, women were also involved in the fighting, as in Sara Martin's 1925 recording of "Down at the Razor Ball":

Down at the Razor Ball, given at the Razor Hall,
Sluefoot Moe and Crosseyed Joe, didn't go at all.
But they hung around outside,
And this is what they spied:
Crap-shootin' Ann was in the Hall, and started in to fight,
Joe got drunk and that ain't all: he went and turned out the light.
Winchester Charley shot Automatic Slim,
'Cause Charlie took his gal and double-crossed him.
The police came and pulled the Hall,
Down at the Razor Ball.[23]

It seems likely that Sara Martin had obtained a song which was already in circulation, or that her recording inspired the Georgia songster Blind Willie McTell, who, a few years later, made his own version of the "Razor Ball." Some of the characters were similar, but the genre seemed to permit a considerable degree of freedom in the description of events, which, in spite of the title, arose out of a

crap game. Accompanying himself on 12–string guitar and recording for the
Columbia Company in Atlanta under the name of Blind Sammie, he sang:

> Down at the Razor Ball, given at the Razor Hall,
> Sluefoot Mose and old Cross-Eyed Joe didn't go in at all.
> They hung around outside, this is what they spied:
> A big crap game in the hall started in to fight,
> Joe got drunk, that wasn't all, he went and turned out the lights.
> And that mark-shootin' Charlie, shot his automatic twin,
> Charlie grabbed his girl and he croaked off ten.
> Police came and filled the Hall.
> Down at the Razor Ball, I mean Ball,
> Down around the Razor Ball.
> Doin' that shimmy-she-wobble and shakin' your—
> Quit that shimmy-she-wobblin', quit shakin' your hips,
> Down at the Razor Ball, I mean Ball,
> Down around the Razor Ball.
> Playin' base-ball and foot-ball and don't get enough
> Playin' base-ball and foot-ball, and struttin' their stuff,
> Down at the Razor Ball, I mean Ball,
> Down at the Razor Ball.
>
> There was another crap game was in the Hall, started in to fight,
> Joe got drunk and that wasn't all,
> Went in and turned out the lights.
> Mighty big Chief shot his automatic twin,
> The high sheriff took the couple and double-crossed ten.
> Rest of them came and got the crowd,
> From down at the Razor ball, I mean,
> Down around the Razor Ball, shootin' crap,
> Down around the Razor Ball, playin' cards,
> Down around the Razor Ball, they was gamblin',
> Down around the Razor Ball, cuttin' on the corner,
> Down around the Razor Ball.[24]

Among the urban singers the "razor ball" was going "out of style," or at least, this
was part of the message projected by Ma Rainey's Boys, Foster and Harris, when
they sang of "Crow Jane Alley" the same year. The recording opens with a

discussion on the risks involved in going to a ball at Miss Susie's house on Crow Jane Alley while carrying money. One of the Boys advises the other, who continually comments, by giving an account of a previous event.

> *I've got a gal, I mean a gal, she's the ugliest woman in town, (tell the truth)*
> *In every place I go, no matter where, she follers me just like a hound.*
> *I was invited out to a ball the other day,*
> *Where all the highbrowns, they give a sway, (sure enough)*
> *You know that woman followed me, all the way,*
> *She likes to ruin them folks' balls, I'd say, (I bet she broke it up)*
> *That's the reason I'm force-ed to say: (what's you gonna say now?)*

> *Partner, Crow Jane is all right with me,*
> *But they've done gone out of style,*
> *They will cut your throat while you sleep,*
> *Boy, look down on your face and smile.*[25]

He concluded that "a Crow Jane is all right with me partner, but they've done gone out of style." By which time the ball might seem to have gone out of style too, but razor cutting and fighting certainly had not. Boasting songs like Louisiana Johnny's "Razor Cuttin' Man" of 1935[26] or Perline Ellison's "Razor Totin' Mama"[27] appear to have been suppressed, the former unissued by Vocalion, the latter recorded by Decca in 1943, but unissued. This would suggest sensitivity on the part of the record companies to the possible offence, and even influence, they might have caused. Yet Bluebird was prepared to issue Washboard Sam's version of "Razor Cuttin' Man" made in December 1936, while Decca had no inhibitions in releasing Charley Jordan's extremely violent "Cuttin' My ABC's" in 1937, a version of "A-Z Blues," first recorded by Butterbeans and Susie (Edwards) in September 1924, and a couple of months later by Billy Higgins, with Josie Miles. In these instances, however, the razor cutting theme was no longer associated with dancing, and may possibly have stemmed from a different lineage than that of the "bully song."[28] Nevertheless, songs about dances continued and there seems to have been a tendency to put a sting in the tail of songs which depicted good times at a ball or similar function.

Most readers will be familiar with Bessie Smith's recording of Wesley Wilson's "Gimme a Pigfoot," which, however, does warn the participants to "check yo' razors and yo' guns, we gotta be rasslin' when the wagon comes . . . ," the "wagon" being the police patrol wagon.[29] Surprisingly, Wesley Wilson's recording of

"Rasslin' til the Wagon Comes" does not shed much light on this, but another less familiar recording of "Gimme a Pigfoot" by Frankie Half-Pint Jaxon is more specific. Jaxon, it should be noted, was a female impersonator on stage. The opening verse follows the Bessie Smith version except that he/she advises:

> *Shake your switch-blades and your guns,*
> *Get yourself ready for a barrel of fun,*
> *Gimme a pig's foot and a barrel of beer.*
> *Send me Gate, I don't care,*
> *Slay me Jack, anywhere.*[30]

In subsequent verses he threatens to "cut you up and down your ear" and "put you six feet under the earth." Jaxon's recording was made in 1940, just two years after Mae Irwin died in 1938, aged 76. The following year we find Washboard Sam evoking the theme of the 1890s in his 1941 recording of "Down at the Bad Man's Hall," though he placed it in a more sedate context; "the ball was given by the Sons of Rest; they boys, they come in they Sunday best."

> *In come a gal, she was big and strong,*
> *A chunk of chewing gum in her mouth,*
> *Her hair was as nappy as a cocklebur,*
> *None of them boys would fancy her,*
> *Down at the Bad Man's Hall, (x2)*
> *Down at the Bad Man's Hall—we sure did have a time.*
>
> *She jumped in the floor and balled up her fists,*
> *"If you want to test your nerve, just jump against this!*
> *If none of you boys don't dance with me,*
> *Then with my razor, I'm gonna break up this jamboree."*
>
> *In come a boy named Slick 'Em Jim,*
> *None of them gals would dance with him.*
> *He reached in his pocket and drew his .32,*
> *Them boys did run. Hot dog, they flew!*[31]

Slick 'Em Jim was arrested "cause all them boys had left but him," and presumably, so had the girl with the cocklebur hair-do and a razor. The term cocklebur refers to a seed pod with burrs. There is a strong possibility of a link between the "bully song" complex and the early "bush ballad" known as "The Bullockies' Ball," which has a broadly similar story line. A team of "bullockies," or bullock-drivers, encamped and had a "grand blow-out." Among the bullockies and their women were:

> *Flash Joe, but Jimmy was flasher,*
> *Hopping Billy, the one-eyed boss,*
> *Brisbane Sal and the Derwent Slasher,*
> *Billy the Bull and Paddy the Hoss.*

A good time was had by all, until "there was ructions." Hunks of food were exchanged in a fight but there were no razors or pistols used: "Blackened eyes and broken noses, Then that wound up the bullockies' ball."[32] Although the origin of the song is unknown, it was traced back some four generations in the 1950s and may have been contemporaneous with May Irwin, or even have derived from a common source.

Though Louis Jordan gave a similar twist to the story in some versions of "Saturday Night Fish Fry," it was something of a surprise to find Howlin' Wolf (Chester Burnett) reverting to the old theme. Not willingly, it seems, for, as Willie Dixon recalled: "I've been real lucky about writing people songs but a lot of times, I'd pick the song, the guy didn't want the song for himself. Muddy didn't want the songs I was giving him and Howlin' Wolf didn't want the ones I was giving him. The one Wolf hated most of all was "Wang Dang Doodle." He hated that "Tell Automatic Slim and Razor-Totin' Jim." He'd say, "Man, that's too old-timey, sound like some old levee camp number.'"[33] The "shack bully" was required to rouse and keep in order the black workers on the levees under the "convict lease" system and was much detested for his brutality.[34] In view of his opinion of the song, Howlin' Wolf made a remarkably effective recording of it. The "Wang" of the song "meant having a ball and a lot of dancing," according to Dixon, though presumably it was a simple adaptation of the traditional term "wing," or "wing-ding" for a country ball. Declaring that "we gonna pitch a wang dang doodle all night long," Howlin' Wolf growled:

> *Tell Automatic Slim, tell Razor-Totin' Jim,*
> *Tell Butcher-knife totin' Annie, tell Fast-talkin' Fannie,*
> *We're gonna pitch a ball down at the Union Hall,*
> *We gonna romp and tromp till midnight,*
> *We gonna fuss and fight till daylight. . . .*[35]

Directing his companions to inform Cooter-Crawling Red, Abyssinia Ned, and Pistol Pete, he promised that the would "break out all the windows" and "kick down all the doors" as they spent the night pitching their wang dang doodle. It may have stemmed from the levee, but "Wang Dang Doodle" clearly drew some of its characters and theme from Sara Martin's "Down at the Razor Ball." Not that Willie Dixon acknowledged it; quite the contrary. "I did write 'Wang Wang Doodle' when I first heard Wolf back in 1951 or 1952 but there's a time for these things. A lot of times you're too far in advance for the people or ideas you're dealing with so maybe a guy can see it at another time." Without intentional irony, John Collis in his history of the Chess record company, referred to it as "an innovative piece of writing, and the Wolf was too set in his ways to appreciate innovation." Before its time, or more accurately, half a century after it, "the last big blues hit the label had was in early 1966 with Koko Taylor's decidedly soul-tinged arrangement of 'Wang Dang Doodle' on Checker." To Koko Taylor herself "it was almost a miracle record . . . before I know anything they said they had sold 100,000 copies right in Chicago."[36]

What was the appeal of the "old-timey levee camp number," as Howlin' Wolf perceptively placed it, some seventy years after the "bully song" appeared? True, the textual theme and the musical theme had parted company by the 1920s, but although there were modifications and transformations in the song narrative, the ball that ended with the threat of a razor slashing, or which anticipated it with advice to be so armed, persisted remarkably. What, we may ask, was the truth behind the theme: what record is there of such events? Perhaps the most immediate description appeared in Zora Neale Hurston's *Mules and Men* of 1935 when she was "doing the slow drag, doing the scronch, Joe Willard doing a traveling buck and wing toward where I stood against the wall facing the open door."

Hurston explained that "Just about that time Lucy hopped up in the doorway with an open knife in her hands. . . . She knew I couldn't get out easily because she had me barred and she knew not many people will risk running into a knife blade to stop a fight." Zora was sick and weak with fear but Big Sweet "was flying at her with an open blade and now it was Lucy's time to try and make it to the door." Then a "double-backed razor flew thru the air very close to Big Sweet's head. Gip, the new skitter man, had hurled it . . . then Joe Willard went for Crip." Violently, Zora was hustled out and bundled into a car, while the "whole place was in motion" with the knife and razor fight. She escaped to New Orleans. . . . The jealousies, bitterness and naked violence at the dance are graphically described. Did she relate (in nearly forty pages) an actual incident? Presumably so, for it is unlikely that Zora Neale Hurston had drawn upon the stereotype to bring the Belle Glade, Florida, episode in *Mules and Men* to a dramatic end.[37]

It is worth a moment's consideration of the recurrent themes and sub-themes in the genre that relate the variants of the "bully song" and its successors to the "Wang Dang Doodle." Clearly, there is the function, generally a ball, to which many people come. Among them are one or two threatening characters whose nicknames are frequently cited. The dancers are often advised to bring their own weapons though a good time is promised. The singer is sometimes razor-wielding and is often female. I have not seen the text of *The Widow Jones*, or any accounts or reviews of it, even though it was considered a major production. Presumably, May Irwin sang the song herself and, if so, this put the threatening razor in her hands as she sought the Bully. Perhaps it was this, in addition to the appeal of the music itself, which made the performance memorable, placing the vengeful female to the fore. This suggests that Mama Lou, the singer at Babe Connor's cabaret who was black and notorious, may have been the source of the razor-wielding woman who recurs consistently in the recorded songs cited here.

Is the razor-totin' female the nemesis of the Bully, or does she become, in turn, the Bully herself? Is the bully a figure of repugnance, or one of fear, or is he or she a figure of admiration? Is the whole story one of rebellion, one of challenging authority, and does it have implications of racial conflict or resistance? It describes good times at the dance, but they also turn sour with the razor slashing or a fight with lethal weapons; does this contrast have symbolic significance and is the whole song cycle one of disillusion, of failed promise? Or is the narrative simply one of accommodation with a far from uncommon experience, which contains no more profound yet covert meanings? Clearly, while it went through subtle changes, the song theme persisted for a lifetime, and could still excite immense numbers of purchasers in the late 1960s. Though one may speculate on the significance of the song and its meaning at different periods, there is no way of knowing for certain what its importance was to individual singers and their audiences. Perhaps a combing through the history of other persistent songs and themes in the broad blues canon may eventually throw more light on these questions. There is much more than the Bully to be "lookin' for."

NOTES

1. Henry Thomas (Ragtime Texas), vo, gtr, "Bob McKinney," October 1927, Vocalion 1138. My sincere thanks to Chris Smith and Guido van Rijn for their invaluable assistance with transcriptions in this article.

2. Paul Oliver, *Songsters and Saints. Vocal Traditions on Race Records* (Cambridge, UK: Cambridge University Press, 1984), pp. 48–49.

3. Cited extracts are from the Charles E. Trevathan version of *Dat New Bully*, 1896.

4. W. C. Handy, *Father of the Blues. An Autobiography* (London: Sigwick and Jackson, 1957), pp. 27–28, 119–20.

5. David A. Jasen and Trebor Jay Tichenor, *Rags and Ragtime. A Musical History* (New York: Dover Publications, 1989), pp. 28–29.

6. Douglas Gilbert, *Lost Chords. The Diverting Story of American Popular Songs* (New York: Doubleday, Doran & Co., 1942), pp. 208–12; David Ewen, *All the Years of Popular Music* (Englewood Cliffs, N.J.: Prentice-Hall, 1977), pp. 117–20.

7. Howard W. Odum and Guy B. Johnson, *The Negro and his Songs* (Chapel Hill: University of North Carolina Press, 1925), pp. 203–205 (collected, 1911).

8. Norm Cohen, notes to *Paramount Old Time Tunes*, JEMF LP 103 (n.d. c.1979), pp. 10–12. Norm Cohen, notes to *Minstrels and Tunesmiths*, JEMF LP 109 (1981), pp. 28–29.

9. Sigmund Spaeth, *Read 'Em and Weep. The Songs You Forgot to Remember* (Garden City, N.Y.: Doubleday, Page & Co., 1927), pp. 212–14; James J. Geller, *Famous Songs and Their Stories* (New York: Macaulay, 1931), pp. 97–99.

10. May Irwin, vo acc. orch., "The Bull," May 1907, Victor 31642.

11. Guthrie T. Meade, Richard Spottswood, and Douglas S. Meade, *Country Music Sources: A BiblioDiscography of Commercially Recorded Traditional Music* (Chapel Hill: University of North Carolina, 2002).

12. Memphis Jug Band, "I'm Looking for the Bully of the Town," June 1927, Victor 20781. Full details of items recorded before 1943 will be found in Robert M.W. Dixon, John Godrich, & Howard W. Rye, *Blues & Gospel Records 1890–1943*, 4th edition (Oxford: Clarendon Press, 1997).

13. Paul Oliver, notes to *Jerry's Saloon Blues. 1940 Field recordings from Louisiana*, Flyright-Matchbox Library of Congress Series, vol. 8, FLY LP 260 (1978); Charles Wolfe and Kip Lornell, *The Life and Legend of Leadbelly* (New York: HarperCollins, 1992), pp. 91–92.

14. Joe Harris and Kid West, gtrs, "Bully of the Town," October, 1940, Library of Congress, Flyright-Matchbox FLY LP 260.

15. Sidney Stripling, vo, bjo, "Lookin' for the Bully in This Town," March 1941, L of C.

16. Leadbelly (Huddie Ledbettter), "Bully of the Town," Folkways FA2942, 1948; John A. Lomax and Alan Lomax, *Negro Folk Songs as Sung by Lead Belly* (New York: Macmillan, 1936), pp. 187–92.

17. Jon W. Finson, *The Voices That Are Gone. Themes in 19th Century Popular Song* (Oxford: Oxford University Press, 1994), pp. 222–23, illus 6.3, 6.4.

18. Mamie Smith, vo acc. Jazz Hounds, "Jazzbo Ball," February 1921, OKeh 4295.

19. Edith Wilson & orch., "Rules and Regulations Signed Razor Jim," June 1922, Columbia A3653.

20. Eddie Hunter, Alex Rogers, vo, acc. pno, "Bootlegger's Ball," November 1923, Victor 19247.

21. Gladys Bryant, vo, acc. Porter Grainger, pno, "The Dark Town Flappers Ball," March 1923, Paramount 12027.

22. Josie Miles, acc. Choo Choo Jazzers, "At the Cakewalk Stepper's Ball," February 1925, Ajax 17127.

23. Sara Martin, vo, acc. trio, "Down at the Razor Ball," November 1925, OKeh 8283.

24. Blind Sammie (Willie McTell) vo, gtr. *Razor Ball*. April, 1930. Columbia 14551 -D.

25. Ma Rainey's Boys (Foster and Harris), "Crow Jane Alley," September 1929, Paramount 12709.

26. Louisiana Johnny, vo, acc. bass, "Razor Cuttin' Man," October 1934, Vocalion unissued.

27. Perline Ellison, vo, acc. Harold Boyce orch., "Razor Totin' Mama," December 1943, Decca unissued.

28. Washboard Sam, wbd, vo, "Razor Cuttin' Man," December 1936, Bluebird BB B6765; Charley Jordan, vo, gtr, acc. pno, "Cuttin' my ABCs," March 1937, Decca 7353.

29. Bessie Smith, vo, acc. Buck and his Band, "Gimme a Pigfoot," November 1933, OKeh 8945; Kid (Wilson) and Coot (Grant), "Rasslin' Till the Wagon Comes," September 1928, Columbia 14363.

30. Frankie Half-Pint Jaxon, acc. quintet, "Gimme a Pig's Foot," April 1940, Decca 7795.

31. Washboard Sam, "Down at the Bad Man's Hall," January 1941, Bluebird B8792.

32. Douglas Stewart and Nancy Keesing, *Old Bush Songs* (Sydney: Angus and Robertson, 1955), pp. 135–36; David Bromley, *Bush Ballads of Australia* (Frenchs Forest, N.S.W.: Reed Books Pty Ltd., 1985), pp. 44–45.

33. Willie Dixon with Don Snowden, *I Am the Blues. The Willie Dixon Story* (London: Quartet Books, 1989), pp. 88, 120–21.

34. John Cowley, "Shack Bullies and Levee Contractors," *JEMF Quarterly* vol. 16, No 60 (1980): 182–93.

35. Howlin' Wolf (Chester Burnett), acc. quartet. *Wang Wang Doodle*. June 1960. Chess 1777.

36. Willie Dixon, John Snowden, Koko Taylor, in Dixon, *op. cit.* pp. 174–75; John Collis, *The Story of Chess Records* (London: Bloomsbury Publishing, 1998), p. 83.

37. Zora Neale Hurston, *Mules and Men* (New York, London: J. B. Lippincott Co, 1935), pp. 86–190.

THAT DRY CREEK EATON CLAN

A North Mississippi Murder Ballad of the 1930s

TOM FREELAND AND CHRIS SMITH

In May 1939, John A. Lomax and his wife, Ruby Terrill, were part-way through a song collecting trip on behalf of the Archive of American Folk Song (now the Archive of Folk Culture) of the Library of Congress. Beginning on March 31, 1939, they were to make recordings in Texas, Louisiana, Arkansas, Mississippi, Alabama, Florida, South Carolina and Virginia, before the field trip ended at the Library of Congress on June 14, 1939. On May 23, Miss Terrill recorded in her fieldnotes that:

> We left Camp #9 of the Arkansas state farm about 2 o'clock and spent the night at Greenville, Mississippi, across the Mississippi River. It was a stormy night; much damage was done by the wind and rain, but the next morning we had clear weather for our drive to Parchman. Mr. Lomax had made his first recording visit to Parchman in 1933. We could not see the Superintendent when we first arrived, but his assistant gave permission for us to visit Camp #10. Rain had set in and the boys could not work. We set up the machine in the wide hall of the barracks that separates the white dormitory from the Negroes. (A high barbed wire fence surrounds the barracks.)[1]

Parchman Penitentiary had been founded to both tighten and perpetuate Mississippi's system of segregation, by one of segregation's most virulent proponents, Governor James Kimble Vardaman. In the thirties, under Jim Crow, the camps in Parchman were segregated.[2] The camps were themselves isolated one from the other on a plantation of just under twenty-five square miles, with each camp separated by the fields its prisoners worked. Camp 10 was the sawmill camp, and, with the women's camp, was one of the two places where whites and blacks labored together, although they were housed in segregated wards.[3] Miss Terrill continues:

> Singers were not plentiful or enthusiastic, but we recorded a few tunes before the rain subsided enough for the boys to chop wood and do other light jobs around the barracks. In the evening we tried again with fair results. We discovered that one barrier was the idea that we were there to make money out of the boys without "divvying-up." This they were told by one of the boys who had made some commercial records. After Mr. Lomax made it clear to them the purpose of the recording and the use which their songs would serve, they were more generous, and helpful.[4]

As it happens, we know the identity of the so-called "boy" who initially obstructed Lomax's attempts to record; his prison nickname was "Barrelhouse," and his real name was Booker T. Washington White (1906–77). He had previously recorded for Victor as "Washington White" in 1930, and as "Bukka White" for Vocalion in September 1937, before being sentenced to life in prison for murder in November of that year.[5] White was to record again for Vocalion in 1940, after his release from Parchman, and he had a further recording career after he was located by researchers in the '60s.[6] The two songs which he recorded on May 23, 1939, "Po' Boy" and "Sic 'Em Dogs On," are probably the best known of the African American material collected during the 1939 field trip, but this paper focuses on a lesser known singer and guitarist, Roger "Burndown" Garrett. Miss Terrill was uncertain whether his surname was Garrett or Garnett, and she put the latter possibility in brackets in her notes. *Blues and Gospel Records 1890–1943* accepts "Garnett," but "Garrett" is the more common surname and will be used in this paper.[7]

As his nickname implies, Garrett was in prison for arson. Miss Terrill gives some background in her fieldnotes:

> "Burndown" gets his nickname from the charge on which he was convicted. According to his and Sergeant Connor's story, he was working for a white man who ordered him to lay kindling and spread oil around an outhouse which was insured for $250.00. Neighbors discovered the fire from the smoke. Burndown and his employer set to work to help put out the fire. Burndown was convicted of arson; his white employer's trial was postponed on an insanity plea. Burndown said he knew he oughtn't to do it, but he thought he had to obey his boss.[8]

That story establishes that Garrett was African American; no white convict in the Mississippi of 1939 would have felt the need to specify the race of his employer. Garrett recorded three songs in May 1939, with Library of Congress accession numbers and titles as follows:[9]

AFS-2675-B-2	Eaton Clan
AFS-2677-A-2	Lighthouse Blues
AFS-2678-A-1	Birmingham Jail

This paper will look chiefly at the first of these songs, but it will be useful to put it in context by examining the other two. Although we know from his fragment of personal history that Garrett was black, this would be far from obvious if our only evidence was his recordings. For the three songs, only the text and performance style of "Lighthouse Blues" are clearly African American:

I moaned and I talked to my faro the whole night long, (x2)
I was trying to teach and show her, now, which-a-way's right from wrong.

My faro got teeth like a lighthouse on the sea, (x2)
Every time she smiles, throw the light all over me.

I'm gonna write me a letter, and mail it in the air, (x2)
I'm gonna tell my faro, I'm on the road somewhere.

I stopped still and listened, I heard somebody calling me, (x2)
Well, it wasn't my regular, but my old-time used-to-be.

The singing and playing on "Lighthouse Blues" seem to be indebted to the popular recordings of the Atlanta-based artist Barbecue Bob. Willie Baker, also presumed to have been from Atlanta, used the "lighthouse on the sea" verse, but it seems to have been in fairly widespread use; variants are found in a number of other recordings prior to 1939.[10]

"Birmingham Jail" is best known from the hit recording by the white singers Tom Darby and Jimmie Tarlton, but it was widespread in white folk music before they recorded it in November 1927.[11] Garrett's text has elements in common with Darby and Tarlton's, but they are not delivered in the same order, and there is little, if any, stylistic debt to Darby and Tarlton:

Here in the jailhouse, down on my knees,
Praying to Heaven, give my heart ease;

Give my heart ease, love, give my heart ease,
Praying to Heaven, give my heart ease.

Write me a letter, send it by mail,
Send it in care of Birmingham Jail;
Birmingham Jail, love, Birmingham Jail,
Send it in care of Birmingham Jail.

Bessie, I love you, and my heart's true,
Bessie, I love you, honest I do;
Honest I do, love, honest I do,
Angels in Heaven know I love you.

Down in the valley, valley so low,
Late in the evening, hear the train blow;
Hear the train blow, love we'll hear the train blow,
Late in the evening, we'll hear the train blow.

Bird in the cage, love, my heart's in pain,
Bessie, my darling, we'll meet again;
We'll meet again, love, we'll again,
Way up in Heaven, we'll meet again.

Apart from Garrett's, the only African American recording of this song appears to be by Lead Belly, who recorded it as "Birmingham Jail" in October 1948.[12]

"Birmingham Jail" is a very familiar song, though uncommon in African American music, and elements of "Lighthouse Blues" can be found in the repertoires of other blues singers, but "Eaton Clan" is only known through Garrett's recording. Its text runs as follows:

I'm quite sure you've heard the story
Of that Dry Creek Eaton clan;
God in Heaven knows they're innocent
Of murdering that revenue man.

They were riding home from Booneville,
When they heard to their surprise,

Screaming roars from many a shotgun,
Then they heard his dying cries.

His face was turned towards the Eatons,
He was shot right in the back;
When the sheriff ran to meet him,
He almost died right in his tracks.

Remembering their reputations,
These Eatons ran away to hide,
Knowing that they was innocent,
By others' hands the man had died.

Officers searched the county over,
Not a sign of them was found;
They called out one hundred soldiers,
Trying to find their hiding ground.

When the soldiers could not find them,
Many a friend was put in jail,
Knowing the Eatons would surrender
When their friends could not make bail.

They are sentenced to the penitentiary
For the rest of their lives,
Leaving their little children,
Their dear old homes and loving wives.

The fieldnotes refer to this song as "a feud ballad," which is self-evidently not correct. Rather, it describes and comments on a murder and its aftermath, events which occurred in northern Mississippi in May 1931. Initially, we give the story of those events as reported in the contemporary press, in Court opinions and in Ruey Eaton's self-published memoir; this composite account is then compared with the ballad.

On Saturday, May 17, 1931, downtown Booneville, Mississippi, was filled with several hundred people in town for the annual singing convention.[13] In the crowd were Ruey Eaton, two of his brothers, and other relatives and friends. The

Eatons lived west of Booneville near Dry Creek, "one of the wildest spots in Mississippi and difficult to penetrate," viewed by federal law enforcement as "a liquor fountainhead" and the area's chief source for alcohol.[14] Ruey Eaton was a major bootlegger in that area. He had been convicted in 1930 for violating the Prohibition Act, served six months in prison, and then resumed bootlegging while on probation. In the first seventeen days of May 1931, he had averaged 250 miles a day in a brand-new Chrysler sedan that was fitted to haul trailers.[15]

In late April of 1931, the federal court had ordered his arrest for parole violations. Ruey had apparently been expecting another arrest; on a trip to Memphis with his girlfriend Alma Gullet in early May, their car had a flat. When Ruey saw another car and concluded it was a Federal Marshal, Ruey said that he "guessed it was the law trying to arrest him and said it took one time to d e and he didn't aim for any law to take him, he knew he had broken parole, but he didn't aim for nobody to take him, . . . and [then he] got his pistol."[16]

When Ruey and the others arrived for Saturday afternoon in Booneville, Clyde Rivers, a Deputy United States Marshal, was also in town, and was intending to arrest Ruey with the help of local law enforcement. A Booneville city marshal first attempted an arrest, but Ruey jerked free and escaped down an alley.

Later in the evening, Ruey was back in Booneville and a local constable again attempted an arrest, but was prevented when Ruey's brother Clovis interfered. Soon afterwards, Ruey, his brothers Clovis and Edgar, their cousin Dell Eaton, and two friends, Tobe Morgan and A. K. Little, all got into Ruey's car, with Ruey driving. They circled the courthouse square a few times, and then stopped at a gas station to put water in the radiator of the car. A witness saw shotguns in the car and that Ruey had a pistol. Ruey was heard to say, "We are going to burn somebody down tonight." A voice in the car responded, "We have got the tools to do it with," and Ruey's brother Edgar replied, "Yes, we'll do it, too."[17]

Deputy Marshal Rivers, in a car driven by Earl Womack, a local deputy sheriff, drove past the gas station and saw the Eaton car leaving, headed west. Rivers and Womack followed out of town for two miles, and came upon the Eaton car, stopped on the right-hand side of the road. As they overtook the stopped car, someone shot at them from it, and two men jumped out and went through a fence beside the road. Womack pulled in front of the Eaton car, and Rivers leapt out, announcing he was a United States Deputy Marshal with a *capias* for the arrest of Ruey Eaton.[18]

Edgar Eaton attacked Rivers, who saw a gun in the Eaton car and shouted to Womack to get it. Rivers struck Edgar on the head with his pistol, knocking him down. At that point, shots were fired from the darkness across the fence where the others had fled. Rivers was struck in the back and side by buckshot, and the Eatons fled.[19] Neither Womack nor Rivers saw who had shot Rivers. Rivers was taken from the scene and died shortly thereafter. He was forty-three and had been a deputy marshal for seven years.[20]

A few minutes later, Ruey and Clovis Eaton showed up at Dave Griscoll's home, near where the killing took place. They hollered from Griscoll's back yard. According to Griscoll, when he came out, they said they had shot a man up the road. Ruey had a pistol and Clovis had a long gun of some sort. One said, "We are going to take your car, you will find it at Pap's in the morning." They took it, and the next morning the car was at Griscoll's father's.[21]

By the next day, the Eatons were being hunted by two posses of fifty men each headed by the United States Marshal, the sheriff from Booneville, and the sheriff and deputies of Coahoma County, 160 miles away in the Delta, which was the home of Deputy Marshal Rivers. The posse arrested Ruey Eaton's father, Pluck, along with three of Ruey's brothers, Oliver, Dewey, and Phipps.[22] In the following days, the posse arrested and brought out friends and family of the Eatons "by the automobile load."[23] Up to fifty were arrested. On Monday, May 19, the state sent a machine gun company of National Guardsmen under the command of Major T. B. Birdsong to Booneville. One of Ruey's cousins, Dell Eaton, surrendered and made a statement admitting that he, Lon Little, and Ruey had been in the car at the time of the attempted arrest, but denying knowledge of the killing.[24]

The manhunt continued for over three weeks. During the first week, it remained front page news in the state capital, with usually a major headline. On June 12, Ruey, his brother Clovis, and their cousin Edgar surrendered to the United States Marshal, accompanied by two friends who had convinced them to surrender.[25] According to newspaper reports, when they surrendered, their hiding place was surrounded by 119 armed troops and they were cut off from supplies, having been pursued by a posse of up to 200 men.[26]

Recounting his flight years later in his memoir, *In Prison. . . . . . and Out*, Ruey Eaton dismissed reports that they had ever been surrounded. He, his brothers, and his cousin hid in the woods near Dry Creek for days, living off boxes of food left at arranged places by family and friends.[27] Finally, he wrote, they walked to nearby Alcorn County, where they spent days hiding in an empty room in a friend's house. Ruey and Clovis's sisters came to meet them and said that their fathers, brothers, and friends would not be released from jail until the

Eatons surrendered. Ruey states that they decided to surrender at this point, got a ride to the Booneville jail, and turned themselves in.[28]

Ruey Eaton was the first brought to trial, on August 12. A star witness was to be his former girlfriend, Alma Gullet, who was rumored to have turned state's evidence in an effort to free Ruey's brother Clovis, who was rumored also to be her lover. She was to be brought in to the courtroom under an armed guard.[29] Her testimony became the prosecution trump card. She had served as a spy for the Eatons in the period up to the killing of Rivers, and had been with them on the day of the killing. She testified that she had not been Clovis Eaton's lover, and that "He was rough with me."

Ruey testified and denied knowing he was a parole violator, or knowing that Rivers was seeking him. He stated that he did not know Rivers and did not shoot him. Ruey was described as "surly and silent" during the trial.

The courtroom was filled with hundreds of county residents, who apparently came as supporters of the Eatons. After they heard Rivers's widow testifying that her husband had told her of a "premonition that he would meet death in the 'bad lands' of eastern Mississippi" while serving the warrant, the Eaton supporters in the crowd were moved and stated that they would "stand by that Clarksdale woman," Mrs. Rivers. After the jury returned a guilty verdict, Ruey was sentenced to life in prison.[30] Clovis Eaton was tried the next day, with the same result and the same sentence.[31] Edgar Eaton's trial resulted in a hung verdict, and he was not retried.[32]

Whoever turned this story into a ballad tracked the Eatons' version of events fairly closely. The ballad's title, "Eaton Clan," echoed state-wide newspaper coverage, which had referred to "the Eaton clan."[33] The ballad began:

I'm quite sure you've heard the story
Of that Dry Creek Eaton clan;
God in Heaven knows they're innocent
Of murdering that revenue man.

The ballad and Ruey Eaton's memoir open with the same theme: the Eatons' innocence of the murder.[34] But the ballad gets the murder victim wrong. Eaton had been bootlegging, but the murder victim was a United States Marshal, not a revenue man. However, the newspaper coverage of the events referred repeatedly to another murder in the southern Mississippi town of Collins, in which a revenue agent had been killed only weeks before the Rivers killing; there was combined coverage of these two killings of federal agents throughout the hunt for Eaton.[35] The ballad continued:

> They were riding home from Booneville,
> When they heard to their surprise,
> Screaming roars from many a shotgun,
> Then they heard his dying cries.

All accounts agree that the Eatons were headed west from Booneville, that is, towards Dry Creek. Ruey wrote that he and his brothers had stopped their car about a hundred yards west of the Booneville city limits and walked to the house of a friend, Dave Billy. Billy's son took Ruey and his brothers to their father's house, where Ruey "got word that a man had been shot near the place where we had left the car . . . and that we were accused of doing the shooting."[36] At trial, the deputy sheriff who accompanied the federal marshal testified that they had followed the Eatons west of Booneville, where the Eaton car stopped. The ballad also has the murder weapon right. The marshal was wounded by one or more shotgun blasts and died soon afterwards.[37]

> His face was turned towards the Eatons,
> He was shot right in the back.
> When the sheriff ran to meet him,
> He almost died right in his tracks.

This does not match Ruey's claim that he was not at the scene. Rivers's wounds were in the side and back. Rivers was facing the Eaton car and Edgar Eaton—who was never convicted of Rivers's murder—when shot from the side of the road. Rivers was with Deputy Sheriff Earl Womack, not the sheriff. However, the sheriff's name was Jerry Womack, and the author of the ballad text may have confused him with Deputy Sheriff Earl Womack.[38]

> Remembering their reputations,
> These Eatons ran away to hide,
> Knowing that they was innocent,
> By others' hands the man had died.

Because "emotions were running high," and convinced they would be "shot on sight," Ruey and his brothers decided to flee "until things cooled off."[39]

Officers searched the county over,
Not a sign of them was found;
They called out one hundred soldiers,
Trying to find their hiding ground.

Both the newspapers and Ruey Eaton report a posse of state and federal law enforcement in the hundreds, including a company of state National Guard soldiers.[40]

When the soldiers could not find them,
Many a friend was put in jail,
Knowing the Eatons would surrender
When their friends could not make bail.

The Eatons' father and other relatives, along with their friends, were arrested and held at some distance from Booneville. The newspapers report up to fifty arrests. During jury qualification, Ruey Eaton's lawyer in the trial attempted to ask the jurors whether they could be impartial knowing that "something like forty" of Ruey's family members had been arrested without basis during the manhunt. Ruey Eaton wrote that there were sixty-five arrests, including his fourteen-year-old nephew. He also states that this led to the decision to surrender.[41]

They are sentenced to the penitentiary
For the rest of their lives,
Leaving their little children,
Their dear old homes and loving wives.

Ruey and Clovis were sentenced to life in prison.[42] As indicated earlier, his brother Edgar's trial resulted in a hung verdict, and he was never retried. Ruey's wife and child, apparently born about the time of Rivers's murder, attended Ruey's trial.[43]

By the time Roger Garrett sang the ballad for John Lomax and Ruby Terrill in 1939, Clovis Eaton had been released from Parchman about five years.[44] Ruey's exit from Parchman in 1932 had been more dramatic, and almost certainly as much of a tale within the prison as the account of his arrest.[45]

It is striking how Ruey's retelling of his story in his self-published memoir parallels that in the ballad. Both the ballad and the memoir present the Eatons as innocent victims of law enforcement (although the memoir at least admits why Ruey Eaton drew the attention of the law, and the ballad admits that it was the Eatons' "reputations" which led them to hide out); both the ballad and the memoir state that family members were arrested and held to force the Eatons to surrender. While newspaper coverage emphasized the number of arrested family and friends, neither the possibility of the Eatons' innocence nor their surrender to obtain the release of family members are even hinted at in that coverage. Both the ballad and the memoir slide past the same problems in Ruey Eaton's account: no coherent explanation is given for the fact that the Eatons just happened to be at the scene of the murder of an officer who happened to be there to arrest one of them, and nothing like an alternative explanation for the murder is provided. In the memoir, Ruey refers to his wife and child;[46] the ballad refers to leaving behind "little children" and "loving wives." Both omit the sensational testimony of Ruey's girlfriend who had been with him on the day of the killing, but who turned state's evidence. This testimony was a prominent part of the newspaper coverage of Ruey's trial.

The ballad that Garrett sang presents the Eatons' version of events. It probably resembled what was presented and argued at the trial in Booneville by the Eatons' lawyers, but not reported in the newspaper coverage. This suggests that the author of the ballad either had access to first-hand information at the trial, or obtained the story from the Eatons or their family and friends in the Dry Creek area.

It also seems certain that the ballad originated closely in time to the trial. Ruey's escape from Parchman in the fall of 1932 generated its own newspaper coverage.[47] It would have been part of any of the stories about the Eatons circulating in Parchman, and would have been a major part of the Eaton story in any account thereafter. This strongly suggests that the ballad was written between the Eaton trials in August 1931 and Ruey Eaton's escape in the fall of the next year.

We now turn to the question of how the ballad was acquired by the African American singer Roger Garrett. It is unlikely that Garrett learned the facts behind this ballad directly in Booneville or Prentiss County. With only a couple of hundred black residents, Prentiss County was one of the whitest counties in the whitest region of the state. In 1930, Prentiss had the fourth lowest black population in percentage terms of Mississippi's eighty-two counties; its neighbors to the east and south, Itawamba and Tishomingo, were second and third, respectively; to the west was Tippah, with the sixth lowest black population, and to the north, Alcorn, with the seventh lowest.[48] Dry Creek itself was overwhelmingly white and was the sort of hill community that was considered very unwelcoming toward blacks.[49]

It is also unlikely that Garrett had direct access to the Eatons' version at Parchman Penitentiary, given the isolation of the camps from each other (Ruey Eaton describes how he was separated from his brother Clovis and had no kind of contact with him while they were both at Parchman[50]), and especially the segregation of prisoners by race. As has been noted, at the time of the recording, Garrett was in Camp 10, where whites and blacks worked together, but Ruey's time at Parchman was in Camp 5, while Clovis was in Camp 6 and then later Camp 5. Camp 6 housed prisoners who worked as both carpenters and farmers, and Camp 5 was purely a farm camp. Both would have held white prisoners exclusively when the Eatons were there.[51] Although it is probable that the Eatons story was widely circulated in the prison, given the state-wide coverage of their manhunt, it does not seem likely that details of the story transmitted via the prison grapevine would remain as close to the original material, or as close to the Eatons' version, as does the ballad.

If Roger Garrett learned the story in the free world but not at first hand, how did he do so? On the evidence of his other songs, Garrett was not a writer of original lyrics, and it seems likely that he learned the story by learning the song itself. As we have demonstrated, the ballad closely tracks the actual events of the murder and its aftermath, while attempting to make a case for the Eatons' innocence. In other words, it is propaganda, attempting to put a favorable spin on unfavorable evidence. This suggests that it is part of the Eaton family's own attempts at self-justification in the face of one-sided newspaper coverage.[52] The close match to the Eatons' version also suggests a closeness between the writer and the community at Dry Creek. That is, the match suggests that the information in the ballad was not transmitted through many intermediate steps. This close match and the fact that the ballad did not incorporate subsequent events also suggest that it was transmitted from its composer to Garrett relatively unchanged between the time of its composition in 1931 or 1932 and the recording in 1939. These facts, and the improbability of Garrett having been at Dry Creek, all suggest that Garrett had a written source for the ballad. We conclude that it is likely that Garrett's source was a printed ballad, although we acknowledge that this hypothesized ballad has yet to be located.

This conclusion raises the question of whether "Eaton Clan," even though sung by a black musician, can be described as black music. This problem of definition is made more complex in the light of the amply-documented musical exchange between the races,[53] and of arguments that the concept of "race" is a construct imposed by white culture.[54] A possible answer, with the merit of simplicity, is that music performed by a black vernacular artist becomes, ready-made, black vernacular music. This argument needs qualifying and refining, however, and both the possible origins of this particular ballad and the distinctions that set "black" lyrics apart from "white" lyrics may be illustrated by comparing "Eaton Clan" with other topical songs recorded by black musicians and with the non-blues repertoire of other black musicians who generally recorded blues.

It could be argued that "Eaton Clan" is African American music in the same way as other songs about local events and local white personalities. Such songs are not common, but in Mississippi, one could note Charley Patton's "Tom Rushen Blues" and "High Sheriff Blues"; in Brownsville, Tennessee, Sleepy John Estes sang about Lawyer Clark and about Tom Mann, on whose land Estes was a sharecropper; in Texas, Mance Lipscomb, Lightnin' Hopkins and others were outspokenly critical of employment conditions on "Tom Moore's Farm."[55] However, the role of the narrator in these songs makes them distinct from "Eaton Clan." The singers of these songs are present as actors in the stories they narrate, whether directly or indirectly; Patton reports on his encounters with local law enforcement, the Texan singers present themselves as having worked on the Moore brothers' land, and in "Lawyer Clark Blues," Estes relates that

Once I got in trouble, I was going to take a ride,
He didn't let it reach the courthouse, he kept it on the outside.

In contrast, Roger Garrett sings "Eaton Clan" as a non-participant, reporting on events in the white community in which he has played no part. Not only that, there seems no room to doubt that he is singing words written by an as yet unidentified white lyricist, and intended for consumption by white listeners. Can it, therefore, be fitted into the spectrum of African American music?

We suggest that it can, albeit perhaps at a far end of that spectrum. There are a number of instances of songs that report on events in the white community in which their African American singers have played no part. The best known and most frequently recorded of these is "Betty and Dupree" (a.k.a. "Dupree Blues"), which in its numerous variants deals with the crime, escape, arrest and trial of Frank Dupree, who was hanged in Atlanta, Georgia, in 1922. Frank Dupree is notable as one of the few white protagonists of a black narrative song; one of us has argued that, initially, Dupree was an appealing subject for African American singers and their audiences because of his youth (he was about 19 when hanged), and his perceived status as a fellow victim of a biased, violent and intimidating legal system.[56] Typical is Willie Walker's "Dupree Blues"[57]:

Betty told Dupree, "I wants me a diamond ring." (x2)
"Now listen, mama, your daddy bring you mostly anything."

He had to killed a policeman, and he wounded a 'tective too, (x2)
Killed a detective, wounded a policeman too,
"See here, mama, what you caused me to do."

Hired him a taxi, said, "Can't you drive me back to Main? (x2)
I've done a hangin' crime, yet I don't never feel ashamed."

"Standin' there wonderin', would a matchbox hold my clothes?" (x2)
Said a trunk was too big, to be bothered on the road.

'Rested poor Dupree, placed him in the jail, (x2)
Yet the mean old judge went and plain refused to sign him any bail.

Wrote a letter to Betty, and this is the way the letter read, (x2)
"Come home to your daddy, I'm almost dead."

Betty went to the jailer, cryin', "Mister jailer, please, (x2)
Please Mister jailer, let me see my used-to-be."

A comparison of "Dupree Blues" with "Eaton Clan" is instructive. White ballads tend to be distinct from black ballads in the particular ways in which the narrative is subjective or objective. The subjectivity of voice in black ballads implies a narrator or observer, in some sort of sympathy with the individual actors in the song. The narrator is morally neutral, and disinclined to sentimentality. Thus Willie Walker, like other narrators of "Betty and Dupree," is implicitly sympathetic towards Dupree, and does not moralize about the crime that is about to result in his hanging; the only actor in the narrative explicitly characterized by the narrator is the "mean old judge" who refuses bail. White ballads have more neutral or omniscient narrative voices, yet the lyrics also tend more often to moralize, and Victorian sentimentality on subjects like family and home is common. The narrator of "Eaton Clan" expresses his partisanship at the start and end of the song, with a conventional invocation of God as his witness to the Eatons' innocence and a conventionally sentimental reference to the wives left behind, faithfully waiting with their children. Willie Walker's Betty, on the other hand already thinks of Dupree as her "used-to-be."

Two other songs in this category of black compositions about events in the white community, are the New Orleans singer Richard "Rabbit" Brown's "Mystery of the Dunbar's Child," about a kidnaping and subsequent events that took place in 1912, and his "Sinking of the Titanic."[58] Unlike "Betty and Dupree," these songs are quite closely comparable to "Eaton Clan" in telling their stories chronologically and for the most part objectively, from the viewpoint of an omniscient narrator. The moral comments made are conventional and sentimental; at the end of "Mystery of the Dunbar's Child," the singer says he is "glad to tell you all that Walters [falsely accused of kidnaping] is now a free man," and in "Sinking of the Titanic," Brown expresses admiration for the perceived heroism of the male passengers, and observes bathetically that "accidents may happen most any time."[59] Brown was a street musician and a singing boatman, who plied his trade among tourists;[60] most of the audience from whom he hoped to gain tips for his singing would have been white, and this probably accounts for his treatment of these subjects.

It seems probable that "Eaton Clan" entered Roger Garrett's repertoire for similar economic reasons. The activities of Mississippi's white underclass are not a common subject for local African American singers. For instance, there are no significant recordings by black musicians of songs about Kinnie Wagner, a contemporary of Ruey Eaton's, and like him an escapee from Parchman, nor, indeed, are there any about Ruey Eaton's own escape.[61] A significant exception, however, is Sid Hemphill's "The Strayhorn Mob," which he recorded in Sledge, Mississippi, for the Library of Congress, many years after the events it describes.[62]

In *The Land Where the Blues Began*, Alan Lomax transcribes this song, making some errors, and "improving" Hemphill's text by making it appear that the chorus line ("Laid him low" and variants) is sung twice.[63] We therefore give our own transcription, which removes the repeated chorus line, and corrects some proper names and mistranscriptions.[64]

Them boys around Strayhorn, they didn't have no job,
Went to Senatoby, they had a big mob,
Laid him low.

They went round to the jailhouse, "Jailer! We wants the key,"
Said, "Boys, if you gets the key, you gwine to have to murder me,"
"We'll lay you low."

Some walked round the jailhouse, stopped in at the gate,
Some of 'em made a shot with a thirty-eight,
They laid him low.

Well, you talk about some runnin' then, all of 'em run just like quails,
Oughta been there to see them run, seen Mister Will Sinquefield,
They laid him low.

Well, they're talkin' 'bout that mob, hasn't been nary one since,
Talkin' 'bout Mister Hunter, when he jumped the courtyard fence,
And laid him low.

Mister Norman Clayton, he told the boys, "Boys, now, if y'all all wait,
We'll soon get back to Strayhorn if we can follow a trottin' gait,"
They laid him low.

Senatoby boys was ragin' mad, but they didn't play so bad,
Scared to fool with the Strayhorn boys, Mister Sam Howell was bad,
He'll lay you low.

These Strayhorn boys, tell you boys, tell you-all a certain fact,
The hounds got on their tracks, and they brought the boys back,
But they laid him low.

When they tried the Strayhorn boys, they did not try 'em here,
Tried the boys most everywhere, but they all sure come clear,
They laid him low.

When they tried the Strayhorn boys, did not try 'em alone,
Tried the boys most everywhere, but they sure come home,
They laid him low.

Mister Norman Clayton, told the boys again, "Boys, if y'all have a little wait,
We'll soon get back to Strayhorn if we can follow a trottin' gait,"
They laid him low.

When the boys got to runnin' there, they didn't run like quails,
Oughta been there to see 'em run, seen Mister Will Sinquefield,
Laid him low.

Lomax states that "The Strayhorn Mob" commemorates a lynching, and reports that he asked, "Who was it they lynched, Sid?" and that Hemphill replied, "Lemme see, now . . . Lemme see . . . You know, I jist fergit who it was!"[65] There is, however, no mention of a lynching in the interview. At the start of the recording, Hemphill says, "What they done, they brought a fellow out of jail." Lomax asks, "Was he Negro or white?" but gets no answer, and goes on to enquire, "When did that happen?" When Lomax asks "Who was the man they got?" (not "lynched") Hemphill responds only, "Lemme see, now [long pause]," and Lomax says, "You-all go ahead and sing the song."

Nevertheless, an attempted lynching was indeed at the root of the events which Hemphill sings about, but its intended victim was not, as Lomax assumed, an African American. David Evans's unpublished research, generously shared with us, establishes that the song is about a mob from Strayhorn, west of Senatobia, Mississippi, who went to the Senatobia jail in April 1905, intending to lynch a white prisoner who was being held, awaiting retrial for murdering the son of one of the mob. When the sheriff opposed them, he was shot and killed. A series of trials of the Strayhorn men resulted in acquittals.[66]

Sid Hemphill's lyrics are entirely consistent with this account, stating that "the jailer" was shot with a .38, and that "the Strayhorn boys . . . all sure came clear" when they were tried. Describing how the song came to be composed, Hemphill says that "one of the men what was in it writ it all down and give it to me and my buddy and told us to make up a song . . . Mister Sam Howell."

Alan Lomax asks, "Did you ever play it for him?"

"Many a time."

"He liked it, huh?"

"Too good . . . You know Mister Norman Clayton? Well, last week he was in, he pitched me fifty cents [to play the song]."[67]

Sid Hemphill was a more dynamic and original composer, lyricist and performer than Roger Garrett; but their ballads about white criminals exhibit very similar properties. "Eaton Clan" and "The Strayhorn Mob" both describe violent events and their aftermath in Mississippi white communities, events in which there was no African American involvement; in both cases, the content of the song was acquired by its black performer from white sources, "The Strayhorn Mob" directly from one of the participants and "Eaton Clan," we hypothesize, from a printed ballad; one song was certainly, and the other probably, sung to solicit payment from white listeners.[68] Both songs also report the events they describe objectively, notwithstanding Alan Lomax's exegesis of "The Strayhorn Mob" as covertly condemning a lynch mob and sympathizing with its African American victim.[69]

"Eaton Clan" seems to fit into Garrett's repertoire in the same way as the ballads by Sid Hemphill and Richard "Rabbit" Brown fit into theirs, with the difference that Garrett acquired "Eaton Clan," rather than composing it. More generally, it is also a member of another category of music performed by African Americans: songs written by white composers, in styles owing little or nothing to black music, and acquired by black musicians in order to entertain and make money from white listeners. As Bill Ferris wrote more than thirty years ago: "Audience is clearly an important influence on a singer's use of material. Though little study has been made of the relation between repertoire and audience, it is a phenomenon which is essential in understanding stylistic differences among black performers. For instance, the use of narrative 'ballads' and songs from the white tradition by black singers may reflect the influence of white audiences."[70]

"Eaton Clan" clearly does reflect the influence of a white audience, and it is possible to produce other examples from Mississippi. In 1943, John W. Work noted that "[p]laying for a white dance at the Stovall plantation . . . [Muddy Waters's] band used the following pieces: "Corinna," "St. Louis Blues," "Jingle, Jangle, Jingle," "Missouri Waltz," "Darktown Strutters Ball," "Darkness on the Delta," and "Wang Wang Blues" . . . For the colored dancers, Morganfield must play blues and music that stems from them, such as "Number Thirteen Highway" and "I'm Goin' Down Slow," his current favorite piece. For the Negroes he plays about one waltz a year."[71]

Scott Dunbar (1904–94), another Mississippian, was a tourist guide like Richard "Rabbit" Brown. For the last third of his life, Dunbar performed exclusively for white audiences.[72] Such of his music as has been issued on LP, and lately reissued on CD,[73] displays a bias towards blues. This no doubt reflects the preferences of producers and purchasers, but Dunbar's repertoire in 1970 included "Wabash Cannonball," "Tennessee Waltz," "Pistol Packin' Mama," "Blue Yodel" and "You Are My Sunshine."[74]

"Eaton Clan" was the first song Roger Garrett sang for John Lomax and Ruby Terrill. This suggests that he thought it was a song which they would want to hear, being white listeners like those he'd performed for in the free world. "Lighthouse Blues," which he recorded some time later, may indicate that Garrett took note of the kind of songs that met with approval when performed by other convicts. It would seem that even an audience of only two people, and a singer with a known repertoire of only three songs, can interact in quite subtle and complex ways.

Violent and somber though its subject matter is, "Eaton Clan" seems to have performed much the same functions for its singer and his original audience as did the pop songs and quasi-blues performed by Scott Dunbar and the young Muddy Waters. Roger Garrett's renditions of "Lighthouse Blues" and "Eaton Clan" have considerable artistic and aesthetic merit. ("Birmingham Jail," it must be admitted, is less impressive.) Nevertheless, "Eaton Clan" in particular is a reminder that, for black musicians under Jim Crow, performing to white audiences was primarily a matter of economics, with self-expression incidental. (Self-expression was not excluded, of course, as the two songs which Bukka White eventually sang for the Lomaxes confirm. However, White's initial reaction to the Lomaxes' presumed commercial motives also confirms the primacy of economic aspects. In the context of Jim Crow, such an explicitly hostile and obstructive response is both unusual and an illumination of White's character and attitudes.)

At the most basic economic level, white listeners could give or withhold payment to a busker, and could hire one band rather than another to play at a function. On at least one occasion, the "who-whom?" of race relations meant that a song came into being at the command of a white man, Mr. Sam Howell, who "writ it all down and . . . *told us* (emphasis added) to make up a song." It's unusual to know so precisely how a song came into a singer's repertoire, and we may never establish exactly what prompted Roger Garrett to learn "Eaton Clan"; but it seems very likely that he did so because in a world of Jim Crow and the Great Depression, it was white people who were likely to have disposable income; singing a song like "Eaton Clan" increased the chance that they might dispose of it in his direction.

NOTES

1. Ruby Terrill, fieldnotes. Ruby Terrill's 23–25 May, 1939 fieldnotes are a part of the collection of the American Folklife Center of the Library of Congress, and may be found within the Library of Congress's American Memory website, "Southern Mosaic: The John & Ruby Lomax 1939 Southern States Recording Trip," whose url is http://lcweb2.loc.gov.ammem/lohtml/lohome.html.

2. William Banks Taylor, *Down on Parchman Farm* (Columbus, Ohio: Ohio State University Press, 1999), pp. 34–40.

3. Ibid., pp. 40, 42–43.

4. Terrill, fieldnotes (see note 1).

5. Gayle Dean Wardlow, *Chasin' That Devil Music* (San Francisco: Mille Freeman Books, 1998), pp. 102–4.

6. Robert M. W. Dixon, John Godrich, & Howard W. Rye, *Blues and Gospel Records 1890–1943* (Oxford University Press: fourth edition, 1997), pp. 1024–25 ; Mike Leadbitter, Leslie Fancourt & Paul Pelletier, *Blues Records 1943–1970, Vol. 2 L to Z* (London: Record Information Services, 1994), pp. 702–4.

7. As this paper was being written, the Social Security Death Index (online at www.familytreemaker.com/fto_ssdisearch.html and numerous other online locations) listed 2,421 Garnetts, of whom only one is named Roger, and 23,603 Garretts, 14 of them named Roger. There was only one Roger Garrett listed whose Social Security number was issued in Mississippi; he was born on January 23, 1913 and died April 16, 1975. We have yet to establish whether this is the musician discussed here.

8. Terrill, fieldnotes (see note 1).

9. Dixon, Godrich & Rye, 287 give this information and show May 23, 1939 as the recording date for all three songs. On record dust jackets Ruby Terrill notes the recording date of "Eaton Clan" as May 22 (which must be a mistake, since the Lomaxes arrived at Parchman on May 23), and that of "Birmingham Jail" as May 24. There is no dust jacket available for "Lighthouse Blues." The dust jackets and Garnett's recordings are a part of the collection of the American Folklife Center of the Library of Congress, and may be found within the Library of Congress's American Memory website, "Southern Mosaic: The John & Ruby Lomax 1939 Southern States Recording Trip," whose url is http://lcweb2.loc.gov.ammem/lohtml/lohome.html.

10. Among them Ida Cox, "Any Woman's Blues," (Paramount 12053, recorded June, 1923) and Willie Baker, "Weak-Minded Woman," (Supertone 9427, recorded January 10 1929) and "Weak Minded Blues," (Gennett 6751, recorded March 11, 1929.) (Dixon, Godrich & Rye, pp. 38–9; R. R. Macleod, personal communication) Cox's recording probably popularized the trope.

11. Darby & Tarlton, "Birmingham Jail" (Columbia 15212, recorded November 10, 1927).

12. See Leadbitter, Fancourt & Pelletier, p. 28. Lead Belly knew the song before Darby & Tarlton recorded it; he played it in 1924 when Texas Governor Pat Neff visited the Sugarland Penitentiary (Charles Wolfe & Kip Lornell, *The Life and Legend of Lead Belly* [London: Secker & Warburg, 1993], p. 86).

13. "Two Dozen Prentiss Farmers Held in Hunt for Murderers," *Jackson Clarion Ledger*, May 18, 1931, p. 1 (downtown filled with several hundred for singing) (*Jackson Clarion Ledger* hereinafter cited as *JCL*); *Eaton v. State*, 140 So. 729, 730 (1932) (events took place in early afternoon). The community singing was mentioned in the newspaper coverage. Ruey Eaton described it as the Annual Singing Convention that weekend. Ruey Eaton, *In Prison. . . . . . and Out* (privately printed, 1977?), p. 3. Singing conventions were regional gatherings of sacred harp singers, who would get together for group singing and dinner-on-the-grounds.

14. "Two Dozen Prentiss Farmers Held in Hunt for Murderers," p. 1 (Dry Creek was hilly and wooded and viewed by law enforcement as the chief source of liquor in the area); "Federal Heads Delay Charges," *JCL*, May 21, 1931, pp. 1, 9 ("wildest spots"); "Girl, Six Men Implicated," *JCL*, May 23, 1931, p. 1 ("liquor fountainhead"); Prentiss County Historical Society, *History of Prentiss County* (Dallas: Curtis Media, 1982), p. 30 (Eatons were from Dry Creek). Ruey's name was consistently spelled "Rouey" in the *Clarion Ledger* and by the Associated Press. It was spelled "Ruey" in his memoir and in the Mississippi Supreme Court opinions.

15. *Eaton*, 140 So. at 730 (served time and was on probation); "Two Dozen Prentiss Farmers Held in Hunt for Murderers," p. 1 (convicted in 1930); "Eatons Spend Quiet Sunday," *JCL*, June 15, 1931, pp. 1, 7 (averaged 250 miles a day); Eaton, *In Prison . . .* , p. 2 (states he was "guilty of selling whiskey, making a little of it, and running from the law where necessary.")

16. *Eaton*, 140 So. 729 at 731. Alma, who testified as quoted in Ruey's trial, had been arrested and initially charged with complicity in murdering the federal marshal. "Girl, Six Men Implicated," p. 1.

17. *Eaton*, 140 So. at 730; "Two Dozen Prentiss Farmers Held in Hunt for Murderers," p. 1 (Ruey's brother Clovis interfered with constable's attempt to arrest).

18. *Eaton*, 140 So. at 730. Rivers was serving a "*capias mittimus*," an order or writ that a law enforcement officer convey the person named to prison. See *Black's Law Dictionary*, 5th ed., s.v. "*mittimus*," "*capias*."

19. *Eaton*, 140 So. at 730; "Federal Bands Hunt Hills of Prentiss Area," *JCL*, May 19, 1931, p. 1 ("shots from the darkness felled the agent"). "The evidence [at Ruey's trial] did not show who fired the fatal shot or shots." *Eaton*, 140 So. at 731. Ruey's memoirs describe Edgar's account of these events, which Ruey claims to have heard the next day: Edgar had been at the scene, where "the man who later got killed" hit Edgar with a pistol, knocking him down and leaving him with "a very bad jaw." At that point the man was shot, and Edgar fled. Eaton, *In Prison . . .* , p. 2.

20. "Two Dozen Prentiss Farmers Held in Hunt for Murderers," p. 7. "The evidence [at Ruey's trial] did not show who fired the fatal shot or shots." *Eaton*, 140 So. at 731.

21. *Eaton*, 140 So. at 730–31.

22. "Two Dozen Prentiss Farmers Held in Hunt for Murderers," May 18, 1931, p. 1; "Mississippi," United States Geological Survey 1:500,000 Series Map (1972).

23. "Federal Bands Hunt Hills of Prentiss Area," *JCL*, May 19, 1931, p. 1.

24. "Machine Gunners Sent to Booneville," *JCL*, May 20, 1931, p. 1. In front page stories, the *Clarion Ledger* reported federal charges brought against six men and Alma Gullet, and conspiracy charges brought against a group that was reported to be from seventeen to twenty. The arrested were jailed across the north part of the state, in Greenwood, Tupelo, Aberdeen, and Booneville. Major Birdsong of the National Guard was later the head of the Mississippi Highway Patrol throughout the civil rights era of the fifties and sixties. John Dittmer, *Local People* (Urbana: University of Illinois Press, 1994), 33, p. 310.

25. "Three Eatons Surrender To State," *JCL*, June 13, 1931, p. 1.

26. "Eatons Spend Quiet Sunday," p. 1; "Three Eatons Surrender To State," p. 1 (Associated Press report of posse of 200 men).

27. Eaton, *In Prison* . . . , pp. 3–9. A young man at one of the farms told his uncle of seeing the Eatons; his uncle reported this to law enforcement, which, Ruey states, got both of them "in trouble." Ibid., pp. 8–9. The *Clarion Ledger* reported that Ruey and Edgar had been reported appearing at a local farm looking for food. "Girl, Six Men Implicated," p. 1.

28. Eaton, *In Prison* . . . , pp. 10–15.

29. "Eaton Witness Threatened by Hill Colonies," *JCL*, August 12, 1931, p. 1.

30. "Rouey Eaton Gets Life Term for Murder," *JCL*, August 14, 1931, pp. 1, 13.

31. "Try Clovis Eaton in Clyde Rivers Slaying," *JCL*, August 15, 1931, p. 1; "Clovis Eaton Is Given Life," *JCL*, August 16, 1931, p. 1.

32. Eaton, *In Prison* . . . , p. 16.

33. "3 Eatons Are Placed in Hinds Jail," p. 1.

34. Eaton, *In Prison* . . . , pp. 1–2.

35. "Two Dozen Prentiss Farmers Held in Hunt for Murderers," p. 7 (reference to Collins killing less than two weeks before in story about Eaton case); "Justice Near Quarry after State Crimes," *JCL*, May 24, 1931, p. 1 (discussing both murder cases and manhunts together).

36. Eaton, *In Prison* . . . , p. 2.

37. See *supra* at nn. 19–21.

38. See *supra* at nn. 19–20, 32; "Federal Bands Hunt Hills of Prentiss Area," p. 1.

39. Eaton, *In Prison* . . . , p. 2.

40. "Two Dozen Prentiss Farmers Held in Hunt for Murderers," p. 1; "Machine Gunners Sent to Booneville, p. 1; Eaton, *In Prison* . . . , p. 4.

41. "Machine Gunners Sent to Booneville," p. 1; *Eaton*, 140 So. at 731; Eaton, *In Prison* . . . , pp. 12, 14–15.

42. *Eaton*, 140 So. at 730; "Clovis Is Given Life," *JCL*, August 16, 1931, p. 1.

43. "Rouey Eaton Gets Life Term for Murder," p. 13.

44. Clovis's early release on a "life" sentence may not have been as strange in its day as it appears from this distance. Mississippi did not have a system of parole and release at the time; release before a term was completed was handled ad hoc. In 1930 and 1931, prison overcrowding had reached a peak sufficient that prisoners were being selected for early release just to free up beds (Taylor, p. 55). Even though Clovis was white, Clovis's release does bring to mind early releases of black inmates (like Bukka White from Parchman a little later), which are often attributed to the intervention of white allies and described as one of the strange attributes of the Jim Crow system.

45. Ruey escaped from Parchman in 1932, using guns that had been smuggled in during cotton picking. He returned secretly the next year to unsuccessfully help his brother Clovis escape. About a year thereafter, Clovis was set free by the state. Eaton, *In Prison* . . . , pp. 28–47, 49–52, 54–55, 62.

46. Eaton, *In Prison* . . . , p. 55.

47. Ibid., p. 42.

48. U.S. Bureau of the Census, *Fifteenth Census of the United States: 1930, Population, Part 1 (Alabama-Missouri)*, vol. III, pp. 1282–87, 1316. The only other counties in this group were two in the Gulf Coast region at the other end of the state. Prentiss's ranking in absolute number of blacks was similarly low.

49. Tom Freeland, personal knowledge.

50. Eaton, *In Prison . . .* , pp. 16–17.

51. Ibid., pp. 17, 52, 82; Taylor, pp. 40, 42–43.

52. Self-justification is also the function of *In Prison . . . . . . and Out*. Attempting to establish his innocence was still a live issue for Ruey Eaton over forty years after the events, at a time when he had become respectable enough to be appointed Mayor of Jumpertown, in the Dry Creek area, and might have been expected to draw a veil over his colorful past.

53. As discussed, for example, in Tony Russell, *Blacks, Whites and Blues* (London: Studio Vista, 1970); reprinted with an afterword in *Yonder Come the Blues: The Evolution of a Genre*, ed. Paul Oliver (Cambridge: Cambridge University Press, 2001).

54. This argument is developed most notably in Grace Hale, *Making Whiteness: The Culture of Segregation in the South, 1890–1940* (New York: Pantheon, 1998).

55. Charley Patton, "Tom Rushen Blues" (Paramount 12877, recorded June 14, 1929) and "High Sheriff Blues" (Vocalion 02680, recorded January 30, 1934); Sleepy John Estes, "Lawyer Clark Blues," (Bluebird B8871, recorded September 24, 1941) and "Tell Me How About It (Mr. Tom's Blues)" (Decca 7766, recorded June 4 1940); Mance Lipscomb, "Tom Moore's Farm" (*inter alia* Candid CJM 8027, recorded June 30, 1960); Lightnin' Hopkins, "Tim [*sic*] Moore's Farm" (Gold Star 640, recorded 1948).

56. Chris Smith, "A Hangin' Crime: A Balladic Blues and the True Story Behind It, Parts 1 and 2," *Blues & Rhythm* 95 (February 1995): 4–7 and 96 (March 1995): 4–8. These articles contain transcriptions of the lyrics of numerous songs in the "Dupree" *corpus* besides the one quoted here.

57. Columbia 14578–D, recorded December 6, 1930.

58. Both Victor 35840, recorded March 11, 1927. Their lyrics are transcribed in R. R. Macleod, *Document Blues-1* (Edinburgh: PAT Publications, 1994).

59. "Sinking of the Titanic" is also unlike many other secular accounts in not introducing a black actor (Shine, the traveling man or Jack Johnson) as a vehicle for satirical comment on the ways of white people. See for example Chris Smith, "The Titanic, a Case Study of Religious and Secular Attitudes in African American Song" in Robert Sacré ed., *Saints and Sinners* (Liège: Société Liégeoise de Musicologie, 1996), pp. 213–27.

60. Samuel B. Charters, *The Country Blues* (New York: Da Capo, 1975), p. 90.

61. Ruey Eaton's brother, Clovis, took food to Kinnie Wagner when he was an escapee, hiding out in the Dry Creek Hills (Eaton, *In Prison . . .* , p. 27). Stories of Wagner's escapes from Parchman are still current in Mississippi folklore (Tom Freeland, personal knowledge); it is ironic, therefore,

that all Mississippi songs by white singers about Wagner seem to derive from recordings by city-billy Vernon Dalhart (as Al Craver) of "Kinnie Wagner" (Columbia 15065–D) and "Kinnie Wagner's Surrender" (Columbia 15098–D), both written by the Atlanta singer-songwriter, Blind Andy Jenkins. See Arthur Hudson Palmer, *Folksongs of Mississippi* (Chapel Hill: University of North Carolina Press, 1936), pp. 243–4, and G. Malcolm Laws, *Native American Balledry* (Philadelphia: American Folklore Society, 1964), pp. 179–80. Donald Hill, "Wade Walton: Blues Singer, Barber, Raconteur" (*Cadence*, vol. 13, no. 8 (August 1987): 22–30) includes stories and a song lyric about Wagner by an African American musician, but the unfinished quality of the lyric suggests that it was improvised on request, rather than being a stable part of Walton's repertoire.

62. "Interview and the Strayhorn Mob," AFS-6671-A-1, recorded August 15, 1942; issued on *Wake Me, Shake Me, Field Recordings Vol. 15, Mississippi 1941–1942* (Document DOCD-5672).

63. Alan Lomax, *The Land Where the Blues Began* (London, Methuen, 1993) pp. 323–24.

64. We are indebted to David Evans for his assistance in making this transcription as accurate as possible. Any errors remaining are our responsibility.

65. Lomax, p. 323.

66. *Senatobia Democrat*, various issues, April 14, 1905 to April 27, 1906.

67. "Interview and the Strayhorn Mob." In Lomax, p. 323, this interview material is para-phrased and embroidered; Lomax has Hemphill describing Howell (mistranscribed "House") as "one of the men in the mob," and Clayton as "in the thing, too." Indeed they were, but Hemphill does not say so in conversation.

68. This was neither Hemphill's only song about the activities of local white people, nor the only one which was commissioned by one of them. "The Carrier Line" (AFS-6670-B-1), about a train wreck on a logging company's railroad, was recorded at the same session as "The Strayhorn Mob." It was written at the request of "Mr. Willard, a white section foreman on the line," and sung, according to Hemphill, "for all the participants in the events except Mr. Carrier himself." The train was driven by "Mister Dave Cowart," identified as white by the honorific. See David Evans, notes to *Afro-American Folk Music from Tate and Panola Counties, Mississippi* (Rounder CD 1515). Sid Hemphill's granddaughter, Jessie Mae Hemphill, says that he did sing the song for Carrier. (David Evans, personal communication.) Hemphill set "The Carrier Line," "The Strayhorn Mob" and a two-part "The Roguish Man" (AFS-6670-A-3, AFS-6670-B-2), which is about Jack Castle, a local black bad man, to the same melody. All were recorded on the same date.

69. Lomax, p. 323.

70. William Ferris, Jr., *Blues from the Delta* (London: Studio Vista, 1970), p. 107.

71. David Evans, notes to *Deep River of Song: Mississippi—The Blues Lineage* (Rounder CD 1825), quoting an anonymous paper in the Alan Lomax archives, believed to be by Work. Two of the songs listed are by African American composers, but this does not affect the thrust of the argument put forward.

72. Ferris, pp. 105–7, includes a categorization of thirty-seven songs recorded by Ferris from Dunbar as "black" (12) or "white" (25); Brett J. Bonner, "Scott Dunbar" [obituary] in *Living Blues* 119 (February 1995): 67.

73. Chiefly on *From Lake Mary*, Ahura Mazda AMS SDS 1 [LP], Fat Possum 80338 [CD].

74. These songs are among many which Dunbar recorded in February and April 1970 (see Mike Leadbitter & Neil Slaven, *Blues Records 1943 to 1970, Vol. 1 A to K* [London, Record Information Services, 1987], p. 368); only "Blue Yodel" has been issued.

COOLIDGE'S BLUES

African American Blues Songs on Prohibition,
Migration, Unemployment, and Jim Crow

GUIDO VAN RIJN

In the twenties the United States was growing economically after the turbulent postwar period. The Harlem Renaissance (1920–1930) was an important period of literary and artistic flowering. The Roaring Twenties brought wealth to many white Americans, and some educated African Americans, but what was the fate of the average African American in the Coolidge era (1923–1928)?

Calvin Coolidge was born on 4 July 1872 in Plymouth, Vermont, the son of a deputy sheriff who owned a successful country store. The Coolidges were of English Puritan heritage. Calvin Coolidge's mother died when he was twelve. In 1895 he graduated from Amherst College in Amherst, Massachusetts and was admitted to the bar two years later. In 1905 he married Grace Goodhue. In 1911 he became United States Senator for Massachusetts and eight years later Governor of the same state. Calvin Coolidge was of the opinion that the government should care for the "defective." The "normal," however, should care for themselves.[1] He distrusted reformers, but not reform itself.[2] Coolidge has been portrayed as slow and reluctant to act, but he could be decisive and even bold when necessary.[3] The Boston Police strike of 1919 won him nationwide fame for his stand on law and order: "There is no right to strike against the public safety by anybody, anywhere, any time."[4] In 1921 Coolidge became Vice President under Warren Harding. Harding died in office, on 2 August 1923, and Calvin Coolidge was sworn in by his father, a notary public, with his hand on the family Bible.[5]

"Silent Cal" was so famous for saying little that a guest at a White House dinner once vowed she could make the President say more than two words. When she told her host of her bet, the president replied: "You lose." "I don't recall any

candidate for president that ever injured himself very much by not talking,"
Coolidge once explained.[6] The irreproachable Calvin Coolidge was experienced as
a relief after the scandal ridden presidency of his predecessor. "Keep Cool with
Coolidge" and "Coolidge or Chaos" were some of the election slogans used in the
1924 Presidential elections which resulted in a major victory for Coolidge. He beat
his Democratic opponent Governor John Davis of West Virginia by a convincing
margin. It was Coolidge and not Roosevelt who first used the new medium of the
radio to good effect. He delivered sixteen radio addresses in five years.[7]

The Eighteenth Amendment to the United States Constitution, which prohib-
ited the making, selling, possession and the consumption of alcoholic beverages
had gone into effect under the Volstead Act of 17 January 1920. Prohibition was
one of the worst mistakes ever made in American social policy. "$2,000,000,000
worth of business was simply transferred from brewers and barkeepers to bootleggers and gangsters, who worked in close cooperation with the policemen and
politicians they corrupted. Blackmail, protection rackets and gangland murders
became all too common, and no one was punished."[8] Coolidge had a simple
response to Prohibition: Congress had passed the Volstead Act, and he would support it. But he also said: "Any law that inspires disrespect for other laws—the good
laws—is a bad law."[9]

Many blues songs from the period deal with the effects of Prohibition.[10] For
some of them I will refer you to *Roosevelt's Blues*.[11] One blues song that was not
discussed there is Jim Jackson's "Bootlegging Blues" of 14 February 1928. In a
humorous way it shows that bootlegging was a risky business both for the bootlegger who always had to be ready to run from the revenue man and for the con-
sumer who never knew what ingredients the concoction contained.

Since corn liquor came in style, there's plenty money to be made,
Just get a job at one of these stills and you surely will be paid.

I'll tell you it's a mighty risk to run and a mighty chance to take,
To spend your money for the corn that the bootleggers make.

(chorus) *The bootleggin' man got his bottle in his hand,*
And all he needs, is a little more speed, so he can outrun the revenue man.

When the bootlegger goes to his still, get ready to make his stuff,
He got his concentrated lye, cocaine and his snuff.

He'll fix you up a drink, just won't quit, it'll make you fight a circular saw,
Make you slap the lady down, and make you pick a fight with your pa.

I went home the other night, I'd swore I wouldn't drink no more,
Until saloons come back with bottled in bond[12] as in the days of long ago.

But I see that will never be, so I've just got drunk again,
I haven't nothin' as long as corn liquor lasts, and I got no money to spend.[13]

In the spring of 1927 four million acres along the Mississippi were inundated causing property losses of $300 million. Herbert C. Hoover, who was Secretary of Commerce from 1923 to 1928, was placed in charge of relief efforts. In December 1927 Hoover asked for flood control legislation. Coolidge indicated that a prime reason why he opposed the measure was that he wanted to withhold assistance not from individuals, but from business interests that would profit from such aid. Congress ignored Coolidge and approved a $1.4 billion flood control measure in April, with all the money coming from the federal government. It set into motion a major program of river and harbor improvements that continued into the Hoover and Roosevelt administrations.[14] Many blues songs were devoted to the disaster and I refer to David Evans's lecture for this conference: "High Water Everywhere: Blues and Gospel Commentary on the 1927 Mississippi River Flood" for an analysis.

Few Presidents were as outspoken on the need to enforce the civil rights of African Americans as Calvin Coolidge: "Numbered among our population are some twelve million colored people. Under our Constitution their rights are just as sacred as those of any other citizen. It is both a public and a private duty to protect those rights. The Congress ought to exercise all its powers of prevention and punishment against the hideous crime of lynching, of which the Negroes are by no means the sole sufferers, but for which they furnish a majority of the victims."[15]

Unprecedentedly, Coolidge delivered the commencement address at Washington D.C.'s historically black Howard University on 6 June 1924:

In a little over half a century since [Emancipation] the number of business enterprises operated by colored people has grown to nearly 80,000, while the wealth of the Negro community has grown to nearly $1,100,000,000. And these figures convey a most inadequate suggestion of the material progress. The 2,000 business enterprises that were in the hands of colored

people immediately following Emancipation were almost without exception small and rudimentary. More than 80 percent of all American Negroes
are now able to read and write; when they achieved their freedom not 10
percent were literate. There are nearly 2,000,000 Negro pupils in the public schools; well-nigh 40,000 Negro teachers are listed, more than 3,000
following their profession in normal schools and colleges. The list of educa-
tional institutions devoting themselves to the race includes 50 colleges, 13
colleges for women, 26 theological schools, a standard school of law, and
two high grade institutions of medicine. The propaganda of prejudice and
hatred which sought to keep the colored men from supporting the national
cause completely failed. The black man showed himself the same kind of
citizen, moved by the same kind of patriotism, as the white man.[16]

Where Coolidge stood on the race issue is clear, but he did not take any concrete
steps to ease the burden of discrimination. Nevertheless, the conservative Coolidge
has had a far better press on the race issue than the progressive Woodrow Wilson,
who was one of the most bigoted persons ever to hold the nation's highest office.

Between 1920 and 1930, 330,000 Southern-dwelling African Americans
moved to industrial cities in the South and especially the North and the West.
By 1940 the total number of migrants had risen to 1,750,000. The reasons for
this massive migration were manifold: military service in World War One had
given many people a broader view of the world and some experience away from
home; boll weevils, droughts, floods and soil erosion had ruined the cotton crop,
and at the same time factories were in sore need of labor, since immigration from
Europe had stagnated after the First World War. At the same time, the brutal
practices of segregation in the South made the North seem like a Promised
Land. To escape Jim Crow, African Americans left parents and other loved ones
behind to try their luck in the cities of the North.

There are many blues songs from the Coolidge era with titles like "Memphis
Bound Blues," "Chicago Bound Blues," "Detroit Bound Blues," etc. Most
of these lament the loss of Southern loved ones, or dream of excitement and
romance in the big city. One fine example is Blind Blake's "Detroit Bound
Blues" from May 1928. The singer, whose real name was probably Arthur Phelps,
may have hailed from Jacksonville in Florida, as recent research by Gayle Dean
Wardlow has proved.[17] In lines five and nine Blake seems to be illustrating the
bustle of life in the city as against the leisurely pace of the country by sudden

changes of tempo. "Detroit Bound Blues" was issued on Paramount 12657 as the B side of "Rumblin' and Ramblin' Boa Constrictor Blues." The copyright files of Chicago Music credit Arthur Blake as the composer and Aletha Dickerson (as Selma Davis)[18] as the lyricist.[19]

I'm goin' to Detroit, get myself a good job,
Tired of stayin' 'round here with the starvation mob.

I'm gonna get me a job up in Mr. Ford's place,
Stop these eatless days from starin' me in the face.

I'm goin' to Detroit, get me a barrelhouse flat,[20]
I would take my baby, but I don't know where she's at.

When I start to makin' money, she don't need to come around,
'Cause I don't want her now, Lord, I'm Detroit bound.

They've got wild women in, in Detroit, that's what I wanna see,
Wild women and bad whiskey, would make a fool out of me.[21]

Henry Ford's assembly lines had revolutionized factory production. Ford offered five dollars for an eight-hour working day since labor was scarce after the Great War. Job conditions were strenuous in the early Ford factories, and Ford reasoned that African Americans who had survived labor under slavery conditions on the cotton plantations would be able to solve his employment dilemma. There were only 5000 African Americans in Detroit in 1910, so Ford sent recruiters down south and thousands of African Americans were lured north. In 1930 there were 120,000 African Americans in Detroit City, and 8.7 percent of the auto workforce of the state of Michigan was African American.[22] The harsh reality was that once they were employed most African Americans did not get work on the assembly lines at all. Instead they held the most dangerous and unpleasant jobs in the factories like forging steel, sanding and spraying cars, cleaning and maintaining the factories.[23] Henry Ford looked with favor on the resurgent Ku Klux Klan and was a sponsor of fiddle contests and the square dance revival, which he viewed as an antidote to jazz with its wicked Negro and Jewish influences. As the years passed, stories of Ford's treatment of African

Americans reached the South and when Bob Campbell recorded his version of Blind Blake's "Detroit Bound" in 1934 the second stanza had been changed into:

Say, I'm goin' down there and get me a job, working in Mr. Ford's place,
Say, that woman told me last night, that you cannot even stand
Mr. Ford's ways.[24]

Recorded blues songs that speak of discrimination as one of the main motives for migration are very rare indeed. However, I have traced a few songs from the Jazz Age in which the singer dares to speak out in an explicit way. Fletcher Henderson (1897–1952) wrote a fascinating song entitled "Back Woods Blues" which he copyrighted under the pseudonym "George Brooks." The first blues singer to record it, on 30 April 1924, was Clara Smith (1894–1935). The song was issued on Columbia 14022. Henderson accompanied the singer on ukulele, with Charlie Dixon (1898–1940) on guitar. It was advertised, with no regard for the actual text, in the *Chicago Defender* of 21 June 1924: "In 'Back Woods Blues' Clara will take you into the deepest, darkest, bluest forest you ever heard of. Even Clara got so lonesome that she made a ukulele come along with the guitar to keep her company." However, we will concentrate on the second recorded version, by Rosa Henderson (no relation to Fletcher), which has two additional verses at the beginning. Rosa Henderson made the recording in May 1924, and it was issued on Emerson 10763. The cornet accompaniment is probably by Howard Scott and the piano stool is again occupied by the composer himself.

Way back down behind Decatur, in an Alabama shack,
There's my mammy and my daddy, wonderin' when I'm coming back.

How I miss them, goodness knows, more and more each day,
That's why I've got these backwoods blues, every since I went away.

Got the backwoods blues, but I don't wanna go back home,
Got the blues so bad, for the place that I came from.

Gonna see my folks, but it's way too far,
To ride in a dusty old Jim Crow car.

Got the backwoods blues, but I don't wanna go back home.

Got the backwoods blues, for a place way down in Bam,
Got the blues, but I'm gonna stay right where I am.

Gonna lay 'round here, right where I'm at,
Where there ain't no grinnin' and snatchin' off my hat.

Got the backwoods blues, but I don't wanna go back home.

I got the backwoods blues, for the folks I left down home,
I got the backwoods blues, for them poor old folks alone.

Yes, I'm from down there and I'm proud to say,
And from down there I'm gonna stay.

Got the backwoods blues, but I don't wanna go back home.[25]

Although Clara Smith hailed from South Carolina and Rosa Henderson had come from Kentucky to New York in 1923, the song specifies Southern poverty by reference to being born in a shack "way back down Decatur" an industrial city in Morgan County in northern Alabama. Memories of Jim Crow are economically evoked by the phrase "no grinnin' and snatchin' off my hat" which vividly pictures a black person being humiliated by white racists. In the last verse the singer says that she is still proud to be from "down there," but that she is going to stay "from down there," meaning that she is remaining in the northern city where discrimination is less harrowing. The faster tempo in stanzas five and six forms a marked contrast with the quiet tempo in the rest of the song. Perhaps Fletcher Henderson, who forces the change on the singer, wanted to illustrate the bustle of life in the city as against the leisurely pace of country life, as we have already noticed in the Blind Blake song analyzed above. This song, with its outspoken social criticism, an extremely rare thing in a recording by an African American artist from the period, vividly shows how traditional family life was subject to disruption by racism.

Maggie Jones, whose real name was Fae Barnes, was born c. 1900 in Hillsboro, fifty miles south of Dallas, Texas. She moved to New York City in the early twenties. "The Texas Nightingale" also recorded an anti-Jim Crow song with Fletcher Henderson at the piano. "North Bound Blues" was recorded on 16 April 1925 and was issued on Columbia 14092. This time the second accompanist

was trombonist Charlie Green (1900–1936) and the song was credited to Maggie
Jones herself.

> Got my trunk and grip all packed,
> Goodbye, I ain't coming back,
> Gonna leave this Jim Crow town,
> Lord, sweet papa, New York bound,
> Got my ticket in my hand,
> And I'm leaving Dixieland.
>
> Going north, child, where I can be free,
> Where there's no hardships like in Tennessee.
>
> Going where they don't have Jim Crow laws,
> Don't have to work there, like in Arkansas.
>
> When I cross the Mason-Dixon line,
> Goodbye, old gallion, mama's gone a-flyin'.
>
> Going to daddy, got no time to lose,
> 'Cause he alone can cure my north bound blues.[26]

Again the song is not geographically autobiographical, for instead of her native
Texas, Tennessee and Arkansas are mentioned as states where Jim Crow reigns.
The references to the Mason-Dixon line and the gallions both refer to slavery
times. The gallions were originally the slave quarters on the plantation. The term
was later applied to the segregated colored sector of a town. Again, the explicit
mention of the Jim Crow laws makes this song exceptional.

There is even a third song from the Jazz Age that takes a stand on racial issues.
It is pianist Charles "Cow Cow" Davenport's (1894–1955) first recorded song
from January 1927, the explicitly titled "Jim Crow Blues." Davenport accompanies himself on the piano and is assisted by B. T. Wingfield on cornet.

> I'm tired of being Jim Crowed, gonna leave this Jim Crow town,
> Doggone my black soul, I'm sweet Chicago bound,
> Yes, sir, I'm leaving here, from this old Jim Crow town.
>
> I'm going up north, where they say money grows on trees,
> I don't give a doggone, if my black soul do freeze,
> I'm going where I won't need no BVDs.

I got a hat, got a overcoat, don't need nothing but shoes,
These old easy walkers, gonna give my ankles the blues,
But when my girlie hear about it, Lord, that'll be sad news.

I'm goin' up north, baby, I can't carry you,
Ain't nothing in that cold country a green girl can do,
I'm gonna get me a northern girl, baby, I am through with you.

Lord, but if I get up there, weather don't suit, I don't find no brown,
Go and tell that bossman of mine,
Lord, I'm ready to come back to my Jim Crow town.[27]

Cow Cow came from Anniston, Alabama, and had come to New York in 1924. His song pictures a country man who intends to leave the racist south for Chicago. The line "I'm going where I won't need no BVDs" is obscure. BVD stands for Bradley, Voorhees and Day, a popular brand of underwear. Why would he not need his underwear in the Windy City? I suggest that he is dreaming of the "brown" woman he hopes to meet in Chicago and who will keep him so warm that he won't need long underwear. Alternatively, Cow Cow perhaps thinks that he will have adequate (steam) heat in his Chicago apartment. The walls of southern shacks were often thin, and they were heated by primitive wood burning stoves. "I didn't need no steam heat by my bed, the little girl I had kept me cherry red," Jimmy Rogers sang in another migration song, "Chicago Bound" from 1954.[28]

Coolidge is now mainly remembered for the phrase "The chief business of America is business." However, in the midst of prosperity for privileged Americans, Coolidge noticed that speculation was getting out of hand on Wall Street. The worried president invited William Z. Ripley, a well-known Harvard economist who sounded warnings about the economy, to the White House. Ripley believed that the trouble had to do with "the dissociation of ownership of property from responsibility for the manner in which it shall be put to use."[29] Both men agreed, however, that nothing could be done as it was a matter for individual states to deal with.[30] White House Secretary Edward Clark asked if Coolidge expected a financial crisis. "I do not attempt to predict anything, but people do not seem to see that while we in this country are increasing production enormously, other countries are closing their doors more and more against our products."[31] Endorsing the Jeffersonian concept of "minimal government," however, he also failed to act in this issue.

The Wall Street Crash took place on 24 October 1929. One year earlier, on 27 October 1928, Georgia blues guitarist Barbecue Bob (1902–1931) recorded a prophetic "Bad Time Blues." The artist has had his share of the good times as well, but now "the panic" has hit hard. He is unemployed and cannot support his girlfriend anymore. The song was issued on Columbia 14461, as the B side of "She's Gone Blues," on 18 October 1929, one year after its recording date and only six days before the crash.[32]

Bad time upon me, tell the world the panic is on,
I feel so disgusted, all the good times done gone.

Everybody is crying, they can't get a break,
Tell me what's the matter, everything seems too late.

When you hear me howlin', then you know something's goin' on wrong,
Bad time has got me, why I sing this song.

I can't make a nickel, I'm flat as I can be,
Some people say money is talkin', but it won't say a word to me.

I ain't had a pay check, since the Devil was a boy,
And if I get a real job, I'd pass out with joy.

Bad time upon me, I can't get a gal,
You know a gal costs money, when she'll be your pal.

Bad times upon me, baby needs some shoes,
Bad luck's hangin' around, keep me singin' bad time blues.[33]

On 18 April 1930, when the Depression was a bitter reality, Barbecue Bob recorded a sequel to "Bad Time Blues," entitled "We Sure Got Hard Times."[34] A lyric transcription and an analysis are to be found in *Roosevelt's Blues*.[35]

As Richard Sobel, Coolidge's biographer concluded: "Had [he] run he probably would have won the 1928 election handily—by an even larger margin than Hoover's." However, in late July 1927 Coolidge handed his secretary, Everett Sanders, a slip of paper on which he had written: "I do not choose to run for president in nineteen twenty-eight."[36] The Wall Street Crash came just half a year after Coolidge left office.

On 5 January 1933, as ex-President Coolidge was preparing to shave, he keeled over and fell to the floor, dead at the age of sixty-one.

Although no blues songs from the Coolidge era mention the President or any of his specific policies or issues of his administration, they show that living conditions were still harsh for the vast majority of African Americans. Very often those in the South dreamed of a flight to the north to escape Jim Crow. The songs emphasize the pain of leaving loved ones. Both Blind Blake's and Cow Cow Davenport's penultimate verses show that heading north was often an opportunity to get out of inconvenient relationships. As we know where the artists hailed from, we can conclude that the songs are not fully autobiographical, although the singers may have had similar experiences themselves. The migrants are very nervous about the great change in their lives and are afraid that they will make fools of themselves as naive country people. The colder weather up north adds to the feelings of uncertainty. The tempo of some of these songs is leisurely when country life is described and impetuous by contrast when city life is depicted. Life in the northern cities is idealized, but the South becomes to some degree romanticized once the different problems of urban life have been experienced.

NOTES

1. Robert Sobel, *Coolidge: An American Enigma* (Washington, DC: Regnery, 1998), p. 84.

2. Ibid., p. 75.

3. Ibid., p. 81.

4. Ibid., p. 144.

5. Calvin Coolidge, *The Autobiography of Calvin Coolidge* (London: Chatto & Windus, 1929).

6. Sobel, p. 304.

7. Ibid., p. 301.

8. Hugh Brogan, *Longman History of the United States of America* (London: Longman, 1985; rpt. 1993), p. 518.

9. Sobel, p. 280.

10. Edward Behr, *Prohibition: The 13 Years That Changed America* (London: BBC Books, 1997).

11. Guido van Rijn, *Roosevelt's Blues: African American Blues and Gospel Songs on FDR* (Jackson, Ms: University Press of Mississippi, 1997), pp. 19, 29 and 79.

12. "Bottled in Bond" is a term used for whiskey that is stored in bonded warehouses, under government supervision, while it ages for at least 4 years. The reasoning behind this system is to delay payment of the excise tax until the whiskey is actually sold and shipped to the retailer.

13. Jim Jackson, "Bootlegging Blues," Memphis, Tn, 14 February 1928; issued on Victor 21268; reissued on Document DOCD 5114.

14. Ibid., p. 315.

15. Ibid., p. 250.

16. Ibid., p. 282.

17. Paul Swinton, letter to the editor of *Blues & Rhythm*, No 171 (August 2002): 20; Gayle Dean Wardlow, "Recording the Blues in Mississippi and the South, 1923–1940," *Blues & Rhythm* 192 (September 2004): 192.

18. Dickerson was the wife of hokum singer Bob Robinson, secretary to Paramount A&R man Mayo Williams and a pianist on or composer of many essential blues sides, including co-compositions with Ida Cox and Ma Rainey.

19. John Cowley and Howard Rye, "Chicago Music and the Unissued Paramounts," in *Storyville 2000–1*, ed. Laurie Wright (Chigwell, Essex, England: Storyville Club, 2001), p. 130.

20. A barrelhouse flat is an apartment turned into a barrelhouse. A barrelhouse contained a row of barrels with a plank counter to form an illicit saloon. The backrooms were often used by good-time girls and gamblers. In this way addresses could quickly be changed to escape the Prohibition police.

21. Blind Blake, "Detroit Bound Blues," Chicago, c. May 1928; issued on Paramount 12657; reissued on Document DOCD 5025.

22. http://www.soulofamerica.com/cityfldr/detroit1.html

23. http://www.sos.state.mi.us/history/museum/explore/museums/hismus/1900–75/erlyauto/workforce.html

24. Bob Campbell, "Starvation Farm Blues," Chicago, 1 August 1934; issued on Vocalion 02798; reissued on Document DOCD 5641.

25. Rosa Henderson, "Back Woods Blues," New York City, May 1924; issued on Emerson 10763; reissued on Document DOCD 5402.

26. Maggie Jones, "North Bound Blues," New York City, 16 April 1925; issued on Columbia 14092; reissued on Document DOCD 5348.

27. Cow Cow Davenport, "Jim Crow Blues," Chicago, c. January 1927; issued on Paramount 12439; reissued on Document DOCD 5141.

28. Jimmy Rogers, "Chicago Bound," Chicago, 13 April 1954; issued on Chess 1574; reissued on Chess LP 407.

29. Sobel, p. 360.

30. Ibid., p. 363.

31. Ibid., p. 373.

32. Dave Moore, *Brown Skin Gal: The Story of Barbecue Bob*, booklet accompanying Agram Blues ABLP 2001 (Ter Aar, The Netherlands: Agram, June 1976).

33. Robert "Barbecue Bob" Hicks, "Bad Time Blues," Atlanta, Ga, 27 October 1928; issued on Columbia 14461; reissued on Document DOCD 5047.

34. Robert "Barbecue Bob" Hicks, "We Sure Got Hard Times," Atlanta, Ga, 18 April 1930; issued on Columbia 14558; reissued on Document DOCD 5048.

35. van Rijn, pp. 19–20.

36. Ibid., p. 368.

ON THE ELECTRONIC TRAIL
OF BLUES FORMULAS

ROBERT SPRINGER

A number of years ago, I published as part of a book (first in French, then in English[1]) a brief thematic study of regional blues repertoires which had allowed me to outline a few of their characteristics, namely, the harshness, frustration and melancholy palpable in Mississippi Delta blues, as opposed to a somewhat more relaxed mood in East Coast/Piedmont blues (not without exceptions though), with Texas blues somewhere in between but closer to Mississippi.

Following this, I began a study of blues lyric formulas to gauge the possibility of retracing them to a particular region and mapping out their migration to other regions. My hope was that, in spite of the influence of sound recordings in the diffusion of the songs,[2] and of the formulas that normally come into their composition, it would be possible to define some regional features, which would reinforce, or so I imagined, the musical and thematic characteristics of regional repertoires.

In his introduction to *Big Road Blues*, David Evans discussed the links and interplay between folk and popular elements, adding that what was true for white folk music was also true for the blues.[3] I soon came to realize that the dissemination of blues records and the relative late date of the first country blues recordings unfortunately preclude the mapping out of a geography of blues formulas, attractive though the idea might have seemed.

Until recently, all the work of tracking down blues formulas had to be done by hand, mainly by delving into Michael Taft's *Blues Lyric Poetry: A Concordance*.[4] In the summer of 2000, however, at an important blues conference organized by Clyde Brooks at Pennsylvania State University, I had the good fortune to meet Ulrich Miethaner, then a doctoral student in linguistics and a graduate assistant at the University of Regensburg, Germany, who had come to inform participants about an on-going database project by the name of BLUR (Blues Lyrics collected at the University of Regensburg), whose ambition it was to collect all blues lyrics and make them available to students, scholars and experts for various types of research, by means of the "wordcruncher" program in particular. Thanks to this database,[5] I have been able to move much faster towards a complete appraisal of formulas. In this paper I want to convey a few preliminary conclusions and illustrate them with a number of selected formulas which may prove or disprove earlier hypotheses. It is noteworthy that some of these conclusions will corroborate those that Paul Oliver, David Evans and—to a lesser extent—Bob Groom,[6] among others, had arrived at without the benefit of an electronic database.

METHODOLOGY

To begin with, what is a formula? According to Albert Lord, who, together with Milman Parry, studied another oral corpus, that of Serbo-Croatian epic singers, it is "a group of words which is regularly employed under the same metrical conditions to express a given essential idea."[7] In the blues, a formula will normally consist of a line, often line A of the rhymed couplet in the twelve–bar blues, to which a B line is fitted. The line may be cut in half, leaving two hemistichs which can themselves function as formulas and may be reversed or recombined with others.[8] Complete two-line formulas are often referred to as floating verses, but I'll use the term formula whatever its length. A formula, in essence, as it is repeated and reused, becomes part of the genre's storehouse or library, so to speak, and is absorbed into the tradition.

In the blues, when we say that certain formulas are traditional, we mean that they circulated in oral tradition before they appeared on phonograph records. How do we know? Largely because of their wide dissemination, and particularly because we have a number of examples collected before the 1920s, mainly in three articles published by Charles Peabody, Howard Odum and W. Prescott Webb in the *Journal of American Folklore*, in 1903, 1911 and 1915, respectively.[9] In the 1910s, the presence of formulas in blues songs published in sheet music form and sung on the vaudeville circuit[10] reinforced their dissemination. Still, some formulas were created after the advent of blues records and spread by this medium, and thus entered the blues tradition via this then new route. A good example is Tommy Johnson's famous "Ain't going down this big road by myself/If I don't carry you, gon' carry somebody else," which he popularized in 1928 with "Big Road Blues," though it had first appeared in "Arkansas Road Blues," recorded by Victoria Spivey a year earlier.[11]

For the purpose of this paper, I will limit myself to a few characteristic items in the vast number of blues formulas in existence. I will not attempt to track down the influence of blues formulas, themselves often borrowed from tradition, to be found in songs issued on sheet music as comparison will only be possible once the database includes them.[12]

In my own database of formulas, I have identified almost 600 (and about 200 of what may be termed "felicitous turns of phrase" which later became part of the blues tradition). The BLUR database is largely prewar, which suits my own views, as I believe, but there is broad consensus on this, that little can be learnt about formulas after the first two decades of commercial blues recordings. So the corpus stretches basically from 1920 to 1942, with a few excursions outside whenever useful.

I must indicate, however, that in the history of blues (and other) recordings, there is a three- to four-year hiatus (broadly speaking, the years 1931 to early 1934) due to the Great Depression, though production did not cease completely. One consequence of this is that it is not infrequent for a formula to be revived on record after the Depression. This would indicate that the influence of pre-Depression records was still active, or that the folk tradition remained alive and filled the recording gap.

In order to have tangible elements at my disposal, I have had to make a number of choices or decisions, which, questionable though they may seem, were practically inevitable due to the strictures of historical circumstances surrounding blues recordings:

1. In trying to retrace the history of blues formulas, I have had no other option than to begin with the recording dates available in *Blues and Gospel Records*.[13] Today, thanks to decades of dedicated, painstaking work by blues record buffs and researchers, the most tangible source of data at our disposal concerns those recordings. The data lend themselves to large- and small-scale analysis and may be the only thing we can rely on with confidence. I have also taken into account the presence of unissued recordings, as this is occasionally of some importance.

2. I realize that blues formulas probably also circulated via itinerant blues musicians, and vaudeville performers, as indicated earlier, but it is clearly impossible to establish the relative importance of each factor, namely, recordings and singing in public. I have thus been compelled to use what is available, i.e., sound recordings. Here, it would have been useful if early interviewers had less infrequently asked

blues singers what records they owned or whom they listened to.[14] Perhaps this was due to the researchers' belief that in person word of mouth transmission was the only rule for folk blues, as if recording artists could have allowed themselves to be tapped for recording purposes without in turn being influenced in the slightest by the new medium.

3. Some of my results confirm Bob Groom's views and the results of Daniel Droixhe's *et al*'s research[15] presented in 2000 at the First International Conference on the Lyrics in African American Popular Music, though my initial purpose was not specifically to study the impact of a seminal recording artist and composer like Blind Lemon Jefferson, as they did. It is clear that his influence ranged far and wide and I do not want to belabor that point. But he was far from alone, as we shall see, and was also influenced by others.

4. In what follows, for the purpose of commenting on blues formulas, I have found it useful to adapt David Evans's own categorization of blues compositions[16]:

– word for word imitation
– combining two (rarely more) formulas
– personalizing or localizing the formula
– using the A line and adding a new B line
– reversing the hemistichs in the A line and adding a new B line (sometimes the reverse)
– garbling.

I. REGULAR PRACTICE AMONG BLUES PERFORMERS

On an almost regular basis, whenever a blues singer released a record with an interesting formula or turn of phrase, within months, at most a year (and we know that it was relatively easy to record just before the Depression[17]), cover versions or partial borrowings would occur. It is difficult to be decide whether this was due to blues artists' awareness that they could thus make their own records sell, or whether talent-scouts and record producers actually goaded them in that direction. In any case, the predominance of a few very popular artists and of their "blues hits" seems to have led to imitation across the South for commercial profit, with record labels competing for potential success.

David Evans has remarked that recordings might have arbitrarily captured only a particular version of a song and then stabilized it.[18] From a folkloristic point of view, one might add that particular formulas were used and reused because they were aesthetically and compositionally satisfying to blues singers, but also because they captured the popular imagination and were meaningful to black people, or, more specifically, to lower-class African Americans of Southern rural extraction.

One may surmise that most of these formulas originated from black folk parlance but, once they had made it onto a record, their existence was perpetuated, whether or not they actually remained in existence otherwise. In other words, they tended to acquire a life of their own.

The availability of records led to a relatively minor phenomenon: the existence of more or less habitual imitators. The less gifted blues artists seemed to venture onto the recording scene only when they felt they were on safe ground, i.e. when they could borrow something that had already worked for another recording artist. Perhaps owing to their relative lack of lyric inventiveness, some deferred to other bluesmen's talents and looked to them as sources of inspiration. But, availing oneself of the tried and true is part of human nature and can be encountered in other types of music and other walks of life. Clearly, some were on the look-out for lyrics to imitate, perhaps mainly in hopes of pecuniary returns, though country blues performers have occasionally claimed that records were merely a way of drumming up custom for their live performances—which was probably true in view of the paltry flat fees, usually without royalties, offered by most record companies for each song recorded.[19] Garfield Akers, for example, seems to have been searching for lyrics to be reused on his own few records; in February 1930, he recorded "Dough Roller Blues" for Vocalion almost a year after Hambone Willie Newbern's "Roll and Tumble Blues" had been cut, and presumably released, by OKeh. The lyrics were virtually identical but the change of title probably fooled Vocalion. Interestingly enough, Akers did not record after that.

However, more often than not, creativity was in evidence, and a given formula would be reworked by other singers who thus, in effect, reappropriated it. The later formulas were rarely carbon copies, though we find many, often clumsy attempts at sounding original, which also often makes it possible to recognize the original formula or turn of phrase, as it is almost invariably the most striking one—in addition to having usually been recorded first. It is often difficult to tell exactly whether the reworking of formulas was the result of the traditional blues process of personalisation[20] or whether it stemmed from a desire to avoid accusations of plagiarism and possible law-suits. The record companies, which "tried to keep from recording such [cover] blues in their efforts to obtain original material,"[21] presumably checked the originality of lyrics, but this was more systematically done by the publishing companies by means of the lead sheets submitted to the copyright office; several publishing companies were controlled by producers like Ralph Peer, J. Mayo Williams and Lester Melrose who might have prevented a song from being issued if it infringed another copyright.[22]

Generally speaking, although it is remotely possible that some short (hemistich) formulas were worked off independently by several performers, the presence of the same rhyme and the same wording is a fool-proof give away of borrowing. Still, there was variation, and I have found that the most successful formulas were those that allowed for variation. In sum, we do witness a certain standardisation and stabilisation, though this does not preclude variation and personalisation, but it is often difficult, if not impossible, to decide whether the variants are really due to the blues' personalisation process or to the artists' attempts at sounding original to the producers.

II. THE INFLUENCE OF THE "CLASSIC" BLUES SINGERS

Concerning the sub-genre of the "classic blues," the BLUR corpus is, at the moment, in embryonic form, and this part of the research had to be done "by hand."

The evidence available indicates that, though Bessie Smith recorded twice as much and started almost a year earlier, Ma Rainey's influence was somewhat stronger. This is clearly due to the more formulaic and traditional quality of her songs. The formulas she put out were certainly reused more frequently.

EX. 1: THE "ROCKING-CHAIR TO ROCK/RUBBER BALL TO ROLL" FORMULA

Ma Rainey, "Jealous Hearted Blues" (Paramount, NYC, c. 15 Oct. 1924)

It takes a rockin'-chair to rock, a rubber ball to roll,
Takes the man I love to satisfy my soul.
Yes, I'm jealous, jealous, jealous-hearted me,
Lord, I'm just jealous, jealous as I can be.

In addition to this formula, in this song Ma Rainey introduced the record-buying public to two other influential ones:

Got a range in my kitchen, cooks nice and brown
All I need is my man to turn my damper down.

and

Gonna buy me a bulldog to watch him while I sleep
To keep my man from making his midnight creep.

Jim Jackson, "Jim Jackson's Kansas City Blues—part 1" (Vocalion, Chicago, 10 Oct. 1927)

It takes a rockin'-chair to rock, a rubber ball to roll,
A nice-looking brown to satisfy my soul.
Then I'll move to Kansas City, (x2)
I'm gonna move to Kansas City, baby, honey, where they don't 'low you.

With this song, the formula, which may have continued an independent career outside the recording medium, became associated with the "Kansas City" song for some time afterwards. However, the original recording was not forgotten, as the following version makes clear.

Charley Lincoln, "Jealous Hearted Blues" (Columbia, Atlanta, 4 Nov. 1927)

It take a rockin'-chair to rock, take a rubber ball to roll,
Takes the gal I love, satisfy my soul.
You know I'm jealous, jealous, jealous-hearted, see,
So jealous, jealous as I can be.

Charley Lincoln's song used Ma Rainey's title and started as a cover version (three out of four stanzas, including this one, are repeated) but then, as often happened, he added material of his own, presumably for purposes of personalization and/or commercial reappropriation.

Lonnie Johnson, "Kansas City Blues—part 1" (OKeh, Chicago, 17 Dec. 1927)

It take a rockin'-chair to rock, a rubber ball to roll,
Takes a nice clean mama to satisfy my soul.
Then I will move to Kansas City,
I'm going to move to Kansas City,
I'm going to move, baby, honey, where they don't like you.

Lonnie Johnson's is an intriguing version. In the formula, "nice clean" seems less natural than "nice-looking." The song was recorded only two months after Jim Jackson's, in Chicago also, and the order of stanzas is the same and the wording virtually identical, as is the case in the sequels ("Jim Jackson's Kansas City Blues—part 2" and "Kansas City Blues—part 2") issued on the flip-sides of the respective records. This cannot be attributed to chance; the chronological and, to some extent, the lyrical evidence indicate that Johnson was probably the imitator. We are obviously presented here with a case of intense commercial competition over a song whose topic was partly located in Memphis and that was clearly very popular in that city and in the rest of the country.

Bo and Sam Chatman, "Back to Mississippi" (OKeh, San Antonio, 10 June 1930)

It takes a rockin'-chair to rock, a rubber ball to roll,
A Mississippi train, now, to satisfy my soul.
And we'll go back to Mississippi,
We'll go back to Mississippi,
We'll go back to Mississippi, honey, where the weather ain't cold.

This is a clear attempt at re-localizing the "Kansas City" song that sounds like a bit of an echoing spoof.

After the Depression, the formula reappears but Ma Rainey and "Kansas City Blues" seem to have faded from memory. It regains life thanks to Kokomo Arnold. Formulas could thus reemerge from tradition, but they could also be imitated, or recycled, whenever an artist chanced upon a 78 rpm recording years after it had first been issued, thus reviving the chain of transmission. In any event, the formula now became associated with Arnold's "Milk Cow Blues," where the depiction of his woman as a milk cow, which males probably found hilarious at the time, was the obvious novelty element.

Kokomo Arnold, "Milk Cow Blues" (Decca, Chicago, 10 Sept. 1934)

Takes a rockin'-chair to rock, mama, a rubber ball to roll,
Takes a little teasing brown, pretty mama, just to pacify my soul.
Lord, I don't feel welcome, please, no place I go,
For the little woman I love, mama, have done drove me from her door.

In a little over a year, three more versions of Arnold's obviously popular formula appeared, two of which under the same title, with only minor changes.

Josh White, "Milk Cow Blues" (Oriole, NYC, 13 Feb. 1935)

That takes a rockin'-chair to rock, mama, rubber ball to roll,
Takes a nice teasing mama just to pacify my soul.
Lord, I don't feel welcome, please, no place I go.
Now, my good gal done quit me, lord, turned me from her door.

Bumble Bee Slim, "Milk Cow Blues" (Bluebird, Chicago, 27 Feb. 1935)

Now, it takes a rockin'-chair to rock, baby, a rubber ball to roll,
Takes a good-lookin' teasin' brown just to satisfy my soul.
'Cause I don't feel welcome, eeh, no place I go.
'Cause the woman I love, mama, she have drove me from her door.

Big Joe Williams, "Wild Cow Blues" (Bluebird, Chicago, 31 Oct. 1935)

It'll take a rubber ball to roll and a rockin'-chair to rock.
The girl I'm lovin', she's talkin' that ole baby talk.
Lord, I don't feel welcome, I said, please, nowhere I go,
Lord, that good girl I'm lovin', she done drove me away from my door.

The title of Big Joe Williams's version is a thin disguise, while the lyrics contain a probable attempt to mix things up a little, with hemistichs reversed in the A line. In addition, the first stanza appears last in his song. Was this the folk process at work or was the singer under the influence of commercialism? The latter interpretation is more likely in this case.

III. RAMIFICATIONS OF A FORMULA

Though often significant as a source of inspiration and imitation, the earliest recorded formula was not systematically the most influential one. Later singers clearly reserved the right to take liberties and make alterations. It remains possible, however, that the source some of the singers started with was not the original recording but an oral version circulated in their community.

EX. 2: THE "WILL A MATCHBOX HOLD MY CLOTHES" FORMULA

In the history of the blues, this formula is indelibly associated with Blind Lemon Jefferson. It was in fact first recorded by Ma Rainey, as Paul Oliver noticed in the 1960s without the benefit of an electronic database.[23]

Ma Rainey, "Lost Wandering Blues" (Paramount, Chicago, March 1924)

I'm standin' here wonderin' will a matchbox hold my clothes
I've got a trunk too big to be bothered with on the road

Whereas her verse makes perfect sense, Jefferson's version, though believed to have been seminal, seems questionable and may even have been a less than successful attempt at reappropriation:[24]

Blind Lemon Jefferson, "Match Box Blues" (OKeh, Atlanta, 14 March 1927 & Paramount, Chicago, c. April 1927)

I'm sitting here wondering would a matchbox hold my clothes
I ain't got so many matches, but I got so far to go.

Before the year was over, Blind Lemon's recordings were followed by three more by different artists.

Luke Jordan, "Church Bells Blues" (Victor, Charlotte, N.C., 16 Aug. 1927)

She wouldn't cook me no breakfast, she wouldn't get me no dinner
She squawk about my supper and she kicked me outdoors.
She had the nerve to ask me would a, a matchbox hold my clothes
Had the nerve to ask me would a, a matchbox hold my clothes.

All that remains of the formula in this version is the felicitous metaphor of the second hemistich in the A line, which here moves to B line position in an otherwise original stanza.

Casey Bill Weldon, "Turpentine Blues" (Victor, Atlanta, 20 Oct. 1927)

Said I wonder would a poor matchbox hold my clothes?
I ain't got so many, Lord, I've got so far to go.

This version would seem to issue from Blind Lemon Jefferson's, if we take into account chronology, recording location and the absence of only one significant word, "matches." However, contrary to its presumed model, its meaning is crystal-clear.

Walter Beasley, "Southern Man Blues" (OKeh, NYC, 30 Nov. 1927)

Lord, I wonder will a matchbox hold my clothes
I ain't got so many, but I got so far to go.

Judging by the lyrics, the source of this version was more likely to have been Casey Bill than Blind Lemon.

Willie Baker, "Weak-minded Blues" (Supertone, Richmond, Ind. Jan. or Feb. 1929 and Champion, 11 March 1929)

I wonder will a matchbox hold my dirty clothes
I ain't got so many but I got so far to go.

Although Baker adds "dirty," he otherwise parallels Weldon and Beasley and there may have been mutual influences at work as Baker and Beasley were from the Atlanta area, while Weldon cut this, his first record there. Intriguingly, this is also where Blind Lemon recorded his first "Match Box Blues."

Ed Bell, "Shouting Baby Blues" (QRS, Long Island, c. April 1929)

You haven't seen her at the station, ain't seen her on the road?
And I'm sitting here wonderin' will a matchbox hold my clothes.

Here the B line is the A line of the Blind Lemon formula, while the A line is totally new.

Willie Reed, "Goin' Back to My Baby" (Columbia unissued, Dallas, 5 Dec. 1929)

I was sitting here wondering would a matchbox hold my clothes
It's dark and raining, she done throwed my clothes

This song is an attempt at originality; starting with Jefferson's exact A line down to the conditional "would" and with possible inspiration from Luke Jordan's 1927 release, it seems to have failed to convince Columbia who decided not to issue it.

Willie Walker, "Dupree Blues" (Columbia 14578-D, Atlanta, 9 Dec. 1930)[25]

Standin' there wonderin' will a matchbox hold my clothes,
Said a trunk is too big to be bothered on the road.

Rather than Blind Lemon, Willie Walker was clearly following Ma Rainey.

Six years later, while the Depression was far from over, the formula resurfaced, first with two singers who, for the first time, used Blind Lemon Jefferson's title, confident probably that the passage of time would protect them. Still, Big Bill Broonzy did produce an original B line,

Big Bill Broonzy, "Matchbox Blues" (ARC, Chicago, 12 Feb. 1936)

Standing here wondering will a matchbox hold my clothes
When I leave this town I don't need no suitcase, I know.

while Black Ivory King remained relatively close to Ma Rainey's original.

Black Ivory King, "Match Box Blues" (Decca, Dallas, 15 Feb. 1937)

I was standing here thinking would a matchbox hold my clothes
Suitcase is too heavy for a poor boy on the road.

Leadbelly, "I'm on My Last Go-Round" (Bluebird, NYC, 15 June 1940)

Sitting down here wondering would a matchbox hold my clothes
I don't want to be bothered with no suitcase on my road

Apart from the substitution of "suitcase" for "trunk," this is the Ma Rainey version. It raises the question of whether Leadbelly had recently acquired her recording of 1924 or had used the formula this way since the 1920s and only had a chance to record the song later.

Interestingly also, between 1944 and 1951, Ralph Willis waxed no fewer than five songs with the "matchbox" formula, three of which ("Church Bells," "Church Bell Blues" and "Worried Blues") were apparently inspired by Luke Jordan and the other two by Blind Lemon Jefferson. All were released, but on four different labels, which may indicate that, in those days, small independent labels were not very discriminating in the release of similar compositions, or not aware of what had been recorded before.

Ralph Willis's, "So Many Days" (20th Cent., NYC c. 1946) contains two stanzas with the formula:

Got me sitting here wondering, great god, will a matchbox hold my clothes
You know, I ain't got so many matches, little woman, great god, got such a
*   long way to go.*

Yeah, got me sitting here wondering, yeah, will a matchbox hold my clothes
Well, I ain't got nobody, great god, to satisfy my soul.

For the first time in the history of blues recording, and almost twenty years later, Blind Lemon's B line was being reused. The second stanza has a semi-improvised B line which rhymes a little awkwardly and has a tenuous link with the A line. In fact, its second hemistich is normally part of the B line of the "rocking-chair/rubber ball" formula examined earlier.

The combined evidence shows that, apart from various reappropriations, this formula produced two B line lineages: one probably initiated by Ma Rainey's record, the other apparently popular in the Atlanta area. The fact that Ma Rainey herself was from Georgia complicates matters further. Concerning Blind Lemon Jefferson's own attempt at originality, two interpretations are possible: either one of the "Atlanta bluesmen" had heard his record(s) and restored some logic to lyrics that Blind Lemon himself had partly adapted from Ma Rainey, or Blind Lemon had come across the "Atlanta version" while he was in the city to record and cut his variant first. In either case, he does not seem to have been the originator and the fact that he titled his song "Match Box Blues" is, in my view, insufficient proof of original coinage.

IV. STABILIZATION AND VARIATION

EX. 3: THE "CRYIN' WON'T MAKE ME STAY" FORMULA

We have just seen that even the reputed trendsetters could be influenced by others, as is rather customary in music. Blind Lemon Jefferson was not averse to borrowing from Papa Charlie Jackson, as we shall see, or from others. As a rule, though the version of a formula that first made it onto shellac was a potential influence on future artists, it was often as a source of inspiration and not necessarily only as a set of words to be memorized and recited verbatim. Thus, the stabilization of a formula did not rule out variation.

Ed Andrews, "Time Ain't Gonna Make Me Stay" (OKeh, Atlanta, late March/early April 1924)

I'm going, I'm going, crying won't make me stay
I'm leaving, walking, talking this very day

This was the first recorded country blues but one should realize that Ed Andrews merely happened to be in the right place at the right time. He was actually never asked to record again. Though he aired the formula first, his second line is a rather idiosyncratic version of the "I'm leaving here walking, talking to myself" formula[26] and was never repeated by another recording artist. Instead, it was Blind Lemon Jefferson's version, contained in "Match Box Blues" and recorded three years later, that apparently initiated a slew of copy-cat recordings. It became one of the most popular and imitated formulas, a perennial formula, one might say.

Blind Lemon Jefferson, "Match Box Blues" (OKeh, Atlanta, 14 March 1927)

I'm leavin' town, cryin' won't make me stay
Baby, the more you cry, the further you drive me away.

Another version of this formula was recorded by Papa Harvey Hull and Long "Cleve" Reed as part of "Two Little Tommies Blues" (Gennett, Chicago, c. 8 April 1927).[27] Three weeks later, Furry Lewis with "Mr. Furry's Blues" reused it. If we assume that Blind Lemon's record was already out, but perhaps not Hull and Reed's, the title seems to have been a thin attempt at personalizing his borrowing.

Furry Lewis, "Mr. Furry's Blues" (Vocalion, Chicago, 20 April 1927)

I'm goin', I'm goin', your cryin' won't make me stay,
For the more you cry, further you drive me away.

Within the same week (if the approximate date can be trusted), Sam Collins waxed a slight variation:

Sam Collins, "Devil in the Lion's Den" (Gennett, Richmond, Va., c. 23 April 1927)

Lord, I'm goin' up the country, for cryin' won't make me stay
More you cry, the further I'll ride away.

Around September of the same year, Frank Stokes, who may very well have got the formula from Furry Lewis (or was it the other way around?), as both lived in Memphis, recorded it in Chicago:

Frank Stokes, "Blues in D" (Paramount, Chicago, c. Sept. 1927)

And I'm goin', I'm goin' and your cryin' won't make me stay
Baby, the more you cry, the further you'll drive me away.

By the end of the year, there was one more apparent copy, with a semi-personal B line however, presumably influenced by Lonnie Johnson's hemistich formula "you'll need my help someday," first recorded in "You Don't See Into the Blues Like Me" (OKeh 8451, NYC, 13 Aug. 1926):

John D. Fox, "The Moanin' Blues" (Gennett, Richmond, 15 Dec. 1927)

I'm goin' to leave you, baby, your cryin' won't make me stay
But it's like I told you, you're gonna need my help someday.

Memphis Jug Band, "Papa Long Blues" (Victor, Memphis, 13 Feb. 1928)

And I'm goin', I'm goin', your cryin' won't make me stay,
And I won't be dead, just won't blow back here no more.

The B line here is a good example of doggerel in the blues, particularly "jug band blues."[28]

Tampa Red, "Big Fat Mama" (OKeh, Chicago, 11 Dec. 1928)

Says, I'm goin' away, baby, cryin' ain't gonna make me stay,
But you just pray to the good Lord your daddy 'll come home some day.

This variation by Tampa Red offers a relatively original B line.

John Hurt, "Big Leg Blues" (OKeh unissued, NYC, 21 Dec. 1928)

I'm goin', I'm goin', cryin' won't make me stay
More you cry, further you drive me away.

Interestingly enough, Mississippi John Hurt's song was unissued at the time, perhaps because it came so close to the Lewis/Stokes/Jefferson formula, little more than a year later.

Within the next decade, after the hiatus due to the Depression, eight more versions of the formula were recorded. So were three unissued songs by Charley Jordan, "Bad Feeling Blues," "Tired Feelin' Blues" and "Low Moan Blues"—all cut during the same session in New York on 10 April 1936—in which he used the first line of the formula and changed the second line in the first two songs, in an apparent attempt at originality, but was probably given the thumbs down by the producer. In the last song, he reverted to the entire Blind Lemon formula with no more success.

V. PAPA CHARLIE JACKSON VS MA RAINEY

Papa Charlie Jackson, by dint of having been one of the first male blues singers to record (although he also sang popular and novelty songs, as the following example will show), was often the starting point for the dissemination of formulas on record. His songs used many traditional ones, but though his name is often associated with the following formula, it is not certain he originated it.

EX 4: THE "WEAR YOU OFF MY MIND" FORMULA

Lottie Beaman/Kimbrough, "Red River Blues" (Paramount, Chicago, c. March 1924)

I'm going away, wear you off my mind
I refuse to stay with the mistreating kind.

This may have been the original version, on record at least, although the B line has a composed sound to it, which may explain why it was never repeated in recording history.

Ma Rainey, "Shave 'Em Dry Blues" (Paramount, Chicago, c. Aug. 1924)

Going away to wear you off my mind,
You keep me hungry and broke, daddy all the time.
Eh hey, daddy let me shave them dry.

Papa Charlie Jackson, "Shave Them Dry" (Paramount, Chicago, c. Feb. 1925)

Now I'm goin' away to wear you off my mind,
You keep me broke and hungry, mama, all the time,
Mama can I holler, daddy wants to shave them dry.

Was the complete formula, with this B line, borrowed from Ma Rainey or did she simply beat Jackson to the Paramount recording studios? The addition of "blues" in her song title, whether she or the producer was ultimately responsible for it, suggests that it was she who did the borrowing. It is possible that Paramount were aware of the existence of what is believed to have been his original composition, even though Jackson had apparently not recorded it yet, if the approximate recording dates available are to be trusted. Whatever the ultimate truth, from that moment, the formula was associated with the "Shave 'em dry" song.[29]

Elzadie Robinson, "Barrel House Man" (Paramount, Chicago, c. Oct. 1926)

Oh, I'm going away just to wear you off my mind
Oh, I've got the blues and I just can't keep from crying.
I've got another papa, keeps me from crying.

This is a different, rather idiosyncratic version.

L. C. Prigett, "Frogtown Blues" (Victor, Savannah, Ga., 26 Aug. 1927)

And I'm going up north, mama, wear you off my mind
You keeps me worried, bothered all the time.

This stanza contains the most common B line, in spite of what may be perceived as an imperfect rhyme. Though it uses the Ma Rainey/Charlie Jackson shell, the adjectives "broke and hungry" have been replaced by "worried (and) bothered," and it was this wording which stabilized the formula. But this, as usual, did not prevent subsequent singers from trying to sound original.

Blind Lemon Jefferson, "Lonesome House Blues" (Paramount, Chicago, c. Oct. 1927)

I'm going away mama, just to wear you off my mind
So if I leave you in Chicago, murder's gonna be my crime.

This time, Blind Lemon again borrowed but, in addition, his wording was not imitated by anyone, probably because his B line—whose second part probably came from a song by Sippie Wallace[30]—here too, was less than clear and had been excessively personalized.

"Blue Coat" Tom Nelson, "Blue Coat Blues" (OKeh, Memphis, 17 Feb. 1928)

I'm going away, baby, to wear you off my mind
For you keeps me worried and bothered all the time.

Nelson here reproduced what may be called the classic version of the formula.

Will Day, "Sunrise Blues" (Columbia, New Orleans, 25 April 1928)

You leave me laughing, some day you'll come back cryin',
You've been gone so long, tryin' to wear you off my mind.

There is little more than the formula's shell in the second hemistich of the B line, as a result of improvisation or garbling.

Henry Spaulding, "Biddle Street Blues" (Brunswick, Chicago,
9 May 1929)

Now, I'm going back to Biddle Street, try and wear you off my mind,
'Cause I have another woman on Biddle Street will treat me nice
*   and kind.*

This stanza is a successful attempt at originality. The rhyme is perfect and the whole could easily be imitated, either by dropping the "Biddle Street" reference or by replacing it with another localizing reference. Though the entire B line never reappeared on wax, and Spaulding's career may have fallen victim to the Depression as this was his only record, he was probably heard by other artists; starting in the 1930s, the second hemistich of his B line was often found on record.

Charlie Spand, "Fetch Your Water" (Paramount, Richmond, Ind.,
6 June 1929)

I'm goin' away, baby, to wear you off my mind,
Now, you keep me worried and bothered, mama, all the time.

This is close to the classic version, as is the following.

Louise Johnson, "Long Ways from Home" (Paramount, Grafton, Wisc.,
28 May 1930)

Well, I'm going, I'm going, daddy, to wear you off my mind
'Cause you keeps me worried, baby, and it's trouble all the time.

Marie Griffin, "Blue and Disgusted" (Paramount, Grafton, Wisc., c. 29 May 1930)

If the blues was liquor, I would stay drunk all the time,
I drink and drink, just to wear you off my mind.

Here, only the last hemistich remains and the whole stanza has been rebuilt, combining elements from another inspirational formula.

Big Bill Broonzy, "Shelby County Blues" (Perfect, NYC, 29 March 1932)

I'm going away just to wear you off my mind
'Cause you keeps me worried, all messed up in mind.

A possibly improvised attempt at sounding original in the second line falls somewhat flat due to the same-word "rhyme." But it might also have been a case of faulty memory.

Black Boy Shine, "Married Man Blues" (Vocalion, San Antonio, 20 Nov. 1936)

Says, I didn't come here to stay no great long time
Says, I just come here, baby, to wear you off my mind.

This stanza is rather paradoxical or even contradictory for, as a rule, wearing someone off one's mind implies going away, unless one imagines the protagonist calling his woman long distance.

To conclude, no matter what the reputation of the recording artist, it was not always the earliest recorded example(s) of a formula which acquired popularity and led to imitation. Blues singers still picked and chose what they liked best and what proved most effective and most aesthetically appealing. A formula could take some time to stabilize and, even then, it remained susceptible to competition and variation, both because of the recording industry's demand for originality, and because of the ongoing folk process of progress, through alteration within a stable, familiar, traditional framework.

As with religious songs, for which recordings also played a major part, blues recordings were an important cultural vehicle for black people, especially rural

Blacks. During the heyday of the blues, sound recordings were clearly a privileged medium of conveyance of witticisms, folk-sayings or aphorisms for African Americans but also of felicitous turns of phrase that were the work of individual artists. It is well-known that Blacks sacrificed other priorities to buy Victrolas and records, or even the latter without the former.[31] Blues was a genuine form of cultural and literary education, and its aural transmission by means of phonograph records was at least as significant as its traditional oral transmission. One certainly should not see the blues as a collection of repeated imitative formulas. Tradition and evolution were constantly at work in the lyrics. In an article published in the *Journal of American Folklore*,[32] Bennison Gray considered that "change is as characteristic of oral literature as is repetition." I believe that Gray's formula can be applied to all folklore, including blues and without excluding recorded blues, though, in this case, commercialism appears to have been an important but often uncontrollable variable.

NOTES

1. Robert Springer, *Le Blues authentique: son histoire et ses thèmes* (Paris: Filipacchi, 1985), pp. 78–80, 97, 100–01, 113–14, 151–53, 167–68; *Authentic Blues: Its History and Its Themes* (Lewiston, N.Y.: Edwin Mellen, 1995), pp. 70–73, 89–91, 99–101, 134–36, 149–50.

2. As early as 1925, Howard W. Odum and Guy B. Johnson had turned their attention to this phenomenon in *Negro Workaday Songs* (Chapel Hill: University of North Carolina Press, 1925).

3. David Evans, *Big Road Blues: Tradition and Creativity in the Folk Blues* (Berkeley: University of California Press, 1982). I am very much indebted to David Evans for providing advice, corrections and expert information for this paper.

4. Michael Taft, *Blues Lyric Poetry: A Concordance* (New York: Garland, 1984).

5. I wish to thank Ulrich Miethaner and Andreas Müller for their permission to use the database.

6. See, for instance, Paul Oliver, *Aspects of the Blues Tradition* (New York: Oak, 1970), pp. 17 *passim*; *The Story of the Blues* (London: Barrie and Jenkins, 1970), pp. 37–38; David Evans, pp. 9 *passim*; Bob Groom, "The Legacy of Blind Lemon," *Blues World*, no. 16 (Sept. 1967): 13; no. 18 (Jan. 1968): 14–16; no. 20 (July 1968): 33–37; no. 21 (Oct. 1968): 30–32; no. 23 (Apr. 1969): 5–7; no. 24 (July 1969): 9–10; no. 25 (Oct. 1969): 9–10; no. 27 (Feb. 1970): 13–14; no. 28 (March 1970): 8–9; no. 29 (April 1970): 8–9; no. 30 (May 1970): 13–14; no. 35 (Oct. 1970): 19–20; no. 36 (Nov. 1970): 20; no. 40 (Autumn 1971): 4–6; no. 50 (1974): 8. Thanks to Luigi Monge for sending me a copy of the latter series of articles.

7. Albert B. Lord, *The Singer of Tales* (Cambridge, Mass.: Harvard University Press, 1964), p. 30, also quoted in David Evans, p. 315.

8. See Jeff Tod Titon, *Early Downhome Blues: A Musical and Cultural Analysis* (Urbana: University of Illinois Press, 1977), pp. 178–82.

9. Charles Peabody, "Notes on Negro Music," *Journal of American Folklore*, 16 (1903): 148–152; Howard W. Odum, "Folk-Song and Folk-Poetry as Found in the Secular Songs of the Southern Negroes," *Journal of American Folklore*, 24 (1911): 255–94, 351–96; W. Prescott Webb, "Notes to Folk-Lore of Texas," *Journal of American Folklore*, 28 (1915): 290–99.

10. I am grateful to David Evans for this addition and most of the contents of note 11 relating to it.

11. I am indebted to David Evans for pointing this out. See also David Evans, p. 272.

12. These songs can be found in three main sources: David A. Jasen, ed., *'Beale Street" and Other Classic Blues (1910–1921)* (Mineola, NY: Dover, 1998), W. C. Handy's *Blues: An Anthology* (New York: Da Capo, 1990), which contains 53 songs, and Richard L. Riley's three-volume *Early Blues* (Roseville, CA: PianoMania, 1996), which compiles over one hundred sheet music reprints (unfortunately, only volume 2 is still in print.)

13. Robert M. W. Dixon, John Godrich & Howard W. Rye, *Blues and Gospel Records, 1890–1943*, Fourth ed. (Oxford: Clarendon P., 1997).

14. As Paul Oliver remarked in 1984 (*Songsters and Saints: Vocal Tradition on Race Records*, Cambridge University Press, 1984, p. 273), "Opportunities have been missed for information that would throw light on the purchasing of records."

15. Daniel Droixhe, Joseph Brems and Jean-Pierre Urbain, "Around Blind Lemon Jefferson's Legacy," paper read at the First Conference on the Lyrics in African American Popular Music, University of Metz, France, 30 September 2000.

16. David Evans, p. 131.

17. This can be concluded from an examination of the years 1927–1930 on the chart of field recordings drawn up by Robert M. W. Dixon and John Godrich in *Recording the Blues* (London: Studio Vista, 1970), pp. 106–07.

18. Ibid., p. 10.

19. On average, country blues performers seem to have been paid about ten dollars per side. In 1926, for instance, Columbia gave Peg Leg Howell fifty dollars plus royalties for his first record (Samuel Charters, *The Bluesmen* [New York: Oak, 1967], p. 182), while, in 1930, Son House only got five dollars per side from Paramount (Francis Davis, *The History of the Blues*, New York: Hyperion, 1995, p. 108.) See also Robert M. W. Dixon and John Godrich, op. cit., pp. 54, 92, 94, 96. These figures can be put in their proper perspective when compared with average sales figures of close to ten thousand for blues (and gospel) records in 1927 and 1928, when they sold for seventy-five cents or so (Robert M. W. Dixon and John Godrich, op. cit., p. 60).

20. David Evans has also remarked that "many blues singers strive for individuality of expression and try to be up-to-date in their music and tastes." (op.cit., p. 7)

21. Ibid., p. 81.

22. David Evans, personal communication. For more on copyright in the blues, see my own "Folklore, Commercialism and Exploitation: the Question of Copyright in the Blues," *Popular Music*, forthcoming.

23. Paul Oliver, *Aspects of the Blues Tradition* (New York: Oak, 1970), p. 18. He also discussed formulas on pp. 17–20.

24. At the conference, David Evans suggested that "matches" might be interpreted as "matches of clothes," which would restore meaning to the second line.

25. At the conference, Chris Smith noticed that this version, rather unaccountably, is absent from the BLUR database.

26. David Evans, personal communication.

27. The existence of this record, also absent from the BLUR database, was pointed out to me by David Evans.

28. See, for instance, in the same song, stanzas 1 and 3, where "wall" is made to rhyme with "bed" and "here" with "now," and stanzas 3 and 4 in the Memphis Jug Band's "Memphis Jug—Blues" (Memphis, 24 Feb. 1927, Victor 20576).

29. See Paul Oliver, *Aspects*, pp. 225–32, for a thorough study of the song. See also note 18 in Randall Cherry's article in this volume.

30. Sippie Wallace, "Murder's Gonna Be My Crime," OKeh, NYC, 22 Aug. 1925. David Evans noticed the absence of this song from the BLUR database.

31. See Jeff Todd Titon, p. 276.

32. Bennison Gray, "Repetition in Oral Literature," *Journal of American Folklore* 84 (1971): 291.

WEST INDIES BLUES

*An Historical Overview, 1920s–1950s—Blues and Music
from the English-speaking West Indies*

JOHN COWLEY

In most contemporary literature, a direct relationship between black music from
the English-speaking West Indies and the United States is considered a twentieth-
century development. Generally, Jamaica is given as the prime example of interchange, but in the region's history the popularity of Jamaican styles is a relatively
recent occurrence.

CULTURAL CONNECTIONS OF LONG STANDING

Before slavery was abolished in the United States, black people in the British
West Indies were perceived as brothers in blood in the fight for Emancipation.
The ending of Apprenticeship in Britain's colonies (1 August 1838) was cause for
annual celebration by enslaved black people in the South, until freedom was
achieved at the end of the Civil War.[1] Cultural influences moved in both direc-
tions. For example, George Liele, a famous black American slave preacher from
the southern states, was instrumental in establishing a mission in Jamaica. By the
early 1800s his Baptist church had tentacles that stretched from black Christian
converts in the United States, to Jamaica, Canada, Britain, and ultimately Sierra
Leone in Africa.[2] In Trinidad (1,000 miles south of Jamaica), one early North
American connection was the Company Villages, where the administration settled black troops who had fought on the side of the British in the War of 1812–14
with the U.S.[3]

In addition to trade, there were many other cultural contacts between the
United States and West Indian islands from their earliest settlement by

Europeans. These ranged from tours by U.S. theatrical companies and circuses to the medicine shows that provided such a rich training ground for black song-sters in North America. The skilled black fiddle player was just as sought after by the plantocracy of West Indian islands as he was by its equivalent in the South. In both instances, he was employed to play the European recreational dances that swept across the Atlantic in fashion after fashion throughout the century, but were later reciprocated by novel American styles. Similar general trends in musical evolution also applied. Jubilee and black-in-black-face minstrelsy laid the foundation stones for the acceptance of later forms of black North American music, and this was also the case in Africa, Europe, and the Antipodes. Obeah and other forms of magic (or "science" in local parlance) were reinforced by the same publications that black Americans purchased in the United States. There are many other links and parallels that intertwine across the nineteenth century.[4]

WEST INDIAN MIGRATION TO THE U.S.A.

It should come as no surprise, therefore, that the United States was viewed as a likely place for migration by aspirant black West Indians. From the early 1900s to the advent of restrictive legislation in 1924—and even afterwards until 1952, whilst they were still counted as British nationals—the primary external focal point for black migration from Britain's then West Indian colonies remained the United States of America.[5]

Documentary evidence for this early- to mid-twentieth century period of emi-gration is especially hard to uncover. Some migration was seasonal, and revolved around the agricultural cycle. For example, after his success as a blues singer, Arthur "Big Boy" Crudup was employed as an overseer for gangs of West Indian transients who worked the crops north from Florida each season, before returning to their islands of origin.[6] There was, of course, similar regional migration both between islands and also to and from the South American mainland. The Panama Canal was built using migrant labor from territories such as Barbados and Trinidad, but primarily Jamaica.[7] Jamaicans traveled to Cuba to cut sugar in the 1920s and 1930s and Laurel Aitken, one of the principal Jamaican calypso/r'n'b/ska performers of the late 1950s and early 1960s, has maternal Cuban ancestry.[8] Before the Second World War, the British journalist William Makin remembered seeing an itinerant blues pianist in Panama City who traveled from North America seeking employ-ment wherever he went, just as others did throughout the South.[9]

A study by Ira De A. Reid shows that between 1899 and 1937 the majority of black West Indian migrants to the United States were from British territories. Their occupations on arrival were split between "male industrial workers and female domestics," likewise the main occupations for urban black people born in the United States. These job opportunities correspond with similar means of employment in the migrants' islands of origin, but as a whole there was a high proportion of skilled artisans and professionals who sought work in the new environment. They also brought their island folklore with them. For example, as early as 1919, Elsie Clews Parsons printed a "West Indian Tale" she had collected in New York City from a Trinidadian migrant named Charles Penny—"Little girl, Mama Glau, and Hummingbird."[10]

The concentration of black West Indian migrants in U.S. conurbations is highlighted in Reid's survey of the characteristics of this group. Thus, in 1930, "there were 91,677 foreign-born Negroes residing in urban areas, 93 per cent of the total foreign-born Negro population," the leading settlements being Boston, Cambridge, New York and Miami.[11] Pinpointed by Gilbert Osofsky, the most important of these locations was New York City where, during the 1920s, "there were ten times as many foreign-born Negroes . . . as in any other urban area" and in the same period "about 25 per cent of Harlem's population was foreign born."[12] Writing in 1928, Wallace Thurman pointed to the difficulty that followed this influx, noting how "the Negro from the British West Indies . . . creates and has to face a disagreeable problem. Being the second largest Negro Group in Harlem, and being less susceptible to American manners and customs than others, he is frowned upon and berated by the American Negro."[13] This friction was to be reflected in local black music.

ENTERTAINERS

As this metropolis was a prime center for musical and theatrical activity, it was inevitable that some West Indian entertainers would try their luck with the city's wider audience. A prototype for success was the famous black vaudeville singer-comedian Bert Williams. Although his minstrel show training was U.S. based, he was born in Nassau, New Providence Island, Bahamas in 1874, but migrated with his family to Riverside, California, in 1885.[14]

During the 1920s, Trinidadians were in the forefront of black entertainers who moved to the United States from the British West Indies. They were undoubtedly encouraged by the success of Lovey's Trinidad String Band, which had toured the country in 1912, making records in New York City for both the Victor Talking Machine Company and Columbia Phonograph Company. Representatives of the Victor organization visited the island in 1914 to record local music, including calypso. Leading his string band, the pianist Lionel "Lanky" Belasco performed numerous pieces before the recording horn. He also cut four piano solos, and his unissued versions of "The Junk Man"—Rag, by Lucky Roberts, and Scott Joplin's "Maple Leaf Rag" might be the earliest examples on gramophone record of these African American compositions by any pianist.[15] Belasco settled in New York by 1915, and for the next thirty-five years his recording career is associated with virtually all the Trinidad entertainers who made the same migration.

Lionel Belasco is a good example of a black West Indian expatriate who was a "professional." His father was of Sephardic descent and his mother a Barbadian creole. Both were musical, and their son inherited this talent.[16] Born circa October 1887, by the early 1900s Belasco was running a small string band in Trinidad. His 1914 string-band recordings mix dreamy Spanish-American influenced dances with occasional "refined" adaptations of the more down-home music of calypsonians. He was conversant also with the defiant or reflective chants of stickfighters (originating in a drum dance known as *kalenda*). The term "calenda," or "colinda," is known in Louisiana, and derives from dances performed across French- and Spanish-speaking Latin America during the slavery period. At the turn of the century, string bands—such as those run in Mississippi by Sid Hemphill, or the Chatmon family—served a similar function to that of Belasco's in Trinidad, some playing to both elite white audiences as well as rural black people. Belasco's unit, however, was closer in organization and status to Armand Piron's New Orleans Orchestra (which performed at elite venues). Like Piron, he was a reading musician, in contrast with members of Lovey's Trinidad String Band, who played by ear.

Island contemporaries did not replicate Belasco's early achievements—he was recorded annually by Victor from 1914 to 1920, sometimes undertaking several sessions per year, usually with American studio musicians. This lull in recording local Trinidad music may have been a result of the economic circumstances of the First World War. Statistics indicate there was no decrease in the flow of West Indian migrants in this period; indeed, by 1917 they were almost certainly welcomed as extra labor for the American war effort.

MARCUS GARVEY'S UNIVERSAL NEGRO
IMPROVEMENT ASSOCIATION

A year earlier (1916) saw the arrival in the United States of the black Jamaican political leader Marcus Garvey (1887–1940). He was one of a line of African American
people who advocated Pan-Africanism. George Liele (1750–1826) might be considered a precursor,[17] but Edward W. Blyden (born in the Danish West Indies in 1832,
died 1912) was one of the most active in the late nineteenth century—on behalf of
his adopted country, Liberia.[18] In the United States, Bishop Henry M. Turner
(1833–1915), of the African Methodist Episcopal Church, was a similar prototype.[19]
The Trinidadian Henry Sylvester Williams coined the term Pan-Africanism in
London, in 1900, when he held a conference on the subject in which delegates
participated from three continents—Africa, the Americas and Europe.[20]

Garvey's message found fertile ground in the United States, and by 1920 he
had established a mass movement based on his Universal Negro Improvement
Association. This included the formation of a steamship company called the
Black Star Line (incorporated in 1919). The rise of the U.N.I.A. took place at the
same time as the advent of the creative period of black culture in New York City
known as the Harlem Renaissance. With the latter in mind, it is probably no
coincidence that the first popular blues cut by black performers were recorded in
New York at the beginning of this decade.

There were other significant black radicals from the Caribbean in Harlem
who shaped the politics of this period. Some prominent in the cultural milieu
include the Jamaican poet and novelist Claude McKay, P. M H. Savory, a
Guyanese physician and (from 1936) co-publisher of the *Amsterdam News*—the
principal black newspaper in New York—and Herbert (or Hubert) Julian, the
Trinidad-born, accident-prone, parachutist and aviator, who became an official in
the U.N.I.A.[21]

TRINIDADIANS RECORD IN NEW YORK—1921

It was not until 1921, a year in which Belasco did not record, that Trinidad musicians again traveled to New York to cut sides for Victor. Walter Merrick (piano)
accompanied the vaudevillian Johnny Walker, whose songs were associated with
recent Carnivals. Merrick's solos ranged from "Creole" and "Venezuelan" waltzes
to interpretations of "Paseos" (or two-steps). According to Theodore van Dam,

Merrick's rendering of the "Tobago paseo" "Bulldog Don't Bite Me" (Victor 73060) is representative of Jelly Roll Morton's "Spanish Tinge" as well as "early blues and boogie woogie" piano styles. He reports also that Walker's "Go 'Way Gal," the "Trinidad Calypso" on the reverse of this record, has Merrick using "very much the 'rolling bass' effects of early [Jimmy] Yancey, [Jack] Dupree, etc." in his accompaniment.[22] These observations await independent aural verification.

Walter Merrick was born in St. Vincent in 1896, but moved to Trinidad at the age of five. He built a reputation as a performing musician and subsequently took up composition. He obtained a Doctorate in medicine at Howard University in Washington, D.C. and reportedly undertook postgraduate training in London and Edinburgh—the latter city's prestigious medical reputation was of great importance among educated British West Indians in the inter-war period. In pursuit of a medical career, however, Merrick did not forsake all of his musical interests.[23]

Harry Pace, the black American entrepreneur, left the music publishing company he ran with blues composer W. C. Handy and launched Black Swan Records in January 1921. This, the first wholly owned black record company in the United States, is generally considered to be another signal for the nascent Harlem Renaissance.[24] By the middle of the year Ethel Waters and Alberta Hunter were among performers on the company's roster. In October, Black Swan reported sales as far afield as the Philippines and the West Indies.[25] It is not surprising therefore that early in 1922 Lionel Belasco's South American Orchestra (again, probably studio musicians) cut six sides for the company with West Indian and Latin American sales in mind.

CHANGING FORTUNES OF THE U.N.I.A.—1922

1922 was a crucial year in the fortunes of Marcus Garvey and the U.N.I.A. The success of this mass movement had created considerable opposition among some black intellectuals and concern in certain quarters of both the U.S. and British administrations. The Black Star Line had suffered numerous setbacks, owing to financial mismanagement, and eventually this was to lead to Garvey's downfall. The annual U.N.I.A. convention was less successful than in previous years and questions were raised regarding a meeting Garvey attended with Ku Klux Klan officials. Above all, his flirtation with the Klan had "turned some of the most influential West Indian Harlemites" against him. Until then, David Levering Lewis notes, "writers Claude McKay and Eric Walrond, bibliophile Arthur Schomburg, numbers king Casper

Holstein, and [fellow Jamaican, the] Marxist W. A. Domingo had overlooked his excesses because of his tremendous potential for success." On 12 January 1922, Garvey was arrested for mail fraud relating to the failed Black Star Line. Released on bail, he did not appear in court until fifteen months later, legal proceedings against him taking the best part of three years. Tried in May 1923, he was convicted on 18 June, remained in jail until September of the same year but was released pending appeal, which was not heard until February 1925. He lost the appeal and spent two years in prison before being deported from the United States.[26]

COMPOSITION OF "WEST INDIES BLUES"

It is against this backdrop that the black American composers Edgar Dowell, Clarence Williams and Spencer Williams wrote their "West Indies Blues." Born in Louisiana, the publisher of this sheet music, Clarence Williams, was a jazz and blues musician who composed and recorded prolifically. Between 1923 and 1928 he was employed as "race-record judge" for the black record catalogue of the General Phonograph Corporation, which traded under the name of OKeh. Although Clarence Williams Music Publishing submitted "West Indies Blues" to the Library of Congress Copyright Office in December 1922, and it was registered on the six-teenth of that month,[27] the song was not recorded until a year later. Such a time lapse is unusual and presumably occurred because of legal sensitivities dictated by Garvey's arrest, trial, conviction, imprisonment, and release (pending appeal).

EXPANSION OF "WEST INDIAN" RECORDING ACTIVITIES—1923

The Victor Talking Machine Company briefly experimented with "Race" records in 1923. It also decided to expand its line of English-speaking West Indian recordings. Sessions were held with a string band led by the talented violinist Cyril Monrose and vocals recorded by a popular Guyanese comedian Phil Madison, with Lionel Belasco supporting on piano. In addition to sales in the Caribbean, the company had recognized the scope for commercial advantage in the United States. A contemporary supplement spells out their reasoning:

The steady increase of the West Indian population along the eastern seaports of the United States has stimulated the interest for West Indian records

issued by the Victor Company. Phil Madison, one of the favorite singers in
the West Indies, is giving a few numbers to the accompaniment of the piano
and ukulele and the Monrose's Orchestra appears with instrumental
selections which are sure to be welcomed by West Indians in this country.

Complementing this up-to-date repertoire (including pieces from the most
recent Trinidad Carnival), Victor advertised items from their back catalogue—
ranging from 1912 recordings by Lovey, to efforts by Walter Merrick made in
1921, plus many sides by Lionel Belasco's Orchestra.

RECORDINGS OF "WEST INDIES BLUES"—1923–24

Following Garvey's conviction, incarceration, and release on notice of appeal, the
initial version of the Dowell, Williams and Williams composition "West Indies
Blues" was cut on 14 December 1923. Intended for purchase by black Americans,
the song was issued in General Phonograph's "Race" series (OKeh 8118). A New
Orleans speciality, accompanied by the Orchestra of Armand J. Piron (in New
York for an engagement), it was sung by Esther Bigeou, a Crescent City vocalist
who toured the vaudeville circuit. A flow of instrumental and vocal versions of
the composition ensued throughout the year, giving some indication of the success
of Garvey's message on the black population and determination by his African
American opponents to minimize the effect of the U.N.I.A. Indeed, during
1922–23, the *Messenger*, a black radical journal from Harlem, ran a "Garvey Must
Go Campaign" with which the circulation of "West Indies Blues" might be associated indirectly.[28] Not strictly a blues, but a blues-based song in "hokum" tempo,
the lyrics of the published version of "West Indies Blues" have been interpreted
by Ira De A. Reid, who points out "how visibility through sheer numbers [of
migrants] leads to ridicule and jest." He notes that "the words" were "written in
the parlance of the Jamaican immigrant [to] indicate the nature of this visibility:

"West Indies Blues"

1. Got my grip and trunk all packed,
Steamship, I'm gwine to take her,
So good-bye old New York Town,
I'se gwine to Jamaica,

When I git on de odder side,
I'll hang aroun' de waters,
I'll make my livin' sure's you born,
A-divin' after quarters.

(chorus) Gwine home, won't be long,
Gwine home, sure's you born,
I'm gwine home, won't be long 'cause I got no time to lose,
Gwine home, I can't wait, gwine home,
Mon, I'm late, I'm gwine home,
I can't wait, 'cause I've got the West Indies Blues,
Got the West Indies Blues, got the West Indies Blues.

2. Done give up the bestes' job,
A runnin' elevator,
I told my boss "Mon" I'd be back,
Sometime sooner or later,
When I get back to dis great land,
You better watch me Harvey,
'Cause 'm gonna be a great big "Mon,"
Like my frien' Marcus Garvey.'[29]

Subtitled "A Calipso" in the sheet music version and a recorded rendition by
Viola McCoy (Vocalion 14801), the six vocal recordings of this song made in
1924 incorporate these standard lyrics, sometimes with chorus variation. Five of
the renderings were performed by vaudeville blues women, with careers founded
in touring theater shows, and each was issued in the "Race" market. McCoy,
however, incorporates an extra verse:

3. I eat my nice big shrimp pelau,
There's nothing dat is better
Just like they have in Barbados,
With plenty salt and pepper.
When I get back there on de dock,
The Queen I will not face her,
'Cause all the people on this side,
They call me the monkey chaser.

(A "monkey chaser" is an African American nickname for a West Indian)

Ukulele Bob Williams cut the most distinctive variant of "West Indies Blues" (Paramount 12247). This also features lyrics that add to the more generalized insults:

3. When I get on de odder side,
If the Queen I have to face her,
Tell her, I don't like it over here,
'Cause they call me the monkey chaser,
I can stay up the whole night through,
I don't cease [for slumber]
I would try to figure out,
How to catch the policy number.

4. Came over here on a banana ship,
I thought that was fine,
I've got plenty of money now,
Goin' back on the Black Star Line,
If I die, don't want no one,
To call that undertaker,
Throw my body in the deep blue sea,
I'd float back to Jamaica.

Ira Reid confirms that there were endless verses to the song, many being parodies depicting the "habits, customs and institutions of the foreign-born Negro:

1. When I get on the other side,
I'll buy myself a Lizzie,
Climb up in a coconut tree,
And knock those monkeys dizzy.

2. Garvey, Garvey is a big man,
To take his folks to Monkey-land,
If he does that, I'm sure I can,
Stay right here with Uncle Sam.

3. When you eat split peas and rice,
You think you eatin' somethin',

But man you ain't taste nothin' yet,
'Till you eat monkey hips and dumplin'.

4. When a monkey-chaser dies,
Don't need no undertaker,
Just throw him in the Harlem River,
He'll float back to Jamaica.

5. When I get on the other side,
I'll buy myself a mango,
Grab myself a monkey gal,
And do the monkey tango."

As can be seen, some of these sentiments relate directly to the additional verses recorded by McCoy and Williams. Garveyism and Jamaica are the focal points for these jibes.[30] The melody of "West Indies Blues," however, appears to be based on a traditional U.S. motif used later for a number of hokum and medicine show pieces recorded by black North American performers, such as the influential 1928 recording "Beedle Um Bum" by The Hokum Boys (Paramount 12714).[31] While antipathy towards Garvey is a most likely interpretation of the lyrics, the direct impact on West Indian migrants is less certain. Some evidence comes from the research of Ted Vincent, who believes the original intention of the lyrics was not derisory. He reports that the band of the U.N.I.A. played "West Indies Blues" in front of Liberty Hall (the organization's headquarters) in August of 1924. While this suggests approval, he notes that, by May of the following year, the Lafayette Theater in Harlem placed a newspaper announcement "asking that patrons refrain from making requests for numbers which 'might express sarcasm towards people from the islands, such as "West Indian Blues".'"[32] Undoubtedly, the common element of the English language is of greater significance in interaction between black people from the United States and their Caribbean counterparts. More concrete, in the words of the song, is the reflection on tensions resulting from mass migration—a maximum of 12,234 people from English-speaking islands sought a new life in the United States during 1924. This was the peak year for British West Indian emigration in the pre-1941 period; presumably because of fear of exclusion on the adoption of the U.S. National Origins Act (which formalized quotas for the first time).[33]

OTHER "RACE" RECORDINGS WITH A SIMILAR THEME—1924

The success of "West Indies Blues" led to a spate of similar compositions in 1924. One was "Black Star Line" by Edgar Dowell and Spencer Williams; subtitled "A West Indian Chant," this was registered for copyright on 26 April. Dowell wrote "Barbado[e]s Blues" with Clarence Williams (registered 18 June). The lyrics to "My Jamaica" (registered 29 May) were written by the black-American composer, vocalist and pianist Porter Grainger, and the melody by S. Monrose (on circumstantial evidence, the Trinidad violin player Cyril Monrose).[34] Each song was recorded for the "Race" catalogs of various gramophone companies; Hazel Meyers being the first woman vaudeville singer to record "Black Star Line" (for Pathé Actuelle: 032053), circa 19 May. The next day, Rosa Henderson cut a version, together with "Barbadoes Blues," for which Dowell provided the piano accompaniment—they were coupled on Vocalion 14825.[35] Henderson's "Black Star Line" was more complete lyrically than that performed by Meyers. As with "West Indies Blues," the words poke fun at Garvey, concentrating on the failed shipping enterprise that brought about his downfall, but which he was endeavoring to revive as the Black Cross Trading & Navigation Company:

"Black Star Line (A West Indian Chant)"

1. Brothers and sisters, country man, you'd better get on board,
Big steamship gwine to sail away, Lord, with a heavy load,
It's gwine to take us all back home, yes every native style
And when we get there what a time, down on West Indies isle.

(chorus) Get on board, country man,
I say, get on board, leave this land,
A-get on board, country man,
Gwine back on de Black Star Line.

2. Take my Bowie knife in hand and lay around de dock,
Jump right in the deep blue sea, pick fights with the sharks,
I'm gwine see Brother Abraham, go catch that "Sly Mongoose,"
I'm going to see my downtown gal, and then we'll raise the deuce.

3. We'll eat monkey hips and rice, tomato, garlic too
Then we'll grab our favorite sport, child, chasing monkey, too,

I done put my lastest dime down on dis great steamship,
Lord, I hope that it won't sink, I wanna take this trip.

A line in the second verse mocks two well-known West Indian songs of the
period. Originating in Barbados, probably during the first ten years of the century, "Buddy Abraham" [rather than "Brother"] had been recorded by the "Banda
Belasco, Trinidad" in 1914. This was not released, although the company issued
Belasco's solo piano rendition made the next year (Victor 67672). He cut a piano
roll (QRS 2657) and registered the tune for copyright in 1924 (attesting to its continuing popularity).[36] Dating probably from the late 1910s, "Sly Mongoose"
reached Trinidad from Jamaica by 1923, and was a Carnival hit that year, also being
recorded respectively by Cyril Monrose and Phil Madison for Victor. Belasco
registered this tune for copyright (December 1923) and the following March cut
a piano roll of the piece (QRS 2544).[37] References in "Black Star Line" to these two
songs, together with derogatory comments regarding "monkey chasers," exem-
plify antagonism between elements in black North American and migrant
groups. The description "country man" is an allusion to Garvey's followers and
his avowed intention of organizing the repatriation of black people to their place
of origin, Africa.

"Barbadoes Blues" takes a different slant on the position of the migrant,
reflecting on homesickness, but also hinting at "primitive" West Indian attitudes
that had no place in the sophisticated streets of black New York:

"Barbadoes Blues"

1. *I tired livin' in this country, oh mon, ain't that no joke?*
The people all act crazy, everywhere you go,
I'm going to a land, where the mammee apples* grow—mm,
Where I can go barefooted,
And they don't have no ice and snow.

2. *I'm gwine back to Barbados, to the shore, to the shore,*
To that place that I'll never, leave no more, leave no more,
Where little monkeys play up in the trees,
All you need to wear is BVDs,
Rain or shine, all the time,
The coconut juice tastes just like wine.

3. I'm gwine back to Barbados, there I'll stay, there I'll stay,
No one there to backbite poor me, I'll soon be free,
I'm gonna fill my rice with salt and pepper,
Tell you, mon, it sure tastes better,
I'm gwine back to Barbados, 'cause I got the Barbados blues.
(speech)
Roll 'em boys, roll 'em, roll 'em.
Play them Barbados blues, boys, play 'em, play 'em.

* mammee apple: mammea americana (Guttiferae)

Columbia Records decided to feature versions of "Black Star Line" and "My Jamaica" in their "Race" catalog when on 3 June they recorded George and Roscoe (George Gray and Roscoe Wilkham) singing to the accompaniment of a ukulele. This instrument (or the banjo) featured in several of these performances (for example, Clara Smith's version of "West Indies Blues"—Columbia 14019–D, made on 17 April), suggesting a deliberate effect on the part of record producers. The Grainger and Monrose composition was subtitled "A West Indian Song" on release (Columbia 14024–D), and its lyrics continue with the derogatory theme of its predecessors:

"My Jamaica (A West Indian Song)"

1. There's a place I wanna go,
Where there ain't no ice and snow,
Where the summer wind him blow,
And the sugar cane she grow,
'Cause the money ain't so much,
But the rent be not so high,
There I can wear my silk [prize] shorts,
Play the cricket 'til I die,

(chorus) *I love my Jamaica,*
I just can't forsake her,
My poor heart I'll break her,
If I don't go where the coconuts grow, there,
There ain't no use in talking,
I'm so tired New Yorking,

Going to that West Indies home,
In my Jamaica.

2. Where the sun he never sets,
On the flag she always flies,
'Tis a British flag you bet,
I trying to love her 'til I die,
Going to have a jolly time,
Simply let myself a-loose,
When I am in this good old land,
I'll be [watch for] Sly Mongoose,

(chorus) It's in my Jamaica,
My ship she will make-a,
'Cause she will ride the breakers,
Sailing on down to where she bound to,
My good old Jamaica,
And don't you muck-rake her,
Down beneath our noble King,
Of my Jamaica.

The words imply that intended purchasers for this record were West Indian, or those that knew something of their culture: mention of cricket, the empire "where the sun never sets," and the British monarch and flag were specialist topics, unlikely to have had much appeal in the South!

LAUNCH OF OKEH'S WEST INDIAN SERIES—1924

At the same time George and Roscoe were cutting their sides, the General Phonograph Corporation made plans to enter the market for West Indian recordings in both the United States and the English-speaking Caribbean. Almost certainly, this was a further consequence of the peak in migration, probable success of similar recordings issued by the Victor Company, and contemporary popularity of West Indian themes in "Race" catalogs. Commencing 18 July, they held three sessions to inaugurate a special series, the first release of which was OKeh 65001 by Slim Henderson. Cut on 30 July, his recordings comprised

another version of "My Jamaica," coupled with "Goofer Dust John," on the
theme of a feared obeah man in Trinidad. The latter was a further "S." Monrose
composition registered for copyright on 29 May (on this occasion with words by
Harvey Hogbin). Accompaniment was by the Fred Hall Orchestra, a standard
white musical unit of the period. It is suggested that Slim Henderson is the
black-American vaudevillian who was married to Rosa Henderson.[38] His version
of "My Jamaica" is virtually the same as that performed by George and Roscoe.
With a West Indian audience in mind, Slim Henderson's two sides emphasize
differences within the migrant English-speaking Caribbean community. "My
Jamaica" disparages the nostalgic sentiments of "small-island" and "small-time"
Jamaicans (in the eyes of the lyricist), while "Goofer Dust John" is altogether
more ominous in its message. It describes how easily the sophisticated "unbe-
liever" will be "fixed" by the power of "old John's" evil magic from miles away in
the Trinidad countryside. Unintentionally, in its portrayal, this established sym-
bolically the more "powerful" position and involvement of Trinidad performers
in the New York record business during this period.[39]

SAM MANNING

The other singer featured in the new OKeh series was Sam Manning, whose
career was to influence recordings of music from the English-speaking West
Indies in the Caribbean, United States, and Britain for the next 35 years. Like
Lionel Belasco and Walter Merrick, Manning almost certainly came from the
black "professional" strata. Born in Couva, Trinidad in either 1898 or 1899, after
schooling he became a jockey and then a chauffeur and motor mechanic, working for a period in British Guyana. At the advent of the First World War he
joined the Middlesex Regiment in England, and was transferred to the British
West Indies Regiment, seeing service in France, Egypt and Palestine. During this
period he took up "concert party work under the Colours." It was this experience in entertainment that led to his stage career, commencing with a minstrel
show tour of Britain following demobilisation and vaudeville engagements in
Trinidad and other West Indian islands.

In the early 1920s, he gravitated to the United States. Settling in New York
City, with difficulty he persuaded the proprietor of a Brooklyn theater to rent
him the premises and proceeded to stage a vaudeville program based on his
Caribbean expertise. Filling the theater with expatriates, who had been aware of

his talents in the West Indies, this successful engagement secured his reputation as an actor and vaudeville specialist. His first Broadway appearance was in 1925 playing Rastus in John Howard Lawson's Theater Guild production *Processional*. The latter, subtitled "a jazz symphony of American life," was an early radical play depicting a strike in West Virginia coal fields.[40]

Manning's two sessions for OKeh in July 1924 set the scene for his recordings during the next ten years; they are a mix of traditional West Indian themes, and songs reflecting on the life of the newly arrived migrant in the U.S.A. Accompaniment by Palmer's Orchestra was in the style of an old-time Trinidad string band. As Steve Shapiro reports, "Susan Monkey Walk" (from Manning's first session, 18 July) "mocks West Indian immigrants being taken in by their own Americanization, but allows for a healthy look at being caught up in faddishness."[41]

"Susan Monkey Walk"

1. There's a girl up Harlem has 'em wild, with her new brand style,
She comes from somewhere down West Indian isle,
Most everybody on the Avenue just crazy to do,
Little Susan's funny "monkey walk."

2. Have you seen Susan "monkey walk?"
Oh, the whole town talk is that "monkey walk,"
Oh, she got 'em beat with her monkey feet,
Her monkey style is what got 'em wild,
Her monkey hips and her monkey dips.

3. Seems to me I know that child, from down West Indian isle,
Her mother, father, bredder, sister too,
But now that she's a Harlem star, she pass by in her car,
And never even say "How-de-do."

4. Have you seen Susan "monkey walk?"
Oh, the whole town talk, that "monkey walk,"
Oh, Susan foot like puss in boots,
But she got 'em beat with her monkey feet,
Her monkey style is what's got 'em wild.

"Amba Cay La' (Under the House)," with which this was coupled, was a Trinidad Carnival piece, sung part in French Creole and part in English (OKeh 65003). For the second session (9 July) there was more of the same: "My Little West Indian Girl" depicts a male grieving for the girl he has mistreated who has gone back to the islands. "Baby" describes the unfortunate changes wrought on a young girl following her first sexual encounter (OKeh 65002).

Accompanied by Fred Hall's Orchestra, the following month Manning was involved in a session for the New York Recording Laboratories' Paramount "Race" series, which featured two significant songs (Paramount 12229). Grace Taylor performed "Sweet Willie," a lyric that Manning revised and recorded several times, later describing it as "a typical St. Lucian beguine."[42] His own "African Blues," however, is firmly in the mold of the other blues-based songs devoted to Garveyism that year: identifying "country man" followers of the U.N.I.A. as romantic idealists, but also emphasizing migrant nostalgia for "home"—whether in the Caribbean or Africa. Not one of Manning's most successful recordings, its intended market was presumably North America, although no evidence is to hand for the export of Paramount's "Race" series.

"African Blues"

1. I was born 'way down in West Indies,
And my dear old mammy taught me,
To love the fields of corn,
Where I was born,
But of late I've got a teaching,
That has set my heart a-yearning
For a land far away across the sea.

2. Country-man, gee! I've got those Africa blues,
Oh, country-man, it's the blues that I can't refuse,
They say the sunny skies just harmonize,
With my ebony skin and my coal-black eyes,
Country-man, true, I've got those Africa blues.

3. Country-man don't try to stop me,
Country-man don't try to block me,
Let me go, where there ain't no ice and there ain't no snow,
When you—when you miss my familiar face I'm gone,

To the land where I belong,
Africa, that land of the blazing sun.

4. Country-man, gee! I've got those Africa blues,
Country-man, it's the blues that I can't refuse,
They say the sunny skies just harmonize,
With my ebony skin and my coal-black eyes,
Country-man, true, I've got those Africa blues.

5. Oh, country-man, get your bundle and come with me,
Country-man, to that land far across the sea,
Ain't no time to be flirtin' around,
Ain't no time to be sheiking the town,
Country-man, gee! I've got those Africa blues.

Along with previous examples from this selection of "compositions," by October each piece had been registered for copyright, submitted by either Manning (sometimes with an associate) or "S." Monrose.[43]

While "African Blues" is probably the first to establish continental repatriation as an objective for some West Indians (note there is no direct reference to black North Americans), its message cannot be said to be wholly positive. Indeed, the ambivalence may have been intentional, so as to appeal to the widest possible audience. Africa is portrayed as utopia in relation to North America and the West Indies, but the "ebony skin and coal black eyes" of the lyricist have a whiff of minstrelsy and the vaudeville portrayal of black people that became the norm among whites in blackface during the nineteenth century. Sam Manning was a master at maximizing the effect of such portrayals, which were also adapted by black entertainers in the Americas, following the U.S. Civil War.

Research in the *Negro World*, the U.N.I.A.'s weekly newspaper, adds a few details regarding Manning's relationship to Garvey's organization. A "Monster Benefit" in aid of the U.N.I.A. was held at Liberty Hall, New York, 16 December 1924. Staged by Manning and Porter Grainger, they also co-composed the song "Back Home on 'The Booker T. Washington'" (about one of the Black Star Line ships) that was featured in the program.[44] Ted Vincent reports that the show included a performance by the black vaudevillian Lena Wilson. Subsequently, he indicates, there was an "Ethiopian Barn Dance" at the same location with "American and West Indian blues," and Manning and Grainger seem to have involved Lionel Belasco in efforts to organize a "club" to recruit artists to play there.[45]

From his earliest recordings, it is evident Sam Manning is significant in the evolution of black music from the West Indies in the United States simply in the light of his repertoire. There was, however, much more to Manning's role than this. His music appealed to U.S. audiences as well as West Indians, as witnessed by the appearance of a number of his records in U.S. "Race" catalogs. In addition, unlike most of his British Caribbean contemporaries who recorded regional music, he was not bound by Trinidad norms, adopting and interpreting songs from other islands, in particular Jamaica.

All these facts indicate that Manning became accepted very quickly by members of the Tin Pan Alley musical hierarchy in New York, both with black and white Americans (who ultimately held the purse strings). A succession of almost 40 recordings for OKeh, Paramount, Columbia and Brunswick between 1924 and 1928 attest to this recognition, as do reports of his capacity as a stage entertainer. Thus Roi Ottley writes, "Sam 'Squashie' Manning, a West Indian comedian achieved considerable popularity on the Harlem stages with his comic distortions of the immigrant Negro."[46]

OKEH'S WEST INDIAN SERIES—1925

OKeh continued with its West Indian series throughout 1925, with three sessions by Sam Manning, and one by Monrose's String Band. On two of his recording dates, the Cole Jazz Trio, or Cole Mentor Orchestra, accompanied Manning. "Mentor" identifies a particular Jamaican dance. In 1910 this was defined "as the 'shay shay' . . . or *mento*," performance of which was "invariably accompanied by words" and ". . . at the height of its popularity [each lyric was] sung and whistled all over the island" with "the air [being] played at every 'practice dance.' "[47] The Trinidad reed player Rupert Cole, who arrived in New York City in 1924, might be the bandleader here. His later playing style, however, does not bear aural comparison with either the clarinet or saxophone on these early sides, suggesting another West Indian musician with the same surname may have been active in the metropolis during this period. Among other bands, Rupert Cole worked with Lucky Millinder's Orchestra in the 1950s.[48] Coincidentally, Walter Merrick appears to have migrated to the U.S.A. in 1925, as did his compatriot Joe Willoughby (another Trinidadian).[49] The latter is possibly the vocalist Lyle Willoughby who recorded with Merrick for Victor in that year, and perhaps the Lyle Lorieo who sang with the Monrose unit for OKeh—Merrick is credited as "composer" on the labels for both sides of this record (OKeh 65006).

Only Manning's repertoire is of direct concern at this point. His first OKeh session in 1925—29 June—was with the Cole Jazz Trio (clarinet or saxophone, guitar and cuatro—a small ukulele-like guitar of Venezuelan origin). This comprises versions of traditional West Indian pieces (65004, 65005). A second session in August, however, included "Englerston Blues," with a composer credit to the "Englerstone Quartette" (OKeh 65007). Accompanied by alto saxophone, guitar and ukulele (according to the label), this is another homily on the Garvey movement and incorporates sentiments from the lyrics to previous songs on the subject. The theme appears to be devoted to a mythical utopia, although Englerston itself is the name of a recently constructed residential quarter to the south of Nassau, New Providence Island in the Bahamas. The settlement of "neat little cottages" had been built "through the enterprise of a citizen of Florida" named "Englerston":[50]

"Englerston Blues"

1. There's a steamboat leaving out today,
For good old [Meto] island,
I'm goin' there to stay for good,
And build me a home it's understood,

(Chorus) I'm goin' home, and it wouldn't be long
Goin' home, as sure's you born,
Goin' home, I can't wait,
'Cause I got that Englerston Blues, Lordy Lord,
I got that Englerston Blues.

2. When I get to Englerston,
Get me a horse and carriage,
Then I'll get me an Englerston gal,
And do that thing called marriage.

3. When I get to Englerston,
You'd better watch me Harvey,
I'm gonna be a great big "Man,"
Like my friend Marcus Garvey.

(chorus)

4. When I settle in Englerston,
I'll get myself a mango,
I'll grab myself an Englerston gal,
And do that shimmy shango,

5. While I live in Englerston,
I'll hang around the waters,
Make my livin' sure as was born,
Divin' after quarters.

(chorus)

6. Now when I get back over there,
I'll write you all about it,
I'll tell you folks about Englerston,
And you can't do without it.

7. Now I was born in old Jamaica,
In a place they call Kingston,
But I'm going to write my people home,
They must come over to Englerston.

(chorus)

8. I've been all over the United States,
Even been to China,
But the best place I have ever been,
Is Englerston of the island.

9. So goodbye all you northern folk,
I'm goin' back to the islands,
I'll make my home in Englerston,
Instead of courtin' asylum.

(chorus)

With the adoption of lines and other elements from "West Indies Blues," the underlying message of the text remains ambivalent towards those who believed that resettlement was the solution to all their problems. This, however, was mitigated by Manning's sympathetic delivery and is one possible reason for his broad-based popularity—having the capacity to appeal to the sentiments of pro- and anti-Garvey audiences, amongst others. The lyrics to the coupling for OKeh 65007, "Home's Delight," mention a "Captain Engler" who might be synonymous with Englerston the benefactor. This piece plays on nostalgia for West Indian food (rice) in contrast with grits from the United States.

SAM MANNING RECORDS FOR COLUMBIA—1925

On 21 September, Manning cut his first session for the Columbia Phonograph Company. Four sides were recorded and released in Columbia's export series—two were Trinidad calypsos but, significantly, one coupling was also issued in the domestic "Race" series: "Let Go My Hand" and "Bungo" (Columbia 14110–D). The former was Manning's first collaboration on record with Porter Grainger, and concerns relations between a male West Indian migrant and a North American girl. Manning is endeavoring to resist the temptation of "Dinah Lee," a black woman of North American parentage. He favors his "sweet West Indian girl," although (verse five) he also retains slight suspicions about the latter.

"Let Go My Hand"

1. Now listen Miss Dinah Lee
Please keep away from me,
I got myself a sweet West Indian girl.

2. She has promised to marry me,
Take me down to the West Indies,
Keep away, Dinah Lee, keep away.

3. Let go my hand, Dinah Lee,
Please let go my hand,
Done got myself this sweet West Indian girl.

4. I've made up my mind to go,
Down where the coconuts grow,
Let go, Dinah Lee, please let go.

5. I know we're gonna be happy, as happy can be,
If she don't make a monkey of me,
Let go, Dinah Lee, please let go.

6. (repeats 3)

7. She come from the land of the calalu,
The goofer dust, and the cascadu,
Let go, Dinah Lee, please let go.

8. Come like [a lion] from the [monkey meat],
Just as gentle and just as sweet,
Let go, Dinah Lee, please let go.

The other side of this record, "Bungo," is a West Indian dance piece. Accompaniment by the Cole Jazz Orchestra is closer idiomatically to black North American jazz and probably it was this, plus the standpoint of the lyrics to "Let Go My Hand," that persuaded Columbia to widen the market for these two recordings.

The third OKeh session was held circa 30 December and concentrated on West Indian repertoire. "Barbadoes Blues," devoted to nostalgia for a particular Caribbean island, however, was another in the mold of popular blues-based songs (OKeh 65009), and a more sympathetic treatment than Edgar Dowell's earlier composition with the same title.

MANNING'S FIRST RELEASES IN THE OKEH "RACE" SERIES—1926

Manning's popularity with black American audiences almost certainly led to his next OKeh release being allocated to their U.S. "Race" series. Recorded in February 1926, this comprises two songs with local appeal, accompanied by his Blue Hot Syncopators. In accordance with OKeh's marketing strategy, the "jazz" element in the backing is particularly pronounced. The lyrics to both songs are North American oriented. "Go I've Got Somebody Sweeter than You" is standard fare, but "Keep Your Hands Off That" has a Harlem theme depicting popular recreations, as well as male-female relations:

"Keep Your Hands Off That"

1. In Harlem's colored section,
[Now] the browns of all complexion,
There's a saying "keep your hands off that,"
In a parlor social, in a cabaret,
It's "keep your hands off that,"

2. Every woman has got that slogan,
"Keep your hands off that,"
It's too bad how she'll get you mad,
Well "keep your hands off that,"
Gee, I'll do the Charleston, the Pigeon Wing,
But it's "keep your hands off that,"
Even Black Bottom, Shake That Thing,
But it's "keep your [hands] off that."

3. Say, how she'll hold you, hug you and squeeze you,
But it's "keep your hands off that,"
She'll call you honey, make you spend your money,
But it's "keep your hands off that,"
And she'll look so temptin' dressed up in satin,
But it's "keep your hands off that,"
And it's aggravatin' when she starts to shakin',
But it's "keep your hands off that."

4. When you take her home, you'll find she don't live alone,
But it's "keep your hands off that,"
You'll hear her laughter, you know you are a sucker,
But it's "keep your hands off that."

Manning cut another session for Columbia's export series on 27 May. Two of the sides were instrumentals and described as "Mentors" on the record labels, although "Hold Him Joe (My Donkey Want Water)" adapted the melody of a

Jamaican "Digging Sing" or work song (Columbia 2409–X).[51] "Oh Emily!," the
sung performances on the reverse of this record, was designated a "Trinidad
Carnival" piece, but "Jamaica Blues" (Columbia 2410–X) is another in the
familiar idiom of nostalgic blues-based songs. This was co-composed with
the Jamaican pianist and bandleader Adolph Thenstead (with assistance
from Spencer Williams, when the song was registered for copyright in
December).[52] The lyrics yet again describe a "country man" tired of "New
Yorking," longing for his island home. The homesick Jamaican also has "the
sweetest Bajan gal," emphasizing the position of both Barbados and Jamaica in
the popular imagination as important points of departure for British West
Indian migrants.

THE IDENTITY OF THE "KING" OF THE ZULUS?

Distinctive differences between black people from the Caribbean and those born
in the United States are the subject of an interjection written into the performance of "The King of the Zulus (At a Chit' Lin' Rag)," recorded by Louis
Armstrong's Hot Five in Chicago, Illinois on 23 June (OKeh 8396). With the
line up of Louis (cornet), Kid Ory (trombone), Johnny Dodds (clarinet),
Johnny St. Cyr (banjo) and Lil Armstrong (piano), this New Orleans oriented
group was at the height of its considerable powers. Although a non-Crescent
City musician received credit as composer—Louis's wife, Lillian Hardin(g)
(Armstrong)—the theme is devoted to the activities of a New Orleans *Mardi
Gras* masquerade band. The Zulu Aid and Pleasure Club had been participating
in *Mardi Gras* since at least 1916, and almost certainly before. Like similar organizations involved in Carnival in Trinidad, the association also acted as a mutual
aid society and held balls and other events to raise funds for these purposes.[53]
King Oliver and his Creole Jazz Band's "Zulus Ball," made in 1923 (Gennett
5275), was the first recording by New Orleans musicians devoted to these functions, but this was purely an instrumental. The interpolation in the Hot Five's
"King of the Zulus" brings into play a stereotype of the Jamaican seen to have
been current in the lyrics of several compositions recorded in North America in
this period. A representation of a Jamaican migrant or perhaps a member of a
ship's crew, (personated by "Clarence Babcock") suddenly arrives at the
Chitterling Rag—held supposedly in a black quarter of New Orleans. His inter-
ruption appears to reinforce perceptions of Jamaican migrants as uncouth, and

believers in the "back to Africa" movement, but also seeking the approval of their black peers in North America:

"The King of the Zulus (At a Chit' Lin' Rag)"

U.S. (band) [instrumental, featuring trombone, with accompaniment]
J. (C.B.) *Wait man, wait, stop, stop, wait!*
U.S. (Lo A.) *What's the matter?—Eh, what you mean by interrupting my solo?*
J. (C.B.) *Man, it 'cause I from Jamaica and I don't mean to
interrupt your party, but one of me "country man" tell me there's a chitterlin'
rag going on here. Madam, fix me one order of those things you call chitterlin'
but I call 'em inner tube, and I play one of me native jazz tune.*
U.S. (Li A.) *Twenty cents-hot for my chitterlin'.*
U.S. (band) [instrumental, featuring cornet and banjo, with accompaniment]
J. (C.B.) *Do you like it, man?*

(Key: U.S.: idiomatic performance by Black person(s) from the United States
J.: representation of a Black person from Jamaica)

This is a highly charged but also enigmatic performance. The vaudeville exchange could be construed to be anti-Jamaican, especially with regard to Garvey and his "country man" followers. The patter, however, is succeeded by one of the most emotional cornet solos ever recorded by Louis Armstrong and at the end the "Jamaican's" request for endorsement gives particular authority to Armstrong's interpretation. The implication of the title, that it represents a performance at a fund raising dance (a chit'lin' rag) held by the preeminent black *Mardi Gras* organization in New Orleans, begs the question as to the identity of the "King of the Zulus." He might be the annually elected symbolic leader of the masquerade band (a position held by Armstrong in 1949) but, conversely, he could be the Jamaican. In both instances, these personalities can be interpreted as representative of the African origin of black Americans and this may be the deeper and emotional significance of the presentation by the Hot Five.

The success of the Armstrong performance can be measured by two cover versions recorded by OKeh's competitors. On 22 October, the Dixie Washboard Band—a Clarence Williams group—recorded "King of the Zulus" for Columbia in New York. The rendering follows the same pattern, although the interjections are far less slick and slightly different. The Jamaican impersonation (said to be by Clarence Todd) is belabored, neither does the speaker seek approval at the end of the performance. Coupled with "The Zulu Blues," a trite song about the *Mardi Gras* band, from the same session, this release might have been aimed at black tourists visiting New Orleans for the Carnival, although the quality of the performances makes this conjecture unlikely (Columbia 14171–D).

Eleven days later (2 November), a New York group led by Thomas Morris, but "masquerading" as the New Orleans Blue Five, cut "The King of the Zulus" for Victor (20316). The same format was used. Again, there is slight variation in the spoken asides and the quest for salutation at the end is omitted.

In addition to being important pointers to the significance of New Orleans Carnival in the history of jazz (and Crescent City blues), these recordings also reflect a continuing ambivalence in this period by some black Americans towards Jamaicans, whether transients or migrants. For example, the proximity of West Indian settlers seems a likely reason for the two New York renderings of "King of the Zulus" placing much greater emphasis on negative stereotypes.

MANNING APPEARS IN HARLEM MUSICALS—1926–27

On 2 October, one month before the session by the New Orleans Blue Five, Buddy Christian, the guitarist with the group, had registered "Charleston Hop" for copyright; this was a joint composition with Sam Manning. Christian was a long-time musical associate of Clarence Williams, whose publishing company handled the proceedings. Coincidentally, just one week after the Thomas Morris unit cut their cover of "The King of the Zulus," the Lafayette Theater in Harlem staged the first night of *Hey Hey*, a musical in which Manning starred. This successful show received mixed press reaction;[54] it also has some notoriety in that it was used to break a strike at the theater by black projectionists.[55] Produced by Amy Ashwood Garvey—the separated first wife of Marcus Garvey—the presentation went on tour at the time she began a suit for divorce against her husband.[56] Thus, by the time the production reached Pittsburgh, with a slightly different cast, but Manning still one of the leading lights, the plot had been altered to a parody of the "rise and fall of Marcus Garvey."[57] This and Manning's alliance with Amy Ashwood confirms Manning's disassociation with Garvey's organization. By January the show was in Chicago.[58] A booking at the Royal Theater Baltimore in May, however, was cancelled at the last minute, leaving

Manning and Amy Ashwood filing suit against the proprietors.[59] Manning remained one of Ashwood's closest allies until his death, while engaged on a joint project, in Ghana circa 1961.[60]

General acclaim in Harlem vaudeville theaters was probably one reason for Sam Manning's next session being released in the OKeh U.S. "Race" series. Recorded on 23 June 1927, the repertoire, however, was Caribbean. There were remakes of three sides cut previously for Columbia—the dance piece "Bongo," and two calypsos, "Lignum Vitae," and "Emily" (in this version, Gwendolyn is identified as a "Bajan girl") and another dance melody, "Pepper Pot." The accompaniment was by Adolph Thenstead's Mentor Boys, the leader being the pianist from Jamaica. A little more than a month later, on 1 August, Lionel Belasco organized the first session by the Trinidad calypsonian Wilmoth Houdini, whom he had brought to New York to record for Victor. This further expanded the export market for British Caribbean repertoire, but had no immediate impact in Harlem. On 15 August, however, to great acclaim, Amy Ashwood Garvey and Sam Manning launched their new show *Brown Sugar* at the Lafayette Theater. Porter Grainger collaborated with Manning on the music and, according to a pre-show advertisement, Fats Waller & His Harlem Serenaders provided musical accompaniment (Waller was house organist at the Lafayette in this period).[61] In a preview of the show, the *New York Amsterdam News* noted Manning was developing "a new character which will be brimful of fun, in that this new departure will show him as an educated colored British West Indian, 'Sir Quashie,' the latter knighted by the King of England and with all the earmarks with which so many are familiar."[62] Undoubtedly this is the origin of Manning's "Mr. Squash," or "Squashie" comedy character for which he became famous. The name "Quashie" has its roots in Africa. A later Amy Ashwood Garvey and Sam Manning presentation, *Black Magic*, was advertised in the *New York Amsterdam News* for "One Week beginning November 21" at the Lafayette Theater. This production starred Manning and Mercay Marquiz, with Anna Freeman, Doe Doe Green, Anabella McGerry, Duckett and Conway and a Beauty Chorus.[63]

PARLOR SOCIALS OR "RENT PARTIES"

Musical extravaganzas were not the only form of popular entertainment or recreation in urban centers, there were the usual cabarets, drinking dives, and dances.

The latter parallel similar functions in country districts throughout the South. In this respect Ira De A. Reid identifies " 'struggles,' 'break-downs,' 'razor-drills,' 'flop-wallies,' and 'chitterling parties.' " Other reports indicate that when activities were held outdoors they were the domain of small bands (string, brass, fife and drum), and might also attract guitar-playing songsters. For small-time entertainment in enclosed locations, the principal instrument was the piano, which for migrants to conurbations became associated with a particular event, the house rent party. These gatherings undoubtedly grew out of collective African American traditions for survival and advancement in situations of extreme deprivation, which existed in the Caribbean as well as the United States. In Harlem, with its mixed population of locals and migrants, from both the South and the Caribbean, there was the potential for a greater variety of music being played on such occasions.

Wallace Thurman sets the scene:

Saturday night comes. There may be only piano music, there may be a piano and drum, or a three or four-piece ensemble. Red lights, dim and suggestive, are in order. The parlor and the dining room are cleared for the dance, and one bedroom is utilized for hats and coats. In the kitchen will be found boiled pigs feet, ham hock and cabbage, hopping John (a combination of peas and rice), and other proletarian dishes.

The music will be barbarous and slow. The dancers will use their bodies and the bodies of their partners without regard to the conventions. There will be little restraint. Happy individuals will do solo specialities, will sing, dance—have Charleston and Black Bottom contests and breakdowns. . . .[64]

Ira Reid made a study of these events in the 1920s and quotes an undated "News Item" (no source given):

Growing out of economic stress, this form of nocturnal diversion has taken root in Harlem—that section known as the world's largest Negro center. Its correct and more dignified name is "Parlor Social," but in the language of the street, it is caustically referred to as a house rent party.

"Parlor Socials" (per Sam Manning's "Keep Your Hands Off That"), "Social Whist Parties," "Social Parties," and similar activities in Harlem are generally associated with the stride piano playing of such performers as James P. Johnson,

Lucky Roberts, and Willie "The Lion" Smith. Undoubtedly, players rooted in a variety of traditions participated—Reid mentions unknowns such as "Kid Professor," "Blind Johnny," and "Kid Lippy"; Rudi Blesh and Harriet Janis elicited stories of others.[65] There were also the West Indians: Lionel Belasco, Walter Merrick, Taffy Palmer (leader of Palmer's Orchestra) and Adolph Thenstead have been mentioned. Other pianists who recorded include Jack Celestain, Berry Barrow and Donald Heywood.[66]

A Trinidadian, Heywood was known principally for his role in the black musical theater.[67] He had recorded solo for Black Swan in 1922 (two popular tunes of the day) and as an accompanist to Marion Harrison. Under the auspices of Ralph Peer (Victor's talent scout) in 1927 and 1928, however, he undertook a series of sessions for the export market. The Victor log labels all these sides as by "Race" artists, although each was issued in the company's West Indian catalogue. They reflect repertoire from the islands or the migrant experience in New York. The first session was held on 9 June 1927, and comprised two instrumentals by Donald Heywood's West Indian Band plus two vocals by "Marsa Langman" accompanied by the same group: Heywood on piano, two saxophonists and a cuatro player. Langman was Sam Manning, who presumably hid his identity in the light of a contract with the Columbia Phonograph Company's recently acquired OKeh label (for whom he recorded two weeks later). One side, "Touch Me All About, But Don't Touch Me Dey," is calypso; its coupling, "Mister Joseph Strut Your Stuff,"(with a Heywood composer credit) is pure black North American vaudeville in execution, though its subject is the Trinidad West Indian in New York and it is sung to an island melody (Victor 80777):

"Mister Joseph Strut Your Stuff"

(sung) *Dea-dad-da-ah-da, de-da-ada,*
Dea-da-dee-dee-da,
De-de-ah-da-de-a-dah-dah.

(spoken) *Oh, do it son,*
Oh, play that thing boy.
Ah-ha,

(sung) *Ah-ha.*

(spoken) *Do you know anybody ever heard about Mister Joseph?—Yeah, Mister Joseph's the boy from Trinidad—And I mean folks, he's just too bad. Mister Joseph works down Down Town—yes sir!; and he runs an elevator. When you sees him on the Avenue you'll think he's a doctor—I mean! Mister Joseph gets his payroll every Saturday evening—yes sir!; fat payroll too—yes boy!—and the girls just wild 'bout him. See him, he standing up at a Hundred-And-Thirty-Fifth-Street corner on Seventh Avenue. And everybody talk. Atta boy!—you hear him talk.*

(sung) *1. See him a-coming a-down the road,*
Walkin' stick, it ain't no load,
Dressed up in the latest style,
He makes the folks in Harlem wild,

(chorus) *Mister Joseph strut your stuff [. . .],*
Strut your stuff like fun,
Call their bluff, you'll win that cake, my son,
Mister Joseph strut your stuff—Lord sir!
Show you come from far,
You certainly make a hit in this America.

1. Now, see him coming a-down that road,
And that walkin' stick, oh, it ain't no load,
Then he's dressed up in the latest style,
He makes the folks in Harlem wild,

(chorus) *[repeats initial chorus]*

(chorus) *Oh Mister Joseph strut—Oh, look on him—Sir!*
Oh strut—walk a jig!
Call their bluff, you'll win the cake my son,
Mister Joseph strut—ha-ha-ha!
Although you come from far,
You'll certainly make a hit in this America.

The compelling desire of the new migrant for success in his new country, and the means employed to this end, are the meat of this caricature, the lyrics of which suggest an extravagant and imposing stage routine in line with Manning's Harlem reputation.

A second Donald Heywood session took place on 27 December 1927 and featured Dan Michaels, who recorded a solo and two vaudeville duets with Hilda Perleno, each with accompaniment by Heywood on piano. Michaels's "Mongoose Hop" is virtually black North American hokum and the setting a New York "Social" (Victor 80778). The words are different, but melodically this is based on the well-known U.S. black dance piece "Ballin' the Jack," which was published in 1913.[68] The setting of the lyrics, with their theme of an "experienced" settler's superiority over his naïve counterpart, however, gives some indication of adaptations made by migrants to their own community, whilst accommodating idioms from the host country. This allowed appeal to the widest audience possible.

"Mongoose Hop"

(sung) 1. *Went down to the dance the "hother" night,*
Saw a new step, filled me with delight,
Almost laughed 'till I cracked my sides,
When Miss "Molinden" tried,
This new invention is fine,
So why don't you get in line.

2. Put your hands on your hips, count one, two, three,
Makes funny motion, like climb the tree,
Put your right foot down, stamp all around,
Do the shimeree, until you touch the ground,
That's what they call the "Mongoose Hop,"
When you start to do it, boy, you can't stop,
So swing your partner, while you may,
Dance 'till the break of day.

(spoken) *Have a good time fellers. Oh, make that girl dance. He's all right baby, why don't you go ahead and dance with him? He hasn't been eatin' "honions." He-he. She feels the music. Lord today! Oh, baby! This girl is a mess! Baby, you must have been livin' in New York a very long time. Boy! Come here, come here, come here boy! Look! Look at her shakin' that thing too! He-he. Boy, I'm goin' to take this gal on home with me. He-ee! Look at her! Look at her! Well, come on boy—this girl is a—MESS!*

(sung) 3. [repeat verse 2]

(spoken) Oh! Listen to that piano. Go ahead, that boy playing that piano too. He-ee! It's too bad boy. Oh no! You better stop playing that piano fool. I'm standing up over here with my old lady. He-he! That's all.

The sophisticated piano accompaniment and Michaels's smooth delivery indicate performers of experience. This is true likewise for the duets with Hilda Perleno, one of which, "Susanne," emphasizes problems encountered by West Indian males in their relationships with North American females.

"Susanne"

D.M. *(sung) Rumour spreading h-all around, I don't understand,*
Everybody seems to take me for a monkey man,
All on account of Susanne, that good for nothing brown,
I don't want no h-alibi, 'cause I'm goin' to call her down.
Oh Susanne, Susanne, you h-ain't treatin' me right,
Susanne, Susanne, you stay out every night,
Susanne, Susanne, you been gettin' my pay
After I've been toiling and sweating every day,
Susanne, Susanne, you loving someone else,
Susanne, Susanne, don't put me on the shelf,
Baby, if you don't stop your cheatin'
I'm goin' to meet you and gi' you a beating,
Susanne, Susanne, you ain't treatin' me right.

D.M. *(spoken) Yes sir, I'm goin' down there and see Susanne, because she sure ain't treatin' me right*

[knocking]

Open that door woman! What you tryin' to do?

H.P. *You here again? Why don't you stay away from here? What's the idea?*
D.M. *What is you trying to do? Keep me out of my home now?*
H.P. *Does this apartment look to you like a coconut tree?*

D.M. *Eh-eh, you tryin' to insult me after I give you all my affection and my love with my whole heart.*

H.P. *I didn't order coal!*

D.M. *No, but you're hard as a sealskin coat. And now I catch you walking out with another sheik and you come tell me 'bout how you didn't h-order no coal. The other day I bought you a player piano and the first thing you play when I first come in the house is "Bye Bye Blackbird." Where did you get that at?*

H.P. *You better get away from here with that vulgarity. Brother—you are dark and unlucky.*

H.P. *Eh-eh.*

D.M. *(sung) [repeats lines 5–13 of initial verse]*

Here the unsatisfactory relationship first identified in Sam Manning's "Let Go My Hand" (Columbia 14110–D) is brought into the open in a way that suggests the subject may have become common in certain black New York vaudeville presentations at this time, a proposal enhanced by the presence of Hilda Perleno, who was in the cast of a number of black musicals during the 1920s and early 1930s.[69] The supposition is also reinforced by similar duets recorded by Sam Manning and Anna Freeman in the year following. Donald Heywood's final session for Victor, in April 1928, concentrates on West Indian repertoire with two other vocalists, Timothy Dunn and Adrian Johnson.

MANNING'S COMIC DIALOGUES WITH ANNA FREEMAN—1928

Sam Manning sustained his recording and stage career in 1928, the former with two new-year sessions for the Brunswick-Balke-Collender Company's Brunswick "Race" series. The first (2 February) incorporated a Trinidad calypso "Woman Sweeter than Man" that had been interpreted in 1927 by Wilmoth Houdini, the Trinidad calypsonian domiciled in New York. Manning's "Woman Sweeter than Man" was coupled with "Bouncing Baby Boy," about the plight of an unmarried mother, once again reflecting on the lives of West Indian migrants in the metropolis. A record company file note indicates that this was "for special release New York territory."

It is, however, Manning's second session for Brunswick (19 March) that is of particular interest in exploring the relationship between black West Indian and North American culture in New York. The occasion comprised a series of four comic dialogues between Anna Freeman (the American woman) and Manning (the West Indian man). Composer credits for these are attributed to Porter Grainger, who accompanies on the piano. His involvement may indicate that this material had been included in *Brown Sugar*, but no particulars have been traced regarding the show's music; Anna Freeman, however, was one of the featured performers in this and the subsequent show *Black Magic*.[70] Grainger had recorded one song, "Nothin' but a Double-Barrel Shot Gun," in a purely black North American context in October of the previous year (OKeh 8516), and it is useful to compare the two versions. The lyrics to his solo rendition are:

"Nothin' but a Double-Barrel Shot Gun"

1. I'm mad, I'm mad today,
I can't see nothing but red,
So mad, yes I'm sad today,
I'd just as doggone soon be dead,
My gal just said she was through with me,
She didn't even say what for,
I know there's been some dirty work,
So here's what I says to her,
"'T ain't nothin' but a double-barrel shot gun,
"Gonna keep me away from you,
"Now sister, you'll think I'm the battle of 'bulls run' [sic],[71]
"If you quit me like you said you do."
Now listen,
"Even if I didn't want you, just get this under your hat,
"'T ain't nobody else gonna have you, so mama that's that,
"'Cause nothin' but a double-barrel shot gun,
"Gonna keep me away from you."

2. Now I'm mean and I'm evil, as a jealous man can be,
When it comes to a piece of furniture what belongs to me,
And I don't mind no funeral, 'cause I ain't scared to die,
And I couldn't be no different, if I doggone try,
Neither lightnin', nor thunder, don't scare me a bit,
Bring on your six-shootin' pistol,
I ain't even bothered about it,
I'll just take my bare hands and hit a lion on its jaw,

Rrrrr,
I ain't even scared of a mother-in-law, no sir,
Now I'll fight a nest of hornets,
With four rattle snakes throwed in,
I'll grab a tiger by its whiskers,
And I'll smack him on his chin,
But two long steel barrels, with the triggers pulled back,
Make me run clean on down the railroad track, yes sir,
But nothin' but a double-barrel shot gun,
Gonna keep me away from you.

This piece has the structure of the "dozens," the black North American tradition of exchanging boastful insults, although Grainger's version does not have the advantage of dialogue with another protagonist. Substantially rewritten for this purpose, it is apparent that "Nothin' but a Double Barrel Shotgun's Gonna Keep Me Away from You" by Manning and Freeman is comic in intent. The content, however, maintains antagonism between the West Indian migrant and black people of local origin, superimposed by the battle of the sexes—like the dozens, violence is never far from the surface. If matrix order is the sequence in which they were recorded, this was the first dialogue. Here, the American woman is seeking to leave her West Indian man:

"Nothin' but a Double Barrel Shotgun's Gonna Keep Me Away from You"

(spoken) S.M. *Don't bother me woman. I'm mad, I'm mad today, and I can't see nothing but red.*
A.F. *Why, you'd better get glad, I mean glad today, 'cause tomorrow you might be dead.*
S.M. *Gal, does you mean to say that you is through with me, after all I have been to you?*
A.F. *Why, that's just exactly what I mean, and please stay away from me too.*
S.M. *Well, nothing doing. 'Cause nothin' but a double-barrel shotgun, gonna keep me away from you.*
A.F. *Is that so?*
S.M. *You think that I am the battle of "bulls run?"* [sic]
A.F. *Guess it's bull's eye!*

S.M. *If you quit me like you said you'd do. Even if I didn't want you, sister, get this under your hat.*

A.F. *What?*

S.M. *'T ain't nobody else gonna get you, so mama, dat's dat. 'T ain't nothin' but a double-barrel shotgun.*

A.F. *Gonna do what?*

S.M. *Gonna keep me away from you. Now, I'm mean, I'm evil.*

A.F. *I know.*

S.M. *As a jealous man can be.*

A.F. *Sure.*

S.M. *When it comes to a piece of furniture that belongs to me.*

A.F. *I'm sorry.*

S.M. *And I don't mind a funeral, 'cause I ain't scared to die*

A.F. *That's so.*

S.M. *Furthermore, I won't be different, hot mama, and I ain't goin' to try.*

A.F. *Now your lightnin' and your thunder don't scare me a bit. Go get your six-shootin' pistol, you know I ain't bothered 'bout it. Now you've been boastin' and you've been bragging, and I've heard it long enough, so I'm ready, Mr. Barrel of Bricks, to call your bluff.*

S.M. *I'll fight a nest of hornets, four rattlesnakes throwed in, grab a tiger by his whiskers and I'll whale him on his chin.*

A.F. *That so.*

S.M. *Woman, don't antagonize me, and your saucy talkin' back, 'cause I'll run and grab a freight train, and drag him off his tracks. You treat me like you think that I ain't nothin' but a joke.*

A.F. *You ain't.*

S.M. *Yet every pay day you is down there, to grab my envelope.*

A.F. *That's what you made for.*

S.M. *You'se talking graveyard language, woman, can't you plainly see, that I'm mad from my A down to my W, X, Y, Z.*

(sung) *Ain't nothin' but a double-barrel shotgun,*
Gonna keep me away from you.

A.F. (spoken) *Be careful.*

This was coupled with the next item in matrix sequence, "Goin' Back to Jamaica" (Brunswick 7027). Here, the American woman is the protagonist, but it is the West Indian man—or, rather Jamaican, or "country man"—who is given the last word:

"Goin' Back to Jamaica"

S.M. (spoken) *Woman, I see what you is going to do. You is going to get me 'cacerated.*
A.F. *Man, what are you talking about, 'cacerated?*
S.M. *I said 'incarcerated.' I mean you is going to put me behind the four walls of the jail house.*
A.F. *Well, you could get cremated for all I care.*
S.M. *That's the way with you 'Merican women. You make a "John" out of my country man and get him down to his last expense or his last farthing. Then you wants to kick him in the pants. But woman, let me tell you something, let me tell you something.*
A.F. *What is it now?*

S.M. (sung) *I'm gonna grab me a steamboat sure,*
Yes, I'm goin' to take her,
Ain't gonna fool with you no more,
I'se gwine back to Jamaica.
Oh, woman, leave me 'lone, leave me 'lone, leave me 'lone,
Oh, woman, leave me 'lone, I don't want you no more.

A.F. *You don't have to get no boat,*
Grab a pick and shovel,
Here's your hat and here's your coat,
Now, go to the devil.
Oh, let me miss you, man, miss you, man, miss you man,
Oh, let me miss you, man, let me miss you now.

S.M. *A wise man, he might change his mind,*
A "coolie" wouldn't change nothin',
Gal you make me so much mad,
I'm gwine land in Sing Sing prison.
Oh, woman, leave me 'lone, leave me 'lone—please leave me 'lone,

A.F. *(spoken) I ain't done nothing.*
S.M. *(sung) Oh, woman, leave me 'lone, you gonna land me in Sing Sing prison.*

(spoken) Woman, you is driving me to the very degradation. You'se fixin' to prohibit me of seeing my poor old pappy and mammy, who's waitin' for me in my beloved Jamaica.

    Listen woman, this cantankerous situation cannot last. Remember these words, what I say, a eye for a eye, a tooth for a tooth—I'm gwine to get even with you some of these days. 'Cause I'm from down the country, where they know the hoodoo. I'm goin' to hoodoo you, woman.
A.F. *Ah-ha, I know exactly what's the matter with you. Man, you're crazy. What you need to do is to go to the bug house instead of to Jamaica. Brother, you'se bugged. You've been a monkey every since I met you.*
S.M. *Don't you call me no monkey chaser. Don't you call me no monkey chaser.*
A.F. *I didn't call you no monkey chaser.*
S.M. *Well, don't you call me no monkey chaser. And, if I is a monkey chaser—you is the monkey.*

The other two matrices in this sequence were respectively the first and second part of "The American Woman and West Indian Man" (Brunswick 7028). As with the previous two titles, this dialogue sometimes takes on the rivalry of the "dozens," although the language of insult is less bawdy. Again, the West Indian man is a Jamaican, or "country man," and he is seen to triumph over his two-timing, scheming, "high yellow" North American woman:

"The American Woman and West Indian Man–pt. 1"

A.F. *(sung) I got a man for spring, I got a man for summer,*
A stick of wood is dumb, but brother you're dumber,
So, "Mr. Chump," be on your merry way,
Your merry way.
Don't stand there actin' like a doggone nut,
'Cause when you open my front door, my back door shut,
So, "Mr. Chump," be on your merry way,
I mean, your merry way.

S.M. (spoken) *Look here, American woman, do you mean to tell me when I make entrance by my front door a gentleman exits by my back door?*

A.F. *I didn't say it was no woman, and he didn't go up no chimney.*

S.M. *Well, let me tell you, while I stand here looking as dumb as a lamb, I ain't so dumb that I can't hear a back door slam.*

A.F. *Well, since you're so wise and heard all of those doors slamming, why don't you do something about it?*

S.M. *Don't excite yourself. I'm gwine to do somethin' about it.*

A.F. *Well, let me know somethin', hot papa, 'cause mama's fixin' to obliterate you from your existence.*

S.M. *I am gwine buy me a razor sure, in my right hand I know she can't fail. I ain't gwine back to Jamaica no more. I'm gwine up to that man' jail, I'm gonna fight that man a duel, if me and you don't stay married. I'm gwine cut his throat from ear to ear, I'm talking about your sweet man Harry.*

A.F. *Say now, papa. Ain't no use for you to get so hot. 'Cause you know that ain't got it. Our mis-marriage was a mistake.*

S.M. *Yeah, but who made the mistake?*

A.F. *Well, who's squawking?*

S.M. *I ain't squawking. I just want you to understand our relationship from now on.*

A.F. *What is it gonna be?*

S.M. *Well! We live like strangers. You sleep by yourself and I'm gwine to be sleepin' by my-self.*

A.F. *Oh-oh! Never no sleep by myself.*

S.M. *Well, you ain't gwine-a sleep with me no more. 'Cause it might be raining sleet and snow, it don't make no difference.*

A.F. *Well, don't you worry 'bout mama, you know. I am able to take care of myself.*

S.M. *Yeah.*

A.F. *Just go out every morning and scuffle—that's your share.*

S.M. *Well, let me tell you somethin'. Another thing, when you walk down the street in the future, you'll walk by yourself.*

A.F. *Yes, and when you make your rules, remember I ain't so old as to be on the shelf. And another thing, I'm gonna get a divorce and alimony from you.*

S.M. *But you done got all my money.*

A.F. *I haven't got half of what I'm gonna get. From now on I'm gonna get every penny that you can make. And if you don't give it to me, I'm gonna see the man.*

S.M. *See what man?*

A.F. *The judge man. And see that he puts you under the jail, you get me?— under the jail!*

S.M. *Yea, and there'll be a whole lot of people up to your house—your mother, your father, all your generation. There will be crashing and gnashing of teeth, and you wouldn't know nothing 'bout it.*

A.F. *What do you mean?*

S.M. *I mean, when I come out from under the jail, I'll take my razor and cut you so low, you'll be walking around with crutches under your ears.*

"The American Woman and West Indian Man–pt. 2"

S.M. (sung) *Say now, look here, American woman.*

A.F. (spoken) *What is it now?*

S.M. (sung) *Have you understand,*
You're flirting with the graveyard,
When you fool with my country man?
I loves you like I don't know what,
Gives you all my dough,

A.F. (spoken) *Got a right to.*

S.M. (sung) *Fool with me, you sure get cut,*
Then "Sing Sung" jail I'll go.

A.F. (spoken) *Oh, oh, hold them dice, brother, hold them dice. You going to "Sing Sing" jail all enough. That is if there is anything left of you when I get through with you. And you gonna shoot somebody—heh!*

S.M. *That's what I said.*

A.F. *Ha! Well brother, if you just as much point a pistol at this pretty yellow woman, you just as well give your heart to the Lord, because your hips are gonna belong to me.*

S.M. *Me hips, me hips? Woman, do you know you is talking under my clothes?*

A.F. *Yes, and that ain't all. I'll be standing over your cold carcass if you try to execute any of them cruel threats.*

S.M. *Calm yourself, American woman, I say be-calm yourself!*

A.F. *Calm myself nothin'! I told you I was gonna quit and I had no right marrying you in the first place, because you West Indian men are too treacherous.*

S.M. *Take that back! I said, take that back! Talking about treacherous; look at what you done!*

A.F. *What did I do?*

S.M. *What you didn't do! Didn't you take out a 10,000 dollars life insurance on my life, then try to stash with me?*

A.F. *You're a "salt water" liar!*

S.M. *"Salt water" liar, the devil! Look what you done—you put starch in my biscuit trying to poison me.*

A.F. *I?*

S.M. *Not "I," "you!" And you know I don't like no starch in my biscuit.*

A.F. *Well, how do you like your biscuit?*

S.M. *I have often told you I like my biscuit rough dry.*

A.F. *Ah ha! Now I have thought this matter over carefully and I think it best that we part because your ways and manners don't ex-suit my taste.*

S.M. *Mm.*

A.F. *Now we are gonna part and from now on you go your way and I'll go mine.*

S.M. *Yea.*

A.F. *For look what you did. You haven't spoken to the pastor of our church since we got married.*

S.M. *Why should I? Why should I?*

A.F. *Well, why not? The pastor hasn't offended you in any way*

S.M. *Oh, go ahead woman, I knows my enemy when I sees him. That man he don't mean me a bit of good.*

A.F. *How come?*

S.M. *How come? Didn't he get me tied up in marriage to you?*

A.F. *Ah ha! Now I, now I know it's best that we part. For in the first place, your vocabulary is limited. Your deportment is shocking. Why you haven't got it in any way.*

S.M. *Well, if you don't want me, I don't want you either, you big fat
good-for-nothing yellow woman.*
A.F. *Oh!*
S.M. *You can't dance.*
A.F. *No?*
S.M. *You can't sing, you can't even shook that thing.*

These sketches are unique in their coverage of what was a particularly potent
issue in Harlem in the 1920s. Manning's capacity to depict the immigrant, and
the American responses by Anna Freeman, emphasize the process of cultural
adjustment between these two segments of the black community (as well as their
relationship to the white majority).

MANNING CONTINUES TO DEPICT WEST INDIAN
CULTURAL ADJUSTMENT

Manning was to record one more piece in this vein in 1928, the final matrix from
four sides made for the OKeh "Race" series on 3 and 4 April. Like a good proportion of his other lyrics, this was an adaptation of a West Indian folk song—in this
instance "Bromley" from Barbados.[72] Accompanied by Jack Celestain and his
Caribbean Serenaders, Manning's "You Can't Get Anything out of Me"(OKeh
8567) transposes an Eastern Caribbean male boasting song into another confronta-
tion between a migrant West Indian male and his black American girl in New York:

"You Can't Get Anything out of Me"

(spoken) *Look here, American girl, why do you keep on bothering me?
Haven't I told you to keep away. You are not going to get anything, you are
not going to get nothing out of me.*

(sung chorus) *Out of me, out of me,
You wouldn't get no fur coat, out of me,
Out of me, out of me,
You wouldn't wear no diamond ring, out of me,*

1. [repeat first chorus]

2. I get up in the morning, half past eight,
Get up on the job, five minutes late,
Boss says, he don't want me no more,
The cold north winds just begin to blow.

3. Now it ain't no joke, when I got no overcoat,
Number playing done got me broke,
Get me rent money, tried to get quit,
Landlord come, in a hell of a fix.

4. [repeat first chorus]

(chorus) *Out of me, out of me,*
You wouldn't get no wedding out of me,
Out of me, out of me,
You wouldn't get no wedding ring out of me.

5. Listen, Miss 'Merican girl,
You wouldn't get no apartment out of me,
Go 'way, Miss 'Merican girl,
You wouldn't get no furniture out of me.

(chorus) *Out of me, out of me,*
You wouldn't keep no sweet man, out of me,
Out of me, out of me,
You'll never make no slavey out of me.

5. Go 'way, Miss 'Merican girl,
You wouldn't make no slavey out of me,
Go 'way, Miss 'Merican girl,
You wouldn't keep no sweet man out of me.

6. [repeats second verse]

7. Ain't no joke, got no overcoat,
Number playing done got me broke,
Took me rent money, played seven-fifty-six,
When the landlord call, I'm in a hell of a fix.

Here is a further presentation of migrant black West Indian mistrust for the black American—overlain with mistrust between the sexes. This apprehension is combined with the problems of employment dictated by the clock, fear of dismissal, poverty, and of North American ghetto life, with its "numbers" rackets offering players a gambler's chance of changing one's lot by "winning" (or, more generally losing) in the local policy game. Such sentiments are also found in blues of the period, although expressed far more introspectively than in this performance.[73]

During the first eight months of 1928, advertisements for variety shows at the Alhambra and other Harlem theaters, together with reports of the same, indicate that Sam Manning kept a busy schedule of engagements in his role as a comedian and singer. This culminated in the successful staging of *Keep Scuffling* at the Lafayette at the beginning of August.[74] Excepting a recording session as featured vocalist with Jack Celestain and his Caribbean Stompers (September), Manning devoted the remainder of the year to his newly chosen field of journalism.[75]

LIONEL O. LICORICH AND THE S.S. VESTRIS—1928

Columbia held a curious session in December 1928, comprising two sides sung by Lionel O. Licorich, a black Barbadian. They were issued in the company's export series, with "Jack 'Sweet Willie' Celestain" on piano and "One String Willie" on one string violin (Columbia 3360–X). "Bajan Girl" is an up tempo piece, while "I Has the Blues for Thee, Barbadoes" is a non-idiomatic, nostalgic and mournful blues-based song:

"I Has the Blues for Thee, Barbadoes"

1. Barbados, Barbados, I am thinkin' of you,
Barbados, Barbados, I am feelin' real blue,
I am saving my money now, so I can come back home,
I will get enough somehow, never more will I roam.

2. I have the blues for thee, Barbados,
Lord, [the moon], what shall I do,
I have the blues for thee, Barbados,
I'll weep, I'll wail the whole night through.

3. Nobody knows my worries and my woes,
Nobody knows which way the wind blows,
Every time I eat of the mangoes,
I have the blues for thee, Barbados.

An undistinguished vocalist, Licorich was Quartermaster on the ill-fated
S.S. *Vestris*, which had sunk ignominiously in November, en route to Barbados
and Argentina. The singer played a special part in the rescue of white travelers and
appears to have been granted the opportunity to record as a result of this heroism.
Unlike the several hillbilly ballads composed and recorded about the sinking,[76]
the market for Licorich's West Indian pieces seems to have been very limited. His
fearlessness in saving passengers and his Bajan origins, however, allowed him a
short period of fame as a performer on the black vaudeville circuit.[77]

MANNING'S WEST INDIAN TOUR AND RETURN TO
THE RECORDING STUDIOS—1929–30

During the last four months of 1928, Sam Manning and Amy Ashwood Garvey
launched the *West Indian Times* (in one source *The American Times and West
Indian Review*), but this experience ended in financial failure and acrimony.[78] By
mid 1929 Manning was back performing, appearing in reviews at both the Lincoln
and Lafayette Theaters in April[79] before taking part in a tour of the West Indies
with the black American vaudevillian Sid Perrin. Amy Ashwood Garvey staged
the show, which visited Jamaica in May,[80] and went on to Panama, Trinidad,
Barbados and probably other islands. The party reached Trinidad on 21 June and
presented their vaudeville program at selected island cinemas until the end of
the month.[81]

The format was based on New York presentations, though Manning introduced newly composed songs relating to each island in which he was performing. "My West Indian Home" was announced in the *Trinidad Guardian* as
"especially written" for the visit.[82] The shows were based on recent Harlem presentations, and Manning also contributed four essays to the *Guardian* on life in
this famous black people's settlement. The content of these treatments is of special interest in the light of his repertoire.

Describing "Deep Harlem" as a "Mecca of 'Big Bluff' " in the first of these articles Manning places the population of this black section in the context of poor

wages and crowded accommodation, deducing that "the average West Indian man and woman in New York . . . realize that they do not 'belong.' Their one desire is to get enough money to get away." Like the Trinidad character in "Mister Joseph Strut Your Stuff," Manning's view was that "Everything is a great big bluff in Harlem. Everybody makes it his business to live a lie."[83]

The enactment of this life of fantasy is explored in Manning's further three columns, beginning with an exposition on the "Lure of 'The Numbers' " in which he describes the mechanics and effect of the game of "policy." Interestingly, he does not use the latter term. The struggle to pay the rent and resort to gambling to bolster income is familiar from his "You Can't Get Anything out of Me." Betting on numbers and use of dream books to identify combinations had become commonplace. Thus he observed: "nearly everyone in Harlem owns a dream book which interprets the meaning of their dreams in numbers. These books, of course, have come since the Numbers craze. Strange to say they have numbers so well combined that they are often correct in their interpretations." Winners, of course, were apt to use "the Big Bluff" to further their advancement in this money-oriented society. Yet, in his view, the effect of the Numbers racket was not all negative, with a welcome circulation of cash and wealth for lucky winners mitigating the corruption.[84]

A further reflection of the means by which Harlem inhabitants maintained themselves in strained circumstances is explored in the third essay: "Orgy of Drinks and Dances." This discusses consequences of alcohol prohibition, with the organization of illicit drinking houses—"gin mills"—and use of "Jump Steady" (home-brewed whiskey). Manning associates the latter with weekend "house rent parties" described as dances "where you pay a quarter at the door, and a piano player and perhaps a noisy drummer greets you with a throbbing noise like the beating of a tom-tom. The piano hammers out a rhythm that most of those present find irresistible in its sensuous appeal. . . . The parlor in which a dance is held is sometimes crowded with as many as thirty couples" and "in the circumstances" of such a confined space "the dancing is just a slow sensuous movement of the body accompanied by a sort of shuffling of the feet. In ten minutes of dancing the dancer hardly moves three feet. But the most amusing part of the show is when the Police arrive. This frequently happens and the host is then forced to pay 'protection money.' If he does not intend to do so, there is a rush for the bathroom to get rid of the drinks." The collective nature of these events in supporting rent payments is identified.[85]

In Manning's final treatment, the secular world of top Harlem night-clubs patronized by "white visitors from Broadway"—the Cotton Club, Small's Paradise, and Connie's Inn—is contrasted with the variety of old and new religious group-ings flourishing within Harlem's boundaries: "Humorous Religion."[86]

After a series of performances in Barbados during the first weeks of July 1929, the movements of the Manning-Perrin company are uncertain, but by January 1930 Manning had returned to New York where he recorded eight titles for Columbia's foreign series.[87] This was in the height of the Depression, and several of these pieces reflect the disillusionment of migrants stranded without resource in the metropolis. They may also represent newly composed repertoire from the West Indian tour. Optimistically, the lyrics to "Back to My West Indian Home"(Columbia 3940–X) recommend a return to the Caribbean as a much better alternative to the financial uncertainty of the U.S.A. This is likely "My West Indian Home," the song he had composed in Trinidad:

"Back to My West Indian Home"

1. Then I'm leaving, leaving, leaving this town today,
Sailing, sailing, like a stowaway,
Empty handed, broken hearted, got no trunks to pack,
But I'm happy 'cause I'm going home and I ain't coming back,
Back to my West India home, where the coconut grow,
Back, back where I belong, never to roam no mo',
I ain't got no money, I've been broke for the longest time,
But the folks will be glad to see me, though I ain't got a dime.

2. Oh, yes, I'm going right back, midst the flowers and the bees,
Oh now, I'm hurrying back, 'neath the coconut trees,
Over there don't have to have the blues,
Don't need no overcoat, I wasn't born with shoes,
I'm just a rolling stone, going back to my West India home.

3. [repeats the last four lines of verse one]

4. [repeats two]

On 9 May, Manning registered twelve of his melodies for copyright—as "Samuel Manning of Great Britain . . . domiciled in New York."[88] This indicates Manning's status, and that of many of his contemporaries, as non-U.S. nationals, the process of naturalization having little social advantage for British West Indian migrants in this period.[89] In June, George Tichenor published a vivid account of a Manning appearance at the Alhambra Theater, on Seventh Avenue and 126th Street in Harlem. In a skit with Ruth Trent entitled "Mr. Squash Meets a Girl," Tichenor notes that:

> Sam Manning comes on the stage wearing a pinkish vest and white top hat. His suit is checkered gray, the trousers fitting close to his stout legs and not quite long enough. It is Sam's favorite costume and is never out-moded, whatever the act he appears in this evening. Sam is ingeniously beguiling, in the hunching way he walks and his Jamaica [sic] accent.

Supporting Manning on this bill were the popular black North American vaudevillians Revella Hughes and Amanda Randolph, and in the orchestra pit New York jazz musicians James "Bubber" Miley (cornet) and Emmet Matthews (saxophone).[90]

MANNING AND LIONEL BELASCO TRAVEL TO BRITAIN—1934

Manning made no recordings for the West Indian export market in 1931 or 1932, Trinidad being catered for principally by Wilmoth Houdini. As with the recording of blues in this period, there was little or no commercial activity during the height of the economic depression. In 1933, however, Manning cut sessions for the Perfect and Bluebird specialist lines for the English-speaking Caribbean. During the same years, changes took place in the organization of the principal Harlem theaters.[91] Thus, by the beginning of 1934, Manning parted company with the lease holder of the Harlem Opera House, where he was a featured performer,[92] a move that coincided with a more aggressive competition policy set by the nearby Apollo Theater.[93] By this time, Manning's special popularity in Harlem was probably on the wane; certainly his repertoire appears to have been directed primarily towards Caribbean sales, when he made further sides for Bluebird, before setting sail for Britain with Lionel Belasco in June 1934. Nevertheless, Manning's virtually unique role in mediating traditionally based black vocal music from the Caribbean, mixed with American jazz, to audiences in the English-speaking West Indies, North America and later Britain paved the way for future crossover performances that began to emerge during the 1930s.[94]

POPULAR TRINIDAD CALYPSONIANS RECORD IN NEW YORK FOR THE FIRST TIME—1934

1934 was a watershed year in recorded music from the English-speaking Caribbean. Two leading Trinidad calypsonians—Atilla the Hun (Raymond Quevedo) and the (Roaring or Metro) Lion (Hubert Raphael Charles)—journeyed to New York to make 24 sides for ARC-Brunswick (March). Subsequently, at the end of the year, the black vaudevillian Bill Rogers traveled from Guyana to the same location to record 30 performances for Bluebird. From this point, a preponderance of recordings by artists based in the Eastern Caribbean became the norm in series aimed directly at this market.

The immediate effect of Atilla's and Lion's visit in the United States was the promotion of authentic calypso via radio broadcast—both states-wide and in the Caribbean, they appeared on the Fleischmann hour with the famous crooner Rudy Vallee. To acclaim, at Vallee's invitation, the two calypsonians also performed with the singer at the Hollywood restaurant and club on Broadway.[95] This varied exposure raised the status of the music—President Roosevelt became a fan—and paved the way for greater acceptability of the style. The growing interest among a general audience, however, would not be felt for several years in the dissemination of equivalent traditional U.S. black music that sold principally to regional purchasers in a segregated market.

THE BALLAD OF "DELIA (GREEN)" IN THE BAHAMAS—1929

There were several ways in which secular black Caribbean music interchanged with its North American counterpart. A particularly interesting case (with respect to the Bahamas) is the African American ballad "Delia (Green)," known more usually but incorrectly as "Delia (Holmes)" (Laws I 8).[96]

In 1928, Robert W. Gordon, the first Archivist at the newly instituted Archive of (American) Folk Song at the Library of Congress, traced the origin of this ballad to Savannah, Georgia.[97] Unfortunately, other aspects of his research remain unpublished, but the event has been identified as taking place at a Christmas Eve party in 1900, when Moses "Coony" Houston shot Delia Green.[98] The song first appeared in print as "One More Rounder Gone" in 1911, obtained between 1906 and 1908 in Newton County, Georgia, by Howard W. Odum.[99] Another folk song collector, Newman Ivey White, printed three variants in his

American Negro Folk Songs (1928), obtained between 1915 and 1924 in Alabama, Georgia, and North Carolina respectively.[100] Chapman J. Milling printed three more versions in 1937.[101] Zora Neale Hurston also collected the ballad in Florida[102] and several south-eastern U.S. field recordings are documented—such as that recorded by Blind Willie McTell in Atlanta for the Library of Congress in 1940—as well as Jimmy Gordon's "Delhia" (Decca 7592), recorded in 1939.

Less well known are the versions from the Bahamas. Amelia Defries printed the earliest in 1929, in a book on the islands:

Rubber tyred buggy, double seated hack,
Carry poor Delia to de graveyard and never bring her back,
Delia gone, Delia gone.[103]

There are also two Bahamian prewar field recordings of this piece held by the Library of Congress, and several post Second World War commercial recordings.[104] Further examples of similar black North American proto blues appearing in English-speaking Caribbean repertoire include "Nobody's Business," which was recorded commercially in Jamaica (and West Africa) after the Second World War.[105]

RECORDED BAHAMIAN REPERTOIRE AND THE U.S.A.—1920s–30s

Inevitably, there was movement of songs in the other direction. A useful example of the adoption and adaptation of West Indian repertoire is the Bahamian song "Mama Don't Want No Peas and Rice," as a formal arrangement has become known. This bears some resemblance to the black American barrelhouse piece "Mama Don't 'Low," adapted for the mayoral campaign of "Boss Crump" in Memphis, Tennessee, in 1909 and recorded by several bluesmen.[106] Perhaps a Caribbean reworking of the earlier composition, "Mama Don't Want No Peas and Rice" is best remembered in jazz circles for recordings by white bandleader Mart Britt and his Orchestra (Victor 22933/Bluebird B4955, recorded 1932) and Cleo Brown (Decca 512, recorded 1935). Most familiar is the "blues" rendition by Jimmy Rushing with the Count Basie Orchestra (Decca 2030, recorded in New York City on 6 June 1938).[107] The Bahamian lyric probably originated during the First World War. At least, this was the view of Van Campen Heilner, who collected a version entitled "Coconut Oil (A Song of the Bahama Islands)" in about 1924:

My mammy don't want no peas, no rice, no coconut oil! (x3)
All she wants a brandy shandy after nine!

During the war the natives of the Bahamas found it extremely difficult to get butter, lard or fat of any kind and the majority of cooking was done in coconut oil. They soon got sick of it and the saying "My mammy don't want no peas and rice with coconut oil" gave rise to the song. A "brandy shandy" can be either a drink or a "hot time."[108]

His variant was published in 1930 but, with the substitution of "Papa" for "Mammy" and other minor differences, had been printed a year earlier by Amelia Defries:

Papa don't want no peas nor rice nor coconut oil, (x2)
All he wants is sugar brandy [sic] all the time.[109]

The "composed" rendition (as sung by Rushing), was not registered for copyright until 1931—in the names of L. Wolfe Gilbert (words), L. Charles and J. Rosamond Johnson (melody).[110]

Working in Florida during the 1930s, the celebrated black American folklorist Zora Neale Hurston recorded a version of this song for the Library of Congress. She attributes its origin to Nassau, New Providence Island in the Bahamas, describing it as a husband's explanation "to the neighbors what is the matter with his wife and why they don't get along better."[111]

DECCA EXPERIMENT WITH WEST INDIAN STYLES IN THEIR U.S. "RACE" SERIES—1938–39

By the late 1930s, popular success of Trinidad calypso recordings in the United States was manifest.[112] The trend was spearheaded by the canny judgements of Jack Kapp who had cultivated the line since he broke from ARC-Brunswick and launched U.S. Decca (with Edward Lewis of British Decca) in August 1934. Encouraged by sales to U.S. tourists in Trinidad, Kapp inaugurated availability of the Decca calypso series in any U.S. record store in August 1938.[113] He was a

master at superimposition of dissimilar musical styles via the gramophone
record and, having produced Sam Manning and Wilmoth Houdini for
Brunswick, was well aware of the crossover potential in marketing West Indian
idioms to different audiences. In September 1938, therefore, he authorized
an offbeat session by Jack Sneed and his Sneezers, which paired a quasi
West Indian vocalist with high-class black American musicians in accompaniment (Joe Guy–trumpet, John Kirby–string bass, O'Neil Spencer–drums,
unknown–piano, unknown–guitar). The "West Indian" repertoire incorporated
a very anti Garvey version of "West Indies Blues," and a semi-bawdy Jamaican
rendering of "Sly Mongoose" (Decca 7566). Its "North American" session mates
comprised "The Numbers Man" (a policy theme), and "Big Joe Louis," a pane-
gyric for the famous boxer (Decca 7522). The playing of policy and Joe Louis's
career as a champion fighter were the subjects of contemporary blues,[114] and Joe
Louis's exploits also featured in several Trinidad calypsos.[115] Notwithstanding,
Sneed's presentation is difficult to interpret. He accentuates mannerisms that
might be Jamaican in origin virtually to the point of parody, but in a black
North American context. This suggests a familiarity with New York cabaret. The
authenticity of his lyrics to "Sly Mongoose," however, suggests knowledge of
Jamaican traditions, and may indicate he was a black New Yorker of West Indian
parentage.[116]

Decca recorded Sneed for a second time in May 1939. Unlike the first
session—issued in the company's "Race" series—one coupling was selected for the
popular line: "Jamaica Mama"/"Sissy in the Barn" (Decca 2529). As the title suggests, the former is a "West Indian" theme in which the "mama" is both "mighty
sweet" and "mighty mean":

"Jamaica Mama"

(sung) *Jamaica mama, Jamaica mama, Jamaica mama,*
Mighty sweet to me.
Jamaica mama, Jamaica mama, Jamaica mama,
Sweet as she can be.

1. Jamaica mama, she cook cou-cou,
Jamaica mama, cook calalu,
Jamaica mama, cook fungee too,
Oh, Jamaica mama.

Jamaica mama, Jamaica mama, Jamaica mama,
Mighty sweet to me.

(spoken*) Ah, toot it*
Yes, yes now
Oh, baby—oh baby
Hi-hi-hi-hi
Ah, toot it
Hi-hi-hi

(sung*) Jamaica mama, Jamaica mama, Jamaica mama,*
Mighty mean to me.
Jamaica mama, Jamaica mama, Jamaica mama,
Mean as she can be.

2. Jamaica mama, she big and stout,
She get mad and poke out she mouth,
She man come home, and he throw me out,
Oh, Jamaica mama.
Jamaica mama, Jamaica mama, Jamaica mama,
Mighty mean to me.

The second title is both a children's game song and a bawdy rhyme, known otherwise as "Sissy and Bob," that was described in the 1940s as an ancient "Virginia reel" by "One Leg Shadow"—Walter Gould, an elderly ragtime pianist.[117] The other two sides (Decca 7621) are also cleaned up versions of bawdy songs: "Paul Revere" and "Ole Chris (Christafo Colombo)."[118] The same backing group accompanied. These are just as enigmatic as the earlier performances by Sneed, and a later group made on 22 August, which might provide further clues to his antecedents, remains unissued. This comprises interpretations of three Trinidad calypsos from Decca's West Indian series, plus "Lyonaise, Potatoes and Porkchops."[119]

"CALYPSO JAZZ"—A PRECURSOR OF "JIVE?"

While the session was never released, it confirms Decca's interest in exploring the market for West Indian repertoire in "jive" tempo. Further evidence comes from an earlier recording date, on 5 July, by Harold Boyce and his Harlem Indians. Six sides were made, and Arthur Herbert, the drummer at the session, considered them to be "played in West Indian Calypso Jazz style" and that they were "ten years ahead of their time."[120] Four are relevant to this assessment. Decca 7636 consists of a variant of Sam Manning's "Sweet Willie"—entitled "Willie, Willie Don't Go from Me"—and "De Bush to Biol [*sic*] Tea":

"De Bush to Biol [sic] Tea"

1. Oh, buy me, for I know the bush to boil tea, (x2)
The [seal] on the leaf is one,
The [tentan] bush is two,
The Minnie root bark is three,
And that will fix the baby.

2. Oh, buy me, for I know the bush to boil tea, (x2)
The Minnie root bush is four,
The yellow hawk seed is five,
The Christmas bush is six
And everything that will fix.

3. Oh, buy me, for I know the bush to boil tea, (x2)
The [seal] on the leaf,
The leaf on the [seal],
The [tentan] bush,
The Gully root bark,
The mahogany seed,
The peach tree root,
And that's the bush to boil tea.
[repeats verse three, excluding the first line]

From these words, the meaning of the theme is obscure, excepting that it appears to be the cry of a street seller of herbs (bushes) used for various remedies (teas). Light is thrown on the full implication of this piece, however, via the repertoire of a blind Caribbean "ballad-monger" named Charles "Johnny" Waters who lived on Nevis. The performer died in 1959, but while working in the island during the early 1960s, Roger D. Abrahams recovered a proportion of his songs from "a chapbook assembled and sold by Waters." One item gives "a recipe for tea to induce abortion" and, as Abrahams notes, the constituents "are names of bushes, except for the addition of ingredients like *crapaud* (frog) gills." The lyrics are related directly to Harold Boyce's recording:

"The Bush to Kill the Baby"

1. Ahoy, come to me, come to me,
Let me teach you bush to boil tea,
Ahoy, come to me, come to me,
The bush to kill the baby.
(chorus) White pine board, mhalodo bush,
Congolala, and the black-sage,
Mahogany bark, cattle tongue leaf,
The bush to kill the baby.

2. Old lady body, pumpkin belly,
Mosquito wing, crapow gill,
Blue fly belly, policeman shoes,
The bush to kill the baby.

3. When she picks up that mixture,
Then she goes to the dance,
Soon she give two little spin 'round,
They sing out she mischance.[121]

The other pertinent Boyce coupling encompasses a version of the Jamaican work song "De Donkey Want Water," and a lament "Bajun Gal" (Decca 7748):

"Bajun Gal"

1. Bajun gal, she gone and left me alone,
Bajun gal, I wish that she would come home,
Boy, she could stir up the cou-cou,
Oh, how I miss the cou-cou,
Want you know, one and all,
I like my Bajun gal.

2. Bajun gal, she travel all 'round the world,
Bajun gal, the sweetest gal in the world,
Boy, she could [fly] up the flying fish,
Oh, how I miss the flying fish,
Want you all, one and all,
I like my Bajun gal.

3. Bajun gal, I just can't do without her,
Bajun gal, I keep on thinkin' 'bout her,
Boy, she could cook up the dumplings,
Oh, how I miss me dumplings,
I want you know, one and all,
I like my Bajun gal!
I like my Bajun gal!

The final two sides have no direct West Indian relationship: "Knock Ya' Self Out"/"So What" (Decca 7696).

Herbert's description of these performances as "Calypso Jazz" is accurate. In contrast to Jack Sneed, the vocals have none of the patronizing affectations associated with his presentations. They are, therefore, particularly important precursors of the "Calypso-Rhythm & Blues" or "Jive" style adopted by Louis Jordan after the Second World War.

THE ROLES OF GERALD CLARK AND GREGORY FELIX IN NEW YORK

There were further factors that supplemented Decca's cultivation of calypso for a wider audience. One was the Trinidad-born bandleader Gerald Clark (Fitzgerald Clarke). If not before, from 1927—when he played guitar on Wilmoth Houdini's first session, for Victor—Clark was involved in a good proportion of the calypso sides recorded in America. Jack Kapp used his band to accompany Atilla the Hun and the Roaring Lion in 1934 and this unit became the house musicians for Decca when they recorded Trinidad calypsos in New York. There was a lull in Clark's Decca recording activities between 1938 and 1940, when the company sent their production team annually to Trinidad for calypso sides. Together with another colleague, Gregory Felix (who was also a bandleader),

Clark sought to expand the interest in Trinidad music in the United States by staging events and extra recording dates.[122] Felix, a clarinet player, had worked in the band of James Reese Europe before the latter's unfortunate death in 1919, and had possibly been with King Oliver circa 1931. Almost certainly, he was Gregory Felix Delgardo, one of the Puerto Rican musicians Reese Europe recruited for his U.S. Army 369th Infantry Band, and took to France at the end of the First World War.[123]

Decca employed Felix and his Krazy Kats, who often accompanied Wilmoth Houdini on his sides, for an unusual set of recordings on 21 February 1938. These were popular songs performed by the band in paseo (or calypso) tempo. Interesting for their lack of jazz influence, the six pieces reversed Jack Kapp's general practice for his calypso sequence—usually different performers were represented on either side of a release. The Krazy Kats, however, were coupled in three 78s for the series and, separately, two were paired in the company's popular line: "Josephine" and "The Dipsy Doodle" (Decca 1856). The singer was Cecil Anderson, a Trinidadian who was to make a career in the United States under the sobriquet Duke of Iron.[124] Anderson was not a true calypsonian, never having achieved status in Trinidad calypso tents, but his diction was clear, and this made him a suitable vocalist for North American audiences as well as migrant West Indians.

By August 1939, Gerald Clark had secured a position for his Calypso Serenaders at the Village Vanguard in Greenwich Village, New York, and virtually remained in residence for a year. He used the Duke of Iron as narrator and vocalist for this cabaret. At the end of 1939 the group cut four sides for Varsity. This was followed in January 1940 with another four titles for the same company in which two more of Clark's vocalists performed: Sir Lancelot (Lancelot Pinard—a trained singer of lieder from Trinidad) and Macbeth the Great (Patrick McDonald).[125] In April, *Life* magazine printed a story on this movement towards attracting a larger audience, with photographs that showed the Duke of Iron accompanied by Gregory Felix on clarinet and characters in masquerade costumes, taken at Shrovetide celebrations in New York.[126]

The closest parallels in jazz and blues at this time were the two *Spirituals to Swing* concerts at Carnegie Hall sponsored by John Hammond in 1938 and 1939 respectively. They form part of a process that was leading to greater acceptability of black culture among white people in the United States. Since the networked broadcasts by Atilla and Lion in 1934, calypsonians had been in the vanguard of this trend and Trinidadians missed no opportunity that presented itself to promote their island's music.

BILL GAITHER'S "BIG TIME TOWN WOMAN"—1939

References to West Indians are very scarce in blues recorded by black North Americans. An exception is Bill Gaither's "Big Time Town Woman" (Decca 7760, made in New York City on 29 June 1939). Here, as the first two verses explain, one of three "big time town" women with whom he is intimate is a "thorough-bread West Indie" living in New York City:

> *1. I once had three women, each lived in a big time town,*
> *I once had three women, each lived in a big time town,*
> *New York, Detroit, and Chicago,*
> *They kept me traveling the whole year 'round.*
>
> *2. The girl in New York, she was a thorough-breaded West Indie,*
> *The girl in New York, was a thorough-bread West Indie,*
> *She had a way of loving,*
> *That would nearly take my breath away.*

By the end of the song, however, Gaither is asking "Somebody tell me what [love] is all about"—indicating that none of the affairs has produced a lasting relationship. His West Indian girlfriend, nevertheless, has positive attributes, in contrast to the negative stereotypes of 1920s pieces. This points to a greater degree of cultural understanding and, obliquely, may reflect a wider acceptance of people from the Caribbean then prevalent in the U.S.A.

WILMOTH HOUDINI'S FIRST 78 RPM CALYPSO ALBUM—1939

While the majority of Jack Sneed's recordings and all of those by Harold Boyce were issued in the Decca "Race" series, the company was also intent on expanding its calypso line with more general purchasers. With this in mind, on 11 September 1939 it recorded the first of three 78 rpm albums devoted to the genre. This three record set was performed by Wilmoth Houdini, the Trinidad calypsonian domiciled in New York since the late 1920s, accompanied by his "Royal Calypso Orchestra." The package was aimed at a growing white audience for the style, with notes containing a puff for the music and its enthusiasts, plus a short history of "Calypso" by Atilla the Hun and lyric transcripts of all six songs. On 9 October, *Newsweek* ran an article on calypso and the imminent distribution of the album, further indicating Decca's public relations endeavor to popularize the music among affluent white purchasers. Several of the compositions had the theme of the recent visit to the U.S.A. by the British monarch and his consort. Album no. 78 (Decca 18005–18007) was released ten days later.[127]

"HE HAD IT COMING"—AN ADAPTATION OF "MURDER IN THE MARKET"

One song—"He Had It Coming"—was to be of particular significance when it was re-recorded after the Second World War. It is based on a Barbadian folk song usually known as "Murder in the Market" or "Payne Dead." According to Atilla, the song reached Trinidad in the early 1910s.[128] The anthropologist Melville J. Herskovits obtained a short version on 15 July 1939, while he was conducting field work in Toco, Trinidad, which was recorded by Louisa Neptune, accompanied by three other women.[129] The fullest text that has been traced, however, was collected in the Panama Canal Zone during the Second World War, from an old Barbadian woman who recalled it from her youth in the island:

"Murder in de Market"

1. Murder in de market murder! (x3)
Hide me, oh Miss Clark, do hide me.

2. Put me under de bed an yo hide me.
Hide me, oh Miss Clark, do hide me. (x3)

3. Betsy tell me what you do before I hide you. (x2)
I went to the market to get beef,
Payne call me a liar an I stab 'im.

4. Payne dead, Payne dead, Payne dead. (x3)
An I wish Grand Session was tomorra.

5. I would answer de judge like a lion, (x3)
For I ain't killed nobody but me husband.

6. Didn't mean to kill him but him stone dead. (x3)
Payne call me a liar an I stab 'im. (x2)[130]

OTHER DECCA 78 RPM "CALYPSO" ALBUMS—1940–42

Just over a year after recording their first calypso album, Decca cut six specially prepared sides for a further presentation by Wilmoth Houdini. This was released in a three record set early in 1941—*Harlem Seen through Calypso Eyes* (Album no. 198). A third collection followed in the first months of 1942, comprising five 78 rpm records made by visiting Trinidad calypsonians the previous April—*Calypso* (Album no. 256). Accompaniment was by Gerald Clark's Orchestra. Finally, Felix and His Krazy Kats performed the same function for Sam Manning's four record album *West Indian Folk Songs*, cut in December 1941. This was released in May 1942 (Album no. 308), by which time the United States was fully engaged in fighting the Second World War.

The advent of full-scale war interrupted the slow build-up in general interest in music from the English-speaking West Indies being cultivated by Decca. This appears to be true also for recordings aimed at a specifically black audience. (The orientation of a session by Boyce's Harlem Serenaders for Decca in October 1941 was in proto-rhythm and blues tempo and, in parallel with the company's second Wilmoth Houdini album, the lyrics focused on Harlem night life.) In any event, the ban on recording by the American Federation of Musicians in the summer of 1942, plus wartime rationing of shellac, brought Decca's carefully laid plans to a snail's pace.

Another reflection of the growing interest in Trinidad music, however, was the preparation of a book of calypsos with musical notation by Massie Patterson and Lionel Belasco, which commenced in 1941. In the same year, Belasco toured California and Oregon as pianist with Sir Lancelot and the singer's motion picture career started as a result of contacts made at this time. Similarly, in New York, the Duke of Iron, and Gerald Clark and his orchestra, began performing regularly for radio broadcasts.[131]

LOUIS JORDAN'S ADOPTION OF CALYPSO REPERTOIRE

During the same period Decca were experimenting with recordings by Jack Sneed and Harold Boyce performing West Indian repertoire, and Felix and his Krazy Kats playing popular American tunes in paseo tempo, they also began speculating with novelty rhythm and blues. Their prime performer was Louis Jordan, whose first coupling under his own name was cut in December 1938

(Decca 7556). This comprised a version of a black American children's game song "Honey in the Bee Ball" (otherwise known as "All Hid") backed by "Barnacle Bill the Sailor" (a cleaned up version of a bawdy song, like three of the items recorded by Jack Sneed in May 1939). Jordan's genial blues and dead pan vocals were to gain in popularity in the market for "Race" records until the start of the 1942 recording ban. At some point, Jordan became interested in the calypsos being performed by Trinidadians in the United States. His earliest known association with the genre is an AFRS Jubilee broadcast made for the American Forces circa August 1943, in which his band accompanied the Duke of Iron singing "Marry a Woman Uglier than You." (Better known as "Ugly Woman," this Roaring Lion speciality had been recorded first by the calypsonian for ARC in 1934 as "Marry an Ugly Woman": Perfect P–735 &c.)

THE U.S.A. AND WORLD WAR II IN TRINIDAD

President Roosevelt signed the Lend Lease agreement with the British in September 1940. One consequence was that U.S. forces began to set up bases in Trinidad during 1941. Similar establishments were situated at several other locations in the Caribbean, including Jamaica, St. Lucia and Guyana on the South American mainland. By the time of the Japanese attack on Pearl Harbor, on 7 December of the same year, U.S. military personnel were firmly entrenched in Trinidad. Bing Crosby had visited the island on 15 October, and several U.S. stars touring in a flying showboat played a date for the troops on 8 November.[132] This pattern of visits by famous U.S. performers to entertain American forces continued throughout the war, following Roosevelt's declaration of hostilities in the wake of the Pearl Harbor debacle.

Calypso singers found ready employment entertaining the American troops, as did Trinidad dance bands. Calypso tents were sanctioned during Shrovetide although, between 1942 and 1945 inclusively, no local Carnival parades were allowed by the island's administration. The full story of Lord Invader's calypso "Rum and Coca-Cola" has been detailed elsewhere. Suffice it to say that it was sung in calypso tents in 1943 and, later in the year, learnt by Morey Amsterdam, a U.S. comedian on a tour entertaining his country's armed personnel. Amsterdam took the song back to New York, made adjustments to the lyrics, and in 1944 introduced the calypso to the city's night spots via the singer Jeri Sullavan. By this time Decca had signed with the American Federation of Musicians and once more were fully engaged in up-to-date recording.

POPULARITY OF "RUM AND COCA-COLA"—1945

For Jack Kapp, in his endeavor to broaden the appeal of calypso, "Rum and Coca-Cola" was the most suitable crossover song he could ever wish for. Its heady subject was the entanglement of American and Caribbean values brought about by the war. Here were GIs and Trinidad women flirting on the beach, drinking a cocktail of one of America's favorite beverages mixed with West Indian rum, in a tropical paradise. This could not fail in the hands of the highly successful threesome, the Andrews Sisters. Recorded in October 1944, released in December, their rendering became an enormous hit (Decca 18636).

The profound effect of "Rum and Coca-Cola" on the popularity of Trinidad music in the United States is most obvious in the ensuing litigation over both the words and melody. This was big business and big money. There were also new opportunities for island calypsonians with reputations in America. Lord Invader (Rupert Grant) was the first to travel to New York, followed shortly afterwards by Atilla the Hun and the Lion. The legal challenge to Morey Amsterdam was foremost in their objectives, but personal appearances and recording dates were also on the agenda. Each made records for Guild/Musicraft and Invader cut further sides for Decca. Other Trinidad singers known from their earlier recordings (Lord Beginner, King Radio, the Growling Tiger) took similar advantage of the new circumstances, as did Trinidad performers living in the United States.[133]

New York-based blues musicians also reacted to "Rum and Coca-Cola" in their repertoire. Champion Jack Dupree, a New Orleans pianist living in Harlem, recorded his "Rum Cola Blues" in May 1945 (Joe Davis 5100), and Brownie McGhee, the guitarist from Tennessee, cut "Rum Cola Papa" the next year (Alert 400). Interestingly, Sam Manning had been instrumental in arranging McGhee's first session in New York following the recording ban, with Savoy Records in December 1944. Another migrant musician, blues pianist Wilbert "Big Chief" Ellis from Alabama, managed a New York bar for 12 years which was owned by Manning's Jamaican business partner, the pianist Adolph Thenstead.[134]

"STONE COLD DEAD IN THE MARKET"–A FOLLOW UP TO "RUM AND COCA-COLA"—1946

Intent on making the maximum of his success with the Andrew Sisters' hit, Jack Kapp took careful stock before his next foray in this particular market. Judging by his action, he endeavored to increase popularity of the genre by making a record that would appeal to both black and white audiences, especially those intent on up-to-date sounds. In consequence, he teamed Ella Fitzgerald and Louis Jordan, two of his well-known black artists, in a version of "He Had It Coming"—retitled for the occasion: "Stone Cold Dead in the Market." This rendition was cut on 8 October 1945, and Houdini registered "He Had It Coming" for copyright on 7 November (there had been no formalities in 1939, when he first recorded the song). The Fitzgerald-Jordan performance was released by Decca in May of the following year and was another huge success (Decca 23546) at which point, using the new title, Houdini re-registered copyright.[135]

In the light of its hit status, the song was soon covered by Bett Mays and her Orchestra, led by Paul Bascomb, with the Duke of Iron performing the duet (Alert 203). Houdini gained accolades in the next year or so by advertising himself as the composer wherever he appeared. Such was the vogue for this piece that Fred Robbins, on behalf of the *Trinidad Guardian*, presented a silver trophy to Fitzgerald and Jordan for their endeavors in popularizing West Indian music. This event was held in New York on 2 February 1947, at an "Afro-West Indian Shango Carnival and Dance" in which Houdini, Lord Invader, the Duke of Iron and Sir Lancelot also took part.[136]

LORD INVADER IN NEW YORK—1945–48

Unlike the other Trinidad calypsonians who traveled to New York in 1945, Lord Invader remained domiciled in the city for over three years, performing and recording with local musicians. He cut a number of sides for Moses Asch's Disc label, several of which were drawn from the repertoire of other calypsonians in Trinidad. One was "God Made Us All," first performed in Trinidad during the calypso season of 1943 by Lord Pretender (Alric Farrell), who is credited with its composition.[137] Invader performed his version at a hootenanny in New York on 9 May 1946,[138] and this version was printed in *People's Songs* in July 1946.[139] Following the acquittal in November 1946 of Linwood Shull (Chief of Police in Batesburg, South Carolina) for beating black war veteran Isaac Woodard and gouging out his eyes, Invader added a verse to cover the incident. The later version is remembered from a calypso concert staged by Alan Lomax at New York Town Hall in December of the same year.[140] Invader recorded the song for Disc in 1947 (5080)[141] and in turn the words were adopted by the famous black American songster Huddie

Leadbetter (Lead Belly), another Asch protégé. Lead Belly's version went under the names of "Nobody in the World Is Better than Us," or "Equality for Negroes," and entered his recorded repertoire in 1948.[142] The songster's adaptation of this theme demonstrates yet another aspect of the process by which black music from the English-speaking West Indies and North America interacted during the immediate postwar period. From his arrival in 1945, Invader was engaged in the court battle over the infringement of his lyrics to "Rum and Coca-Cola." This was won in February 1947, and upheld on appeal at the end of the year. Invader was back in Trinidad by Shrovetide 1949, but the damages were not paid until 1955![143] The general American interest in calypso and Trinidad performers was sustained throughout 1947 with at least two special shows staged at Carnegie Hall and further recordings. Undoubtedly, this was one factor that led both Jack Kapp and Louis Jordan to consider more material for the singer-saxophonist's successful stream of recordings for Decca. Jordan also developed an affinity for the genre.

WALTER MERRICK, JOE WILLOUGHBY, LOUIS JORDAN AND "RUN JOE"—1948

Possibly as a result of Lord Invader's litigation against the publishers of "Rum and Coca-Cola," or the parallel case brought by Lionel Belasco, who contested the melody, Decca officials were reminded of the calypso "composing" abilities of Walter Merrick. In any event, a song prepared by Merrick and one of his "boyhood pal[s] . . . from Trinidad" (Joe Willoughby) was selected for Jordan's next calypso recording in Rhythm & Blues tempo. This was "Run Joe," cut in New York on 23 April 1947 and released in 1948 (Decca 24448). Like "Stone Cold Dead in the Market," the piece was almost certainly an interpretation of an old Caribbean song. The clue is an unissued piano solo by Merrick, cut for Victor on 19 May 1921: "Come Quick, the Man at the Door"–Grenada Paseo.[144]

Merrick and Willoghby [sic] had registered an unpublished version of "Run Joe, de Man at the Door" for copyright on 18 April, just under a week before Jordan recorded the piece: all three registered a revised version of the words and melody (simply called "Run Joe") on 15 May. The song's title encompasses a masquerade which many U.S. citizens may not have realized, for in Trinidad during the war "Joe" became parlance for an American male on the "make"!

Historical evidence shows the story "Louis Jordan Visits Doc: Leaves with Hit Tune" is apocryphal.[145] This was published soon after the release of "Run Joe" and maintained "when band leader Louis Jordan visited Dr. Walter Merrick last summer for a physical check-up, little did he realize he would walk out of the medic's office with a batch of calypso tunes" and that "Run Joe" had been "waxed just before the recording ban last year" [commencing 31 December 1947].

It is possible Merrick had a private practice, but when he appeared as an expert witness for Lionel Belasco (1948), he was head director of the department of physical medicine and assisting visiting neuro-psychiatrist at Harlem Hospital.[146] The romantic ring of the *Defender*'s story was probably record promotion hyperbole!

The Merrick-Willoughby-Jordan partnership continued after the recording strike ended in December 1948. In April 1949, Louis cut "Push Ka Pee Shee Pie (The Saga of Saga Boy)" which had been written by all three (Decca 24877). A Trinidad "saga boy" is synonymous with zoot-suited swaggers of the 1940s in the U.S.A., and part of the same war-time phenomenon. There were other Willoughby-Jordan collaborations, notably "You Will Always Have a Friend" (Decca 27620) recorded almost two years later, on 1 March 1951, just before Louis and his band set out for their tour of the West Indies.

LOUIS JORDAN TOURS THE WEST INDIES—1951

This trip took Jordan and his group to Jamaica, Trinidad and Guyana in the English-speaking Caribbean, and his trumpet player Aaron Izenhall recalled they also played in Haiti.[147] The tour "was a huge financial success and further stimulated Jordan's interest in West Indian music." While in Trinidad, Louis collected calypsos on his portable wire recorder, and was "captivated" by King Radio's "Brown Skin Girl" (which tells of a Trinidad woman being left with children by a demobbed U.S. service man). Sometime after his return to the United States, Jordan told the *New York Amsterdam News* that he believed calypso would be very big in America, but for the pronunciation of the singers. He endeavored "to make calypso understandable to Americans and yet preserve that West Indian flavor that makes it so unique."[148]

CALYPSO IN THE U.S.A. DURING THE 1950S

Jordan's objective was shared by others in the U.S. music business who were involved in recording calypso and other forms of West Indian music during the

1950s, either for export, New York sales, or widespread American consumption. The latter culminated in the late 1950s with the attempt to subvert the popularity of rock 'n' roll by introducing West Indian songs, epitomized in the sanitized repertoire of Harry Belafonte.

These developments do not concern this discussion. More pertinent is Dinah Washington's recording of Walter Merrick's "Since My Man Has Gone and Went" (Mercury 70284, recorded circa July 1953), or Louis Jordan's support for the genre, which continued into the decade. Of the Trinidadians who gained popularity in the U.S. in the late 1930s, the Duke of Iron had a significant recording career throughout the 1950s, and Sir Lancelot made several films.

PATTERNS OF CULTURAL INTERACTION

There were differing developments in Trinidad and Jamaica that parallel and intertwine with the British and U.S. music establishments across the 1950s. These can be seen as part of a long-standing pattern that began with the coercion of slaves to work plantations in the Americas. The same general trends in the development of black music in the United States are observable in the Caribbean. In addition, it is evident that particular characteristics relate to unique aspects of colonial heritage. A case in point might be the discernible style of playing the clarinet (apparent in representative commercial recordings from the 1920s–1930s) in locations that came under French cultural influence—Martinique, Trinidad, New Orleans. Interchange in the words to children's game songs crosses the boundaries of many English-speaking territories in the Americas.[149] The adoption and adaptation by black people of certain English ballads in the U.S.A. is true also for Jamaica (and other islands),[150] but like the United States, in the Caribbean, the composition of new creole ballads and other novel song forms is the norm. Some evidence suggests that, during the mid-1890s, African American contract workers from Virginia originated "John Henry"—the most famous of all black North American ballads—in Jamaica.[151] The most recent research, however, implies that the ballad probably originated in Alabama in the late 1880s.[152] How the evidence for the existence of the ballad in Jamaica came to be uncovered and its implications remain open questions notwithstanding. This is yet another strand in the complex relationship between black culture in the Caribbean, Africa, the Americas and Europe.

During the nineteenth and early twentieth centuries, in British controlled areas, black soldiers in the British West India Regiment, which had its headquarters in Jamaica, augmented the circulation of local songs. (The pattern of membership for this military unit included Africans who were posted in the British Caribbean, and African-Caribbeans who served in British Africa.)

From colonization, the culture of each of the Caribbean islands was influenced by a flow of theatrical presentations, circuses, and other forms of entertainment originating both in Europe and the Americas. The latter were analogous to and sometimes the same as touring organizations that traversed the Southern United States in both centuries. The absorption and modification of particular European musical styles and instruments are a further parallel with the U.S.A., as are common forms of music—work songs, topical songs, Christian religious repertoire (allied to particular denominations), etc. Yet all of these trends were subject to geographical variation and local circumstances: for example, the African American religious practices of Shango in Trinidad (of Yoruba origin), and Kumina in Jamaica (of Congo origin).

With the influx of black migrants from the English-speaking Caribbean to the United States, from the turn of the century, it was inevitable that island-based music would form a component of the burgeoning U.S. record business. This commenced with recordings by Lovey's Trinidad String Band in New York in 1912, but was interrupted by the First World War. Migration to the Eastern seaboard of America, however, did not cease during the War and the population domiciled there and in English-speaking Caribbean islands proved a ready market for recordings of indigenous music. There was opportunity also for the direct interchange between black West Indian and black American music that is the subject of this treatment. It is apparent this was not a one-way process and that the development of black musical styles in the English-speaking West Indies is as complex as equivalent traditions in North America. Knowledge of each informs the other and allows greater perception of their significance as strands of American music in the twentieth century. More can be written, but enough has been stated to introduce another important facet of black American musical values that remains in the shadow of contemporary understanding.

ACKNOWLEDGMENTS

For help in assembling the information and recordings in this article, I thank in the U.S.A.: Matthew Barton (Alan Lomax Archive), Pat Conte, David Evans,

Ray Funk, John Garst, Don Hill, Don Kent, Jeff Place (Archivist, Smithsonian-Folkways) and Stephen Wade. In addition to allowing me access to recordings, Steve Shapiro and Dick Spottswood provided useful comments on the manuscript. Steve Shapiro also undertook additional newspaper research in periodicals not available in Britain. We collaborated equally in the research and notes for the two CDs of Manning's early recordings issued by Jazz Oracle in 2002. This work received a 2003 Association for Recorded Sound Collections Certificate of Merit for Excellence in Historical Recorded Sound Research. Lise Winer, in Canada, and Guido van Rijn, in the Netherlands, commented on the lyric transcriptions. In Britain, support has been received from: Alan Balfour, Bruce Bastin, Alisdair Blazaar, John Chilton, Ruth Edge (EMI Archives), Keith and Janet Fanshawe, Jeff Green, Reg and Claire Hall, Scott Hastie, Graham Johnstone, Vanessa Knights, Chris Mobbs (National Sound Archive), Richard Noblett, Paul and Valerie Oliver, Mike Rowe, Howard Rye, Joe Swain, Malcolm Taylor (Vaughan Williams Memorial Library), and Marika Sherwood. I apologize to any person or organization inadvertently omitted from these acknowledgments. All views expressed are my own.

NOTES

1. William H. Wiggins Jr., "'Lift Every Voice': A Study of Afro-American Emancipation Celebrations," *Journal of African and Asian Studies* 9, nos. 3–4 (1974): 85; Susan G. Davis, *Parades and Power: Street Theater in Nineteenth-Century Philadelphia* (Philadelphia: Temple University Press, 1986), p. 46.

2. Beverley Brown, "George Liele: Black Baptist and Pan-Africanist 1750–1826," *Savacou* 11–12 (1975): 58–67.

3. Bridget Brereton, *A History of Modern Trinidad 1783–1962* (London: Heinemann, 1982), pp. 68–69.

4. John Cowley, *Carnival, Canboulay and Calypso: Traditions in the Making* (Cambridge: Cambridge University Press, 1996).

5. Ira De A. Reid, *The Negro Immigrant: His Background Characteristics and Social Adjustment, 1899–1937* (New York: Columbia University Press, 1939); Reed Ueda, "West Indians," in *Harvard Encyclopaedia of American Ethnic Groups*, ed. Stephan Thernstrom (Cambridge, Mass.: Harvard University Press, 1980), pp. 1020–27; Maldwyn Allen Jones, *American Immigration* (Chicago: University of Chicago Press, 1960), pp. 276–77.

6. Mike Leadbitter, "Big Boy Crudup, Pt. [3]," *Blues Unlimited* 77: 19 (1970): 19; Mike Leadbitter, n.d., personal communication.

7. Malcolm J. Proudfoot, *Population Movements in the Caribbean* (Port of Spain: Caribbean Commission, 1970).

8. Chris May, "Rudi Kept Pushing," *Black Music and Jazz Review* 2, no. 11 (1980): 18; Mel Hirst, n.d., personal communication.

9. William J. Makin, *Caribbean Nights* (London: Robert Hale, 1939), p. 271.

10. Elsie Clews Parsons, "A West-Indian Tale," *Journal of American Folklore* 32, no. 125 (1919): 442–43.

11. Reid, *The Negro Immigrant*, p. 91.

12. Gilbert Osofsky, *Harlem: The Making of a Ghetto: Negro New York 1890–1930,* (New York: Harper & Row, 1971), p. 131.

13. Wallace Thurman, *Negro Life in New York's Harlem* (Girard, Ks: Haldeman-Julius Publications, [1928]), pp. 18–19.

14. Eric Ledell Smith, *Bert Williams: A Biography of the Pioneer Black Comedian* (Jefferson, N.C.: McFarland & Co, 1992), pp. 1–5.

15. Richard K. Spottswood, comp., unpublished MS, "A Discography of Recordings from the English-speaking West Indies."

16. Donald R. Hill, *Calypso Calaloo: Early Carnival Music in Trinidad* (Gainesville: University Press of Florida, 1993), p. 171.

17. Brown.

18. Hollis R. Lynch, *Edward Wilmot Blyden: Pan-Negro Patriot 1832–1912* (London: Oxford University Press, 1967).

19. Edwin S. Redkey, *Black Exodus: Black Nationalist and Back to Africa Movements 1890–1910* (New Haven: Yale University Press, 1969).

20. Tony Martin, *The Pan-African Connection: From Slavery to Garvey and Beyond* (Dover, Mass.: Majority Press, 1983), pp. 3–46.

21. Winston James, *Holding aloft the Banner of Ethiopia: Caribbean Radicalism in Early Twentieth-Century America* (London: Verso, 1998); Jervis Anderson, *Harlem: The Great Black Way 1900–1950* (London: Orbis Publishing, 1982), p. 302; Roi Ottley, *Inside Black America* (London: Eyre & Spottiswood, 1948), p. 37; David Levering Lewis, *When Harlem Was in Vogue* (New York: Vintage Books, 1982), pp. 111–12.

22. Theodore van Dam, "The Influence of the West African Songs of Derision in the New World," *Record Changer* (April 1954): 7.

23. Louis Nizer, *My Life in Court* (London: William Heinemann, 1962), pp. 241–42.

24. Roi Ottley and William J. Weatherby, eds., *The Negro in New York: An Informal Social History* (New York: New York Public Library and Oceana Publications, 1967), pp. 232–35; Helge

Thygesen, Mark Berresford and Russ Shor, *Black Swan: The Record Label of the Harlem Renaissance* (Nottingham (U.K.): VJM Publications, 1996).

25. R. M. W. Dixon and J. Godrich, *Recording the Blues* (London: Studio Vista, 1970), p. 13.

26. Amy Jacques Garvey, *Garvey and Garveyism* (New York: Collier Books, 1970); Lewis, pp. 34–45; Ottley and Weatherby, pp. 209–33; Judith Stein, *The World of Marcus Garvey: Race and Class in Modern Society* (Baton Rouge: Louisiana State University Press, 1986), pp. 145–46, 192–207.

27. *Library of Congress Catalog of Copyright Entries*, Pt. 3, 1922, Washington, D.C.: Library of Congress.

28. Thomas Kornweibel Jr., *No Crystal Stair: Black Life and the Messenger 1917–1928* (Westport, Conn.: Greenwood Press, 1975), pp. 132–70.

29. Reid, *The Negro Immigrant*, p. 114.

30. Ibid., pp. 114–15.

31. Paul Oliver, *Songsters and Saints: Vocal Traditions on Race Records* (Cambridge: Cambridge University Press, 1984), pp. 84–85.

32. Ted Vincent, *Keep Cool: The Black Activists Who Built the Jazz Age* (London: Pluto Press, 1995), p. 132; *Negro World* (2 May 1925), p. 10.

33. Reid, *The Negro Immigrant*, p. 235.

34. *Library of Congress Catalog of Copyright Entries*, Pt. 3, 1924.

35. Robert M. W. Dixon, John Godrich and Howard Rye, comps., *Blues & Gospel Records 1890–1943*, 4th ed. (Oxford: Clarendon Press, 1997).

36. See note 34.

37. John Cowley, "'L'Année Passée': Selected Repertoire in English-speaking West Indian Music 1900–1960," *Keskidee*. 3 (1993): 31.

38. Sheldon Harris, *Blues Who's Who: A Biographical Dictionary of Blues Singers* (New Rochelle, N.Y.: Arlington House, 1979), pp. 222–23; Henry T. Sampson, *Blacks in Blackface: A Sourcebook on Early Black Musical Shows* (Metuchen (N.J.): Scarecrow Press, 1980), pp. 103, 157, 163, 457, 472, 486.

39. Richard K. Spottswood, comp., *Ethnic Music on Records: A Discography of Ethnic Recordings Produced in the United States, 1893 to 1942* 5, Section 39, West Indian: 2887–923 (Urbana: University of Illinois Press, 1990).

40. John Howard Lawson, *Processional: A Jazz Symphony of American Life in Four Acts* (New York: Thomas Seltzer, 1925); "Processional." Program folder. New York Public Library.

41. Steve Shapiro, "Calypso Recordings 1912–mid-1930s." Paper presented to the Seminar on the Calypso, St. Augustine, Trinidad, University of the West Indies, January 6–10, 1986, p. 9.

42. *West Indian West Indian Folk Songs Sung by Sam Manning*, booklet notes to the 78 rpm album of the same title, Decca A-308 (New York: Decca Records Inc., 1942), p. 4.

43. See note 34.

44. *Negro World* (20 December 1924): 10.

45. Vincent, pp. 117–19, 130.

46. Ottley, p. 35.

47. H. G. De Lisser, *In Jamaica and Cuba* (Kingston, Jamaica: The Gleaner Co., 1910), p. 109.

48. John Chilton, *Who's Who of Jazz: Storyville to Swing Street* (Philadelphia: Chilton Book Co., 1972), p. 78.

49. Nizer, p. 243 ; "Life and Love," *New Yorker* (13 April 1957): 34–35.

50. Mary Mosely, *The Bahamas Handbook* (Nassau: Nassau Guardian, 1926), p. 43.

51. Walter Jekyll, *Jamaican Song and Story* (London: David Nutt, 1907), p. 183.

52. *Who's Who Jamaica 1941–1946* (Kingston, Jamaica: Who's Who [Jamaica] Ltd, *ca.* 1946), p. 586; *Library of Congress Catalog of Copyright Entries*, Pt. 3, 1926.

53. Samuel Kinser, *Carnival American Style: Mardi Gras at New Orleans and Mobile* (Chicago: University of Chicago Press, 1990), pp. 46–47, 232–35, 247.

54. *New York Amsterdam News*, 10 November 1926, p. 11; Sampson, pp. 221, 495; *Messenger*, vol. 8 no. 12 (1926): 362.

55. Harold Cruse, *The Crisis of the Negro Intellectual* (London: W. H. Allen, 1969), pp. 73–82.

56. *New York Amsterdam News*, 8 December 1926, p. 1.

57. *Pittsburgh Courier*, 11 December 1926, sec. 2, p. 2.

58. *Chicago Defender*, 22 January 1927, pt. 1, p. 6.

59. *Baltimore African American*, 14 May 1927, p. 10; 21 May 1927, p. 8.

60. Lionel M. Yard, *Biography of Amy Ashwood Garvey 1897–1969: Co-founder of the Universal Negro Improvement Association* ([U.S.A.]: Associated Publishers Inc., n.d.), p. 159.

61. *New York Amsterdam News*, 17 August 1927, p. 11; *New York Age* 20 (August 1927): 6 ; Sampson, p. 168 ; Laurie Wright, *"Fats" in Fact* (Chigwell, U.K.: Storyville Publications, 1992), p. 36.

62. *New York Amsterdam News*, 3 August 1927, p. 12.

63. *New York Amsterdam News*, 19 November 1927, p. 6.

64. Thurman, p. 42–43.

65. Ira De A. Reid, "Mrs. Bailey Pays the Rent," *Ebony and Topaz: A Collectanea*, ed. Charles S. Johnson (New York: Urban League, 1927), pp. 144–48; Willie "The Lion" Smith with W. George Hoefer, *Music on My Mind* (London: Jazz Book Club, 1966), pp. 152–57; Rudi Blesh and Harriet Janis, *They All Played Ragtime*, 4th ed. (New York: Oak Publications, 1971), pp. 191–204; Aaron Siskind, *Harlem Document: Photographs 1932–1940* (Providence, R.I.: Matrix Publications, 1981), pp. 71–73; Tom Davin, "Conversations with James P. Johnson," in *Ragtime: Its History, Composers and Music*, ed. John Edward Hasse (London: Macmillan, 1985), pp. 166–77.

66. Spottswood, *Ethnic Music*; *Trinidad Guardian*, 1 February 1929, p. 13; *Port of Spain Gazette*, 14 February 1937, p. 23; *ASCAP Biographical Dictionary* (New York: R. R. Bowker Co., 1980), p. 227.

67. Sampson, 1980; Bruce Kellner, ed., *The Harlem Renaissance: A Historical Dictionary for the Era* (New York: Methuen, 1987).

68. Marshall and Jean Stearns, *Jazz Dance: The Story of American Vernacular Dance* (New York: Schirmer Books, 1979), pp. 98–99.

69. Sampson, pp. 153–55, 158–60, 228–30, 235, 252–53, 259–60, 307–8, 490, 496, 505.

70. *New York Amsterdam News*, 10 August 1927, p. 10; 19 November 1927, p. 6.

71. Bull Run was a battle in the U.S. Civil War.

72. Wilfred Redhead, "Songs of the Islands II," *The Bajan* 5, no. 2: 15 (1957): 15; "Barbadian Folk Songs," *The Bajan* (November 1959), p. 15; Clarence Lynch, *The Barbados Book* (London: André Deutsch, 1964), pp. 189–90.

73. Paul Oliver, *Screening the Blues: Aspects of the Blues Tradition* (London: Cassell, 1968), pp. 128–47.

74. *New York Age*, 11 August 1928, p. 6.

75. *New York Amsterdam News*, 1 August 1928, p. 6.

76. Donald Lee Nelson, "The Sinking of the *Vestris*," *John Edwards Memorial Foundation Quarterly* 9, no. 1 (1973): 11.

77. *New York Amsterdam News*, 19 December 1928, p. 12.

78. *New York Amsterdam News*, 1 August 1928, p. 6; *Inter-State Tattler*, 4 January 1929; *New York Amsterdam News*, 20 February 1929, p. 1 ; Hill, pp. 182–83.

79. *New York Age*, 6 April 1929, p. 6; *New York Amsterdam News*, 10 April 1929, p. 13.

80. *Gleaner* (Jamaica), 1 May 1929, p. 10; John Cowley, "Cultural 'Fusions': Aspects of British West Indian Music in the U.S.A. and Britain 1918–51," *Popular Music* 5 (1985): 83.

81. *Trinidad Guardian*, 22 June 1929, p. 1; *Port-of-Spain Gazette*, 22 June 1929, p. 3.

82. *Trinidad Guardian*, 28 June 1929, p. 1.

83. *Trinidad Guardian*, 26 June 1929, p. 8.

84. *Trinidad Guardian*, 27 June 1929, p. 8.

85. *Trinidad Guardian*, 28 June 1929, p. 8.

86. *Trinidad Guardian*, 29 June 1929, p. 8.

87. Spottswood, *Ethnic Music*, pp. 2195–96.

88. *Library of Congress Catalog of Copyright Entries*, Pt. 3, 1930.

89. Reid, *The Negro Immigrant*, p. 160.

90. George Tichenor, "Colored Lines," *Theater Arts Monthly* no. 14 (1930): 486. Further particulars of Manning's career and his repertoire can be found in John Cowley and Steve Shapiro, booklet notes to the Compact Discs *Sam Manning*, Volume 1, 1924–1927, Jazz Oracle BDW 8028; *Sam Manning*, Volume 2, 1927–1930, Jazz Oracle BDW 8029 (Ontario, Canada: Jazz Oracle Phonograph Record Co., 2002).

91. Ted Fox, *Showtime at the Apollo* (London: Quartet Books, 1985), pp. 39–66.

92. *New York Amsterdam News*, 3 January 1934, p. 7.

93. *New York Amsterdam News*, 17 January 1934, p. 7.

94. John Cowley, "London Is The Place: Caribbean Music in the Context of Empire," *Black Music in Britain: Essays on the Afro-Asian Contribution to Popular Music*, ed. Paul Oliver (Milton Keynes: Open University Press, 1990), pp. 58–76.

95. *Trinidad Guardian*, 18 March 1934, p. 1; 22 March 1934, p. 1.

96. G. Malcolm Laws Jr., *Native American Balladry*, rev. ed. (Philadelphia: American Folklore Society, 1964), pp. 248–49.

97. Debora Kodish, *Good Friends and Bad Enemies: Robert Winslow Gordon and the Study of American Folksong* (Urbana: University of Illinois Press, 1986), p. 163.

98. John Garst, personal communication, 8 July 2001.

99. Howard W. Odum, "Folk-Song and Folk-Poetry as Found in the Secular Songs of the Southern Negroes," *Journal of American Folklore* 24, no. 94 (1911): 353–54.

100. Newman Ivey White, *American Negro Folk Song* (Cambridge: Harvard University Press, 1928), pp. 215–16.

101. Chapman J. Milling, "Delia Holmes—A Neglected Negro Ballad," *Southern Folklore Quarterly* 1, no. 4 (1937): 3–8.

102. Pamela Bordelon, ed., *Go Gator and Muddy the Water: Writings by Zora Neale Hurston from the Federal Writers' Project* (New York, W. W. Norton, 1999), p. 73.

103. Amelia Defries, *The Fortunate Islands* (London: Cecil Palmer, 1929), p. xx. The two further verses in this particular text are on the theme of the "untrustworthy" black preacher.

104. John Cowley and Richard Noblett, comps., unpublished MS, West Indian Recordings 1945–1962: An Exploratory Discography.

105. Cowley, *Carnival*, p. 193.

106. Oliver, *Songsters and Saints*, pp. 72–73.

107. Brian Rust, comp., *Jazz Records 1897–1942*, vol. 1, *A-Kar* (Chigwell, U.K.: Storyville Publications, 1970), pp. 189, 200, 116.

108. Van Campen Heilner, *Beneath the Southern Cross* (Boston: Gorham Press, 1930), pp. 194–95.

109. Defries, p. xxi.

110. *Library of Congress Catalog of Copyright Entries*, Pt. 3, 1931.

111. Bordelon, p. 173; description and performance in Library of Congress AFS 3139 B. 1.

112. *Trinidad Guardian*, 18 March 1934, p. 1; William C. White, "The Calypso Singers: You May Not Understand Their Trinidad Accent but Their Songs Have a Rhythm You Can't Forget," *Esquire* 37 (September 1937): 46, 109; *Billboard*, 16 December 1939, pp. 9–10.

113. *Time*, 29 August 1938, p. 21.

114. Oliver, *Screening the Blues*, pp. 148–63.

115. Spottswood, "A Discography."

116. Cowley, " 'L'Année."

117. Bordelon, p. 102 ; *Check-List of Recorded Songs in the English Language in the Archive of American Folk Song to July 1940* (Washington, D.C.: Library of Congress, 1942), p. 366; Blesh and Janis, p. 190–91.

118. Ed Cray, comp., ed., *Bawdy Ballad* (London: Anthony Blond, 1970), pp. 94, 114, 179–80.

119. Spottswood, *Ethnic Music*, p. 2922.

120. Carl Kenzidora, "Behind The Cobwebs," *Record Changer* (July 1952): 8.

121. Roger D. Abrahams, "Charles Waters—West Indian Autolycus," *Western Folklore* 27, no. 2 (1968): 90–91.

122. Nizer, p. 238; Herman Hall, "In Search Of Gerald Clarke: The Calypso Pioneer in the U.S.A.," *Everybodys* 2, no. 4 (1978): 25–26.

123. Bertram Stanleigh, notes to *Calypso: With Gerald Clark And His Original Calypsos*, Musicraft N 9 [78 rpm album]: U.S.A. [ca. 1946]; Walter C. Allen and Brian A. L. Rust, *King Joe Oliver* (London: Jazz Book Club, 1957), p. 29; Ruth Glasser, *My Music Is My Flag: Puerto Rican Musicians and Their New York Communities 1917–1940* (Berkeley: University of California Press, 1995), p. 54–70; William A. Shack, *Harlem in Montmartre: A Paris Jazz Story between the Great Wars* (Berkeley: University of California Press, 2001), pp. 15–21; R. Reid Badger, *A Life in Ragtime: A Biography of James Reese Europe* (New York: Oxford University Press, 1995), p. 294.

124. Spottswood, *Ethnic Music*, p. 2901.

125. Sam Abbott, "Village Vanguard, New York," *Billboard*, 30 September 1939, p. 17; Hill, pp. 161–64, 186 ; Meyer Berger, "About New York," *New York Times*, 11 March 1940.

126. "Old Calypso Songs from Trinidad Are Now Becoming a New U.S. Fad," *Life*, 8 April 1940, pp. 98–99.

127. "Strange Art of Calypso: Topical Songs from Trinidad Become a Record Vogue," *Newsweek*, 9 October 1939, p. 33.

128. Raymond Quevedo, *Atillas Kaiso: A Short History of Trinidad Calypso* (St. Augustine, Trinidad: University of the West Indies, 1983), p. 17–18.

129. John Cowley, comp., unpublished MS, Artist Discography of Recordings made during the Melville and Frances Herskovits Field Expedition to Toco, Trinidad, 1939.

130. Louise Cramer, "Songs of West Indian Negroes in the Canal Zone," *California Folklore Quarterly* (1946): 264–65.

131. Cowley, " 'L'Année," p. 19; Hill, pp. 189, 186.

132. C. B. Franklin, comp., *The Trinidad and Tobago Yearbook, 1943* (Trinidad: Yuilles Printerie, 1943), pp. A29–A32.

133. Cowley, " 'L'Année," pp. 19–28; 8–9.

134. Paul Crawford, " 'Blues Is Truth,' Brownie McGhee in Conversation," *Guitar*, 9, no. 6 (1981): 21; Richard K. Spottswood, ed., booklet notes to the long playing record, *Songs of Love*

Courtship And Marriage: 9, Music in America, vol. 2, LBC 2 (Washington, D. C.: Library of Congress, 1976), p. 9.

135. *Library of Congress Catalog of Copyright Entries*, Pt. 3, 1946; 1947; Dave Colebeck, "Louis Jordan Discography," *Blues Unlimited* 143 (1982): 15.

136. *New York Amsterdam News*, 25 January 1947, p. 21.

137. *Sunday Guardian* (Trinidad), 17 January 1943, p. 5.

138. John Cowley, *Lord Invader: Calypso in New York; The Asch Recordings 1946–1961*, booklet notes to the compact disc of the same title, Smithsonian-Folkways CD 40454 (Washington D.C.: Smithsonian Folkways Recordings, 2000).

139. *People's Songs* (July 1946): 7.

140. Donald R. Hill and John Cowley, *Calypso after Midnight: The Live Midnight Special Concert, Town Hall, New York City 1946*, booklet notes to the compact disc of the same title, Rounder CD 1841 (Cambridge, Mass.: Rounder Records Corp., 1999).

141. *People's Songs* (July-August 1947): 8; Cowley and Noblett; Hill, p. 165.

142. Charles Wolfe and Kip Lornell, *The Life and Legend of Leadbelly* (New York: HarperCollins, 1992), pp. 245, 315–20.

143. Cowley, "'L'Année," pp. 22–23; Raymond Quevedo, ed., *Souvenir of Trinidad Calypsoes, 1949* (Port of Spain: M. A. Lee Lung, [1949]).

144. Spottswood, *Ethnic Music*, p. 2917.

145. *Chicago Defender*, 19 June 1948, p. 26.

146. Nizer, pp. 241–42.

147. John Chilton, letter to author, 10 October 1991.

148. *Trinidad Guardian*, 6 September 1951, p. 7.

149. J. D. Elder, *Song Games from Trinidad and Tobago*, revised ed. (Port of Spain, Trinidad: National Cultural Council, 1973).

150. Oliver, *Songsters and Saints*, pp. 229–56; Martha Warren Beckwith, "The English Ballad in Jamaica: A Note upon the Origin of the Ballad Form," *Publications of the Modern Language Association of America* 39 (1924): 455–83.

151. MacEdward Leach, "John Henry," *Folklore and Society: Essays in Honor of Benjamin. A. Botkin*, ed. Bruce Jackson, (Hatboro: Folklore Associates, 1966), pp. 93–106; Norm Cohen, ed., *Long Steel Rail: The Railroad in American Folksong* (Urbana: University of Illinois Press, 1981), p. 73; Brett Williams, *John Henry: A Bio-Biography* (Westport: Greenwood Press, 1983), pp. 26–29, 50–51, 65–66.

152. John Garst, "Chasing John Henry in Alabama and Mississippi: A Personal Memoir of Work in Progress," *Tributaries: Journal of the Alabama Folklife Association*, no. 5 (2002): 92–129.

ETHEL WATERS

"Long, Lean, Lanky Mama"

RANDALL CHERRY

Ethel Waters (1896–1977) was one of America's most prolific and multifaceted entertainers. Successively, a blues singer, one of the first true jazz vocalists to record, a Broadway star and an acclaimed film actress, her heyday could easily be any one of dozens of high points in a career that spanned the end of the 1910s to her years of semi-retirement in the early 1970s. She made her debut around 1917 as a singer of blues and novelty songs—as well as a celebrated shimmy dancer—under the stage name "Sweet Mama Stringbean."[1] Famous for being the first professional female singer to introduce W. C. Handy's now classic "St. Louis Blues" on the black vaudeville circuit,[2] she built her reputation mainly on the strength of songs of that sort, that is, "vaudeville blues" consisting of a mix of folk blues and theatrical influences, as she became a leading star at clubs and theaters catering almost exclusively to black audiences. In 1921, benefitting from a blues vogue sparked the preceding year by the success of Mamie Smith's "Crazy Blues," Waters became one of the first black blues artists to record, cutting sides for the Cardinal label and then, later that same year, signing up with the Black Swan label, run by the first black-owned and -operated record company. At a time when the record industry had begun to create specially segregated "race labels" and "race series" aimed at black audiences, she shone prominently among a constellation of black, female blues artists.

Waters started her career in a small club near in her hometown of Chester, Pennsylvania, but quickly graduated to black vaudeville houses in Baltimore, Maryland, and, notably, the famed Standard Theater in Philadelphia. Eventually she scored her first major recording hit, "Down Home Blues"/"Oh Daddy" (Black Swan #2010, 1921) before moving on to the Paramount, Vocalion and

264

Columbia labels throughout the 1920s. Releasing other notable titles including "There'll Be Some Changes Made" (Black Swan #2021, 1921), "Shake That Thing" (Columbia #14116-D, 1925) and "Maybe Not at All" (Columbia 14112-D, 1925), Ethel Waters crafted her own distinctive style. Specifically, in these and other blues or blues-inflected songs, she showed off her irrepressible personality and her matchless "sweet-sounding" voice, in contrast to Gertrude "Ma" Rainey's "raw" folk sound or Bessie Smith's majestic, gospel-influenced approach, or "shouting" as Waters termed their styles somewhat dismissively.[3]

This paper will focus on the lyrics of a handful of songs,[4] beginning with a few of the above-mentioned signature songs, before turning to songs written or co-written by Ethel Waters herself. In each case, I will stress how the lyrics allowed her to crystallize her stage persona at the height of the so-called Negro or Harlem Renaissance of the 1920s. This persona had two important aspects. First, the lyrics themselves highlighted Waters's image as a young black woman who flaunted the conventions of the day, particularly by portraying her as a rambunctious, free spirit who was unafraid to address issues of female sexuality openly and did so while purveying especially risqué blues. Second, while rival female singers shared a similar image, Waters succeeded in setting herself apart from them through her unique delivery of songs, tailor-made lyrics and savvy marketing on the part of her record companies.

These particular facets of Sweet Mama Stringbean's image as a liberated blues mama may come as a surprise to those who know her only from her later years when, as a serious actress in the 1940s and 1950s, Waters took on roles as a God-fearing, matronly type, ranging from Petunia in *Cabin in the Sky* to her moving, Oscar-nominated portrayal of Aunt Dicey in *Pinky* and her performance as Berenice in *Member of the Wedding*. As early as 1940, she already began to forsake her earlier image, admitting that, although she had sung "ungodly raw" songs at the start of her career and particularly when appearing regularly at Edmond's Cellar, a Harlem dive, from around 1919 to 1923, she had done so almost unwillingly, only to please club patrons. In her words, she specialized in low-down blues "because they didn't come up to Harlem to go to church." "I wanted to sing decent things," she claimed in retrospect, "but they wouldn't let me. They didn't even know I could—I who at home, to get things off my chest, would rip loose with a good, rousing spiritual."[5] Her "Sweet Mama Stringbean" persona might seem more surprising still for those who recall Waters from her period of semi-retirement in the 1960s and 1970s, when she had become an ardent Christian performing in the choir of evangelist Billy Graham's crusades. For all intents and purposes, she had refashioned herself as a gospel singer identified most closely with the inspirational song "His Eye Is on the Sparrow" (which served as the title of her acclaimed 1951 autobiography). By that point, as rumor would have it, she blocked attempts on the part of record companies to reissue her old blues songs, citing religious grounds.

I would like to focus, first and foremost, on the image of Ethel Waters as the young Sweet Mama Stringbean, who relied on blues songs as well as slightly "blue" popular dance songs to forge a memorable stage personality. But she was not only a blues diva. She was also a black jazz flapper, as she alternated chameleon-like and with considerable ease between songs that portrayed her as a young innocent from the South, a hard-nosed blues mama bent on setting her "papa" straight, or a street-smart city girl infusing her pop-blues-jazz recordings with wit and urbane sophistication that was uniquely her own. In a word, the songs examined below shed light on key moments that seem to best reveal her piquant humor, sexual abandon, and unsinkable personality, thanks to a perfect marriage of lyrics and performer.

The first real indication of Waters's original approach to the blues came to light when she performed on the same bill as Bessie Smith at the 91 Theater on Decatur Street in Atlanta, Georgia, around 1918. According to Waters's account of her appearance, taken from her autobiography, her sweet sound struck the black audience as a fresh, viable alternative to Smith's brand of singing:

Bessie Smith was booked into 91 Decatur Street while I was working there. Bessie was a heavy-set, dark woman and very nice-looking. Along with Ma Rainey, she was undisputed tops as a blues singer. When she came to Atlanta she'd heard a good deal about my low, sweet, and then new way of singing blues.

Bessie's shouting brought worship wherever she worked. She was getting fifty to seventy-five dollars a week, big money for our kind of vaudeville. The money thrown to her brought this to a couple of hundred dollars a week. . . . Bessie was in a pretty good position to dictate to the managers. She had me put on my act for her and said I was a long goody. But she also told the men who ran No. 91 that she didn't want anyone else on the bill to sing the blues. I agreed to this. I could depend a lot on my shaking, though I never shimmied vulgarly and only to express myself. And when I went on I sang "I Want to Be Somebody's Baby Doll so I Can Get My Lovin' All the Time." But before I could finish this number the people out front started howling, "Blues! Blues! Come on, Stringbean, we want your blues!"[6]

Seeking to quiet down the tumult, the theater manager implored Bessie Smith to let Waters sing one of her blues numbers. Bessie finally acquiesced—but not without mumbling within Waters's earshot "These Northern bitches."[7] Waters proceeded to sing "St. Louis Blues" to enormous cheers and garnered the same sort of reaction in the subsequent shows. For Waters, the import of her breakthrough was clear: "Now nobody could have taken the place of Bessie Smith. People everywhere loved her shouting with all their hearts and were loyal to her. But they wanted me, too." In an effort to assuage Smith, Waters did her best to remain respectful:

I remained courteous and deferential to her, always addressing her as "Miss Bessie." I was crazy about her shouting as everyone else, even though hers was not my style, but I didn't enjoy the conflict. It was just more of the contentiousness I'd known all my life. Besides, I sensed this was the beginning of the uncrowning of her, the great and original Bessie Smith. I've never enjoyed seeing a champ go down, and Bessie was all champ.[8]

Of course, Bessie Smith's career was far from over, and she was in fact on the verge of becoming perhaps the most admired and successful blues singer of the time. But the real point is, for our purposes, that Waters had made her first inroads into Bessie's territory and would be considered one of the few singers worthy of comparison as a serious rival, although, by the mid-1920s, their musical paths would diverge starkly. Moreover, Waters's triumph would embolden her to go so far as to actually invite comparisons between her and Bessie's styles. Waters did this to great effect using songs that allowed her to play up the fact that she could, if need be, elicit a southern blues flavor or perhaps even "shout" like her blues-singing rivals—a point that had not been lost on the reviewer from the black newspaper the Baltimore *Afro American* when reviewing one of Waters's early tours for Black Swan. "Miss Waters' voice," the article read, "is of mezzo quality with that moanful sweetness that is regarded as characteristic of the Southern Negro."[9]

With the blues song "Georgia Blues" (Black Swan #14120-B, 1922) and again, most notably, with her recording of "Maybe Not at All" (co-written with Sidney Easton), Waters demonstrated that, while she was no stranger to the southern blues style, she preferred to convey her own northern sound. That point is well illustrated by the way she introduced "Georgia Blues," which she showcased in the musical revue *Oh Joy* in 1922. Noting that Ma Rainey had often made her entrance onto the stage by stepping out of a mock-up of a Victrola record machine, Waters came up with what she considered a classier opening. It consisted of remaining in the back of the theater, out of the audience's view, while another artist, in this case the dancer Ethel Williams, entered onto the stage and called out to her partner in vain: "Where's that Ethel Waters? What can be keeping her? How can I start that act without that gal?" Peering out into the darkness, looking toward the back of the room, Williams would then call out, "Are you Ethel Waters?" That was Waters's cue to make a grand, blustering entrance down the aisle, and as she approached the stage, she would yell, "I ain't Bessie Smith!" Then, she would step onto the stage dressed in a plain, gingham dress, wearing a straw hat, as if she were a simple girl from the South, and sing "Georgia Blues" (written by Higgins and Overstreet)[10]:

> *I feel bad, and I feel sad,*
> *'Cause [sic] it won't be very long before I'll be feeling glad,*
> *I just sigh, why, I could die—but I hope I don't*
> *'Cause I've got the Georgia blues and I'm too darn mean to cry. . . .*
>
> *Gee, would I be happy to have my mammy by my side.*
> *I heard that whistle blow. I guess it's time to go.*
> *Because my train is waitin', I've got no time to lose . . .*
>
> *Now, a certain party that I know*
> *Has offered me a ticket to Chicago.*
> *But he can have it. I don't want it*
> *'Cause I've got the Georgia blues.*[11]

As Waters had announced implicitly in her build-up to the song, her message was that she would not sing such blues in the expected "Southern" style, in the manner of Bessie Smith. But the contrast between her style and Smith's is brought home even more sharply in Waters's "Maybe Not at All." Here, Waters adopts her signature clear-as-a-bell, sunny voice and immaculate enunciation in the first verse:

> *Jim Johnson took me home last night,*
> *'Twas the first time that we'd met,*
> *He claimed to be a small-town sheik,*
> *And all his jive he bet,*

He rest his hat and coat and said, "Here I'll stay."
But his feathers fell when he heard me say:

Not on the first night, baby! Ain't knowed you long enough!
Don't you think you're kind of hasty to pull that kind of stuff!
Don't slam my front door, please, when you go out,
Just because there was nothin' doin' what you was thinkin' about,
Not on the first night, baby! Or maybe not at all!

In the following verses, she stops in mid-song to talk and announce that she is about to imitate Bessie Smith ("I'm gettin' ready for the Empress, Miss Bessie Smith, Lawd!"). Suddenly, the rhythm slows down to the point of bordering on a dirge and Waters lowers her register as she growls out lines (basically the same as in the first verse). As if her convincing parody of the Empress's voice were not enough, she alters a few words in relation to the first verse, to convey a brassier sound and a southern twang: "long" becomes "loooong" and "you're kind of hasty" is stretched out to sound like "you kinda hay-stee."

We might interpret this either as the sincerest form of flattery or as out-and-out derision; however, given the way that Waters introduces her parody of the "Empress" (giving special emphasis to the word "L-A-W-D"), it is perhaps best to consider that Waters did, in fact, want to convey some degree of reverence for her presumed rival. However that may be, Waters undoubtedly was concerned less with pointing up their rivalry than with placing herself on equal footing with Smith, by daring to make fun of her and giving a clear demonstration of how different their approaches really were.

Of course, the differences between Waters and Smith had always been readily apparent, not only in their vocal approaches but in their choice of material. While it is not possible to treat this point in detail, let it suffice to say that, although their repertoires occasionally overlapped (including songs like "Midnight Blues," "Oh, Daddy ["Oh Papa"] Blues," and "St. Louis Blues," to name only a few), their stage personas were entirely antipodal. Smith's repertoire consisted mainly of vaudeville blues, along with a sprinkling of popular songs to which she succeeded in giving a blues flavor. Waters, unlike Smith, rarely sang blues dealing with floods, boll-weevil infestations or alcohol; and while Waters occasionally performed songs allowing her to portray a variation on a girl from the South, her repertoire included a large variety of popular songs, musical comedy numbers and blues that verged on self-contained comedy routines. Moreover, Waters's songs seemed, overall, more upbeat, jazzier, in tune with a "citified" sensibility, containing words or music that presented her as a kind of black jazz flapper; and, it must be said, there were in particular a number of songs that seemed designed to play up Waters's special image as a black icon of beauty and sexuality. To cite only three particularly revealing examples, let us consider songs such as "Pleasure Mad," "Long Lean Lanky Mama," and "Shake That Thing."

In "Pleasure Mad" (music by legendary trumpeter Sidney Bechet and lyrics by Rousseau Simmons), which Waters recorded for the Vocalion label in 1924 [#14860], she added her distinctive voice to those of the increasing rank of female recording artists, and black blues artists in particular, who vaunted an unprecedented sense of brazenness more commonly associated with world-wise girls from the big city:

I'm never sad, . . . cause I'm 21, far from done, just begun. . . .

. . . And I always get what I want, too.
Good times is my passion,
I must be glad.
Ain't got no time to sit and pine,
Just pleasure mad.

. . . 'Cause I'm livin' to conquer,
And I know it's bad.
I must have my thrills, can't keep still
Just pleasure mad.

Why, I'm the reason why boys leave home.
. . . I'm always round . . .
Just pleasure mad.

In "Long Lean Lanky Mama" (#14458-D, Columbia 1929),[12] Waters adopted virtually the same, liberated attitude, but now her undaunted hedonism—and in particular her suggested insatiability—was put in decidedly more sexually explicit terms:

I've always had my own ideas as to what a boy should be,
Now I've begun to have my fears they don't want my company
Blonds, brunets, and red-heads, too
Of each I've had quite a few,

And now I want the world to know
I'm lookin' for a brand new beau.

Cause I'm a long, lean, and lanky mama, lookin' for a lovin' man
I want a big, strong and healthy papa to come and hold my hand
I've had sweeties by the score, but I never get what I'm lookin' for
Cause I'm a long, lean and lanky mama lookin' for a lovin' man . . .

In the last verse of the song, Waters proclaims, "I want a syncopatin', ejaculatin', never-hatin' papa," . . . "Of course, he don't have to be of the best, just as long as he can stand the endurance test." To blues audiences, her delivery of such lyrics was all a part of the kind of titillation they had come to expect of her on stage: she regaled in boldly asserting her own needs, sexual and otherwise, and she was not beneath flaunting her charms and teasing men in the audience who would often call out to her, although she was certain to pull away at the last minute, almost demurely, as if to remind them that she was, after all, still a lady.

Another interesting thing about "Long Lean Lanky Mama" is that, on the basis of the title alone, it seemed tailor-made to call attention to Waters's distinctively tall, slender figure—as opposed to the corpulent frames and less winsome appearance of most of her blues singing rivals. That is, although it was nearly impossible to undermine the loyalty and respect that Bessie Smith's and Ma Rainey's vocal gifts had garnered them among their fans, the mix of Waters's then-new "sweet" blues sound, beguiling personality and pleasing looks made her a serious contender for the crown of "Queen of the Blues" in the eyes of the blues-buying public—a public that seemed to be hungry for the kind of "northern" sophistication Waters was bringing to blues music. Cabaret singer Bobby Short understood this implicitly and recalls how, as a youngster, these qualities made Waters stand out among her peers:

Ethel Waters was a true blues singer. She was elegant, and she was tall and slender and pretty, . . . as opposed to Ma Rainey, who was none of those things. Bessie Smith didn't like her because she was a Northerner. And so Ethel paid her dues as a young girl out there up against competition like Bessie Smith and Mamie Smith. Mamie Smith was pretty, but Bessie Smith was not considered a pretty woman, but I thought she was very handsome. Ma Rainey was certainly not pretty at all.[13]

While such statements seem less pertinent today, now that these blues singers' reputations rest primarily on their recorded legacy, it must be borne in mind that these women's physical appearance was often of utmost importance in an age when live performances were their primary avenues of exposure. Record making was hardly lucrative for black recording artists. Indeed, Waters and Smith earned on the order of a few hundred dollars per two-sided disk but could earn as much from a week or so of work on the black vaudeville circuit. As a result, recording was seen primarily as a privileged form of advertisement for live performances, not to mention a means of enhancing the artist's reputation as a "recording star."

Certain aspects of these songs accentuating Waters's appearance and sensuality may be seen as a logical outgrowth of the kind of promotional effort that had been adopted years earlier by Black Swan, which had promoted Waters's records in black newspapers in tandem with "Madame Hightowers' Beauty Product" (a pomade), vaunting the singer as a standard of black beauty. One ad, which included a product testimonial by Waters herself, announced: "'Queen of Blues Singers' Ethel Waters tells how Madame Mamie Hightower's 'Golden Brown' beauty preparations have made her the most famous and beautiful of Our Race Stars."[14] Black Swan had also used another ingenious tactic to exploit Waters's enormous appeal to men in particular. It consisted in announcing that the company had made her the highest paid blues star of the time (this being about two years before Bessie Smith was signed up by Columbia Records and Ma Rainey by Paramount), while stressing that it had included a provision in Waters's contract forbidding her to marry. As might be expected, this generated much ballyhoo in the black press, where articles, such as the one below, stressed that the provision was intended to fend off the numerous marriage proposals Waters had received encouraging her to give up her singing career:

> "Ethel Must Not Marry—signs contract for big salary providing she does not marry within a year. . . . It was due to numerous offers of marriage, many of her suitors suggesting that she give up professional life at once for domesticity . . ."[15]

It was undoubtedly this unusual contractual stipulation that inspired Waters's self-penned "Ain't Gonna Marry, Ain't Goin' to Settle Down" (#14145-B, Black Swan) in 1923, as she seemed to incarnate a northern girl spurned by her lover and who was prepared, as a result, to defy conventional views on marriage by refusing to marry:

> *I ain't gonna marry, ain't goin' to settle down,*
> *Because the man I love is Alabama bound.*

And he broke my heart, just for his own sweet sake,
So now he wants it back again but it's too late
'Cause he promised to be faithful until the end,
When I caught him making love to my best friend
. . .

Married life is mighty sweet, but a single-life person is so hard to beat . . .
Since that right one ain't easy found, I ain't gonna marry nor settle down.

To be sure, songs dismissing marriage or even risqué songs were not at all uncommon in the repertoires of blues women of the time. As regards the latter songs, some singers, such as "Ma" Rainey and Lucille Bogan, for example, sang tunes like the infamous "Shave 'Em Dry" that were out-and-out bawdy. Moreover, many white singers of the day, ranging from Gilda Gray and Sophie Tucker to Ruth Etting and Annette Hanshaw, often performed or recorded highly suggestive bluesy numbers like "Last of the Red Hot Mamas" or variations on the "Black Bottom" theme (versions of which had been recorded by Ma Rainey ["Ma Rainey's Black Bottom"], Ethel Waters ["Take Your Black Bottom Outside"] and Trixie Smith ["Black Bottom Hop"], among others), expropriating the black singers' reputation for indulging in "raw" material. Songs charged with sexual innuendo also allowed these singers, black and white alike, to exult in a new-found liberty to flaunt the loosening of sexual inhibitions. Waters was surely an exemplar of this trend; but it should also be added that she was ever mindful of the age's persistent Puritanism. For every "Pleasure Mad" or "Long Lean Lanky Mama," there were songs, usually much more blatantly comedic, in which she contested any suggestion that she was an easy sexual conquest. Note the underlying message of the following lines from "Brother, You've Got Me Wrong" (Geise and Hall) [#140564–5, 1925]: "Ain't nobody around here told you nothin' about me . . . I'm as hard as nails!" or "When it comes to dishing out this figure, I'm the only boss."

In "Brother" and "Go Back Where You Stayed Last Night" [#140790–1] (co-authored by Sidney Easton and Waters and recorded by her on the Columbia label in 1925), Waters also demarcated another area of authority: she was much more prone than most blues singers to include half-talked, half-spoken lines in her songs, giving her the opportunity to show that, more than being merely a singer, she was an inimitable comedienne. In "Go Back," which is worthy of the type of singing-talking routines associated with great black vaudeville acts like Butterbeans and Susie, Waters takes up what by then had become a common theme in her repertoire: reading the riot act to her two-timing "papa," while informing him that she herself has found someone new. In this case, as she intones, "Charlie" is her regular now:

> *Go back where you stayed last night, get away from my door!*
> *Charlie's my reg'lar now, and I don't want you no more;*
> *In another candy shop, aargh, get your lollipop*
> *Be on the hop, papa, 'cause I'm through with you.*
>
> *I've been a chump long enough, from now on I'm gonna be mean.*
> *So find another station to get your supply of gasoline.*
>
> *. . . Right back where you stayed last night,*
> *'Cause I don't want you no more.*
>
> *Take it where you had it last night*
> *Boot away from that door or I'll call the law!*
> *Charlie's elected now, and he's in right sure.*
>
> *. . . So take it where you had it last night, mama can't use it no more . . .*

What the song lacks in the bawdiness of, say, "Lanky Mama" is compensated by a very acute sense of humor and a masterful mix of great comedic timing and perfect delivery of seemingly ad-libbed lines. At one point she sings, "Now you're 'round here preaching and whining for a chance, . . . but that's history, that's history," while actually *speaking* the throwaway lines "that's history, that's history" for added emphasis. In the last verse, as she delivers a sort of *coup de grâce*, she dismisses her former lover in a humorous, sexually-charged line that amounts to metaphoric emasculation: "You're just an old banana that has been peeled . . . Mama can't use it no more." In a word, these lyrics reveal Waters to be a main stem of the blues mama tradition which served as a forum for "smart talk" intended to set men straight.

Yet, for all the bravura and unbridled sexual energy generated by Waters's sometimes scorching lyrics—which were certainly accentuated by her provocative shimmies, sexual posturing and knowing looks on stage—the fact remains that she was known, above all, for her ability to make the most torrid lines and otherwise lascivious movements seem respectable. As regards the delivery of her songs, critics often noted that she, more than almost any other contemporary blues singer, somehow managed to elicit charm from blues lyrics, as is stressed in the following assessment which appeared in the *Philadelphia Tribune* in 1926, regarding *Vanities*, one of Ethel Waters's musical revues. "The peerless Ethel Waters gets off her songs in her own inimitable way and proves herself again the only singer who gets real sweetness and charm out of Blues songs."[16] What is even more impressive is that such assessments were often made concerning some of her "lowdown" blues. For example, noted Harlem Renaissance writer James Weldon Johnson seemed to be especially sensitive to the fact that Waters's immaculate diction, allied with her sunny soprano voice, her poise and refined stage presence, afforded her an uncanny ability, on record or on stage, to purify even the most provocative blues lyrics. Remarking on early performances by Waters he had witnessed at Edmond's Cellar, Johnson observed, first of all, that she had an alluring appearance that, in keeping with the blues commonplace, would "surely make a preacher put his bible down"; but, equally noteworthy, she seemed to have a special disarming quality that allowed her to put over blues lyrics in a genuine, black southern style without ever being truly "raw," all the while investing them with her own originality. To understand how she managed to reclaim songs almost miraculously from the brink of raunchiness, one needed, continued Johnson, merely listen to her sing "Shake That Thing."[17]

To understand the import of Johnson's comment, it must be borne in mind that, while "Shake That Thing" would be a huge hit for both Waters and the male folk blues singer, Papa Charlie Jackson, around the same time, in 1925,[18] Waters's rendition is noteworthy for having been a success not only among blues enthusiasts and Harlemites (who had usually been somewhat reluctant to embrace "lowdown" blues) but also among white audiences for whom she performed it in the context of the first musical revues she presented before white audiences (*Ethel Waters' Vanities*, *Miss Calico*, to name only two). The song became so closely identified with her that the trade magazine *Variety* proclaimed it her signature song.[19] Importantly, it was a hit despite being widely criticized for its unsavory overtones elicited by the double-entendre lyrics, earning her vers on the dubious distinction of being named the "Lowdown Song of the Year."[20] The song owed no small part of that distinction to Waters's slow, sultry delivery. Indeed, the combination of the suggestive lyrics and Waters's performance added overtones that were accentuated more than in Jackson's animated, banjo-backed version. Waters slowed down the tempo and relied on a sparse piano accompaniment, and while she may have sapped some of the tune's folk flavor, she drew more attention to the lyrics themselves.

The controversy surrounding Waters's tune has been related by Bobby Short, who remarked that, although he loved the song and implored his mother to buy the recording for him, she refused to do so, arguing that it was totally unfit to be played in a respectable black household. Thankfully for Waters, many record-buyers clamored for the record precisely because of its sexual overtones—and because it was simply a great dance song. As a reading of the lyrics suggests, the song owed its notoriety to the ambiguous meaning of that "thing":

Down in Georgia, got a dance that's new,
Ain't nothin' to it, it's easy to do;
Called Shake That Thing! . . .
I'm getting sick and tired of telling you to shake that thing!

Now, the old folks start doing it, the young folks, too
But the old folks learn the young ones what to do
About shakin' that thing
Ah, shake that thing
. . .

Why, there's old uncle Jack, the jellyroll king,
He's got a hump in his back from shakin' that thing,
Yet, he still shakes that thing,
For an old man, how he can shake that thing,
And he never gets tired of tellin' young folks: go on and shake that thing! . . .

Bobby Short has suggested that the "thing" in question was no doubt the hindquarters of the dancer who is the subject of the song; but, given the allusion to "jelly roll" (the blues euphemism for the male sexual organ or for sexual intercourse) and the predominant reference to men, the listener is given to understand that other sexual connotations may be at work. But what really makes the song work is the coy playfulness—often wordless—that Waters elicits through the sultriness of her voice. On the one hand, the double meanings behind the lyrics allow Waters to feign innocence, claiming to be singing merely about a dance; but her tone and the song's rhythm leave no doubt as to covert references to sexual acts. Waters belts out the first line "Down in Georgia, got a dance that's new" in the manner of Bessie Smith, then she gradually slows down the pace to sensually utter the words "Shake That Thing." At another point—the song's climax—she slows down the proceedings yet another notch and simply hums "m-m-m-m-m," leaving it to the listener to imagine it as a sign of a sensual pleasure that escapes expression in words.

Although Waters's inimitable way with provocative blues songs confirmed her status as a first-rank vaudeville blues artist, a number of factors would lead her to alter her repertoire and all but abandon the kind of blues she had been associated with. For one thing, the blues vogue had already begun to wane by the mid- to late-twenties. Sales figures for blues race records slumped in general and especially in the North, though the phenomenon had no immediate effect on an artist like Bessie Smith, who was able to buck the trend owing to the fact that she continued to have her strongest audience base in the South. For an artist like Waters, who sang an exceptionally broad mix of southern blues and smoother, urban popular songs and novelty songs, it was not difficult to make the transition toward the types of songs that had now become the rage in Harlem. Basically, these consisted of tunes being written by black songwriters and composers who, in the wake of the enormous success of the black musical comedy *Shuffle Along* in 1921, aspired to have their material performed in the black musical revues now cropping up regularly in Harlem or on Broadway. Setting her sights on these musical scenes, Waters's main rival was less Bessie Smith than *Shuffle Along*'s star, Florence Mills.

In fact, Ethel Waters and, reportedly, even Bessie Smith, had auditioned—unsuccessfully—for a part in the ground-breaking production of *Shuffle Along*. However, as Waters suggests in her autobiography, she was rejected because of her affiliation with the unseemly Edmond's Cellar, a reputed hangout for prostitutes and drug dealers, not to mention the fact that Waters had gained a reputation for being a "honky-tonk" singer of "lowdown" blues.[21] Perhaps this rejection, along with encouragement from her pianist at Edmond's and, later, her manager Earl Dancer to diversify her choice of material, are what encouraged Waters to add more non-blues songs to her repertoire. In any event, by 1925, Waters was recording far more popular songs and musical comedy numbers than blues. Even so, she was still being advertised in Columbia's catalogue as one of the label's leading blues stars (alongside Bessie Smith and Clara Smith).

It was around that time, too, that Waters started to come under criticism from various members of the black community, including the intellectual and guiding spirit of the Harlem Renaissance, Alain Locke, who felt that she had begun to turn away from her blues roots. Alluding to her increasing appeal to white audiences and record-buyers (Columbia had even switched her from its race catalogue to its popular music catalogue while failing to mention her color), Locke also echoed those critics who suggested that she had "sold out" to commercialism.[22] But what seemed to have been ignored was the fact that what Waters's songs lost in blues flavor they gained in jazz vocalizing. There are perhaps many reasons why Waters's place in jazz has never been adequately assessed. Most prominent among them is the fact that, just as interest in vaudeville blues was waning and interest in jazz music and swing was on the rise (around the time of the Great Depression), Waters was launching into a new phase of her career as a star of musical comedies on Broadway. As a result of her new reincarnation as Broadway star, Waters's importance to blues and to jazz seemed to have been obscured entirely, as she found herself overshadowed by newcomers to the music scene in the 1930s such as Billie Holiday and Ella Fitzgerald. That helps to explain why, only belatedly, her disks were recognized, notably by Chris Ellis and Gary Giddins, to be among the first real examples of modern, vocal jazz recordings.

Indeed, music critic Chris Ellis and, more recently, Gary Giddins have made the case for Waters's importance as a seminal artist who fused blues and popular song traditions to create modern jazz vocalizing. For Ellis, Waters's earliest blues recordings from 1921 already showed that she was in command of a style of singing that, in his words, "made her recorded contemporaries sound decidedly square." Admitting that Waters's voice was smaller and lighter textured than "classic blues shouters of the Bessie Smith tradition," he emphasized that Waters exhibited a wide range and a tremendous flexibility. What was most impressive about her singing, in his view, was her sense of swing and rhythm that revealed her to be well ahead of her contemporaries:

[It] is the rhythmic subtlety and freedom of her phrasing that make a profound impact on today's listener. To put it in a nutshell—Ethel swings! She swings, what is more, in a manner that is ten years ahead of its time. Even Bessie Smith herself sounds stolid and heavy by comparison, at least until, in the twilight of her recording career, she produced such wonderful pieces of jazz singing as "Moan You Moaners" and "He's Got Me Going." This is no criticism of Bessie Smith, rightly named Empress of the Blues. To clarify a little no-one would claim that Bessie swings in the way that one would apply that word to Ella Fitzgerald, and indeed Ella's kind of singing is regarded as dating from the 1930s. Yet this is precisely the way Ethel was singing as far back as 1921. Certainly, Ethel Waters was the first to take pop songs and turn them into jazz.[23]

It would appear that Waters's reputation has suffered as a result of her open-ness to a variety of musical styles. As Gary Giddins has pointed out, she, and other popular singers of her generation, did not feel any obligation to make a pledge to sing only jazz or blues songs. She simply sang what pleased her and what seemed to suit her voice, without any real consideration of what that might mean in terms of crossing boundaries of generic categories (often imposed retro-spectively by latter-day music critics):

> Bessie Smith and Ethel Waters on the far side, Louis Armstrong and Bing Crosby on the nearer side, who grew up, who were born rather, in the 1890s, the first ten or fifteen years of this century—they discovered music either live or on records with none of the prejudices that virtually every generation afterwards came with. . . . So Ethel Waters didn't think that to become a jazz singer she had to sign some kind of pledge to only sing a certain kind of song. I think that you could put together an album of jazz performances that would qualify as some of the best jazz—and some of the earliest if not THE earliest jazz singing on record going back to 1923. But it's only a small part of what she did then. She was also, of course, a blues singer and a very influential one, and she was a theatrical singer and a diva of the stage.[24]

Furthermore, even as a theatrical singer and diva of the stage, Waters occasion-ally performed songs in the style of her early blues songs, frequently written especially for her by the same writer, Andy Razaf, who penned, for example, "Handy Man" (Columbia 1928) and "My Handy Man Ain't Handy No More," which Waters performed in the Broadway musical *Blackbirds of 1930*.

Ethel Waters's influence was so wide-reaching, her repertoire so diverse, that it is simply not possible to evoke, solely in the context of her song lyrics, the true dimensions of her profound contribution to American music. Nonetheless, lyrics were of great importance to her, and one of her great gifts was her supreme elo-quence, that is, her ability to convey lyrics with feeling and invest them with just the right comic touch, infusing them with her personality. Lyrics were the tools of her trade that she used in order to tell stories and to shape her persona on stage or in recordings. They also were a source of defiance or rebellion, a means of flouting convention or simply marking her individuality. Waters dared to utter lyrics that many contemporaries would have shied away from or that, quite simply, others would not have known how to convey in a way that would have been acceptable to the general public. As a master of "smart talk" and repartee, she seemed to speak out and rebel on behalf of women who longed to voice their opinions about men or about love and sexuality. Finally, she relished the opportunity to show that, in relation to artists like Bessie Smith or Papa Charlie Jackson for example, she was not content to convey lyrics in the expected way.

Any real understanding of Ethel Waters's place in music history must start with a consideration of her songs from the 1920s, when she forged a then new blues and jazz sound, while lending credence to the assessment of her made by white Harlem Renaissance chronicler Carl Van Vechten. In his view, Waters and poet Langston Hughes were the two true geniuses of the Harlem Renaissance.[25] It is fitting, then, to see her as not merely a great singer but as one of the era's masters of language.

NOTES

1. No clear chronology is presented in Ethel Waters's autobiography, *His Eye Is on the Sparrow*, written in 1951; moreover, the date of her professional debut remains dubious, given that Waters originally gave her year of birth as 1900 but admitted in the second instalment of her autobiography, *To Me It's Wonderful* (New York: Harper & Row, 1972) that she was in fact born in 1896. It is generally accepted, however, that Waters made her first professional appearance at Jack's Rathskeller in Philadelphia in 1917 and began touring that same year as part of the Braxton & Nugent vaudeville unit being billed as a singer and dancer under the stage name "Sweet Mama Stringbean." This date is confirmed in Sheldon Harris's *Blues Who's Who* (New York: Da Capo Press, 1979), p. 540.

2. Commenting on her association with "St. Louis Blues," Waters states: "I wanted to sing a new number I'd once heard Charles Anderson, a very good female impersonator, do. Braxton and Nugent said it was a restricted song and I'd have to get permission from the copyright owners, Pace and Handy, in Memphis, Tennessee, before I could sing it on stage. . . . The song I wanted to sing was "St. Louis Blues." Pace and Handy answered my letter by granting me permission. That was how I, a seventeen-year-old novice, became the first woman—and the second person—ever to sing professionally that song which is now a classic and, according to many people, the greatest blues ever written." See Ethel Waters, *His Eye Is on the Sparrow* (New York: Da Capo, 1992), p. 73. Waters's association with the song had been mentioned, as well, by Zora Neale Hurston: "At fifteen, [Waters] introduced the "St. Louis Blues" to the world. She saw a sheet of music, had it played for her, then wrote to W. C. Handy for permission to use it. Handy answered on a postal card and told her to go as far as she liked, or words to that effect. If W. C. Handy had only known

at that time the importance of his act!" See Zora Neale Hurston, *Dust Tracks on a Road* (1942, reprint London: Virago Press, 1981), p. 247.

3. *Sparrow*, pp. 91–92.

4. The texts of all songs have been transcribed by the author on the basis of the compact disk series *Chronological Classics: Ethel Waters* issued in 1992 and 1993 by the French-based record company MPO: Classics 796 (1921–1923), Classics 775 (1923–1925), Classics 721 (1929–1931).

5. "Harlem's Ethel Waters," *New York Times*, 10 November 1940.

6. *Sparrow*, pp. 91–92.

7. *Sparrow*, p. 91.

8. Ibid., pp. 91–92.

9. Baltimore *Afro American*, 2 December 1921, p. 4.

10. *Sparrow*, p. 151.

11. Waters recorded two versions of this song: #14120 recorded in 1922 for Black Swan and #14565-D in 1929 on the Columbia label, the latter being the basis for this transcription.

12. Author identified only as Rich, in liner notes of Chronological Classics "Ethel Waters 1929–1931."

13. Bobby Short: personal interview, New York, 13 December 2001.

14. From an ad printed in the *Chicago Defender* on 25 August 1923.

15. *Chicago Defender*, 24 December 1921, p. 7.

16. *Philadelphia Tribune*, 14 August 1926.

17. James Weldon Johnson, *Black Manhattan* (New York: Da Capo, 1991), p. 210.

18. As Paul Oliver points out, Papa Charlie Jackson had a runaway success with his version of "Shake That Thing" in May 1925 and is credited with having written the song; however, Waters maintained that she had been performing it on stage since 1921, even though she did not record it until December 1925. See Paul Oliver, *Songsters & Saints* (London: Cambridge University Press, 1984), p. 85.

19. An article in *Variety* from 1927 proclaimed "Shake That Thing is to Ethel Waters what 'I Don't Care' is to Eva Tanguay. It's her trademark." Clipping from the archives of the New York Public Library, Schomburg Center for Research in Black Culture.

20. Barbara Kukla: Personal interview, Newark, New Jersey, 2000. Kukla, a journalist, is the author of *Swing City: Newark Nightlife, 1925–50* (Philadelphia: Temple University Press, 1991.) See also Abel Green and Joe Laurie, Jr., *Showbiz: from Vaudeville to Video* (New York: Holt, 1951), p. 313.

21. According to Waters: "The *Shuffle Along* producers still classed me as a Fifth Avenue honky-tonk performer. . . . [In] Harlem it was the street of about-to-be forgotten entertainers." *Sparrow*, p. 138.

22. Alain Locke wrote: "The only contemporary blues singer who retains much of [the] earlier effectiveness and folk flavor [of the blues] is Ethel Waters, and she has been forced by managerial

control or suggestion too far out of the line of the original tradition. The older generation sang not for the night clubs and "hot spots" of Harlem and its Broadway imitations that have spread all over the world of commercialized entertainment, but to the folky people for whom this racy idiom was more of a safety valve of ribald laughter than a neurotic stimulant and breaker of Puritan inhibitions." Alain Locke, *The Negro and His Music* (First edition 1936; reprint, New York: Arno Press and *The New York Times*, 1969), p. 87–88.

23. Chris Ellis, "Ethel Waters—Jazz Singer," *Storyville* 22 (April-May 1969): 128–30.

24. Personal interview with Gary Giddins, New York City, 16 October 2000.

25. See letter by Van Vechten to Blanche Knopf, dated 14 December 1932: "I have long believed that Ethel Waters and Langston had more genius than any others of their race in this country and I think Langston will in the end have as wide a success as Ethel." Bruce Kellner, ed., *Letters of Carl Van Vechten* (New Haven: Yale University Press, 1987), p. 129. Van Vechten reaffirms his claim in a letter addressed to Langston Hughes: "I have been shouting for you and Miss Waters ever since the day you came along and it gives me great pleasure to be snooty to those unfortunate people who believed more in Florence Mills and Countee Cullen. In fact, I was RIGHT." Emily Bernard, ed., *Remember Me to Harlem* (New York: Alfred A. Knopf, 2001), p. 115.

CONTRIBUTORS

RANDALL CHERRY, a professional translator and writer based in Paris, was educated in the U.S. (New York University) and in France (Ph.D. University of Paris). His publications include two English-language translations of philosophical works printed by Zone Books (MIT Press) and various articles on Ethel Waters.

JOHN COWLEY, a Visiting Fellow at the Institute of Commonwealth Studies, University of London, writes on blues and West Indian vernacular music. Author of *Carnival, Canboulay and Calypso* (Cambridge, 1996), with Paul Oliver he edited the *New Blackwell Guide to Recorded Blues* (Blackwell, 1996). His essays appear in scholarly and popular books and periodicals, and he compiles and edits CDs for labels such as Smithsonian-Folkways and Rounder Records.

DAVID EVANS is Professor of Music at the University of Memphis. After graduating from Harvard, he began fieldwork in the southern states in 1965. He received his M.A. (1967) and his Ph.D. (1976) in folklore from the University of California, Los Angeles. He is the author of *Tommy Johnson* (1971) and *Big Road Blues: Tradition and Creativity in the Folk Blues* (1982), as well as many articles in specialist magazines and in scholarly journals, and book chapters on various aspects of African American folk music. He is also a blues musician (vocal and guitar), has played concerts and festivals throughout the United States, and toured as a solo performer or accompanist in Europe and South America.

TOM FREELAND is a lawyer and freelance writer in Oxford, Mississippi. He has written about the music and history of the American South for *Living Blues*, the *Oxford American, Blues and Rhythm*, and other magazines, and spoken about prewar Mississippi blues at the U.S. Folk Alliance, the Rock and Roll Hall of Fame, and elsewhere.

LUIGI MONGE is a freelance teacher and translator in Genoa, Italy. In 1985 he graduated in Foreign Modern Languages from the University of Genoa with a dissertation whose Italian title translates as "Black English and the Blues: A Critical Analysis of Some Lyrics." He is one of the founders and secretary of the Cultural Association "Liguria Blues–Genova," a member of SIdMA (Italian Society of African American Musicologists), and a blues lecturer. In Italian he has written for the magazine *Il Blues*, for SIdMA's journal *Ring Shout*, for the on-line magazine *All About Jazz Italy* and for *World Music Magazine*. In English he has published articles in *Black Music Research Journal* and for Peter Lang. He has contributed entries to *The Encyclopedia of the Blues* and the *Encyclopedia of American Gospel Music*, both forthcoming from Routledge.

PAUL OLIVER is Professor of Vernacular Architecture at Oxford Brookes University. He pioneered blues research with fieldwork in the U.S.A. and in Africa in the 1960s. He is the author of innumerable liner notes and articles in the specialist press and in scholarly journals, and of *Bessie Smith* (1959), *Blues Fell this Morning* (1960, 1990), *Conversation with the Blues* (1964, 1997), *Screening the Blues* (1968, 1988), *The Story of the Blues* (1969), *Savannah Syncopators* (1970), *Blues Off the Record* (1984, 1988), *Songsters and Saints* (1984), and *Yonder Come the Blues* (2001); co-author of *The New Grove Gospel, Blues and Jazz* (1986); and co-editor of *Black Music in Britain* (1990) and of *The Blackwell Guide to Blues Records* (1996).

CHRIS SMITH is a freelance writer and researcher living on Out Skerries in the Shetland Islands. Former editor of *Blues Link* and *Talking Blues*, he is the author of many LP and CD notes, numerous articles and reviews for the specialist blues press, and discographies of Big Bill Broonzy, and Sonny Terry and Brownie McGhee. He was proof reader for the fourth edition of *Blues & Gospel Records, 1890–1943* and translated Sebastian Danchin's biography of B.B. King from French for publication by the University Press of Mississippi.

ROBERT SPRINGER is Professor of American Civilization at the University of Metz, France. He has contributed articles, interviews with blues performers and reviews to such specialist magazines as *Blues Unlimited, Living Blues* and *Jefferson*. He is the author of various scholarly articles and of *Le blues authentique, son histoire et ses thèmes* (1985), whose English translation, with André Prévos, appeared as *Authentic Blues: Its History and Its Themes* (1995), and of *Fonctions sociales du blues* (1999). He convened the 2000 and 2002 conferences on The Lyrics in African American Popular Music at the University of Metz and edited the proceedings of the former under the same title (2001).

GUIDO VAN RIJN is a teacher of English at Kennemer Lyceum in Overveen, the Netherlands. In 1970 he co-founded the Netherlands Blues and Boogie Organization, whose work culminated in the annual Utrecht Blues Estafette. He has published many articles in specialist magazines like *Blues Unlimited*, *Blues & Rhythm*, *Juke Blues* and *Living Blues*, and has produced eighteen LPs and CDs for his own Agram label. His Ph.D. dissertation from Leiden University was revised as the award-winning *Roosevelt's Blues: African American Blues and Gospel Songs on FDR* (1997). A sequel entitled *The Truman and Eisenhower Blues* was published in 2004. He is now at work on *Kennedy's Blues*.

INDEX

West, Kid, 113
West Indian Times. See Manning, Sam
West Indies, 187–263 passim;
    Americanization and relations with
    Americans, 203, 209, 217, 221–32, 234,
    254–55; Baja(n)/Bajun, 212, 215, 233,
    243–44; Carnival(s), 191, 199; emigration/
    (im)migrants from, 188–89, 190, 197, 203,
    204, 212, 219, 235; "paseo(s)," 191, 192, 245,
    248, 252; popular music, 187–263 passim
"West Indies Blues," 193–97, 200, 208, 240
"We Sure Got Hard Times," 160
"When the Levee Breaks," 57–59
"Where Were You When the Archeta River
    Went Down?," 22
Whistlin' Pete, 40
White, Bukka (Booker T. Washington), 127,
    144, 147n44
White, Josh, 25, 172
White, Newman Ivey, 237
White, Walter, 7
Whitt, Little, 101
Whittaker, Hudson. *See* Tampa Red
"Who Stole the Lock," 111
Widow Jones, The, 112, 123
"Wild Cow Blues," 172
Wild Palms, The, 12
"Wild Water Blues," 21
Wilkham, Roscoe. *See* George and Roscoe
Willard, Joe, 122
Williams, Bert, 189
Williams, Big Joe, 172
Williams, Clarence, and Music Publishing,
    193, 194, 198, 213, 214
Williams, Elmo, 99
Williams, Ethel, 268
Williams, George, 24
Williams, Henry Sylvester, 191
Williams, Mayo, 162n18, 169

Williams, Robert Pete, 39
Williams, Spencer, 193, 194, 198, 212
Williams, Ukulele Bob, 196, 197
"Willie, Willie Don't Go from Me," 242
Willis, Ralph, 176
Willoughby, Joe (Lyle?), 206, 252, 253
Wilson, Edith, 114
Wilson, J. P., 112
Wilson, Lena, 205
Wilson, Wesley, 119
Wilson, Woodrow, 154
Wingfield, B. T., 158
Wingin'/winging (dance/ball), 109, 114
Witherspoon, Jimmy, 25
Womack, Earl, 131, 132, 134
Womack, Jerry, 134
"Woman Sweeter than Man," 221
Woods, Harry, 16
Woodward, Isaac, 251
Work, John Wesley, III, 88, 113, 143, 149n71
"Worried Blues," 176
Wright, Willie, 98

Yancey, Estelle Mama, 108
Yancey, Jimmy, 192
Yates, Blind Richard. *See* Richards, Uncle
    Charlie
Yazoo City, Miss., 9
Yazoo River, 4
"You Are My Sunshine," 143
"You Can't Get Anything out of Me," 230–32,
    234
"You Don't See Into the Blues Like Me," 178
"You Will Always Have a Friend," 253

Zeno Mauvais Music Co., 111
Zulu Aid and Pleasure Club, 212
"Zulu Blues, The," 214
"Zulus Ball," 212

Printed in the United Kingdom by
Lightning Source UK Ltd., Milton Keynes
136539UK00001B/181/A